Selected **Bed** and **Breakfast** in
FRANCE 2001

Selected **Bed** and **Breakfast** in FRANCE 2001

Featuring the unique 'sun' rating system

Every B&B included in this book has been visited and allocated between 1 and 4 'suns' by our experienced team of examiners.

✸✸✸✸

See page 5 for more details

Welcome Guides

Selected **Bed** and **Breakfast** in
FRANCE 2001

Your guide to a great welcome in France

Published by Thomas Cook Publishing
The Thomas Cook Group Ltd

PO Box 227
Thorpe Wood
Peterborough PE3 6PU
United Kingdom

Telephone: 01733 503571
email: books@thomascook.com

Text:
© Bed & Breakfast (France) 2001

Maps:
© 2001 Thomas Cook Holdings Ltd

ISBN 1 841570 77 X

Publisher: Donald Greig

Manager, Special Projects:
Bernard Horton

Text design, imagesetting and layout by
PDQ Digital Media Solutions, Bungay

Printed and bound by Stamford Press Pte
Ltd, Singapore

Why Bed & Breakfast in France?

It is fashionable to have a 'Mission Statement' these days, but nevertheless it is important for a guide to clearly identify and mark out its position in the market.

There are thousands of B&B's in France, and it is clear to us that the quality varies enormously, and that there is a need for a good guide at a sensible price which sorts out the wheat from the chaff. The coverage of the country needs to be good, but a vast database-style directory giving no guidance on quality or style is confusing and of little help in making a choice on grounds of quality, atmosphere and welcome. On the other hand, an exclusive selection of a few homes inevitably means that there is unlikely to be one close to where you want to stop and, if there is, it is probably going to be full.

Thomas Cook Publishing, in cooperation with Bed & Breakfast, France, have therefore decided not to concentrate only on those at the top of the market, where the price is also pitched accordingly. This guide aims to bring you a wide selection, from simple farm-houses right up to the grandest châteaux, where all offer comfortable, clean accommodation and where above all, you are really made to feel at home by an outstanding welcome. Our classification by 1, 2, 3 or 4 'suns' reflects the warmth of the welcome that radiates from our hosts, just as much as the quality of the property. In some quarters the French have a reputation for being abrupt and unfriendly, but with our hosts you will be received like a friend of the family and feel completely at ease.

We love France. Our team is mainly French, essential to build up a really good rapport with our hosts, but sprinkled with British and other nationalities so that the views of overseas visitors are reflected in the guide. This keeps us tuned into the demands of clients outside France, and also keeps the French on their toes. All hosts are members of the French Bed & Breakfast Association (Bed & Breakfast France) to which they pay a small membership fee. We work with our hosts as partners to improve their welcome for the benefit of both clients and hosts alike. However, low standards or a poor welcome are not tolerated, and each year our inspections mean applicants are rejected, and your comments may also result in some being weeded out if standards fall. 'Would I be happy to stay there?' is our inspector's ultimate test, not a check-list of standard facilities that guarantee an official rating.

'Le B&B' is an internationally recognised term for guest rooms in private homes, and brings this uniquely French style of accommodation to a wider audience. We urge you to try it. Any language barriers will melt away and you will make many new friends and our mission will be accomplished.

CONTENTS

HOW TO BOOK

There are two options, choose whichever suits you best.

Book direct with your host
Option 1

Telephone or mail the 'book direct' letter at the back of this guide. If hosts also have faxes and E-mail, this is indicated. Your host will reply, advising you on their procedure for confirming a booking. Some hosts may ask you to send them a deposit in French francs or Euros to hold rooms for you. If you book direct, we advise you to confirm in writing to your host, and to give them a phone call about 24 hrs before you arrive.

TO PHONE HOSTS IN FRANCE
From outside France:
Dial +33 then the number of your host. Remove any zero before the first number.
(e.g.: from U.K. 00 33 1 34 68 83 15)

From within France:
Dial the number of your host
(e.g.: 01 34 68 83 15)
It is cheaper to phone after 6pm. Do not forget to take account of time differences if phoning in the evening.

Each host is located in a 'Région', in relation to the nearest main town. The map of each 'Région' shows the 'Départements' (counties) with their number, the main towns and the main roads. Use this in conjunction with a detailed road map. Each host has a Code Number which is made up of two parts. The first part is the number of the 'Département' and the second part is the number of that host in its 'Département'. There is a description of each host giving general facilities for each bedroom. You can see the facilities contained in each room immediately, thereby avoiding any unpleasant surprises. This enables you to request a specific room when you book, often by name.

Use the Bed & Breakfast (France) Central Reservations Office
Option 2

Bed & Breakfast (France) can make your bookings for you and save you time, language problems and the complications of sending payment to France. This is essential for Paris hosts. There is a booking fee for this service.

a)   Decide on the dates of your stay and the number of persons in your party and complete the Reservation Form on page 573.

b)   Select your hosts.

Give a first and second choice and quote the host numbers. In the unlikely event that all your choices are full, we will always come up with the nearest available to your requirements. There may also be hosts that have joined us since this guide went to press, but with this number of hosts, you will never be far from

PRICES

After the description of each room, the two prices shown are the costs of THE ROOM in French francs per night including breakfast.

The first price is for two people sharing the room, the second price is based on the maximum capacity of the room not including extra beds that can be added.

You will find places as low as FF90 per person per night, right up to FF550 per person per night.

NB: Not all hosts had their year 2001 prices available as we went to press, so please check room rates carefully when you make a reservation; prices are liable to alteration.

OTHER REDUCTIONS/DISCOUNTS

– Reductions for a long stay :

Many hosts offer good discounts for stays of several nights. This is indicated on their entry.

– Reductions for children :

Many hosts accept babies free of charge or offer reductions for children.

– Off-Peak Discounts:

Some hosts offer good discounts for stays out of the main season. This is indicated on their entry.

– Family Rooms: These are much cheaper where available.

your first choice. Your trip will be more enjoyable and less tiring if you stay more than one night at each host, which will also give you the opportunity to get to know them and the area better.

c)   Send the Reservation Form and the deposit to Bed & Breakfast (France).
The Reservation Form indicates the various ways to pay.

d)   You will be sent a Provisional Booking.
As soon as your Reservation Form and the deposit are received, a Provisional Booking will be made. This will give brief details of the hosts that have been booked, the balance to pay and the latest date by which payment should be received.

e)   Confirm your booking.
In order to confirm your booking, you should pay the balance to Bed & Breakfast (France) no later than the date indicated. Alterations can be made to your Provisional Booking until you are happy with it and confirm it. However, an administrative charge of £25 will be made for the following alterations, once the Provisional Booking has been issued: changes to dates, reduction in number of persons in your party or a reduction in the total number of nights booked.

f)   Bed & Breakfast (France) will send you a Confirmation Voucher.
Once the full balance of your payment has been received, you will be sent a Confirmation Voucher, which will give the full details of your hosts and directions on how to find them. If you are leaving home several weeks before your arrival in France, your Confirmation Voucher can be sent to another address if you request it.

It is not possible to make changes to your booking once the Confirmation Voucher has been issued.

After this point, a booking has to be cancelled and re-booked again and cancellation fees apply. Booking fees are non-refundable. A booking is only confirmed and guaranteed when the final balance has been received before the payment-date given. We regret that last minute reservations cannot be guaranteed if the final payment arrives too late.

You can also book by telephone or fax using a credit card.

If calling from Britain :
Tel : 01491 578803 - Fax : 01491 410806

If calling from outside Britain :
Tel: + 44 1491 578803 - Fax : +44 1491 410806
E-mail: bookings@bedbreak.demon.co.uk
The service is quick and efficient and the total cost can be charged to a Visa or Mastercard.

The Reservations Office is open Mondays to Fridays from 9.30am to 6pm UK time. Outside of these hours, you may leave your reservation request on the voice-mail service or send a fax or E-mail.

At certain times of the year, if you need an answer in less than 48 hours, you will have to use the EXPRESS SERVICE, for which there is a surcharge of £25. You will be advised if this surcharge is applicable when you book.

Book via the Internet

This service is also available on the Bed & Breakfast (France) website: www.bedbreak.com

Conditions of Reservation of Bed & Breakfast (France)

1. Role of Bed & Breakfast (France)
Bed & Breakfast (France) acts only as a booking agent. It makes the reservations as agent for the person(s) providing the accommodation and does not accept liability in connection with these reservations.

2. Deposit
(a) The deposit of £30 is non-refundable, but will be deducted from the total cost of a reservation when it is confirmed by the client.
(b) If you state that only certain specified hosts are acceptable to you, and we are unable to find you accommodation with any of these hosts, your deposit will be refunded.

3. Payment
All reservations must be pre-paid, and a reservation is not confirmed until full payment is received by Bed & Breakfast (France). We do our best to rush through last minute reservations, but cannot take any responsibility for problems arising due to reservations being confirmed at the last minute or payment not reaching us in time. If hosts have to collect payment from you (except for extras e.g. dinner, etc.), a £25 administration fee will be charged.

4. Recommended forms of payment
(a) Bookings made through our office in Britain
– Valid VISA or MASTERCARD
– Sterling cheque/draft on UK bank (sender to pay all charges)
– Eurocheque in Sterling under £700
– Bank transfer in Sterling to our account at: LLOYDS TSB BANK, Henley-on-Thames, UK. Account number: 115779. Sort code: 30-94-13. Account Name: Bed & Breakfast (France). Please mark "Advise and Pay", and add £25 to cover bank charges.
– Sterling travellers cheques (signed twice please)
All other forms of payment: Surcharge of £25 per booking.
(b) Bookings made through our office in France
– Valid VISA or MASTERCARD
– Cheque in French francs or euros on a French bank
– Cheque in euros on a Euroland bank (add 38.11 euros to cover bank charges)
– Bank transfer in euros to our account at: CREDIT AGRICOLE IDE DE FRANCE, Place

Seguin, 95470 Fosses, France. Account Name: Bed & Breakfast (France). Account number: 18206 00139 56129828150 52 CRCA FOSSES (add 38.11 euros to cover bank charges) All other forms of payment: Surcharge of 38.11 euros per booking.

5. Alterations

Alterations can be made to your Provisional Booking until you are happy with it and confirm it. However, an administrative charge of £25 will be made for the following alterations, once a Provisional Booking has been issued:
– changes to dates
– reduction in total number of persons in your party
No alteration can be made to confirmed bookings.

6. Re-Instatement

If a booking is released because you have not paid the balance to us on time or delay your stay, a re-instatement fee of £25 will be charged if we have to re-book the accommodation for you.

7. Cancellations

If you cancel a booking before it is confirmed, only your deposit is lost, unless condition No. 2(b) applies.

If you cancel a confirmed booking, notice must be received by Bed & Breakfast (France) by letter, fax or e-mail. The following cancellation charges apply to cancellations received as follows:
– 15 days or more before the first night booked: 30% or deposit paid, whichever is the greater.
– 14 to 4 days before the first night booked: 97%
– less than 4 days before the first night booked: 100%
NB. The "first night booked" is the earliest date on your Confirmation Voucher, and applies to the whole itinerary, and not individual stops. You must be covered by Cancellation Insurance to cover these charges.

8. Reservation Fee

A reservation fee is charged by Bed & Breakfast (France). This is 10% of the total cost of the accommodation (excluding insurance), with a minimum of £30.00. Any additional fees charged by travel agents are not the responsibility of Bed & Breakfast (France).

9. Confirmation

Please check carefully that you are happy with your Provisional Booking before you confirm it, as confirmation of your reservation by you commits you to a firm booking that cannot be altered. You are advised to check the location of the hosts reserved in relation to your planned itinerary, especially if travelling by public transport.

10. Express Services

At certain times a £25 non-refundable fee is payable on bookings or alterations that require priority treatment ahead of other clients. You will be advised of this when you book.

11. Circumstances beyond our control

Bed & Breakfast (France) cannot be held liable for problems and delays resultng from circumstances beyond their control (force majeure) e.g. strikes, postal delays, transport delays, etc.

12. Extra Services

Bed & Breakfast (France) cannot be held liable for payment of additional charges for extra services and facilities not included in the basic price paid to Bed & Breakfast (France). It is the client's responsibility to settle these charges before departing from the establishment.

13. Quality of Hosts
Bed & Breakfast (France) has taken all reasonable care to ensure the quality of the hosts and accommodation reserved for clients, and cannot be held liable for any dissatisfaction the clients may have with the hosts or accommodation. Any complaints must be registered with your hosts before departure, so that they have the opportunity to put matters right.

14. Errors and Omissions
Every care has been taken in the production of the guide and all information is correct at time of going to press. However Bed & Breakfast (France) cannot accept liability for errors or omissions it may inadvertently contain.

15. Telephone Bookings
Bookings made by telephone are accepted on the clear understanding that Bed & Breakfast (France) cannot accept liability for errors or misunderstanding that may occur. We advise you to leave sufficient time for written documents to reach you.

16. Responsibility
Bed & Breakfast (France) shall have no liability in contract, tort or otherwise for death, injury or loss to clients except to the extent that such liability is imposed by law and cannot be excluded or restricted.

17. Dispute
Any dispute or claim against Bed & Breakfast (France) or the person(s) providing accommodation shall be governed by English Law and subject to the exclusive jurisdiction of English Courts.

Cancellation Insurance
Bed & Breakfast hosts are small, private homes, and if you cancel a confirmed reservation they may not be able to re-let the room and will expect to be paid. For your protection, Bed & Breakfast (France) have arranged a special insurance scheme with travel insurance specialists PJ Hayman & Company Limited to cover all clients booking with us. The small premium is mandatory, and will be added to your balance to pay when you confirm your reservation, unless you provide written proof that you already hold valid cancellation insurance. You must be covered, either by your own policy or this one. Full details will be supplied with your reservation.

HELPLINE

When in France our **HELPLINE** is available to you
if you have a problem with a reservation.

Tel: 01 34 68 83 15 (office hours only).

If you require a reservation, at least 48 hours notice must
be given.

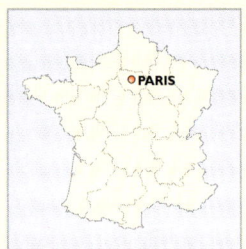

PARIS

CENTRAL PARIS

All Central Paris hosts have to be booked via our reservations office and cannot be booked direct.

Tel: 01491 578803
Fax: 01491 410806
E-mail: bab@bedbreak.com
http//www.bedbreak.com

Full addresses and directions will be notified on booking.

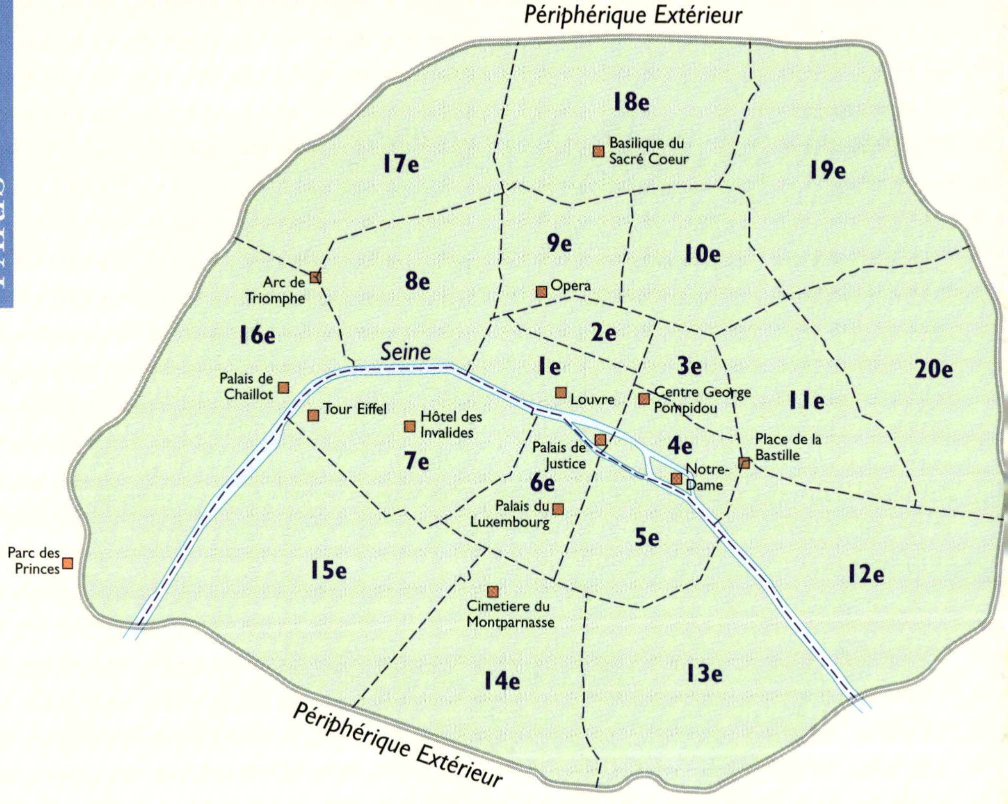

Périphérique Extérieur

18e

Basilique du
Sacré Coeur

17e

19e

9e

10e

Arc de
Triomphe

8e

Opera

16e

2e

Seine

1e

3e

20e

Palais de
Chaillot

Louvre

Centre George
Pompidou

11e

Tour Eiffel

Hôtel des
Invalides

Place de la
Bastille

Palais de
Justice

4e

7e

6e

Notre-
Dame

Palais du
Luxembourg

5e

Parc des
Princes

15e

12e

Cimetiere du
Montparnasse

14e

13e

Périphérique Extérieur

14

80

Abbeville

AMIENS

St. Quentin

02

76

Laon

ROUEN

PICARDIE
page 306

Beauvais

Compiègne

Soissons

27

60

NORMANDIE
page 328

Senlis

Auvers-sur-Oise
page 46

95

Meaux
page 46

51

Evreux

Mantes

Pontoise

93

78

92

PARIS

Disneyland
pages 41-44

CHAMPAGNE
ARDENNE
page 251

Versailles

75

94

77

Dreux

Evry

Rambouillet
page 47

28

ILE DE FRANCE

91

Melun

10

Chartres

Fontainebleau
page 45

Troyes

Sens

Châteaudun

Montargis

ORLÉANS

45

Auxerre

89

endôme

41

CENTRE
page 209

Blois

BOURGOGNE
page 122

37

18

Vierzon

58

Bourges

Nevers

Mona

Tel: +33 1 34 68 83
15/+44 1491 578803

Fax: +33 1 34 72 29
31/+44 1491 410806

E-mail:
bab@bedbreak.com

Apartment

Châtelet - Hotel de
Ville - Marais
PARIS 1e
nearest metro:
Châtelet-Les Halles
airport: PARIS 20km

PRICE STRUCTURE

1 Bedroom
along corridor bathroom
with wc, twin beds: FF420

Capacity: 2 people

75.38 PARIS

Mona's place is warm and lively. A charming and pretty bedroom is furnished so as to give you maximum privacy. In a very quiet street in the centre of Paris. An excellent address.

PROPERTY

hosts have pets, pets not accepted, closed: 1/12–2/01 &
8/07–7/09

Fluent English spoken

75.46 PARIS

In the centre of Paris, this apartment offers comfort, space, and peace and quiet. You can walk to the Louvre, to the Opéra and to Châtelet. If you are music lovers, so is your hostess. The kitchen is available, where you prepare your own breakfast.

PROPERTY

lounge, pets not accepted, kitchen, non-smoking, 10 years old minimum age, 2 nights minimum stay

Fluent English spoken

PRICE STRUCTURE
2 Bedrooms
first room: television, shower room with wc along corridor, 2 single beds: FF400

second room: double bed: FF400

Capacity: 4 people

Brigitte

Tel: +33 1 34 68 83 15/+44 1491 578803

Fax: +33 1 34 72 29 31/+44 1491 410806

E-mail: bab@bedbreak.com

Apartment

Opéra
PARIS 1e
nearest metro: Pyramides
airport: PARIS 20km

75.59 PARIS

This superb apartment is quietly situated in a beautiful, Haussmann-designed building. It is very practical, as you are at the heart of the République area, near to Le Marais and 5 minutes from the Pompidou Centre (Centre Beaubourg). You will particularly appreciate the kindness of your hostess.

PROPERTY

pets not accepted, non-smoking, 12 years old minimum age

Adequate English spoken

PRICE STRUCTURE
1 Bedroom
television, bathroom with wc along corridor, double bed: FF370

Extra Bed: FF150

Capacity: 2 people

Hélène

Tel: +33 1 34 68 83 15/+44 1491 578803

Fax: +33 1 34 72 29 31/+44 1491 410806

E-mail: bab@bedbreak.com

Apartment

République
PARIS 3e
nearest metro: Temple

Lélia

Tel: +33 1 34 68 83
15/+44 1491 578803

Fax: +33 1 34 72 29
31/+44 1491 410806

E-mail:
bab@bedbreak.com

Apartment

Quartier Latin -
Jardin des Plantes
PARIS 5e
nearest metro:
Austerlitz
airport: PARIS 20km

PRICE STRUCTURE

2 Bedrooms
first room: television,
shower room with wc,
double bed, single bed:
FF390 (2 people)
FF540 (3 people)

second room: double bed:
FF340

Capacity: 5 people

75.31 PARIS

A small, cosy apartment, quietly situated, with extensive views from the lounge. The nearby 'Jardin des Plantes' is ideal for strolling in. You can continue to the Rue Mouffetard via the typical small streets of the Latin Quarter.

PROPERTY

pets not accepted, telephone, 1 shared bathroom with wc,
2 nights minimum stay

Fluent English spoken

75.35 PARIS

Brigitte will give you a warm welcome to her charming apartment in this 18th century building, a short walk from Notre Dame. The bedroom is independent, and is quiet and pleasant. There are also two extra beds for children. A great base from which to wander through the Latin Quarter.

PROPERTY

pets not accepted, 2 nights minimum stay

Fluent English spoken

PRICE STRUCTURE
1 Bedroom
television, bathroom with wc along corridor, double bed + en-suite room Mezzanine: 2 single beds (children size): FF400 (2 people) FF600 (4 people)

Extra Bed: FF100, Capacity: 4 people

Brigitte

Tel: +33 1 34 68 83 15/+44 1491 578803

Fax: +33 1 34 72 29 31/+44 1491 410806

E-mail: bab@bedbreak.com

Apartment

Quartier Latin - Notre Dame - PARIS 5e
nearest metro: Maubert Mutualité & St Michel

75.45 PARIS

Karen is a sculptress, and you may be able to watch her at work in her studio and admire some of her creations. Her apartment, which is very close to the Jardin des Plantes, is particularly quiet and relaxing and the atmosphere is easy-going and friendly.

PROPERTY

hosts have pets, 1 shared bathroom with wc, 4 years old minimum age, 3 nights minimum stay

Fluent English spoken

PRICE STRUCTURE
1 Bedroom
twin beds: FF350

Capacity: 2 people

Karen

Tel: +33 1 34 68 83 15/+44 1491 578803

Fax: +33 1 34 72 29 31/+44 1491 410806

E-mail: bab@bedbreak.com

Apartment

Quartier Latin - Jardin des Plantes PARIS 5e
nearest metro: Austerlitz
airport: PARIS 20km

Tel: +33 1 34 68 83
15/+44 1491 578803

Fax: +33 1 34 72 29
31/+44 1491 410806

E-mail:
bab@bedbreak.com

Hotel

Champs-Elysées PARIS 8e
nearest metro:
Franklin-Roosevelt
airport: PARIS 20km

75.02 PARIS

This 2 star hotel is pleasant and comfortable. It has 36 rooms and is situated on a corner of the Champs-Elysées. The rooms are of a good standard and very charming, all with private bathrooms, mini-bar, television, telephone and security box.

PROPERTY

tv lounge, telephone

✸ ✸ ✸

PRICE STRUCTURE
36 Bedrooms

Each room: television, telephone, bathroom with wc

Single: single bed: FF478 (1 person), Double: double bed: FF568

Twin: twin beds: FF578

Triple: double bed, single bed: FF668 (3 people)

Marie-Carmen

Tel: +33 1 34 68 83
15/+44 1491 578803

Fax: +33 1 34 72 29
31/+44 1491 410806

E-mail:
bab@bedbreak.com

Apartment

Grands Magasins
PARIS 9e
nearest metro: Liège
airport: PARIS 20km

75.03 PARIS

An ideal place in a quiet cul-de-sac in the theatre district between the Place Clichy and the large department stores. Chez Marie-Carmen the rooms are basic and clean. Warm Spanish hospitality.

PROPERTY

hosts have pets, dinner available, 1 shared bathroom with wc, closed: 25/12–02/01

PRICE STRUCTURE
3 Bedrooms

double bed: FF300 (2 people) FF450 (2 people)

twin beds + room single bed: FF300 (2 people) FF450 (3 people)

Capacity: 5 people

75.16 PARIS

A recently renovated hotel, conveniently situated opposite the Gare du Nord (Eurostar) and several métro and RER lines (direct to Charles-de-Gaulle airport:). Good rooms with private facilities and TV. Take your breakfast in the room.

PROPERTY

telephone

Tel: +33 1 34 68 83 15/+44 1491 578803

Fax: +33 1 34 72 29 31/+44 1491 410806

E-mail: bab@bedbreak.com

Hotel

PRICE STRUCTURE

Each room: television, telephone, bathroom with wc
Single: single bed: FF440 (1 people), Double: double bed: FF490
Twin: twin beds: FF490
Triple: double bed, single bed: FF680 (3 people)

Gare du Nord
PARIS 10e
nearest metro: Gare du Nord

75.40 PARIS

A very charming welcome from Maryse, a teacher. Her small apartment is warm and cosy, and you are in the heart of Paris. Ideal for a young student.

Maryse

Tel: +33 1 34 68 83 15/+44 1491 578803

Fax: +33 1 34 72 29 31/+44 1491 410806

E-mail: bab@bedbreak.com

PROPERTY

lounge, 1 shared bathroom with wc

Adequate English spoken

Apartment

PRICE STRUCTURE
1 Bedroom

single bed: FF200 (1 person)

Capacity: 1 people

République PARIS 11e
nearest metro:
République
airport: PARIS 20km

75.58 PARIS

Michèle

Tel: +33 1 34 68 83
15/+44 1491 578803

Fax: +33 1 34 72 29
31/+44 1491 410806

E-mail:
bab@bedbreak.com

Apartment

The bedroom has been completely refurbished, as has the bathroom, which is on the same floor and shared with your hostess Michèle, who is very friendly. You are very close to Oberkampf and Charonne, which are the latest 'in' places for Parisians.

PROPERTY

pets not accepted, non-smoking

Basic English spoken

PRICE STRUCTURE
1 Bedroom
shower room with wc, double bed: FF300

Capacity: 2 people

Bastille - Nation
Père-Lachaise
PARIS 11e
nearest metro: Temple

75.51 PARIS

Catherine

Tel: +33 1 34 68 83
15/+44 1491 578803

Fax: +33 1 34 72 29
31/+44 1491 410806

E-mail:
bab@bedbreak.com

Private Home

This flat is in the recently rebuilt area of Bercy, with its Palais Omnisport (sports and pop concerts) and its enormous public park, ideal for jogging! Your hostess knows all about this area. The rooms are basic but practical and very quiet.

PROPERTY

off street parking, tv lounge, hosts have pets,
pets not accepted, kitchen

Adequate English spoken

PRICE STRUCTURE
1 Bedroom
shower room with wc, double bed: FF300

Capacity: 2 people

Nation - Gare de Lyon
PARIS 12e
nearest metro: Reuilly
Diderot ou Montgallet

75.55 PARIS

This flat is in the fashionable area between Nation and Bastille and contains a bedroom with its own pretty sitting room. The atmosphere is quiet, friendly and pleasant. Your hostess is a lecturer and art lover and will be delighted to chat with you. She knows everything there is to know about Paris.

PROPERTY

tv lounge, 1 shared bathroom with wc

Fluent English spoken

PRICE STRUCTURE
1 Bedroom
lounge, television, double bed: FF330

Capacity: 2 people

Patricia

Tel: +33 1 34 68 83
15/+44 1491 578803

Fax: +33 1 34 72 29
31/+44 1491 410806

E-mail:
bab@bedbreak.com

Apartment

Bastille - Nation
PARIS 12e
nearest metro:
Faidherbe-Chaligny

75.56 PARIS

Jeannine lives in the same building as Catherine, in the recently rebuilt area of Bercy. The old wine-trading centre of Paris, its warehouses and pavilions are undergoing a major transformation into a cultural centre called Bercy-Village, which will be fascinating to explore.

PROPERTY

tv lounge, hosts have pets, kitchen, 1 shared bathroom with wc

Adequate English spoken

PRICE STRUCTURE
1 Bedroom
television, double bed: FF330

Capacity: 2 people

Jeannine

Tel: +33 1 34 68 83
15/+44 1491 578803

Fax: +33 1 34 72 29
31/+44 1491 410806

E-mail:
bab@bedbreak.com

Apartment

Bercy - Nation
PARIS 12e
nearest metro: Bercy
airport: PARIS 20km

Tel: +33 1 34 68 83
15/+44 1491 578803

Fax: +33 1 34 72 29
31/+44 1491 410806

E-mail:
bab@bedbreak.com

Hotel

Place d'Italie PARIS 13e
nearest metro:
Place d'Italie
airport: PARIS 20km

75.32 PARIS

This hotel is very well placed in a quiet street, in the pleasant area near the Place d'Italie. It is between the Chinese Quarter and the Latin Quarter, 10 minutes walk from the Rue Mouffetard. They have 37 basic, comfortable rooms with TV. There is a special lounge for smokers.

PROPERTY ✴ ✴

telephone

Fluent English spoken

PRICE STRUCTURE
37 Bedrooms
Each room: television, telephone, bathroom with wc
Single: single bed: FF395 (1 person), Double: double bed: FF467
Triple: double bed, single bed: FF567 (3 people)

Catherine

Tel: +33 1 34 68 83
15/+44 1491 578803

Fax: +33 1 34 72 29
31/+44 1491 410806

E-mail:
bab@bedbreak.com

Apartment

Montparnasse
PARIS 14e
nearest metro: Plaisance
airport: PARIS 20km

75.54 PARIS

A nice quiet place, with a charming host. Close to the métro, in an area where you will find all you need. Ideal for students.

PROPERTY

tv lounge, pets not accepted, kitchen, non-smoking, 1 shared bathroom with wc, 2 nights minimum stay

Adequate English spoken

PRICE STRUCTURE
1 Bedroom
single bed: FF250 (1 person)

Capacity: 1 person

75.48 PARIS

This well-equipped, quiet studio is on the ground floor overlooking the courtyard. You are a short distance from the Palais des Expositions at Versailles and your hostess, who is lively and very friendly, will be delighted to chat with you.

PROPERTY

✸✸

tv lounge, pets not accepted

Basic English spoken

PRICE STRUCTURE
1 Apartment
Studio: television, kitchen, bathroom with wc, double bed: FF330

Capacity: 2 people

Juliette

Tel: +33 1 34 68 83 15/+44 1491 578803

Fax: +33 1 34 72 29 31/+44 1491 410806

E-mail: bab@bedbreak.com

Apartment

Porte de Versailles
PARIS 15e
nearest metro: Porte de Versailles

Nathalie

Tel: +33 1 34 68 83
15/+44 1491 578803

Fax: +33 1 34 72 29
31/+44 1491 410806

E-mail:
bab@bedbreak.com

Apartment

Bois de Boulogne -
Auteuil PARIS 16e
nearest metro: Exelmans
airport: PARIS 20km

75.49 PARIS

A classy, charming and typically Parisian apartment, furnished with antiques. 5 minutes from the Bois de Boulogne. Nathalie is always in great form, and as a guide Lecturer will be delighted to show you round Paris. Her passions are history and French cuisine.

PROPERTY

lounge, pets not accepted, dinner available, kitchen, 15 years old minimum age, 3 nights minimum stay

Fluent English spoken

PRICE STRUCTURE
2 Bedrooms

Rose: television, bathroom with wc and shower along corridor, 2 single beds: FF370

Jaune: single bed: FF290 (1 person)

Capacity: 3 people

Tel: +33 1 34 68 83
15/+44 1491 578803

Fax: +33 1 34 72 29
31/+44 1491 410806

E-mail:
bab@bedbreak.com

Hotel

Montmartre - Clichy
PARIS 17e
nearest metro: Rome
airport: PARIS 20km

75.12 PARIS

René and Jacqueline welcome you warmly to their comfortable 32-room family-run hotel. In a convenient location with garage, private facilities, TV, telephones, bar. Practically in Montmartre.

PROPERTY

private parking, telephone

PRICE STRUCTURE
32 Bedrooms

Each room: television, telephone, bathroom with wc

Single: single bed: FF445 (1 person), Double: double bed: FF445,

Twin: twin beds: FF445, Triple: double bed, single bed: FF600 (3 people)

75.14 PARIS

Danièle and Franck welcome you to their flat in this well-to-do building, typical of Paris, opposite the métro. Montmartre is nearby. Be sure to visit the famous cemetery where many well-known artists and writers rest.

PROPERTY

private parking, tv lounge, 1 shared bathroom with wc

PRICE STRUCTURE
1 Bedroom
double bed: FF300

Capacity: 2 people

Danielle

Tel: +33 1 34 68 83
15/+44 1491 578803

Fax: +33 1 34 72 29
31/+44 1491 410806

E-mail:
bab@bedbreak.com

Apartment

Montmartre - Marché
aux Puces PARIS 17e
nearest metro:
Guy Moquet

75.53 PARIS

Monica, Philippe and their daughter live in a luxurious flat only 10 minutes walk from the Champs-Elysées. The bedroom is very attractive and quiet, with its own separate entrance. A warm family welcome and, as Monica is a language teacher, she will be delighted to organise tours of Paris for you.

PROPERTY

private parking, tv lounge, pets not accepted, non-smoking, shared wc, 18 years old minimum age, 2 nights minimum stay

Fluent English spoken

PRICE STRUCTURE
1 Bedroom
television, shower, double bed: FF660

Capacity: 2 people

Monica & Philippe

Tel: +33 1 34 68 83
15/+44 1491 578803

Fax: +33 1 34 72 29
31/+44 1491 410806

E-mail:
bab@bedbreak.com

Apartment

Pereire - Etoile
PARIS 17e
nearest metro: Pereire
airport: PARIS 20km

ILE DE FRANCE

PARIS

Tel: +33 1 34 68 83
15/+44 1491 578803

Fax: +33 1 34 72 29
31/+44 1491 410806

E-mail:
bab@bedbreak.com

Hotel

Gare du Nord
PARIS 18e
nearest metro: La
Chapelle-Gare du Nord

75.17 PARIS

A warm smile welcomes you to this modern hotel, conveniently situated behind the Gare du Nord (Eurostar), served by several métro lines and the RER (direct to Charles-de-Gaulle airport:). Spotless rooms with private facilities. Pleasant lounge in the basement.

PROPERTY

✷ ✷

lounge

PRICE STRUCTURE
34 Bedrooms

Each room: bathroom with wc

Single room: FF495 (1 person)

Double room or Twin room: FF530

Triple room: double bed, single bed: FF665 (3 people)

Quadruple: double bed, 2 single beds (child-size): FF800 (4 people)

Geneviève

Tel: +33 1 34 68 83
15/+44 1491 578803

Fax: +33 1 34 72 29
31/+44 1491 410806

E-mail:
bab@bedbreak.com

Apartment

Place du Tertre -
Sacré Cœur
PARIS 18e
nearest metro:
Abesses
airport: PARIS 20km

75.18 PARIS

You may have dreamt of the Place du Tertre, of a clear view over Paris and an open fire. Voilà! Geneviève's place offers all this. She is relaxed, loves art and culture, museums and animals. The flat reflects her character and has a soul.

PROPERTY

tv lounge, hosts have pets, dinner available,
1 shared bathroom with wc

Fluent English spoken

PRICE STRUCTURE

1 Bedroom
double bed: FF400

Capacity: 2 people

Barbara

Tel: +33 1 34 68 83
15/+44 1491 578803

Fax: +33 1 34 72 29
31/+44 1491 410806

E-mail:
bab@bedbreak.com

Apartment

Montmartre - Sacré
Coeur - Place du Tertre
PARIS 18e
nearest metro: Anvers

75.50 PARIS

Barbara comes from the world of entertainment and she has decorated her apartment with great taste and orginal ideas. It is spacious, quiet, bright and very attractive. You are at the foot of the Sacré Coeur, almost in a village setting. As it is on the 5th floor with no lift, you need to be fit!

PROPERTY

hosts have pets, pets not accepted, non-smoking, 1 shared bathroom with wc, 10 years old minimum age, 2 nights minimum stay, closed: 26/12–02/01

Adequate English spoken

PRICE STRUCTURE
2 Bedrooms
first room & Chambre Trône: double bed: FF330
Extra Bed: FF100

Capacity: 4 people

Danièle & Bernard

Tel: +33 1 34 68 83
15/+44 1491 578803

Fax: +33 1 34 72 29
31/+44 1491 410806

E-mail:
bab@bedbreak.com

Apartment

Buttes Chaumont -
Belleville PARIS 19e
nearest metro: Belleville
airport: PARIS 20km

75.47 PARIS

Bernard and Danièle left the south of France to spend their retirement in Paris. This is a lively quarter, Belleville and Ménilmontant are traditionally the areas that the 'Titi Parisien' (the Parisian equivalents of Oliver Twist), come from. Be sure to take a walk to Buttes-Chaumont, from where there is a fantastic view over Paris.

PROPERTY

tv lounge, pets not accepted

Basic English spoken

PRICE STRUCTURE
1 Bedroom
shower room with wc, double bed: FF400

Capacity: 2 people

75.13 PARIS

Soufiane is a young doctor who has now settled down after travelling the world with Médécins sans Frontières. The rustic look of the decor, from the '20s and '30s, reflects the style of this quarter, where Maurice Chevalier lived and which is now in vogue again. The wood, the floor tiles and knick-knacks Soufiane has collected all complement the style.

PROPERTY

tv lounge, non-smoking, mountain bikes available

Fluent English spoken

PRICE STRUCTURE
1 Bedroom
bathroom with wc, double bed: FF360

Extra Bed: FF145

Capacity: 4 people

Soufiane

Tel: +33 1 34 68 83
15/+44 1491 578803

Fax: +33 1 34 72 29
31/+44 1491 410806

E-mail:
bab@bedbreak.com

Apartment

Ménilmontant - Père Lachaise PARIS 20e
nearest metro:
Ménilmontant

ILE DE FRANCE

PARIS

Florence & Bruno

Tel: +33 1 34 68 83
15/+44 1491 578803

Fax: +33 1 34 72 29
31/+44 1491 410806

E-mail:
bab@bedbreak.com

Apartment

Père Lachaise -
Nation PARIS 20e
nearest metro:
Porte de Montreuil

PRICE STRUCTURE

1 Bedroom
bathroom with wc, double
bed: FF360

Extra Bed: FF100

Reduction:

01/11–30/11 &
01/02–28/02 and 7 nights
and children

Capacity: 2 people

75.43 PARIS

Florence and Bruno have 3 small children, a dog and a cat. Their very pleasant apartment is organised so that guests are quite independent with their own private garden... a dream come true for Parisians! The welcoming smiles of Florence and little Nicolas will make you feel at home. The room is bright, with direct access to the garden and is comfortable and tastefully decorated.

PROPERTY

garden, tv lounge, hosts have pets, pets not accepted, babies welcome, free cot, 2 nights minimum stay

Adequate English spoken

75.52 PARIS

This family residence provides the quiet charm and ambiance of Parisian homes in the old style. The garden, the terrace and the bedrooms furnished with antiques, create the ideal oasis of peace in Paris.

PROPERTY

private parking, garden, tv lounge, dinner available, kitchen

Fluent English spoken

Donald & Chantal

Tel: +33 1 34 68 83 15/+44 1491 578803

Fax: +33 1 34 72 29 31/+44 1491 410806

E-mail: bab@bedbreak.com

Private Home

PRICE STRUCTURE
2 Bedrooms and 1 Suite
Rouge: bathroom with wc, double bed (queen size), single bed: FF360 (2 people) FF440 (3 people) + Petite chambre: 2 single beds: FF200

Bleue sur jardin: shower room with wc along corridor, double bed: FF330

Extra Bed: FF80,

Capacity: 7 people

Père Lachaise
PARIS 20e
nearest metro:
Porte de Bagnolet

ILE DE FRANCE

PARIS

Jean & Françoise BULOT

30, Chemin des Valences

78740 VAUX-SUR-SEINE

Tel: (0) 1 34 74 84 91

Fax: (0) 1 34 92 02 33

Residence of
Outstanding Character

35 km - W - PARIS
Vaux-sur-Seine
hosts can collect
from station,
railway station: 1km
airport: PARIS 30km

PRICE STRUCTURE

3 Bedrooms and 1 Suite
Myosotis: bathroom with wc,
twin beds + room single
bed: FF290 (2 people)
FF520 (3 people)

Lilas: shower room with wc,
double bed: FF290

first floor – Suite: shower
room with wc, twin beds +
en-suite room 2 single beds:
FF280 (2 people)
FF480 (4 people)

Extra Bed: FF100
Reduction: 01/11–31/12
and 10 nights

Capacity: 9 people

78.02 PARIS

Two hours from Calais and 30 minutes from Paris, this beautiful, spacious villa is in a residential area, only 10 minutes walk from the station. They have a swimming pool, a boules pitch and a billiard table, to help you relax after sight-seeing in Paris, Versailles, Auvers/Oise, Giverny....

PROPERTY

off-street parking, garden, tv lounge, dinner available,
swimming pool, hiking

Basic English spoken

——A13, Exit 9. At Meulan, follow Vaux-sur-Seine (D190) towards St-Germain-en-Laye. Pass the station (on right) & the railway bridge. After 150m, 2nd on the right (hairpin bend). The road undulates, ending in a cul- de-sac on the left. (From A15, exit Courdimanche Follow signs to Menucourt & Vaux/Seine).

Christine & Thierry

RAYNAUD

'La Petite Maison'

33, rue Numance Bouël

91800 BRUNOY

Tel: 01 60 46 36 08

Fax: (0) 1 60 46 36 08

Private Home

17 km - S E - PARIS
Brunoy: hosts can
collect from station,
nearest metro:
RER D 1km
airport: Paris-Orly

91.01 PARIS

This friendly family home is quiet, and is a good place to relax after visiting Paris, which is only 20 minutes by RER (fast suburban train). The comfortable accommodation is in a separate house in the garden. Take Christine's advice on what to visit, particularly the châteaux of Fontainebleau or Vaux le Vicomte.

PROPERTY

off-street parking, garden, tv lounge, pets not accepted, dinner available, babies welcome, free cot, hiking, cycling, fishing 1km, mushroom-picking 1km, golf course 8km

——From Paris, A4 towards Metz and Nancy, Exit Créteil (A86). Head towards Provins/Troyes. Then take the N19 and, at Boissy-St-Léger, head towards Yerres. In front of the château turn left and go right to the end of the avenue Raymond Poincaré. When you reach the abbey, turn left at the roundabout, left into the rue de Villecresnes and, at the traffic lights, turn right.

PRICE STRUCTURE

2 Bedrooms
lounge, television, shower room with wc along corridor, twin beds + room double bed:
FF350 (2 people)
FF580 (4 people)

lounge, television, shower room with wc along corridor, twin beds + room double bed:
FF350 (2 people)
FF580 (4 people)

Capacity: 8 people

Céline

Tel: +33 1 34 68 83
15/+44 1491 578803

Fax: +33 1 34 72 29
31/+44 1491 410806

E-mail:
bab@bedbreak.com

Apartment

5 km - S W - PARIS
Meudon
nearest metro:
RER A - Meudon

92.07 PARIS

This well-equipped, charming, small apartment will give you complete independence. The town of Meudon is pretty and fairly quiet and you are only 2 minutes from the RER station, then 15 minutes to the centre of Paris. However, do not miss the nearby attractions of this area, such as Versailles and Monet's Giverny.

PROPERTY

lounge, babies welcome, free cot, 2 nights minimum stay

Fluent English spoken

PRICE STRUCTURE
1 Apartment
lounge, television, kitchen, shower room with wc, double bed, cot: FF440

Extra Bed: FF100

Capacity: 2 people

Ruth

Tel: +33 1 34 68 83
15/+44 1491 578803

Fax: +33 1 34 72 29
31/+44 1491 410806

E-mail:
bab@bedbreak.com

Apartment

(N W) - PARIS
Neuilly-sur-Seine
nearest metro:
Pont de Levallois

92.04 PARIS

Ruth is a painter, sculptor and tourist guide. Some of her works are in her apartment which is bright and very quiet, in the chic residential area of Neuilly.

PROPERTY
lounge, shared wc

Fluent English spoken

PRICE STRUCTURE
1 Bedroom
shower along corridor, double bed: FF360

Capacity: 2 people

92.05 PARIS

This apartment at the Porte Maillot is at garden level, with direct access to the terrace from bedroom 1. Everything is supplied, including a computer. Ideal for students.

PROPERTY

lounge, pets not accepted, non-smoking, 1 shared bathroom, with wc

Adequate English spoken

PRICE STRUCTURE
2 Bedrooms
first room: shower, single bed: FF245 (1 person)
second room: single bed: FF245 (1 person)

Capacity: 2 people

92.01 PARIS

Cecilia will welcome you with great warmth and kindness. Her house is quiet and next to the station (from where you can reach the Place de l'Opéra in 10 minutes). She loves Italian culture, and also speaks Hebrew. You will appreciate the relaxing garden after a tiring day's sightseeing!

PROPERTY

garden, hosts have pets, pets not accepted, non-smoking, wheelchair access

Fluent English spoken

PRICE STRUCTURE
2 Bedrooms and 1 Suite and 2 Apartments
television, bathroom with wc along corridor, double bed FF390 + room television, single bed: FF330 (1 person),
Chasse & Châlet: television, kitchen, shower room with wc, double bed: FF423,
British: television, kitchen, shower room with wc along corridor, double bed: FF423
Extra Bed:110FF, Capacity: 11 people

Claire

Tel: +33 1 34 68 83 15/+44 1491 578803

Fax: +33 1 34 72 29 31/+44 1491 410806

E-mail: bab@bedbreak.com

Apartment

(N W) - PARIS
Neuilly-sur-Seine
nearest metro:
Porte Maillot

Cécilia

Tel: +33 1 34 68 83 15/+44 1491 578803

Fax: +33 1 34 72 29 31/+44 1491 410806

E-mail: bab@bedbreak.com

Private Home

(N W) - PARIS
Asnières
hosts can collect from
railway station

Annie BUNOD

'La Fraternité'

17, rue de la Fraternité

93160 NOISY-LE-GRAND

Tel: (0) 1 43 03 51 29

Fax: (0) 1 43 03 51 29

annie.bunod@wanadoo.fr

http://perso.wanadoo.fr
/b-and-b-paris-fraternite

Private Home

15 km - E - PARIS
Noisy-le-Grand
nearest metro:
RER D - Noisy-le-
Grand

ILE DE FRANCE

PARIS

PRICE STRUCTURE

2 Bedrooms
(2 rooms) shower room
with wc, 2 double beds:
FF320

Extra Bed: FF100
Reduction: 7 nights

Capacity: 4 people

93.01 PARIS

In the quiet of a large garden, Annie welcomes you in her **home, away from city pollution. Ideal for kids. Situated near to the autoroute, mid-way between Paris and Disneyland. About 30–45 mins. from the centre from Paris by public transport, or 20 mins. by car. Fleur de Soleil member.**

PROPERTY

private parking, garden, pets not accepted, swimming pool

——Take the RER, line A towards Marne-la-Vallée. Get off at Noisy-le-Grand Mont d'Est. Contact your hosts for directions or a map.

94.04 PARIS

Charming house in a quiet area, near to Orly (but without aircraft noise). A charming bedroom and a secluded garden. Easy access to central Paris, 'La Vallée aux Loups' and Sceaux Park with its French-style gardens are only 10 mins. away.

PROPERTY

off-street parking, garden, tv lounge

PRICE STRUCTURE
2 Bedrooms
shower room with wc, double bed + room with single bed: FF330 (2 people) FF460 (3 people)

Monique

Tel: +33 1 34 68 83 15/+44 1491 578803

Fax: +33 1 34 72 29 31/+44 1491 410806

E-mail:
bab@bedbreak.com

Private Home

10 km - S - PARIS
Rungis
airport: Orly 5km

ILE DE FRANCE

PARIS

Aline MATHIEU

69, Av du Général de Gaulle

94240 L'HAY-LES-ROSES

Tel: (0) 1 45 46 16 50

jean-louis.mathieu3
@libertysutf.fr

Private Home

5 km - S - PARIS
l'Hay-les-Roses
bus station
airport: Orly 7km
car essential

PRICE STRUCTURE

3 Bedrooms
Jaune: television, shower room with wc, double bed: FF280

Rose: television, shower room with wc, double bed: FF280

Verte: television, shower room with wc, 2 double beds: FF280 (2 people) FF400 (4 people)

Extra Bed: FF80
Reduction: children

Capacity: 8 people

94.01 PARIS

This young couple and their three small daughters will welcome you with an aperitif. The rooms are in a separate house in the garden. Do not miss the rose garden at l'Haÿ. Within easy reach of Paris. On sale: Honey.

PROPERTY

off-street parking, garden, tv lounge, hosts have pets, dinner available, babies welcome, free cot, interesting flora

Fluent English spoken

——At the Porte d'Italie, follow the signs to A6 (Lyon) but do not take the autoroute. Instead, head for Arcueil-l'Haÿ-les-Roses for 5km. At l'Haÿ turn left, towards the Continent hypermarket.

Philippe & Jeanne
MAUBAN

'Ferme de Vert St Père'

77390 CRISENOY

Tel: (0) 1 64 38 83 51/
06 85 40 88 51

Fax: (0) 1 64 38 83 52

mauban.vert@wanadoo.fr

Residence of
Outstanding Character

30 km - S -
DISNEYLAND
Crisenoy
airport: Orly 40km
car essential

77.02 DISNEYLAND

A farmhouse, restored with great taste, with beautiful old furniture and a large, pleasant garden. Ideal location for Disneyland and the forest of Fontainebleau. Paris is less than 1 hour away (Autoroute A5 and RER nearby). On sale: Competition horses.

PROPERTY

private parking, garden, tv lounge, hosts have pets, pets not accepted, telephone, kitchen, babies welcome, free cot, closed: 24/12–01/01, riding

Fluent English spoken

——In Melun, N36 towards Meaux. (From Paris, A4 Metz-Nancy, Exit N104 towards Troyes then take the A5. First Exit after the 'péage' (toll). On the N36 towards Meaux, after the St Germain-Laxis roundabout (Exit of the A5), turn right on to the 2nd road towards Crisenoy. Cross Crisenoy and head towards the 'Tennis' and the 'Stade'. The farm is just after the village.

PRICE STRUCTURE

**1 Bedroom
and 1 Apartment**

Verte: shower along corridor, wc, double bed, single bed:
FF300 (2 people)
FF400 (3 people)

Apartment: kitchen, shower room with wc, double bed, single bed + en-suite room single bed:
FF390 (2 people)
FF550 (4 people)

Extra Bed: FF100

Reduction: 4 nights

Capacity: 7 people

Patrick & Marie-Josephe
VANDEWEGHE

'Ferme de Forest'

Forest

77390 CHAUMES-EN-
BRIE

Tel: (0) 1 64 06 27 35

Fax: (0) 1 64 06 25 33

Residence of
Outstanding Character

25 km - S -
DISNEYLAND
Chaumes en Brie
airport: Orly 40km
car essential

PRICE STRUCTURE
6 Bedrooms

(2 rooms) television,
bathroom with wc, double
bed: FF270

(1 room) television,
bathroom with wc, double
bed, single bed:
FF240 (2 people)
FF370 (3 people)

(1 room) television, shower
room with wc, double bed:
FF255

(2 rooms) television,
bathroom with wc, double
bed, 2 single beds:
FF240 (2 people)
FF470 (4 people)

Extra Bed: FF100

Reduction: 5 nights

Capacity: 17 people

77.04 DISNEYLAND

A friendly couple, of Belgian origin, welcome you to their cereal growing farm, built of chestnut wood in the Vietnamese style. Pleasant, quiet rooms and beautiful bathrooms. Ideal for Paris, Disneyland and the châteaux.

PROPERTY

private parking, garden, hosts have pets, pets not accepted, kitchen, babies welcome, free cot, wheelchair access, hiking

Basic English spoken

——Leave the A4 at the Exit Melun/Nancy par RN (A104). After 8km follow the signs to Nancy (N4). Exit in the direction of Melun Fontenay Trésigny (N36). After 6km turn left towards Chaumes-en-Brie then right towards Forest. Follow signs 'chambres d'hôtes'.

BORDESSOULE Thierry
BESSELIEVRE Stephane

'La Hérissonière'

Place de l'église –
4, rue du Barrois

77580 CRECY-LA-
CHAPELLE

Tel: 01 64 63 00 72/
06 11 24 16 93

Fax: (0) 1 64 63 00 72

Private Home

12 km - E -
DISNEYLAND
Crécy-la-Chapelle:
railway station: 1km
airport: Orly 40km
car essential

77.15 DISNEYLAND

We have no hesitation in saying that, if there is a heaven, this must be part of it. This charming house overlooks the river, has pretty bedrooms and a romantic little garden with a pergola and, above all, a small bridge, a magical spot for a romantic dinner. Chez Stéphane and Thierry, you can enjoy a gently harmonious lifestyle, or head into Paris or to Disneyland for something completely different.

PROPERTY

off-street parking, garden, tv lounge, hosts have pets, pets not accepted, telephone, dinner available, babies welcome, free cot, cycling, fishing, hiking 4km, interesting flora 4km, mushroom-picking 4km, golf course 10km

——After the 'peage' (toll) on the A4, Exit 16 Crécy-La-Chapelle. Then take the N34 towards Crécy and follow Crécy-Centre. Continue straight on to rue Serret. At the end of this street (there is a Kodak photo shop on the corner), the rue Barrois is on the left.

PRICE STRUCTURE

5 Bedrooms

Each room: tv, telephone:

Le Lavoir: shower room with wc, double bed (king size), single bed: FF340 (2 people) FF460 (3 people)
Le Clocher: shower room with wc, double bed (king size): FF340
Le Brasset: bathroom with wc, double bed (king size), single bed: FF340 (2 people) FF460 (3 people)
L'Ecluse: bathroom with wc, double bed (king size): FF340
Les Séquoïas: shower room with wc, double bed (king size) (king size), 2 single beds (child-size): FF400 (2 people) FF580 (4 people)

Reduction: 7 nights
Capacity: 14 people

Patrick & Isabelle
GALPIN

'Bellevue'

77610 NEUFMOUTIERS-
EN-BRIE

Tel: (0) 1 64 07 11 05-06
08 25 59 88

Fax: (0) 1 64 07 19 27

Residence of
Outstanding Character

14 km - S -
DISNEYLAND
Neufmoutiers:
hosts can collect
from station,
railway station: 7km
car essential

PRICE STRUCTURE
6 Bedrooms

television, shower room
with wc, washbasin, double
bed, 3 single beds:
FF295 (2 people)
FF560 (5 people)

(3 rooms) television, shower
room with wc, washbasin,
double bed, 2 single beds:
FF275 (2 people)
FF475 (4 people)

television, shower room
with wc, washbasin, 3 single
beds: FF275 (2 people)
FF355 (3 people)

television, shower room
with wc, washbasin, double
bed, 2 single beds:
FF395 (2 people)
FF585 (4 people)

Extra ed: FF90

Reduction: 7 nights

Capacity: 24 people

77.11 DISNEYLAND

You will be warmly welcomed by Isabelle and Patrick in their beautiful 19th century house, typical of the Brie region. It is in a quiet little village overlooking the plain, with beautiful walks in the nearby forest. You are only 30 mins. from Paris and 10 mins. from Disneyland.

PROPERTY

off-street parking, garden, lounge, hosts have pets, telephone, dinner available, wheelchair access, hiking

Adequate English spoken

——From the A4 Exit Villeneuve-le-Comte. In Villeneuve, head in the direction of Neufmoutiers. At Neufmoutiers, follow signs to 'chambres d'hôtes' and 'Bellevue'.

Jeannine PERRIN

'La Tourelle'

65, Av de la Forêt

77590 BOIS-LE-ROI

Tel: (0) 1 60 69 52 73
Fax: (0) 1 60 69 52 73

jeanineperrin
@minitel.net

Residence of
Outstanding Character

8 km - N W -
RAMBOUILLET
Poigny-La-Forêt:
hosts can collect
from station,
railway station: 8km,
car essential

77.09 FONTAINEBLEAU

Jeannine and her husband, a warm and courteous couple, invite you into their beautiful home dating from the start of the 20th century, situated on the edge of the Fontainebleau forest, near to the main road. Walk in the majestic forests, and be sure to visit the châteaux of Fontainebleau.

PROPERTY

private parking, garden, lounge, hosts have pets, telephone, babies welcome, free cot, 1 shared shower room with wc, hiking

Fluent English spoken

PRICE STRUCTURE

3 Bedrooms

Rose: double bed: FF260

Bleue: double bed: FF240

Enfants: 3 single beds (child-size): FF200 (2 or 3 people)

Extra Bed: FF80

Reduction: 5 nights

Capacity: 7 people

10 km - N - FONTAINEBLEAU
Bois-le-Roi: car essential
——At the Croix de Vitry crossroads, on the N6 between the A6 and Fontainebleau, take the D138 towards Champagne-sur-Seine.
In the centre of Bois-le-Roi turn left. The house is on the corner on the right.

Denise WOEHRLE

44, rue du Chef de Ville

77440 ARMENTIERES-
EN-BRIE

Tel: (0) 1 64 35 51 22

Fax: (0) 1 64 35 42 95

Private Home

10 km - E - MEAUX
Armentières-en-Brie
hosts can collect
from station,
railway station 12km,
airport: Roissy
30km, car essential

ILE DE FRANCE

MEAUX

PRICE STRUCTURE

4 Bedrooms

(1 room) bathroom with wc,
double bed: FF340

(2 rooms) bathroom with
wc, double bed: FF280

(1 room) shower room with
wc, double bed: FF280

Chambre enfant: single bed
(child-size):
FF180 (1 person)

Extra Bed: FF100

Capacity: 9 people

77.07 MEAUX

Remember Alexandre Dumas from your school days? Well it appears that the magnificent fireplace here once belonged to him. You will find refinement, charm and good humour here. You are also close to the famous town of Bossuet, l'Aigle de Meaux, and only 20 mins. from Disneyland.

PROPERTY

extensive grounds, tv lounge, hosts have pets, telephone,
babies welcome, free cot, golf

Fluent English spoken

——From the A4, Exit 18 and head towards Paris on the N3.
Go through St-Jean-les-Deux-Jumeaux and then take the D17
on the right to Armentières. Go straight through the village,
pass in front of the church and the house is the last but one
on the right, in a cul-de-sac.

François le BRET

'Le Château de Poigny'

2, rue de l'Eglise

78125 POIGNY-LA-FORET

Tel: (0) 1 34 84 77 63

Fax: (0) 1 34 84 74 38

Château

8 km - N W - RAMBOUILLET
Poigny-La-Forêt:
hosts can collect
from station,
railway station: 8km,
car essential

78.03 RAMBOUILLET

If you are not able to get in at the Château de Poigny at your first attempt, then re-arrange your trip! It would be a great pity to miss this wonderful place. Quality and simple, original ideas, featuring travel souvenirs, make up the wonderful interior decor. The bedrooms are charming and amusing, especially the Coca-Cola room, and the grounds are a veritable wildlife park. Sometimes a barbecue is held under the majestic trees. You will never have seen a breakfast like the one served here, a spectacle in itself. To call this an 'excellent address' by no means does justice to the pleasure of an evening chez François and Taieb.

PROPERTY

off-street parking, extensive grounds, tv lounge, hosts have pets, pets not accepted, telephone, babies welcome, free cot

——At Rambouillet take the D936 towards Montfort l'Amaury and the D107 as far as Poigny. Follow the 'chambres d'hôtes' signs. The house adjoins the church.

PRICE STRUCTURE

5 Bedrooms and 1 Suite

Louis XIII: bridal room, shower room with wc along corridor, double bed: FF395 + en-suite room
Indonésienne: double bed: FF395

Marocaine: shower room with wc, double bed: FF395

Coca-Cola: bridal room, shower room with wc, double bed: FF395

Collection: shower room with wc, double bed: FF395

Rustique: shower room with wc, washbasin, double bed + en-suite room Empire: wash-basin, 3 single beds: FF395 (2 people)
FF720 (5 people)

Extra Bed: FF90

Capacity: 15 people

Monique & Charles
Henri GUEGUEN

23, rue des Fichets

95300 HEROUVILLE

Tel: (0) 1 34 66 22 84-06
82 33 83 00

Fax: (0) 1 34 66 22 84

Private Home

4 km - N W -
AUVERS- SUR-OISE
Hérouville: railway
station: 10km,
car essential

95.01 AUVERS-SUR-OISE

Here, you can feel the presence of Van Gogh, so close to the landscapes that he immortalised and the inn where he lived. On your return from exploring, you will certainly appreciate Monique's wonderful meals. The swimming pool is very welcoming. Paris is only 30 mins. away.

PROPERTY

off-street parking, garden, tv lounge, hosts have pets, dinner available, babies welcome, free cot, non-smoking, 1 shared shower room with wc, swimming pool, hiking

PRICE STRUCTURE
3 Bedrooms
(2 rooms) double bed: FF280

twin beds: FF280

Extra Bed: FF50

Capacity: 6 people

BELGIUM

LUXEMBOURG

GERMANY

Sedan

02
Laon
08
Rethel
Reims
Thionville
Verdun
Sarreguemines
METZ
55
57
Haguenau
CHÂLONS
LORRAINE
67
51
Vitry
Bar-le-Duc
Nancy
pages 52-53
STRASBOURG
St. Dizier
54
Lunéville
Barr
page 50
CHAMPAGNE-
ARDENNE
page 251
Neufchâteau
St. Die
ALSACE
Troyes
88
Epinal
page 54
Colmar
52
Chaumont
68
10
Langres
Auxerre
70
90
Mulhouse
page 51
89
Vesoul
Belfort
BOURGOGNE
page 122
21
DIJON
25
58
BESANÇON
FRANCHE-COMTE
71
Autun
Dole
pages 55-56
SWITZERLAND
Beaune
Chalon-sur-
Saône
Pontarlier
39
Lons
Macon
Bourg
03
01
74
Chamonix
Roanne
69
Annecy
ny
RHÔNE-ALPES
page 499
42
Aix-les-
Bains
Albertville
ITALY

Tilly & Gérard
HAZEMANN
'Tilly's & Café d'Alsace'
28, rue Principale
67140 LE HOHWALD
Tel: (0) 3 88 08 33 34
/30 17
Fax: (0) 3 88 08 30 17

Private Home

15 km - W - BARR
Le Hohwald:
railway station: 14km
airport:
STRASBOURG
35km
car essential

PRICE STRUCTURE

3 Bedrooms
first room: television,
kitchen, bathroom with wc,
washbasin, double bed:
FF456

second room: television,
kitchen, bathroom with wc,
washbasin, twin beds: FF426

third room: television, along
corridor bathroom with wc,
twin beds: FF420

Reduction: 01/09–30/06
and 3 nights and groups

Capacity: 6 people

67.02 BARR

Quite an experience. Of course this area is magnificent but you will also breathe its pure air deeply, and go for unforgettable walks. Here, in the heart of Alsace, the area is steeped in European culture. The bedrooms are spacious with beautiful bathrooms.

PROPERTY

private parking, pets not accepted, dinner available, packed lunch, kitchen, babies welcome, free cot, hiking, cycling, fishing, hunting, interesting flora, mushroom-picking, bird-watching, winter sports

Fluent English spoken

——On the A36 from Strasbourg towards Colmar take the Barr Exit. Follow Andiau. Le Hohwald is on the D425.

Jean Louis & Monique
PROBST
2, route de Ferrette
68480 WERENTZHOUSE
Tel: (0) 3 89 40 43 60
Fax: (0) 3 89 08 22 18

Working Farm

35 km - S -
MULHOUSE
Werentzhouse:
railway station: 18km
airport:: 20km

68.03 MULHOUSE

A really warm welcome awaits you in this typical old farmhouse near the Swiss border, in the heart of the Sundgau region, between the Rhine and the Vosges. Horses, goats and, above all, their delicious Pinot Gris wine from Alsace and the local speciality 'la Carpe frite' (fried carp). On sale: Wine from Alsace.

PROPERTY

private parking, garden, lounge, hosts have pets, telephone, dinner available, babies welcome, free cot, closed: 01/01–31/01, hiking, cycling, mushroom-picking, fishing 5km, interesting flora 5km, bird-watching 5km, golf course 10km, sea or lake watersports 10km, riversports 20km, winter sports 40km

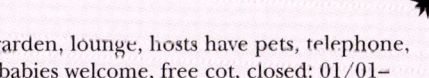

——In Mulhouse, take the D432 to Altkirch and then go to Ferette. In Ferette go towards Bâle. The farm is near the church.

PRICE STRUCTURE

4 Bedrooms
(2 rooms) shower room with wc, double bed, 2 single beds: FF240 (2 people) FF360 (4 people)

second room: shower room with wc, double bed: FF240

third room: shower room with wc, 2 double beds, 2 single beds: FF240 (2 people) FF480 (6 people)

Extra Bed: FF60

Reduction: 01/09–30/06 and 3 nights and groups

Capacity: 16 people

Jacques DURIN
37, rue François Richard
54300 LUNÉVILLE
Tel: (0) 3 83 73 75 26-06
08 58 30 62

Private Home

30 km - S E - NANCY
Lunéville: hosts can
collect from station,
railway station: 3km
airport:
NANCY 50km

PRICE STRUCTURE

4 Bedrooms
first room: lounge,
television, shower room
with wc, washbasin, double
bed: FF260

second room: shower room
with wc, washbasin, double
bed: FF260

third room: shower, wc,
washbasin, double bed:
FF260

fourth room: shower room
with wc, washbasin, double
bed: FF260

Extra Bed: FF100

Reduction: 01/10–31/05

Capacity: 8 people

54.01 NANCY

Just the place for garden lovers. Jacques is a landscape gardener so flowers, bridges, streams and ponds are all part of the decor. Immaculate bathrooms, lovely bed linen, and a warm welcome. Mediterranean-style swimming pool.

PROPERTY

private parking, garden, tv lounge, hosts have pets, telephone, dinner available, packed lunch, kitchen, babies welcome, free cot, swimming pool, cycling, fishing, hiking 1km, riversports 3km, gliding 3km, mushroom-picking 5km, golf course 30km, interesting flora 40km, bird-watching 40km, sea or lake watersports 40km

——Exit Lunéville-Château from the A33 and take the N4 for 10km. In Lunéville straight on to roundabout. Head towards Château Salins (on left a square with trees). 70m after square take small street on left. 500m on left.

LORRAINE

NANCY

54.02 NANCY

Anne Marie lives in a house on an estate on the edge of the forest. She is a friendly, interesting lady, particularly when she talks about her numerous travels from the North to the South Pole, via Japan and Indonesia....

PROPERTY

private parking, garden, dinner available, babies welcome, free cot, hiking, cycling, mushroom-picking, interesting flora 3km, fishing 5km, sea or lake watersports 5km, riversports 5km, golf course 10km, winter sports 100km

Adequate English spoken

PRICE STRUCTURE
2 Bedrooms

first room: double bed (queen size): FF204

second room: twin beds: FF204

Reduction: 2 nights

Capacity: 4 people

Anne-Marie RICHARDIN

'Maéva'

Clair-Lieu – 2, allée des Églantiers

54600 VILLERS-LES-NANCY

Tel: (0) 3 83 90 33 60

Private Home

5 km - S E - NANCY
Villers-les-Nancy:
railway station: 6km
airport: 10km
——From Nancy, head for Nancy-Brabois (2b). Stay in the left-hand lane. At the third set of traffic lights, turn left towards Villers-Maron. Continue straight on for 2 km and then turn left (Maron/Villers). When you are on the estate (lotissement) of Clair-Lieu, turn right at the fourth set of traffic lights, and then immediately left. You will see an English telephone box in front of you!

Annie & Claude CORNU

Route de Ruaux

88370 PLOMBIERES-
LES- BAINS

Tel: (0) 3 29 66 08 13

Working Farm

LORRAINE

EPINAL

35 km - S - EPINAL
Plombières-les-Bains:
hosts can collect
from station,
railway station: 10km
car essential

PRICE STRUCTURE

3 Bedrooms
(4 rooms) shower, wc,
double bed: FF250

Reduction: 3 nights and
children

Capacity: 6 people

88.02 EPINAL

A well-known spa town in the Vosges Mountains (Alt. 550m). An old farmhouse, typical of the Vosges, with country views. Farm animals: mixed livestock, sheep, poultry, donkeys, horses, dairy cattle, pigs. Local activities: hiking, mountain biking, riding, fishing, excursions and visits to the spa. On sale: Poultry, eggs and terrines.

PROPERTY

off-street parking, garden, hosts have pets, dinner available, hiking, cycling, fishing 4km

——From Epinal, take the N57 towards Remiremont then at Plombières take the direction for Ruaux.

Giovanni PROEITTO

'Arche Novum'

Domaine Château Bellevue

39700 CHATENOIS

Tel: (0) 3 84 72 82 35

Fax: (0) 3 84 82 67 48

arche.novum @wanadoo.fr

Château

10 km - N - DOLE
Chatenois: hosts can collect from station, railway station: 10km airport: 15km
car essential

39.02 DOLE

This place is on a large estate, geared towards organic and vegetarian produce. They have everything for a relaxing stay, particularly with children who will enjoy the library, the water features, table tennis... or maybe you can persuade them to come with you to explore the forest, the rivers and the charming little villages around Dôle.

PROPERTY

off-street parking, garden, lounge, pets not accepted, telephone, dinner available, packed lunch, babies welcome, free cot, non-smoking, 4 shared shower rooms with wc, hiking, cycling, fishing 5km, bird-watching 5km, sea or lake watersports 10km, riversports 10km, golf course 15km, gliding 15km, vineyard 30km

——From the A36, Exit Dôle-Nord. At the 'Stop' sign, turn right, and then right again to 'Archelange'. At the next 'Stop' sign, head for Chatenois.

PRICE STRUCTURE

10 Bedrooms and 1 Suite
Dormitory – 3 showers, kitchen, 30 single beds: FF130 (per person)

(8 rooms) 2 single beds: FF380

(1 room) 3 single beds: FF380 (2 people) FF480 (3 people)

(2 rooms) lounge, 2 single beds. FF380

(1 room) lounge, double bed, 2 single beds: FF700 (2 people) FF700 (4 people)

(1 room) lounge, double bed: FF380

Extra Bed: FF100

Reduction: groups

Capacity: 59 people

Guy HOYET
'La Maison Royale'
70140 PESMES
Tel: (0) 3 84 31 23 23
Fax: (0) 3 84 31 23 23

Château

24 km - N - DOLE
Pesmes: hosts can
collect from station,
railway station: 25km
airport: 48km

PRICE STRUCTURE

9 Bedrooms
(7 rooms) bathroom with
wc, double bed: FF450

(1 room) bathroom with wc,
twin beds: FF450

(1 room) bathroom with wc,
3 single beds:
FF450 (2 people)
FF500 (3 people)

Extra Bed: FF100

Reduction: 2 nights

Capacity: 19 people

70.01 DOLE

This superb listed building from the 13th century offers comfort, perfect taste, exceptional furniture, a warm welcome and great class. The medieval village of Pesmes is one of the 100 most beautiful villages in France, situated on the border between Franche Comté and Bourgogne.

PROPERTY

private parking, garden, lounge, pets not accepted, packed lunch, 5 years old minimum age, closed: 1/10–31/03, hiking, cycling, fishing, hunting, interesting flora, mushroom-picking, bird watching, riversports, gliding 18km, golf course 50km

Fluent English spoken

——From the A36, take the Exit for Dole. Join the D475 and turn right towards Gray. From the A39, take the Auxonne exit, head for Auxonne then take the D20, D112 and D475 towards Gray.

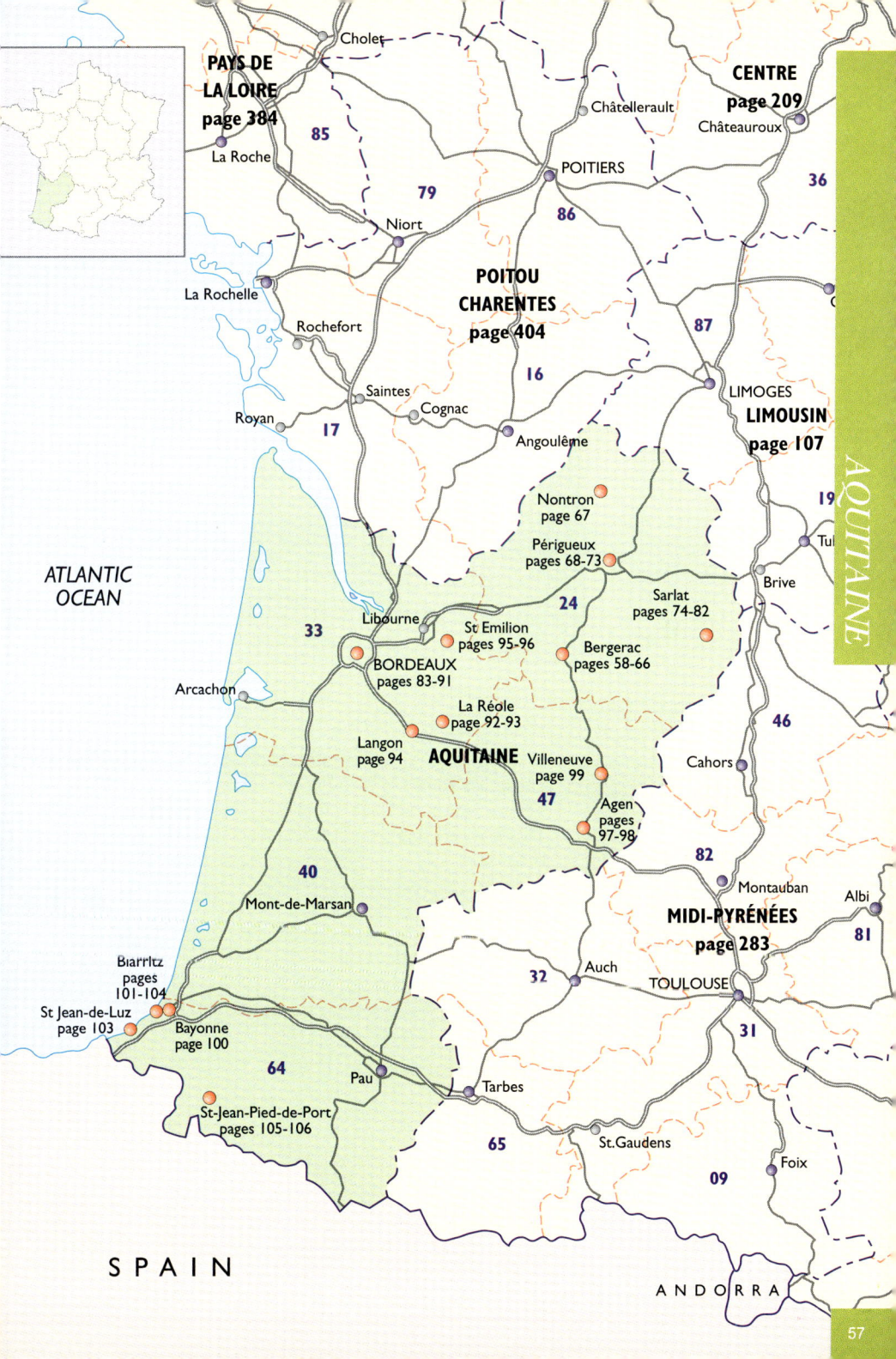

PAYS DE
LA LOIRE
page 384

Cholet

Châtellerault

CENTRE
page 209

85

La Roche

79

Niort

POITIERS

Châteauroux

36

86

La Rochelle

POITOU
CHARENTES
page 404

Rochefort

16

87

Saintes

LIMOGES

Royan

17

Cognac

Angoulême

LIMOUSIN
page 107

19

ATLANTIC
OCEAN

Nontron
page 67

Tul

Périgueux
pages 68-73

Brive

Libourne

24

Sarlat
pages 74-82

33

St Emilion
pages 95-96

Arcachon

BORDEAUX
pages 83-91

Bergerac
pages 58-66

46

La Réole
page 92-93

Langon
page 94

AQUITAINE

Villeneuve
page 99

Cahors

47

Agen
pages
97-98

82

40

Mont-de-Marsan

Montauban

Albi

MIDI-PYRÉNÉES
page 283

81

Biarritz
pages
101-104

St Jean-de-Luz
page 103

Bayonne
page 100

32

Auch

TOULOUSE

31

64

Pau

Tarbes

St-Jean-Pied-de-Port
pages 105-106

65

St.Gaudens

09

Foix

SPAIN

ANDORRA

Joséphine MORAL

'Les Mazeaux'

24520 LAMONZIE-
MONTASTRUC

Tel: (0) 5 53 23 41 83

Residence of
Outstanding Character

10 km - N E -
BERGERAC
Lamonzie-
Montastruc:
hosts can collect
from station,
railway station: 10km
airport: 13km

PRICE STRUCTURE

6 Bedrooms
(3 rooms) bathroom with
wc, double bed: FF250

fourth room: bathroom with
wc, double bed, single bed:
FF250 (2 people)
FF330 (3 people)

fifth room: double bed:
FF230

sixth room: 2 single beds:
FF170

Extra Bed: FF80

Reduction: 1/03–1/06 &
1/11–31/12 and 3 nights

Capacity: 13 people

24.02 BERGERAC

In the heart of a secret valley, you will discover this Périgord house, surrounded by its own beautiful grounds. There is a terrace with a barbecue, and a conservatory full of flowers. This is a relaxing place, near many châteaux. Fluent Flemish is spoken.

PROPERTY

off-street parking, extensive grounds, tv lounge, hosts
have pets, closed: 01/01–28/02, fishing 2km, sea or lake
watersports 10km

Adequate English spoken

——In Bergerac, take the N21 towards Périgueux. After 6km
turn right on to the D21E. Follow the signs.

Nicole VANHEMELRYCK

'Les Rocailles'
RN 21
24520 LAMONZIE-
MONTASTRUC

Tel: (0) 5 53 58 20 16/
06 85 43 04 70

Fax: (0) 5 53 58 20 16

Residence of
Outstanding Character

10 km - N E -
BERGERAC
Lamonzie-
Montastruc: hosts
can collect from sta-
tion, railway station:
10km
airport: 14km

24.38 BERGERAC

You will be charmed by this authentic 18th-century Périgourdine farm, which has been completely restored. Nicole, who is Belgian, will welcome you with a smile, and help you plan your trips. The pool is ideal for 'swimming off' the vast amounts of foie-gras you are bound to consume! An excellent address.

PROPERTY

off-street parking, extensive grounds, tv lounge, hosts have pets, kitchen, wheelchair access, swimming pool, closed: 30/10–30/03, hiking, fishing, interesting flora, mushroom-picking, golf course 8km, cycling 10km, riversports 40km
Fluent English spoken

——From Bergerac, take the N21 towards Périgueux. After Lembras, continue for 5km towards Campsegret. Follow the signs on the main road. From there go up to the hill for 250m.

PRICE STRUCTURE

2 Bedrooms and 1 Suite
Caractère: bridal room, lounge, television, bath-room with wc along corri-dor, double bed, twin beds:
FF325 (2 people)
FF505 (4 people)

ground floor: television, bathroom with wc, double bed: FF270

Suite: lounge, television, bathroom with wc, twin beds + en-suite room twin beds: FF325 (2 people)
FF505 (6 people)

Extra Bed: FF90

Reduction: 01/04–30/06 & 1/09–30/10 and for chil-dren

Capacity: 9 people

Germaine PETIT

'Le Repos'

24240 ROUFFIGNAC-DE-
SIGOULÈS

Tel: (0) 5 53 24 96 91

Residence of
Outstanding Character

6 km - S -
BERGERAC
Rouffignac-de-
Sigoulès: hosts can
collect from station,
railway station: 7km
airport: 7km
car essential

PRICE STRUCTURE

4 Bedrooms
(4 rooms) bathroom with
wc, double bed: FF300

Extra Bed: FF90

Reduction: 4 nights

Capacity: 8 people

24.39 BERGERAC

Discover the informal courtesy of Germaine and her son, who invite you to their old wine-growing estate, dating from the 19th century, nestling in the heart of the famous Monbazillac vineyards. This elegant residence, with large, tree-filled grounds, deserves its name.

PROPERTY

private parking, extensive grounds, lounge, hosts have pets, telephone, babies welcome, free cot, hiking, vineyard, cycling 3km, sea or lake watersports 3km, golf course 10km

Basic English spoken

——From Bergerac, head towards Mont de Marsan on the D933. Continue for 7km along the winding road. Go past 'La Grappe d'Or' restaurant. The house is 200m on the right.

Jennifer LYON

'Château Les Merles'

Résidence des Golfeurs

24520 MOULEYDIER

Tel: (0) 5 53 63 13 42

Fax: (0) 5 53 63 13 45

lesmerles@aol.com

www.Golf-lesmerles.com

Château

10 km - E -
BERGERAC
Mouleydier:
railway station: 15km
airport: 15km
car essential

24.43 BERGERAC

This château, dating from 1677, is situated in magnificent surroundings. It has been renovated and modernised and provides an elegant setting for the numerous activities available on site such as golf, tennis and swimming. Do not miss out on Bergerac, the ancient capital of Bergerac, and its festival. An excellent place to relax. Do not forget that this place specialises in golf! Golfing package, including green fees: FF395 per person, per night.

PROPERTY

off-street parking, extensive grounds, tv lounge, hosts have pets, telephone, kitchen, babies welcome, free cot, wheelchair access, swimming pool, tennis court, hiking, golf course, interesting flora, mushroom-picking, bird-watching, fishing 1km, cycling 2km, hunting 10km, gliding 12km

——From Bergerac, take the D660 towards Sarlat. Go through Mouleydier then, at Tuilières, turn left on to the D36 towards Clause de Clérans. The château is 200m further on.

PRICE STRUCTURE

6 Bedrooms and 1 Suite

Rose & Pivoine: telephone, bathroom with wc, double bed: FF550
Iris: telephone, bathroom with wc, double bed: FF550
Marguerite: telephone, bathroom with wc, shower, twin beds: FF550
Coquelicot: telephone, shower room with wc, twin beds: FF550
Lys: telephone, shower room with wc, double bed: FF550
Suite: telephone, shower room with wc, double bed + en-suite room single bed: FF600 (2 people) FF700 (3 people)

Extra Bed: FF100

Capacity: 15 people

Paulette & Jacques
MOLINIE

'La Gentilhommière'

24140 CAMPSEGRET

Tel: (0) 5 53 61 87 94

Fax: (0) 5 53 61 87 94

Residence of
Outstanding Character

15 km - N E -
BERGERAC
Campsegret:
railway station: 16km
airport:: 22km
car essential

PRICE STRUCTURE

6 Bedrooms
(2 rooms) bathroom with
wc, double bed: FF320

(4 rooms) shower room
with wc, double bed: FF290

Extra Bed: FF80

Capacity: 12 people

24.47 BERGERAC

This former hotel, amongst the fields, is now a spacious house with plenty of character. There is a lake, inhabited by unusual ducks, a secluded swimming pool and a quiet summer house. Here, you will experience all the charm of Le Périgord.

PROPERTY

off-street parking, extensive grounds, lounge, hosts have pets, pets not accepted, babies welcome, free cot, swimming pool, closed: 01/10–30/04, hiking, fishing, hunting, mushroom-picking, cycling 15km, riversports 20km

Basic English spoken

——Campsegret is on the N21, between Bergerac and Périgueux. From the village, follow the signs to 'La Gentilhommière' for 2km.

Françoise MAGNAN &
Gilles VIVIER

'Château de Lanquais'

24150 LANQUAIS

Tel: 05 53 61 24 24

Fax: (0) 5 53 73 20 72

Château

16 km - E -
BERGERAC
Lanquais: hosts can
collect from station,
railway station: 20km
airport:: 20km
car essential

24.50 BERGERAC

The towers, covered walkways and fortifications bear witness to the strength of this castle during the 100 Years War. Once they have closed their doors to the public at 6pm, the place is yours, and you will be enchanted. There is the Blue Salon with its magnificent fireplace, the Music Room, and the apartments, which are lavishly furnished. François and Gilles make a point of ensuring you really experience château life.

PROPERTY

✳ ✳ ✳ ✳

off-street parking, garden, lounge, hosts have pets, pets not accepted, kitchen, closed: 1/11–01/03, hiking, fishing, hunting, sea or lake watersports, vineyard 5km, golf course 6km, cycling 8km, riversports 15km

Fluent English spoken

——From Bergerac, take the D660 towards Sarlat for 15km. At St-Capraise-de-Lalinde, cross the Dordogne towards Varennes, then Lanquais. The château is signposted in the village.

PRICE STRUCTURE

2 Bedrooms
Vendée-Baldaquin:
bathroom with wc, twin
beds, single bed:
FF790 (2 people)
FF840 (3 people)

Suite Louis VI: shower room
with wc, double bed +
en-suite room single bed:
FF690 (2 people)
FF740 (3 people)

Extra Bed: FF50

Reduction: 1/04–1/06 &
1/09–1/11 and 8 nights

Capacity: 6 people

Philippe COMALADA

'Domaine les Jourdis'

Les Jourdis

33220 LES-LEVES-ET-
THOUMEYRAGUES

Tel: (0) 5 57 41 22 35

Fax: (0) 5 57 41 22 35

COMALADA
@net-up.com

Château

30 km - W -
BERGERAC
Les-Lèves-et-
Thoumeyragues:
railway station: 7km
airport:: 25km
car essential

PRICE STRUCTURE

1 Bedroom and 2 Suites
Suite Acacias: lounge,
television, telephone,
shower room with wc,
bathroom, double bed
(queen size) + en-suite
room 2 single beds:
FF590 (2 people)
FF950 (4 people)

Suite Mexique: bridal room,
lounge, television,
telephone, shower room
with wc, bathroom, double
bed + en-suite room double
bed: FF590 (2 people)
FF950 (4 people)

La Romana: lounge,
television, telephone, shower room with wc, twin beds,
single bed: FF480 (2
people) FF630 (3 people)

Reduction: 1/09-31/03

Capacity: 11 people

33.29 BERGERAC

This is a fortified 16th century house in solid stone, set on a hill overlooking the vineyards. The bedrooms are modern, and the décor is really inspired. Philippe welcomes you with great enthusiasm and will tell you about the wines of Bordeaux with even greater enthusiasm, take you to visit wine cellars or teach you how to drive a 4-wheel drive vehicle....

PROPERTY

private parking, extensive grounds, tv lounge, hosts have pets, pets not accepted, telephone, dinner available, babies welcome, free cot, swimming pool, riversports, hiking, cycling, fishing, riversports 7km, gliding 7km, golf course 10km, vineyard 50km

Fluent English spoken

——At Bergerac, head towards Ste-Foy-la-Grande, and there take the D672 towards Pellegrue for 7km. In the village, take the small road on the right of the church towards the 'Cave Cooperative'. Then first left and the lane on the left.

Henri & Françoise
PEYRE

'Château de Pechalbet'

47800 AGNAC

Tel: (0) 5 53 83 04 70

Fax: (0) 5 53 83 04 70

Château

25 km - S -
BERGERAC
Agnac: hosts can
collect from station,
railway station: 30km
airport:: 30km

47.16 BERGERAC

Here in the Périgord Pourpre you will be welcomed to this magnificent 17th century gentilhommière, typical of this region. It is surrounded by 40 hectares of woods and fields. Be sure to try the local dishes as you are in foie-gras country.

PROPERTY

✸ ✸ ✸ ✸

private parking, garden, tv lounge, hosts have pets, dinner available, babies welcome, free cot, wheelchair access, swimming pool, closed: 05/01–25/03, hiking, cycling, hunting, interesting flora, mushroom-picking, fishing 2km, riversports 2km, sea or lake watersports 15km, golf course 18km

Fluent English spoken

PRICE STRUCTURE

4 Bedrooms and 1 Suite
(1 room) bathroom with wc, double bed: FF550

(2 rooms) shower room with wc, double bed: FF390

Suite: shower room with wc, double bed + en-suite room 2 single beds (child-size): FF550 (2 people)
FF650 (4 people)

fifth room: shower room with wc, twin beds: FF550

Extra Bed: FF100
Reduction: 01/10–01/05 and 3 nights and groups

Capacity: 12 people

——At Bergerac take the D933 towards Marmande. 1km after Eymet follow the signs.

Françoise & Christian
LEMARCHAND

'Ferme de Monplaisir'

Cavarc

47330 CASTILLONNÈS

Tel: 05 53 36 84 91
06 82 57 29 60

Fax: (0) 5 53 36 82 82

Working Farm

25 km - S W -
BERGERAC
Cavarc: hosts can
collect from station,
railway station: 25km
airport:: 17km
car essential

PRICE STRUCTURE

5 Bedrooms
Jaune: wheelchair access,
shower room with wc, twin
beds, 2 single beds (child-
size): FF280 (2 people)
FF380 (4 people)
Verte: wheelchair access,
shower room with wc, twin
beds, 2 single beds:
FF280 (2 people)
FF380 (4 people)
Rose: wheelchair access,
shower room with wc, twin
beds: FF250
Bleue-1: shower room with
wc, twin beds, 3 single beds:
FF280 (2 people)
FF380 (5 people)
Bleue-2: shower room with
wc along corridor, twin
beds: FF250

Extra Bed: FF50; Reduction:
groups; Capacity: 17 people

47.17 BERGERAC

**If you like good humour, good food and 'la bonne vie', this is
the place for you. You will receive a genuine Périgord
welcome in this farmhouse, where Françoise will spoil you
with her healthy, traditional dishes. The bedrooms are really
cosy, converted from an old wine cellar. This is an excellent
base for visiting the châteaux and 'bastides' of this region, or
following the many footpaths and tourist trails.**

PROPERTY

off-street parking, garden, hosts have pets, dinner available,
packed lunch, kitchen, babies welcome, free cot, wheelchair
access, hiking, cycling, mushroom-picking, fishing 2km, vineyard 10km, sea or lake watersports 11km, interesting flora
15km, bird-watching 15km, golf course 20km, riversports 25km

Basic English spoken

——At Bergerac, take the N21 towards Agen for 11km. Then
left on to the D14, via Issigeac, and head towards Villeréal for
5km. Then turn right, and continue as far as Cavarc, and
then follow signs to the farm.

Michel & Sheila
BRASSEUR

'Le Petit Cousset'

24360 VARAIGNES

Tel: (0) 5 53 56 52 58

Private Home

15 km - N W -
NONTRON
Varaignes: hosts can
collect from station,
railway station: 32km
car essential

24.24 NONTRON

Situated between the Dordogne and Charente, near the Angoulème-Périgueux road, Michel and Sheila's place offers a great place to stay in a self-contained apartment with every comfort. Ideal for a family or two couples. There are also two rooms on the first floor of the house. Sheila is English.

PROPERTY

private parking, extensive grounds, tv lounge, hosts have pets, telephone, dinner available, packed lunch, babies welcome, free cot, 1 shared shower room with wc, hunting, mushroom picking, hiking 1km, cycling 1km, fishing 1km, sea or lake watersports 10km, golf course 20km, interesting flora 30km, riversports 30km

Fluent English spoken

——At Nontron, take the D75 towards Angoulème. 'Le Petit Cousset' is signposted 2km after Javerlhac. Coming from Angoulème, take the D939 towards Périgueux. 4.5km after Soyaux, take the D4 then the D75 towards Marthon-Nontron. On this road, 2km after the Route Varaignes, turn left to 'Le Petit Cousset' (signposted 500m. on the left).

PRICE STRUCTURE
2 Bedrooms and
1 Apartment
first room: double bed, cot:
FF210

second room: double bed:
FF180

Apartment: lounge, television, kitchen, shower room with wc, double bed + 1st en-suite room double bed, 2nd en-suite room double bed, 2 single beds:
FF250 (2 people)
FF680 (8 people)

Extra Bed: FF70
Reduction: children

Capacity: 12 people

Yvette MERILLOU

Avenue André Maurois

24310 BRANTOME

Tel: (0) 5 53 05 74 04

Private Home

22 km - N - PERIGUEUX
Brantôme:
railway station: 25km
airport:: 30km
car essential
——At Périgueux, take
the D939 towards
Angoulème. Cross
Brantome, heading
towards Angoulème. As
you leave the town, after
the bridge, turn right
towards Thiviers, and
then take the first
country lane on the left.

24.27 PERIGUEUX

Very basic, but the warm kindness of Yvette and the picturesque village of Brantome, (the little Venice of the Périgord), more than compensates. Be sure to ask for the room with private bathroom; the other room has not been classified by us.

PROPERTY

off-street parking, garden, telephone, babies welcome, free cot, wheelchair access, hiking, cycling, fishing, hunting, mushroom-picking, riversports, golf course 20km, gliding 32km

PRICE STRUCTURE
2 Bedrooms

first room: television, shower room with wc, 2 single beds: FF203
Extra Bed: FF51,50

Capacity: 2 people

Jacqueline & Gérolf
JACOBS

'La Ferme de
Laubicherie'

Laubicherie

24270 SARLANDE

Tel: (0) 5 53 52 69 90

Fax: (0) 5 53 52 69 90

Gerolf@wanadoo.fr

Working Farm

50 km - N E -
PERIGUEUX
Sarlande: hosts can
collect from station,
railway station: 8km
airport:: 50km
car essential

24.30 PERIGUEUX

On the main Limoges-Sarlat road, you will find this friendly
Belgian couple. Jacqueline will no doubt tell you of her love
of cats. In their restored farmhouse, they make bread, foie-
gras and Belgian beer! You will have the opportunity to taste
their own produce at dinner. On sale: Summer fruit, poultry,
rabbits, foie-gras, lambs.

PROPERTY

private parking, garden, tv lounge, hosts have pets, pets not
accepted, dinner available, 1 shared shower room with wc,
hiking, cycling, fishing, interesting flora, mushroom-picking,
sea or lake watersports 7km, riversports 10km, golf course
40km

Fluent English spoken

——At Limoges, take the D704 as far as St-Yriex-la-Perche,
which you should cross, heading towards Périgueux. After
6km, you are in the Dordogne, and you should take the first
on the left and follow the daisy signs 'Bienvenue à la Ferme'.
(At Périgueux, N21 towards Limoges. At Sarliac, D705 on the
right then D704 towards Limoges).

PRICE STRUCTURE

6 Bedrooms

Amanda: bathroom with wc,
double bed, 2 single beds
(1child-size): FF245 (2
people) FF320 (4 people)
Bleuet: shower room with
wc, double bed, single bed
(child-size): FF230 (2
people) FF305 (3 people)
Vanille: shower room with
wc, double bed, 2 single
beds (child-size): FF230 (2
people) FF330 (4 people)
Faïence: shower, wc, 2 single
beds (child-size): FF230
Pistache: shower, washbasin,
twin beds: FF230
Melon: shower room with
wc, twin beds: FF280

Extra Bed: FF75

Reduction: groups

Capacity: 17 people

PERIGUEUX

Jean-Claude SALIVES

'Peyssut'

24330 LADOUZE

Tel: (0) 5 53 06 72 92

Working Farm

18 km - S E -
PERIGUEUX
Ladouze: hosts can
collect from station,
railway station: 18km
airport:: 14km
car essential

PRICE STRUCTURE

6 Bedrooms
(5 rooms) shower room
with wc, washbasin, double
bed, single bed:
FF240 (2 people)
FF315 (3 people)

(1 room) shower room with
wc, washbasin, double bed:
FF260

Extra Bed: FF75

Capacity: 17 people

24.31 PERIGUEUX

Claude and Claudine will give you a hearty welcome to their livestock farm surrounded by fields and woods. There are caves and medieval towns to visit, and after a hard day's sightseeing, you will enjoy unwinding beside the swimming pool. On sale: Wine, Pineau, Cognac, honey.

PROPERTY

off-street parking, garden, tv lounge, hosts have pets, pets not accepted, telephone, babies welcome, free cot, wheelchair access, swimming pool, hiking, cycling, interesting flora, mushroom-picking, golf course 10km, fishing 12km, riversports 20km

——At Périgueux head towards Cahors (N89) then turn right to Le Bugue, Sarlat (D710). Peyssut is on the D710.

AQUITAINE

PERIGUEUX

Stuart SHIPPEY
& Robert CHAPPELL

'Le Moulin Neuf'

Paunat

24510 STE ALVERE

Tel: (0) 5 53 63 30 18

Fax: (0) 5 53 73 33 91

moulin-neuf@usa.net

www.francedirect.net

Residence of
Outstanding Character

30 km - S -
PERIGUEUX
Paunat:
railway station: 6km
airport:: 40km
car essential

24.33 PERIGUEUX

Guests are accommodated in an old house which is separate from the mill. Robert and Stuart have given a touch of English charm to this place, and the garden is delightfully designed with flowers, a lake, weeping willow and a stream. Really cosy, very pleasant and near to Sarlat. Small pets accepted by arrangement.

PROPERTY

off-street parking, extensive grounds, tv lounge, hosts have pets, telephone, hiking, cycling, fishing, interesting flora, mushroom-picking, bird-watching, riversports 5km, sea or lake watersports 6km, golf course 20km

Fluent English spoken

——At Périgueux, N89 towards Cahors.Right on to the D710 as far as Le Bugue. Then D31 towards Limeuil. After the 'cingle', go downhill. At the crossroads straight on towards Ste-Alvère. After 100m turn left. It is 2km further on, on the left.

PRICE STRUCTURE

6 Bedrooms
(2 rooms) bathroom with wc, double bed: FF434

(2 rooms) shower room with wc, twin beds: FF434

fourth room: bathroom with wc, double bed, single bed: FF434 (2 people)
FF586 (3 people)

fifth room: shower room with wc, double bed: FF434

Extra Bed: FF154

Capacity: 13 people

Jacqueline GARNERO

'Les Combarelles'

24510 PAUNAT

Tel: (0) 5 53 22 75 74
06 70 91 23 37

Fax: (0) 5 53 22 75 74

Private Home

30 km - S - PERIGUEUX
Paunat:
railway station: 10km
airport:: 40km
car essential
——At Périgueux, take
the N89 towards Cahors,
then the D710 on the
right as far as Le Bugue.
Then take the D703
towards Ste. Alvère for
10km (do NOT go to
Paunat). Then take the
little road on the left,
opposite the D2 (the D2
goes towards Ste. Alvère,
so do NOT take it).
Continue along this
small road for 1km.

24.49 PERIGUEUX

Jacqueline have just taken over this place which is quite a treasure trove in the heart of the Périgord Noir. The 'Or' bedroom, has a romantic decor, while the 'Pin' bedroom and the 'Provençal' apartment (beside the solar-heated swimming pool) are more self-contained. This haven of peace will exceed your expectations.

PROPERTY

off-street parking, extensive grounds, lounge, pets not accepted, telephone, dinner available, kitchen, wheelchair access, swimming pool, hiking, mushroom-picking, cycling 10km, golf course 10km

Fluent English spoken

PRICE STRUCTURE
1 Bedroom and 1 Suite and 1 Apartment

Pin: wheelchair access, bathroom with wc, double bed: FF350

Or: wheelchair access, bathroom with wc, double bed, cot + en-suite room twin beds, single bed: FF350 (2 people) FF650 (5 people)

Provençal: wheelchair access, lounge, television, kitchen, shower, wc: FF350 (2 people) FF650 (5 people)

Extra Bed: FF100

Capacity: 11 people

Michel & Claude
DUSEAU

'Château de La Borie'

24530 CHAMPAGNAC-
DE-BELAIR

Tel: (0) 5 53 54 22 99

Fax: (0) 5 53 08 53 78

chateau-de-la-borie-
saulnier@wanadoo.fr

Château

30 km - N -
PERIGUEUX
Champagnac-de-
Belair: hosts can
collect from station,
railway station: 50km
airport: 30km

24.07 PERIGUEUX

A totally authentic 13th-century fortress, restored and furnished with period furniture. Spend your day visiting the caves and the Abbey of Brantome and, on summer evenings, dine under the stars in the inner courtyard of the château.

PRICE STRUCTURE

4 Bedrooms and 1 Suite
Jaune: bathroom with wc, double bed, single bed:
FF480 (2 people)
FF590 (3 people)

Verte: bathroom with wc, double bed: FF490

Turquoise: bathroom with wc, twin beds, single bed: FF450

Bleu: shower room with wc, double bed + en-suite room
Rose: double bed, single bed: FF450 (2 people)
FF690 (5 people)

Grise: bathroom with wc, twin beds: FF390

Extra Bed:130FF

Reduction: 6 nights and children

Capacity: 15 people

PROPERTY

private parking, extensive grounds, tv lounge, hosts have pets, telephone, dinner available, swimming pool, tennis court, closed: 01/01–01/02, cycling, fishing, riversports, golf course 30km

Basic English spoken

——In Périgueux, take the D939 towards Angoulême. In Brantome, go in the direction of Angoulême, Montron. Before the Total petrol station, take the road 'chez Ravailles' (VC3) for 3.5km.

Françoise HERPIN
FORGET

'Le Verseau'

49, route des Pechs

24200 SARLAT-LA-
CANEDA

Tel: (0) 5 53 31 02 63-
06 88 78 48 24

Private Home

SARLAT:
railway station: 1km
airport:: 50km
——From the centre of
Sarlat, go to the railway
station. Turn left towards
'Les Pechs' and continue
for 1.2km. The house is
on the right.

Danielle BARILLEAU

La Gendonie - Vignera
24200 SARLAT-LA-
CANEDA

Tel: (0) 5 53 59 30 65

SARLAT
Sarlat: hosts can collect
from station,
railway station: 1km
airport: 50km
——From Sarlat, go
towards Bergerac, then
Domme. Opposite the
Casino supermarket,
right towards Le Bugue.
After 100m, left into the
1st small road towards
Vignera. The house is
the 2nd on your left.

24.15 SARLAT

Sarlat is a great place to live, and Françoise will help you enjoy every minute of it during your stay. Her house, in typical Périgord style, is set in grounds with magnificent trees and views over the valley of Sarlat. Be sure to try a trip in a horse-drawn carriage and visit La Dordogne, the châteaux, the prehistoric caves and the medieval villages.

PROPERTY

private parking, extensive grounds, hosts have pets, pets not accepted, babies welcome, free cot, 1 shared shower room with wc, sea or lake watersports 6km, cycling 10km, golf course 10km, riversports 10km

Basic English spoken

PRICE STRUCTURE
6 Bedrooms
1st room: shower room with wc, double bed, twin beds: FF320 (4 people); 2nd room: double bed, single bed: FF235 (3 people); 3rd room: single bed: FF125; 4th room: shower room with wc, double bed, single bed: FF265 (3 people); 4b: television, shower room with wc, double bed: FF230; 5th room: television, bathroom with wc, double bed: FF250

Extra Bed: FF55; Capacity: 15 people

24.23 SARLAT

Danielle is charming, and her pleasant house is in verdant surroundings. The small individual lodges ensure that you can relax and take your breakfast in complete privacy, and you are only 15 mins. walk from the centre of the beautiful town of Sarlat.

PROPERTY

private parking, extensive grounds, hosts have pets, 3 nights minimum stay: (1/05–1/07), closed: 01/10–01/05, hiking, cycling, mushroom-picking, sea or lake watersports 6km, fishing 8km, riversports 8km, golf course 10km

Basic English spoken

PRICE STRUCTURE
4 Bedrooms
Marron: bathroom with wc, 3 single beds: FF240 (2 people) FF305 (3 people)
Verte: bathroom with wc, double bed: FF240
Jaune: bathroom with wc along corridor, double bed: FF240
Lambris-Indépendante: shower room with wc, double bed: FF210

Extra Bed: FF65

Capacity: 9 people

William & Michèle
VIDAL D'HONDT

'Château du Pas du Raysse'

Le Raysse

24370 CAZOULES

Tel: (0) 5 53 29 84 41

Fax: (0) 5 53 59 62 16

Château

24 km - E - SARLAT
Le Raysse: hosts can collect from station, railway station: 3km airport:: 35km
car essential

24.28 SARLAT

This is a real discovery. Peace and quiet pervades William and Michèle's château which melts into the soft landscapes of the Dordogne. You will be enchanted as you taste William's fine cooking and his wines chosen with skill. We fell in love with this place and gave it an extra sun.
On sale: Foie-gras, wine.

PROPERTY

✴ ✴ ✴ ✴

private parking, extensive grounds, tv lounge, dinner available, babies welcome, free cot, wheelchair access, swimming pool, 3 nights minimum stay: (01/07–31/08), closed: 15/09–15/10 & 20/12–15/01, hiking, fishing, cycling 3km, riversports 3km, mushroom-picking 4km, golf course 5km

Fluent English spoken

——In Sarlat take the D704A and then the D703 towards Souillac. As you enter Cazoulès turn left by the sign on the left to 'chambres d'hôtes'. Then climb up the little road at right angles and, when facing the gate, take the unmade road.

PRICE STRUCTURE

3 Bedrooms and 2 Suites

first room: shower room with wc, double bed, single bed: FF490 (2 people) FF590 (3 people)
second room: shower room with wc, double bed: FF490
Suite first floor: shower room with wc, double bed + en-suite room twin beds: FF490 (2 people) FF690 (4 people)
Suite second floor: shower room with wc, double bed + en-suite room twin beds: FF690 (2 people) FF690 (4 people)
extra room second floor: shower room with wc, single bed: FF390 (1 person)

Extra Bed: FF100
Reduction: 01/10–30/06 and groups
Capacity: 14 people

Konrad & Elisabeth
HOLLEIS

'Le Jaonnet'

Liabou Bas

24250 NABIRAT

Tel: (0) 5 53 29 59 29

Fax: (0) 5 53 29 59 29

Residence of
Outstanding Character

16 km - S E -
SARLAT
Liabou Bas:
airport:: 150km
car essential

PRICE STRUCTURE

5 Bedrooms
Fermain: shower room with
wc, washbasin, double bed,
single bed:
FF320 (2 people)
FF405 (3 people)

Icart: bathroom with wc,
double bed, single bed:
FF300 (2 people)
FF385 (3 people)

Portelet: lounge, bathroom
with wc, twin beds: FF300

Saints: shower room with
wc, double bed: FF300

Moulin Huet: shower room
with wc, double bed: FF300

Extra Bed: FF85

Capacity: 12 people

24.29 SARLAT

**Owned by a charming couple from Guernsey. Konrad is a
professional chef (his 'zabaglione' is fantastic). Their old
farmhouse has been restored with great charm, and the
dining room, with its solid oak gallery, is very attractive.**

PROPERTY

off-street parking, garden, lounge, pets not accepted, dinner
available, babies welcome, free cot, non-smoking, wheelchair
access, 3 nights minimum stay: (01/06–30/09), closed: 01/11–
1/03, hiking, interesting flora, sea or lake watersports 2km,
cycling 5km, riversports 5km, golf course 8km, gliding 12km

Fluent English spoken

——In Sarlat take the D704 towards Gourdon-Cahors. 2km
after the Dordogne river, turn right (D50), continue towards
Domme for 50m. At La Poste of Grolejac, turn left towards
Nabirat. 2nd turning on left (signposted).

Chantal GAYRARD

'Domaine des Tourelles'

Le Poujol

24590 ST-CREPIN-ET-CARLUCET

Tel: (0) 5 53 31 09 38

Fax: (0) 5 53 31 09 38

Château

13 km - N - SARLAT
Le Poujol:
railway station: 11km
airport:: 38km
car essential

24.40 SARLAT

In this 18th century former winery, guests are welcome to make full use of the swimming pool and tennis court. It is set in the heart of an attractive tourist area, and peace and quiet is guaranteed.

PROPERTY

private parking, extensive grounds, tv lounge, babies welcome, free cot, swimming pool, tennis court, 14 years old minimum age, hiking, cycling, interesting flora 7km, golf course 9km, fishing 10km, hunting 10km, riversports 15km

Adequate English spoken

PRICE STRUCTURE

2 Bedrooms
Bleu: bathroom with wc, shower, double bed: FF535

Fleurs: bathroom with wc along corridor, shower along corridor, double bed: FF535

Extra Bed: FF150

Capacity: 4 people

——From Sarlat, take the D704 towards Montignac. After 9km, turn left on to the D60 in the direction of Salignac. Continue for 4km as far as 'Le Poujol' then follow the signs for 'Domaine des Tourelles'.

Nicole & Jean QUERRE

'Les Granges Hautes'

St Crépin

24590 ST-CREPIN-ET-CARLUCET

Tel: (0) 5 53 29 35 60

Fax: (0) 5 53 28 81 17

jquerre@aol.com

Residence of
Outstanding Character

13 km - N - SARLAT
St-Crépin-et-Carlucet:
railway station: 10km
airport:: 35km
car essential

AQUITAINE

SARLAT

PRICE STRUCTURE

5 Bedrooms

Toscane: bathroom with wc, double bed, single bed:
FF520 (2 people)
FF625 (3 people)

virginie: bathroom with wc, twin beds: FF520

Irina: shower room with wc, double bed, single bed:
FF480 (2 people)
FF615 (3 people)

Oiseaux: shower room with wc, double bed, twin beds:
FF480 (2 people)
FF770 (4 people)

Pamela: shower room with wc, twin beds: FF480

Reduction: 10 nights
Capacity: 14 people

24.44 SARLAT

This beautiful Périgord house is set in superb grounds. Each room is different, and has its own individual style which will transport you to Italy, the Orient.... A delicious breakfast, an excellent swimming pool and the warm welcome of your hosts all add up to an enchanting place.

PROPERTY

off-street parking, extensive grounds, tv lounge, pets not accepted, telephone, packed lunch, babies welcome, free cot, swimming pool, closed: 01/10–1/04, hiking, cycling, interesting flora 10km, golf course 15km, fishing 15km

Basic English spoken

——At Sarlat, take the D704 towards Montignac. After 9km, turn right and take the D60 towards St. Crépin and Carlucet. In the village, follow the signs to 'Les Granges Hautes'.

Olivier Le ROUX

'Manoir de la Moissie'

La Moissie

24170 BELVES

Tel: (0) 5 53 30 31 97

Fax: (0) 5 53 29 15 34

sunset.creation
@wanadoo.fr

Residence of
Outstanding Character

30 km - S W -
SARLAT
Belvès: hosts can
collect from station,
railway station: 2km
airport:: 75km
car essential

24.45 SARLAT

Here, you will get a really warm, genuine welcome in the centre of Belvès, a listed medieval village. This former 16th-century hunting lodge is surrounded by extensive, and very attractive, wooded grounds. Your rooms are in a comfortably restored little house in the grounds, with the bedrooms in the tower of the 'pigeonnier'.

PROPERTY

✹ ✹ ✹ ✹

off-street parking, extensive grounds, tv lounge, pets not accepted, dinner available, kitchen, babies welcome, free cot, wc, hiking 2km, cycling 2km, mushroom-picking 2km, golf course 3km, fishing 5km, fishing 10km

Fluent English spoken

——At Sarlat, take the D57 and then the D703 for Bergerac. At Siorac, take the D770 on the left as far as Belvès. Head towards Monpazier. Turn right immediately after the municipal swimming pool, and it is the first lane on the left in front of a small wall. Go up this lane (following signs to 'La Moissie').

PRICE STRUCTURE

1 Bedroom and 1 Apartment

Studio: kitchen, shower, twin beds + room Ambre: shower, double bed: FF340 (2 people)
FF480 (4 people)

Extra Bed: FF60

Reduction: 10 nights

Capacity: 4 people

Marie-France CAPY

'Ferme du Syndic'

46300 PAYRIGNAC

Tel: (0) 5 65 41 15 70

Fax: (0) 5 65 41 15 70

Working Farm

12 km - S E - SARLAT
Payrignac: hosts can collect from station, railway station: 5km airport:: 180km car essential

PRICE STRUCTURE

5 Bedrooms and 1 Suite

Orchidée & Les Iris: shower room with wc, washbasin, double bed: FF280

Les Violettes & Roseraie: along corridor shower room with wc, double bed: FF250

Les Genêts:shower room with wc along corridor , double bed, 3 single beds: FF250 (2 people) FF450 (5 people)

Brin de Muguet: shower room with wc, double bed + en-suite room double bed: FF280 (2 people) FF480 (4 people)

Extra Bed: FF90

Capacity: 17 people

46.09 SARLAT

Marie-France's large house sits proudly on the top of a hill, set back from the working farm. You will take breakfast and dinner on the terrace, with its beautiful view over the countryside. There are flowers everywhere, and the bedrooms are also named after them.

PROPERTY

off-street parking, garden, tv lounge, hosts have pets, pets not accepted, telephone, dinner available, non-smoking, hiking, mushroom-picking, fishing 2km, riversports 5km, golf course 15km

——At Sarlat, take the D704 towards Cahors. 'La Ferme du Syndic' is signposted on your right, 5km before Gourdon.

Peter KERKHOFF

'Les Maurelles'

Le Bourg

46300 MILHAC

Tel: (0) 5 65 41 48 59

Fax: (0) 5 65 41 66 21

maurelles@wanadoo.fr

www.maurelles.com

Private Home

19 km - S E -
SARLAT
Milhac: hosts can
collect from station,
railway station: 7km
airport: 150km
car essential

46.13 SARLAT

This young couple have faithfully restored the old solicitor's house in this little stone hamlet parts dating from the 17th century. The welcome is warm and hearty and together with the Dordogne this green, peaceful location will conspire to make you extend your stay. On sale: Walnuts, local produce.

PROPERTY

✸ ✸

off-street parking, garden, tv lounge, hosts have pets, telephone, dinner available, packed lunch, babies welcome, free cot, 1 shared bathroom with wc, swimming pool, hiking, cycling, fishing, mushroom–picking, sea or lake watersports 5km, riversports 7km, golf course 17km

Fluent English spoken

PRICE STRUCTURE

3 Bedrooms
first room: shower room
with wc, double bed: FF400

(2 rooms) shower room
with wc, double bed,
2 single beds:
FF400 (2 people)
FF480 (4 people)

Extra Bed: FF50
Reduction: 01/10–31/05
and 7 nights and groups
and children

Capacity: 10 people

——In Sarlat, take the D704 towards Gourdon. In Groléjac, turn left towards Milhac. As you enter the village, the house is on the left.

Jane Elisabeth BARKER

'La Pinière'

Sous la Plaine

46350 MASCLAT

Tel: (0) 5 65 32 29 80

Fax: (0) 5 65 32 29 80

piniere@hotmail.com

Private Home

AQUITAINE

SARLAT

20 km - S E - SARLAT
Masclat: hosts can collect from station, railway station: 10km airport: 150km

PRICE STRUCTURE

3 Bedrooms
first ground-floor room: lounge, bathroom with wc, double bed: FF420

second ground-floor room: shower room with wc, double bed: FF420

third room: bathroom with wc, double bed: FF350

Extra Bed: FF100
Reduction: 01/01–30/06 & 01/09–01/12

Capacity: 6 people

46.26 SARLAT

This is a really peaceful house, full of character in the woods. The rooms are homely and comfortable, with their own terrace and separate access. Jane Elisabeth is English and an ex-chef, and will prepare delicious local dishes for you.

PROPERTY

off-street parking, extensive grounds, lounge, pets not accepted, telephone, dinner available, non-smoking, swimming pool, hiking, mushroom-picking, fishing 1km, riversports 5km, cycling 10km, golf course 10km

Fluent English spoken

——From Sarlat, take the D704 towards Souillac. In Roufillac, cross the Dordogne towards St-Julien-de-Lampon, then Masclat. In Masclat, follow the signs to 'La Pinière'.

Michèle TARDAT

'Cantemerle'

9, Rue des Châtaigniers - Bourdin

33180 VERTHEUIL-MEDOC

Tel: (0) 5 56 41 96 24
06 08 98 71 02

Fax: (0) 5 56 41 96 24

Residence of
Outstanding Character

55 km - N W - BORDEAUX
Vertheuil:
airport: 60km
car essential

33.06 BORDEAUX

A beautiful house in the Spanish Moorish style, in the heart of the Médoc vineyards. Here you will find peace and quiet and an outstanding decor that reflects your hosts' love of travelling. Nearby are the famous Médoc wine châteaux, beaches and the wine museum. On sale: Wine.

PROPERTY

private parking, extensive grounds, tv lounge, hosts have pets, pets not accepted, dinner available, babies welcome, free cot, non-smoking, cycling, vineyard, fishing 1km, sea or lake watersports 35km

Fluent English spoken

——In Bordeaux, take Exit 7 on the A630 then the D1 towards Le Verdon/Soulac. In Castelnau, take the N215 in the same direction, for 25km. Turn right on to the D205 towards Cissac and take the D104 towards Vertheuil where you turn left by the church, towards Bourdin. The property is on your left as you leave the hamlet. Can be reached by the Royan–Pointe des Graves ferry: N215 to Lesparre then the D204 to Vertheuil.

PRICE STRUCTURE

2 Bedrooms
Tour: shower room with wc along corridor, twin beds: FF320

Bleue: bathroom with wc along corridor, double bed: FF300

Extra Bed: FF100
Reduction: 01/11–28/02 and children

Capacity: 4 people

Valérie & Philippe
BASSEREAU

'Château de la Grave'

33710 BOURG-SUR-
GIRONDE

Tel: 05 57 68 41 49

Fax: (0) 5 57 68 49 26

chateau.de.la.grave
@wanadoo.fr

www.chateau.de.la.grave.
com

Château

30 km - N -
BORDEAUX
Bourg sur Gironde:
railway station: 15km
airport: 45km

PRICE STRUCTURE

3 Bedrooms
Les Tournesols: shower
room with wc, 2 double
beds: FF300 (2 people)
FF400 (4 people)

Les Blés: shower room with
wc, twin beds, single bed:
FF300 (2 people)
FF400 (3 people)

Les Cyprès: shower room
with wc, double bed, single
bed: FF300 (2 people)
FF400 (3 people)

Extra Bed:no charge

Capacity: 10 people

33.30 BORDEAUX

Refreshed by a good night's sleep, you will have your breakfast in the large, white stone dining room. You will then be ready to go walking through the maze of vines and then to cool off beside the pool and take in the superb view over the valleys covered in vines. Valérie will be there, relaxed and full of smiles, to serve you a refreshing drink. You are sure to leave with a few bottles of her own wine as a souvenir, and great memories of this château. Its superb location earns it four 'suns'. Excellent value for money.

PROPERTY

private parking, extensive grounds, tv lounge, hosts have pets, pets not accepted, swimming pool, closed: 15/08–1/09 & 1/02–1/03, hiking, vineyard, cycling 2km, fishing 5km, bird-watching 20km, golf course 35km, sea or lake watersports 50km *Fluent English spoken*

——From Bordeaux on the A10, Exit Bourg sur Gironde. At Bourg, head towards Blaye, and then turn right towards Berson. Then take the second on the right and follow the signs to 'Château de la Grave'.

33.27 BORDEAUX

Alice is a retired anaesthetist and welcomes you to her house right in the centre of Bordeaux. She only has one room, decorated the colour of bordeaux (what else?), which is cosy and comfortable. After days of serious sightseeing and wine tasting, you will appreciate relaxing in her attractive garden. Essential to book in advance.

PROPERTY

private parking, garden, tv lounge, hosts have pets, pets not accepted, telephone, kitchen, 2 years old minimum age, golf course 8km, cycling 10km, interesting flora 50km, sea or lake watersports 60km

Fluent English spoken

PRICE STRUCTURE

television, shower, bathroom, wc, double bed: FF350

Capacity: 2 people

Alice BONDONNY

61, rue Leberthon

33000 BORDEAUX

Tel: (0) 5 56 94 59 11

Fax: (0) 5 56 94 59 11

Private Home

BORDEAUX:
railway station: -
airport: 8km
——In Bordeaux, head towards the Place de la Victoire, Cours de l'Argonne (towards Bayonne) and then take the third street on the right.

AQUITAINE

BORDEAUX

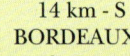

AQUITAINE

BORDEAUX

Yolande BONNET

'Gravelande'

7, Chemin du Bergey

33850 LEOGNAN

Tel: (0) 5 56 64 72 04

alexbonnet@aol.com

Residence of
Outstanding Character

14 km - S -
BORDEAUX
Léognan: hosts can
collect from station,
railway station: 15km
airport: 20km
car essential

PRICE STRUCTURE

1 Bedroom and 1 Suite
Vanille: kitchen, bathroom
with wc, shower, double
bed: FF350

Laura: shower room with
wc, double bed (queen size)
+ en-suite room Led:
(queen size) 2 single beds:
FF350 (2 people)
FF500 (4 people)

Extra Bed: FF100
Reduction: 4 nights

Capacity: 6 people

33.07 BORDEAUX

Only 20 mins. from the centre of Bordeaux, this house is surrounded by impressive grounds in the heart of the famous Pessac-Léognan vineyards. You will find very difficult to tear yourself away from Yolande's wonderful, warm hospitality, so allow plenty of time to relax and enjoy it.

PROPERTY

private parking, extensive grounds, tv lounge, hosts have pets, pets not accepted, dinner available, babies welcome, free cot, swimming pool, 2 nights minimum stay, closed: 15/10–15/05, vineyard, golf course 10km, sea or lake watersports 50km

Fluent English spoken

——In Bordeaux, take Exit 18 on the A630 towards Léognan. There, on the square, take the D214 towards Cestas. Take the fourth lane on the right, and the first gate on the left.

Alain GENESTINE

'Domaine Les Sapins'

Bouqueyran

33480 MOULIS-EN-MEDOC

Tel: (0) 5 56 58 18 26-06 80 22 45 07

Fax: (0) 5 56 58 28 45

Residence of Outstanding Character

25 km - N W - BORDEAUX
Moulis-en-Médoc:
railway station: 4km
airport: 24km
car essential

33.08 BORDEAUX

Here the atmosphere is cosy and you feel like one of the family. The large house dates from the beginning of the 19th century and is set amongst vines, surrounded by beautiful grounds. Nathalie, who is a Cordon Bleu cook, will serve you her specialities and Alain will share his expertise in wine with you. You will love this place. On sale: Wine.

PROPERTY

off-street parking, extensive grounds, tv lounge, telephone, dinner available, babies welcome, free cot, hiking, vineyard, cycling 1km, hunting 1km, mushroom-picking 1km, golf course 12km, fishing 20km, interesting flora 25km, sea or lake watersports 25km, bird-watching 60km

Fluent English spoken

——At Bordeaux, on the A630 take Exit 7 and the D1 towards Le Verdon sur Soulac. In Castelnau, take the N215 in the same direction, for 3km. In Bouqueyran, you turn left (large sign).

PRICE STRUCTURE
5 Bedrooms and 1 Suite

Hortensia: bathroom with wc, double bed (king size) + en-suite room Albarose: double bed, single bed: FF400 (2 people) FF650 (5 people)
Marguerite: shower room with wc, double bed (king size): FF350
Menuet: shower room with wc, double bed (king size): FF350
Country: shower room with wc, 2 double beds: FF350 (2 people) FF450 (4 people)
Charleston: shower room with wc, double bed, single bed: FF350 (2 people) FF550 (3 people)
Chinatown: shower, washbasin, double bed (king size): FF300
Extra Bed: FF150
Reduction: 01/11–30/11 & 01/01–15/03 and 5 nights
Capacity: 18 people

Blanche MAINVIELLE

'Château de Grand Branet'

859, Branet Sud

33350 CAPIAN

Tel: (0) 5 56 72 17 30

Fax: (0) 5 56 72 36 59

Château

30 km - S E - **BORDEAUX**
Capian:
railway station: 25km
airport: 30km
car essential

PRICE STRUCTURE

4 Bedrooms and 1 Suite
Rose: lounge, bathroom with wc, double bed: FF345

Bleuet: shower room with wc, twin beds, single bed: FF295 (2 people) FF375 (3 people)

Pivoine & Jonquille: shower room with wc, double bed, single bed: FF345 (2 people) FF425 (3 people)

Iris: lounge, shower room with wc, double bed + en-suite room 2 single beds: FF345 (2 people) FF505 (4 people)

Extra Bed: FF80

Capacity: 12 people

33.12 BORDEAUX

This château, which has recently been restored, has large, comfortable rooms and king-size beds. Its vineyard produces Premières Côtes de Bordeaux. Enjoy the 5 hectares of peaceful grounds and try to fit in a few châteaux visits between the wine tasting! On sale: Wine 'Premières Côtes de Bordeaux'.

PROPERTY

off-street parking, extensive grounds, tv lounge, pets not accepted, telephone, dinner available, packed lunch, kitchen, hiking, cycling, hunting, mushroom-picking, vineyard, fishing 8km, golf course 30km

Basic English spoken

——Take Exit La Brède from the A62, and then the N113 towards Agen, and then the D115 towards Langoiran as far as the D10. Then turn right towards Cadillac. At Pied-du-Château, turn left towards Capian. At the top of the hill, turn right and then take the 5th made-up road on the left. Continue 200m to the château.

Jean-Pierre & Marie-Ange
FROMENT

18, Route de Soulac

33930 VENDAYS-
MONTALIVET

Tel: (0) 5 56 41 73 52

Private Home

70 km - N W -
BORDEAUX
Vendays-Montalivet:
hosts can collect
from station, railway
station: 6km
airport: 75km

33.13 BORDEAUX

Marie-Ange and Jean-Pierre, 'young' senior citizens, will give you a warm welcome in their beautiful villa, with its beautiful gardens in the heart of the Médoc, famed for its 'grands crus'. They are only 10km from beautiful, sandy beaches. (Please note, bedroom 'Verte' has a shower in the room.)

PROPERTY

private parking, extensive grounds, lounge, hosts have pets, babies welcome, free cot, wc, sea or lake watersports 7km

Basic English spoken

——At Bordeaux, on the motorway take Exit 7 and follow the D1 towards Le Verdon. At Castelnau, take the N215 towards Soulac-Le Verdon. Turn left on to the D102 towards Vendays. At La Mairie, towards Soulac, the house is on the left, 300m after the traffic lights.

PRICE STRUCTURE

4 Bedrooms
Rez de Jardin: shower room with wc along corridor, double bed, single bed:
FF340 (2 people)
FF400 (3 people)

first floor – Blanche-Baldaquin: shower, double bed: FF300

first floor – Bleue: double bed, single bed:
FF320 (2 people)
FF380 (3 people)

first floor – Verte: shower, washbasin, double bed:
FF300

Extra Bed: FF90

Capacity: 10 people

Jeannette SENELAR

'Domaine de Fauquey'

33670 LA SAUVE

Tel: (0) 5 56 23 01 41

Fax: (0) 5 56 23 01 41

Château

AQUITAINE

BORDEAUX

20 km - S E - BORDEAUX
La Sauve:
railway station: 15km
airport: 30km
car essential

PRICE STRUCTURE

3 Bedrooms
Verlaine: bathroom with wc, twin beds: FF350

Claudel: shower room with wc, double bed, single bed:
FF350 (2 people)
FF450 (3 people)

Ronsard: shower room with wc, 2 double beds:
FF350 (2 people)
FF550 (4 people)

Reduction: 01/10–31/05 and 3 nights

Capacity: 9 people

33.17 BORDEAUX

Chez Jeannette, you are in a quiet and pleasant spot, and you will find a very warm welcome. The bedrooms are spacious, comfortable and pleasantly furnished. Stabling for horses is also available.

PROPERTY

off-street parking, extensive grounds, tv lounge, hosts have pets, pets not accepted, dinner available, packed lunch, babies welcome, free cot, swimming pool, riding, cycling, interesting flora, hiking 1km, mushroom-picking 2km, golf course 5km, fishing 5km, bird-watching 20km, sea or lake watersports 50km

Adequate English spoken

——From Bordeaux, go towards Bergerac. Take the D671 towards Créon. Follow the D671 towards La Sauve-Sauveterre. When you are 2 km from Créon and 1 km from La Sauve-Sauveterre, turn left. The house is the first on the right, 800 m further on.

Liliane & Michel
KORBER

'Petit Hotel Labottière'

14, rue Francis Martin

33000 BORDEAUX

Tel: (0) 5 56 48 44 10

Fax: (0) 5 56 48 44 14

Château

BORDEAUX:
railway station: -
airport: 11km

33.25 BORDEAUX

Do not miss this place in the centre of the elegant city of Bordeaux. It is a long story, but this magnificent 'hotel particulier' originally belonged to an 18th-century batchelor gentleman of good taste. The building is listed, and combines refined comfort with an authentic heritage. Your host will be delighted to show you around the house.

PROPERTY

Private parking, garden, lounge, telephone, 8 years old minimum age, golf course 15km, sea or lake watersports 60km

Fluent English spoken

PRICE STRUCTURE

2 Bedrooms
(2 rooms) television, telephone, shower room with wc, bathroom, double bed: FF1,000

Capacity: 4 people

——From the Place Tourny, take the Rue Fondaudège. At the fourth set of traffic lights, turn right into the Rue St. Laurent and, at the end, turn immediately left into the Rue Francis-Martin.

Mieke BORREMANS

'Manoir du Gaboria'

5, le Gaboria

33580 STE-GEMME

Tel: (0) 5 56 71 99 57

Fax: (0) 5 56 71 99 58

manoir@gaboria.com

www.gaboria.com

Château

15 km - N E - LA REOLE
Ste-Gemme:
railway station: 15km
airport: 60km
car essential

AQUITAINE

LA REOLE

PRICE STRUCTURE

3 Bedrooms
Jaune : lounge, television, telephone, kitchen, shower room with wc, double bed (super king size): FF500

Bleu: lounge, television, telephone, shower room with wc, double bed (queen size): FF400

Verte: lounge, television, telephone, bathroom with wc, double bed, twin beds: FF400 (2 people) FF600 (4 people)

Extra Bed: FF100

Capacity: 8 people

33.26 LA REOLE

Another haven of peace. You will know straight away that you have picked the right place because this house breathes comfort and calm. Everything is just right in the large bedrooms, which are uncluttered, bright, pleasant and with a superb view.

PROPERTY

off-street parking, extensive grounds, tv lounge, hosts have pets, pets not accepted, telephone, babies welcome, free cot, non-smoking, swimming pool, hiking, cycling, riversports 4km, golf course 25km

——From La Réole, head towards Monségur on the D668. In Monségur, take the D16 for 4km towards Ste-Gemme. Then turn left towards St-Vivien-de-Montségur, and continue for 400m. Then turn left (by the cross) and immediately take the first on the left towards Gaboria.

Monique BAUGÉ

'Au Canton'

1, Le Canton

33190 ST-SEVE

Tel: 05 56 61 04 88-06 85 10 31 95

Fax: (0) 5 56 61 04 88

Private Home

4 km - N - LA REOLE
St-Sève:
railway station: 4km
airport: 70km

33.31 LA REOLE

This farmhouse dates from the 18th century and has been completely restored. It is surrounded by the quiet vineyards of Bordeaux, near to the ancient town of La Réole. Monique will help you get to know the historical and architectural heritage of this area. Her lovely warm welcome and attention to your every need will have you lingering over breakfast under the large, shaded terrace.

PROPERTY

✸ ✸ ✸

off-street parking, extensive grounds, tv lounge, hosts have pets, telephone, dinner available, babies welcome, free cot, hiking, cycling, hunting, interesting flora, bird-watching, vineyard, fishing 4km, riversports 4km, sea or lake watersports 15km, golf course 18km

Basic English spoken

——From La Réole, take the D670 towards Libourne. At the roundabout, take the D21 towards St-Sève for 2km. After St-Sève, take the first road on the right at the sign 'Au Canton', and continue for 100m. Then take the first lane on the right.

PRICE STRUCTURE

3 Bedrooms

television, shower room with wc, double bed, single bed: FF300 (2 people) FF380 (3 people)

television, shower room with wc, bathroom, double bed, single bed: FF300 (2 people) FF380 (3 people)

television, shower room with wc, bathroom, double bed, 2 single beds: FF300 (2 people) FF460 (4 people)

Reduction: 1/09–30/06

Capacity: 10 people

Béatrice & Pierre
LABUZAN

'Château de Monbazan'

Place de l'Eglise

33720 LANDIRAS

Tel: (0) 5 56 62 42 82
Fax: (0) 5 56 62 54 47

chateaudemonbazan
@worldline.fr

Château

15 km - W - LANGON
Landiras:
railway station: 15km
airport: 45km
car essential
——From the A62, Exit
2, take the D11 towards
Landiras for 6km. In
Landiras, the house is
opposite the church,
next to the petrol
station. The entrance to
the car park is from the
Cabanac road.

33.21 LANGON

This is a wine grower's house, in the heart of the Graves vineyards, 6km from Sauternes. Pierre and Béatrice are into organic farming, and will be delighted to show you round their property. The redecorated bedroom is excellent value and an ideal place for spending several days. On sale: Organically produced wine, grape juice.

PROPERTY

private parking, garden, lounge, hosts have pets, pets not accepted, babies welcome, free cot, non-smoking, hiking, cycling, mushroom-picking, bird-watching, vineyard, cycling 6km, fishing 6km, riversports 6km, golf course 15km, sea or lake watersports 25km

Fluent English spoken

PRICE STRUCTURE
1 Bedroom

shower room with wc, washbasin, double bed, cot: FF220

Reduction: 3 nights

Capacity: 2 people

Jacqueline & Wilfrid
FRANC de FERRIERE

'Château de Carbonneau'

33890 PESSAC SUR
DORDOGNE

Tel: (0) 5 57 47 46 46

Fax: (0) 5 57 47 42 26

carbonneau@wanadoo.fr
chateau-carbonneau.com

Château

20 km - S E -
ST-EMILION
Pessac-Sur-
Dordogne: hosts can
collect from station,
railway station: 12km
airport: 60km
car essential

33.24 ST-EMILION

Vineyard vacations! In this 19th century château on a family estate of 50 hectares, you will savour the peace and quiet of this place. Wilfred and Jacquie, a New Zealand couple, will be delighted to tell you about their wine growing business. On sale: Wine.

PROPERTY

off-street parking, extensive grounds, tv lounge, hosts have pets, telephone, babies welcome, free cot, wheelchair access, swimming pool, closed: 15/11–1/03, hiking, fishing, interesting flora, bird-watching, vineyard, cycling 2km, riversports 2km, sea or lake watersports 10km, golf course 18km

Adequate English spoken

PRICE STRUCTURE

3 Bedrooms
Telephone: bathroom with wc, twin beds: FF300

Master bedroom: bathroom with wc, double bed: FF300

Pigeonnier: shower room with wc, twin beds, single bed: FF300 (2 people) FF400 (3 people)

Extra Bed: FF100

Capacity: 7 people

——At St-Emilion, go towards Bergerac (D936). At La Tête Noire, turn right on to the D9 towards Gensac, Pessac. In the village, follow the signs.

Michel MORTEYROL

'Château de Courtebotte'

33420 ST-JEAN-DE-BLAIGNAC

Tel: 05 57 84 61 61-06 83 07 18 25

Fax: (0) 5 57 84 68 68

michel.morteyrol @wanadoo.fr

Château

9 km - S - ST-EMILION
St-Jean-de-Blaignac:
railway station: 12km
airport: 45km

PRICE STRUCTURE

4 Bedrooms and 1 Suite
shower, double bed: FF600

Suite – Baldaquin-Dordogne: lounge, shower room with wc, bathroom, double bed + en-suite room suite: twin beds:
FF1,100 (2 people)
FF1,600 (4 people)

Double-Dordogne: shower room with wc, twin beds: FF800

Bali-Baldaquin: shower room with wc, bathroom, double bed: FF900

Terrasse: bridal room, lounge, bathroom, double bed (queen size): FF1100

Extra Bed: FF200

Capacity: 12 people

33.28 ST-EMILION

This château, with the evocative name of 'Coutebotte', was built beside the Dordogne in the reign of Henri IV. The views are outstanding and Michel, who is a photographer and landscape gardener, pulls out all the stops to make you feel at home. Life is never dull here, there is always something new to discover – the excellent cooking, the style and originality of the bedrooms, the gardens, the swimming pool or the relaxing walks in the forest. On sale: Wine, foie-gras.

PROPERTY

private parking, extensive grounds, tv lounge, pets not accepted, dinner available, babies welcome, free cot, wheelchair access, swimming pool, cycling, fishing, mushroom-picking, bird-watching, vineyard, sea or lake watersports 15km, riversports 15km, golf course 20km

Adequate English spoken

——At St-Emilion, take the D670 towards La Réole. At St-Jean-de-Blaignac, follow the D119.

Maria VAN STRAATEN

'Le Marchon'

47130 BAZENS

Tel: (0) 5 53 87 22 26

Fax: (0) 5 53 87 22 26

Private Home

22 km - W - AGEN
Bazens: hosts can
collect from station,
railway station: 4km
airport: 22km

47.06 AGEN

Maria and sculptor Henri welcome you, around the fire in cool weather. They try to cater for everybody's individual tastes – organic and vegetarian dishes and excellent wine, some home-made, can be provided. This region is rich in caves and châteaux.

PROPERTY

off-street parking, extensive grounds, tv lounge, hosts have pets, dinner available, non-smoking, 1 shared shower room, wc, swimming pool, closed: 01/11–01/04, hiking, cycling

Fluent English spoken

——In Agen take the RN113 towards Bordeaux, for 20km. Turn right towards Bazens (D118) and D231 towards Galapian until you reach the sign.

PRICE STRUCTURE

5 Bedrooms

shower room with wc, twin beds: FF280

bathroom with wc, double bed, 2 single beds:
FF280 (2 people)
FF410 (4 people)

bathroom with wc, double bed: FF280

washbasin, twin beds: FF240

washbasin, double bed, single bed:
FF240 (2 people)
FF300 (3 people)

Extra Bed: FF65

Reduction: 01/09–30/06 and 2 nights

Capacity: 13 people

Danièle SPIRITELLI &
Daniel RAUST

'Clos Muneau'

28, rue Victor Hugo

47190 AIGUILLON

Tel: (0) 5 53 79 59 84
06 03 35 51 47

Fax: (0) 5 53 79 59 83

clos-muneau@wanadoo.fr
www.clos-muneau.com

Residence of
Outstanding Character

30 km - N W - AGEN
Aiguillon:
railway station: -
airport: 30km
car essential

AQUITAINE

AGEN

PRICE STRUCTURE

4 Bedrooms

Beauregard: shower room
with wc, double bed: FF300

Victor Hugo: bathroom with
wc, double bed: FF300

Marine: lounge, kitchen,
shower room with wc, dou-
ble bed, single bed:
FF300 (2 people)
FF400 (3 people)

Marinette: shower room
with wc, double bed: FF300

Extra Bed: FF100

Reduction: 16/09–14/06
and 3 nights and children

Capacity: 9 people

47.14 AGEN

You will be charmed by the spacious and airy rooms in this residence, dating from the start of the 20th century. The large conservatory opens on to a beautiful wooded garden with a swimming pool. Danièle and Daniel use all their 'savoir faire' and kindness to make you feel at home. A super place, on the edge of the countryside.

PROPERTY

private parking, garden, tv lounge, hosts have pets, dinner available, babies welcome, free cot, swimming pool, closed: 15/12–31/01, cycling, fishing 2km, hiking 3km, sea or lake watersports 5km, hunting 10km, mushroom-picking 10km, interesting flora 15km, riversports 15km, golf course 20km

Adequate English spoken

——Exit 6 from the A62. When you reach the square, facing the Château d'Aiguillon, take the rue Thiers on the left and continue straight on. Cross a small square and you are in the rue Victor Hugo. Number 28 is on the right.

'Le Pré Joli'

Moncheyroux

47290 CANCON

Tel: (0) 5 53 01 78 62

Residence of
Outstanding Character

20 km - N -
VILLENEUVE-SUR-LOT
Cancon:
railway station: 47km
airport: 36km
car essential

47.11 VILLENEUVE-SUR-LOT

Here, in magnificent countryside, is a very pleasant house, furnished with taste and with a very cosy atmosphere. There is a large dining room with a fireplace and the bedrooms are spacious. The atmosphere is enhanced by a collection of old photographs of actors. On sale: Foie-gras, cous farcis (stuffed goose neck).

PROPERTY

private parking, extensive grounds, tv lounge, hosts have pets, telephone, dinner available, 2 years old minimum age, closed: 30/09–30/04, hiking, cycling, riversports, sea or lake watersports 4km, golf course 5km, fishing 12km

Basic English spoken

PRICE STRUCTURE

4 Bedrooms
first room: kitchen, bathroom with wc, twin beds: FF270

second room: bathroom with wc, double bed: FF270

third room: television, bathroom with wc, twin beds: FF270

fourth room: bathroom with wc, double bed: FF270

Extra Bed: FF60

Capacity: 8 people

——At Villeneuve, take the N21 towards Bergerac. The house is on the N21 before Cancon.

Noëllie ANNIC
& Jean-Luc SOT

'Villa Ty Gias'

1, Avenue Hilton Head

40510 SEIGNOSSE

Tel: (0) 5 58 41 64 29
06 80 06 14 77

Fax: (0) 5 58 41 64 29

tygias@wanadoo.fr
http://perso.wanadoo.fr
/tygias/

Private Home

30 km - N -
BAYONNE
Seignosse:
railway station: 30km
airport: 30km
car essential

AQUITAINE

BAYONNE

PRICE STRUCTURE

4 Bedrooms
television, shower room
with wc along corridor,
double bed: FF450

television, shower room
with wc along corridor, twin
beds: FF450

Pavillon: lounge, television,
bathroom with wc along
corridor, double bed +
room twin beds:
FF450 (2 people)
FF900 (4 people)

Extra Bed: FF150

Reduction: 05/02–14/07 &
1/09–31/12 and 2 nights
and groups

Capacity: 8 people

40.11 BAYONNE

It is not surprising that Noëllie is in great demand, as her modern villa, built with traditional materials, is in the middle of the pine forest typical of les Landes, but near to the golf course, lakes and the ocean. The coast near Hossegor is known by surfers the world over. The house overlooks the 13th hole on the undulating golf course at Seignosse. If you like outdoor activities, do not miss staying here.

PROPERTY

private parking, garden, hosts have pets, pets not accepted, dinner available, packed lunch, babies welcome, free cot, 1 shared bathroom with wc, cycling, fishing 3km, sea or lake watersports 3km, interesting flora 5km, mushroom-picking 10km, riversports 15km, gliding 15km, winter sports 80km

Fluent English spoken

——From Bayonne, on the A63, Exit 7. Then go to Benesse Marenne, Hossegor, Seignosse le Lenon, and go to the golf course.

Annette ROCAFORT

20 bis, rue de Tartillon

64600 ANGLET

Tel: (0) 5 59 03 55 68

j.rocafort@wanadoo.fr

Private Home

BIARRITZ
Anglet: hosts can
collect from station,
railway station: 5km
airport: 4km

64.19 BIARRITZ

Annette will give you a warm welcome to her home, which is situated in a residential area. This is a very quiet place, and you will love relaxing in her pleasant little garden after exploring the Basque country. Biarritz is 3km away, and the beach 2km away.

PRICE STRUCTURE

2 Bedrooms
first room: double bed,
single bed (child-size):
FF240

second room: twin beds:
FF240

Extra Bed: FF80

Capacity: 5 people

PROPERTY

off-street parking, garden, tv lounge, pets not accepted, telephone, kitchen, 1 shared bathroom, 1 shared shower room, 3wc, 2 nights minimum stay, cycling, fishing, hunting, mushroom-picking 2km, hiking 3km, sea or lake watersports 4km, bird-watching 5km, golf course 7km, riversports 30km

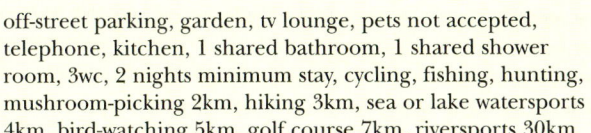

——From the A63, take the Biarritz La Négresse Exit. Head towards Anglet, Cinq Cantons, Plage de la Chambre d'Amour.

Pierre & Bernadette
MENDIONDO

'Villa Arrosen-Artean'

Chemin d'Ithulrraldia

64210 AHETZE

Tel: (0) 5 59 41 93 03

Fax: (0) 5 59 41 93 03

bernadette.mendiondo
@freesbee.fr

Private Home

6 km - S - BIARRITZ
Ahetze:
railway station: 5km
airport: 8km
car essential
——On the A63 take the
Biarritz Exit. Take the
N10 towards Bidart for
3km. At the set of traffic
lights by 'Monsieur
Bricolage', turn left
towards Ahetze for 4km.
At the church, go
towards St-Peel-sur-
Nivelle for 300m. Turn
right on to the 'chemin
d'Ithurraldia' then take
the 2nd lane on the left.
The house is at the end.

64.13 BIARRITZ

The welcome is very warm and the view over the valley and the village is uninterrupted! A very relaxing spot near the beach. The shower is in the room in the Jaune, Bleue and Green bedrooms. In the little neighbouring restaurants you can try 'piperade' or 'poulet basquaise'. Basque pelota, traditional dances and surfing are worth seeing. On sale: Eggs, vegetables.

PROPERTY

off-street parking, garden, tv lounge, hosts have pets, pets not accepted, dinner available, 10 years old minimum age, closed: 1/11–1/03, cycling, hiking 3km, golf course 3km, cycling 5km, fishing 5km, mushroom-picking 5km, bird-watching 15km, riversports 20km, gliding 20km

Basic English spoken

PRICE STRUCTURE

5 Bedrooms

Rose: double bed, single bed: FF300 (2 people) FF400 (3 people)

+ room Saumon Baldaquin: double bed, single bed: FF300 (2 people) FF400 (3 people)

Jaune & Bleue & Verte: shower, washbasin, double bed: FF280 (2 people)

Extra Bed: FF50

Reduction: 01/09–30/06 and 2 nights and groups

Capacity: 12 people

Eliane CHARDIET

'Villa Erresinolettean'

4, rue de la Tour

64500 CIBOURE

Tel: (0) 5 59 47 87 88

Fax: (0) 5 59 47 27 41

www.waqui.com/hotes/64
/chardiet.htm

Private Home

1 km - S W -
ST-JEAN-DE-LUZ
Ciboure:
railway station: 2km
airport: 15km
car essential

64.17 ST-JEAN-DE-LUZ

You have a choice of views from this beautiful modern house: either the bay of St-Jean-de-Luz or the Pyrenées. A warm welcome with embroidered sheets on your bed, quality furniture and decor, real silver, porcelain from Paris and spacious bedrooms. Fleur de Soleil member.

PROPERTY

Private parking, garden, hosts have pets, pets not accepted, dinner available, packed lunch, babies welcome, free cot, 1 shared bathroom with wc, cycling, fishing 3km, sea or lake watersports 3km, interesting flora 5km, mushroom picking 10km, riversports 15km, gliding 15km, winter sports 80km

——On the A63 towards Spain Exit number 2, St-Jean-de-Luz-Sud and follow the signs towards Ciboure. 400m after the traffic-lights, turn left and follow signs to Tour de Bordagain. 100m before the tower, look for the blue gate with the weeping willow.

PRICE STRUCTURE

3 Bedrooms
Hortensia: lounge, television, shower room with wc, double bed (queen size): FF450

Louis XIII: lounge, television, shower room with wc, bathroom, double bed (queen size): FF450

Romantique: bridal room, television, bathroom with wc, double bed (queen size): FF450

Extra Bed: FF200/2 people.

Capacity: 6 people

Sylvie LUPO

'La Musica'

4, rue Thalie - Les
Champs d'Anglet

64600 ANGLET

Tel: (0) 5 59 42 24 97
06 13 67 16 87

LA.MUSICA@wanadoo.fr

Private Home

BIARRITZ
Anglet: hosts can collect
from station,
railway station: 4km
airport: 3km
——From the A63, Exit
Anglet-Bayonne Sud.
Head towards Anglet-
Centre - Les Plages.
Then phone for
directions.

Marie-Jeanne BACHOC

'Maison
Etchemendigaraya'
64780 SUHESCUN
Tel: (0) 5 59 37 60 83
bruno.bachoc
@wanadoo.fr
Working Farm

12 km - N - ST-JEAN-
PIED-DE-PORT
Suhescun:
railway station: 12km
airport:: 45km
car essential
——In St-Jean-Pied-de-
Port go towards St-Palais,
turn left on to the D22
towards Lopeinea and
Suhescun. In the village,
go towards the sign for
'Camping'.

64.22 BIARRITZ

Sylvie is open and full of smiles and welcomes you to her Basque house, close to Biarritz and Bayonne. This area is famous for its surfing beaches and the Basque country offers numerous contrasting activities: beaches, countryside, skiing, the rich culture of this proud people, homes with traditional style and comfort, and unique culinary traditions.

PROPERTY

garden, tv lounge, hosts have pets, telephone, dinner available, babies welcome, free cot, closed: 1/12–31/01, hiking, cycling, hunting, mushroom-picking, bird-watching, riversports, vineyard, fishing 5km, winter sports 15km, golf course 40km

Basic English spoken

PRICE STRUCTURE
3 Bedrooms

Bleue: television,bathroom with wc along corridor , double bed: FF330

Rustique: television,shower room with wc along corridor , double bed: FF330

Garçonnière: television, shower room with wc, double bed (queen size): FF330

Reduction: 2 nights
Capacity: 6 people

64.10 ST JEAN PIED DE PORT

This beautiful farm, with lots of character, dates from the 17th century and is in the heart of the Basque country. A warm farmhouse welcome awaits you. Go to St-Jean-Pied-de-Port (with its numerous restaurants) and try your hand at 'pelote Basque' (a local game). On sale: Farm produce.

PROPERTY

off-street parking, extensive grounds, tv lounge, hosts have pets, telephone, dinner available, packed lunch, babies welcome, free cot, 1 shared shower room, wc, closed: 15/11–15/12, hiking, cycling, interesting flora, mushroom-picking, fishing 1km, vineyard 1km, riversports 4km, hunting 12km, bird-watching 12km, winter sports 15km

Fluent English spoken

PRICE STRUCTURE
2 Bedrooms and 1 Suite

(2 rooms) shower room with wc, double bed: FF220

Suite: along corridor bathroom with wc, double bed + en-suite room 2 single beds: FF220 (2 people) FF440 (4 people)

Extra Bed: FF50; Capacity: 8 people

Mireille & Eric LEVITTE

'Maison E. Bernat'

20, rue de la Citadelle

64220 ST-JEAN-PIED-DE-PORT

Tel: 05 59 37 24 07/ 06 84 24 30 79

Fax: (0) 5 59 37 23 10

Elmh@wanadoo.fr

Residence of Outstanding Character

ST-JEAN-PIED-DE-PORT
airport: 50km

64.24 ST JEAN PIED DE PORT

This place is right in the centre of this typical old town and should not be missed. In fact, the house which dates from 1662, backs on to the citadel and is very quiet. There is also a view over the mountains and the vineyards of IrouLegy. Here, the welcome is pleasant and very professional, as your hosts also own a restaurant.

PROPERTY

off-street parking, garden, tv lounge, hosts have pets, telephone, dinner available, packed lunch, kitchen, babies welcome, free cot, hiking, cycling, riversports 10km, winter sports 30km

——The rue de la Citadelle is the main street and, as you would expect, leads up the citadel.

PRICE STRUCTURE

4 Bedrooms
Iraty: television, bathroom with wc along corridor, double bed, single bed:
FF320 (2 people)
FF390 (3 people)

St-Jean de-Luz: television, bathroom with wc, double bed, single bed:
FF400 (2 people)
FF470 (3 people)

Bayonne & Espelette: television, bathroom with wc, double bed, single bed:
FF350 (2 people)
FF420 (3 people)

Extra Bed: FF70
Reduction: 5 nights

Capacity: 12 people

Patrick BROUQUE

'Arrostegia'

Route d'Arnéguy

64220 UHART CIZE

Tel: 05 59 37 06 22
06 71 25 35 01

Fax: (0) 5 59 37 06 22

Residence of
Outstanding Character

1 km - W - ST-JEAN-PIED-DE-PORT
Uhart Cize: hosts can
collect from station,
railway station: 50km
airport: 50km

PRICE STRUCTURE

5 Bedrooms

(2 rooms) shower room with wc, double bed: FF220

Suite: along corridor bathroom with wc, double bed + en-suite room 2 single beds: FF220 (2 people) FF440 (4 people)

Extra Bed: FF50; Capacity: 8 people

Louis XV: television, bathroom with wc, double bed: FF450

Restauration: television, shower room with wc, twin beds: FF450

Louis XVI & Meneau: television, double bed: FF420

Baldaquin: television, single bed: FF300 (1 person)

Extra Bed: FF30; Reduction: 1/01–30/03; Capacity: 9 people

64.23 ST JEAN PIED DE PORT

It is worth noting that the medieval town of St-Jean-de-Port is listed as a site of world importance. Patrick's 17th century house is a very pleasant spot with antique furniture, evenings around the piano, a jacuzzi and traditional Basque cuisine. On sale: Antiques, objets d'art, foie gras, confits.

PROPERTY ✳ ✳ ✳ ✳

off street parking, extensive grounds, tv lounge, hosts have pets, telephone, dinner available, packed lunch, babies welcome, free cot, 1 shared shower room, wc, closed: 15/11-15/12, hiking, cycling, interesting flora, mushroom picking, fishing 1km, vineyard 1km

Fluent English spoken

——Take the D15 towards St-Etienne-de-Baïgorry and turn right.

Châteaudun

45

ORLÉANS

Montargis

Sens

10

Auxerre

89

BOURGOG│
page 12│

21

D

Blois

41

37

Vierzon

CENTRE
page 209

Bourges

Nevers

18

58

Autun

Beau

Chalon-su
Saôn

71

Châtellerault

36

Châteauroux

Moulins

POITIERS

86

POITOU
CHARENTES
page 404

Guéret

23

87

Montluçon

Montmarault
pages 108-109

03

Vichy
page 110

Roanne

69

16

LIMOUSIN

LIMOGES
page 121

CLERMONT-
FERRAND
page 118

Thiers
page 117

63

RHÔNE-
ALPES
page 499

LYON

Angoulême

19

Tulle
page 120

Issoire
page 116

AUVERGNE

42

Vienne

St.-Etienne

Périgueux

Brive
page 119

15

43

Puy-en-Velay
page 115

Valence

07

24

Bergerac

AQUITAINE
page 57

Aurillac
pages 111-114

Privas

46

Cahors

Mende

48

84

Villeneuve

47

Agen

Rodez

12

Millau

Alès

30

Avignon

13

82

Montauban

Albi

MIDI-PYRÉNÉES
page 283

81

LANGUEDOC-
ROUSSILLON
page 260

Nimes

Arles

32

Auch

TOULOUSE

Castres

Béziers

34

MONTPELLIER

31

Michèle & Olivier BAES

'La Roche'

03240 TRONGET

Tel: (0) 4 70 47 16 43

Working Farm

15 km - N E -
MONTMARAULT
Tronget:
railway station: 25km
airport: 50km
car essential
——From the autoroute
A71, take the Exit
Montmarault, then the
N145 towards Moulins.
From the village of
Tronget, take the D230
towards Gipcy for 3km,
then turn right towards
'La Roche'.

03.10 MONTMARAULT

Michèle and Olivier know how to receive guests in style. Their Charolais beef farm is set in rolling countryside, where wooded hills, lazy streams and green pastures abound. Naturally, Michèle uses only the best farm produce in her cooking.

PROPERTY

off-street parking, garden, lounge, hosts have pets, dinner available, non-smoking, hiking, mushroom-picking, fishing 4km, bird-watching 15km, sea or lake watersports 20km, hiking 25km, golf course 30km, interesting flora 30km, winter sports 60km

Fluent English spoken

PRICE STRUCTURE
3 Bedrooms

first room: shower room with wc, double bed, cot: FF230

second room: shower room with wc, double bed, single bed: FF230 (2 people) FF300 (3 people)

third room: bathroom with wc, washbasin, double bed, 2 single beds (child-size): FF230 (2 people) FF370 (4 people)

Extra Bed: FF70

Capacity: 9 people

Dominique
PESSAR-MAZET

'Château du Max'

Le Max

03240 LE THEIL

Tel: 04 70 42 35 23

Château

15 km - N E -
MONTMARAULT
Le Max: hosts can
collect from station,
railway station: 35km
airport: 90km
car essential

03.12 MONTMARAULT

It is always a great pleasure to stay in a moated château, with parts dating from the 13th and 15th centuries. In addition, you will be welcomed with great warmth and kindness by Dominique. Add to this the calm and the quiet of the countryside, a certain gentle and relaxed lifestyle, the distinctive and authentically furnished bedrooms and you have all the ingredients for a restful and relaxing stay.

PROPERTY

private parking, extensive grounds, tv lounge, hosts have pets, telephone, kitchen, babies welcome, free cot, wheelchair access, hiking, cycling, fishing, mushroom-picking, vineyard 10km, riversports 15km, golf course 20km

Basic English spoken

——From the A71, take Exit 11 Montmarault. Then take the D46 towards St-Pourçain. At Voussac, take the D129 on the left towards Le Theil. The château is on the left, after the lake.

PRICE STRUCTURE

2 Bedrooms and 1 Suite
Rome-Baldaquin: wheelchair access, lounge, television, kitchen, shower room with wc, double bed, single bed:
FF400 (2 people)
FF450 (3 people)

Verte: television, bathroom with wc, twin beds: FF400

Suite: lounge, television, bathroom with wc, wc, double bed, single bed + en-suite room double bed:
FF450 (2 people)
FF600 (5 people)

Extra Bed: FF50

Capacity: 10 people

Marie-Claude MARTIN

'Les Printanières'

23 rue Harpet

03200 VICHY

Tel: 04 70 98 03 26

Fax: (0) 4 70 98 20 04

mcmb@infonie.fr

www.ifrance.com/
mcmartin

Apartment

VICHY
Vichy: hosts can collect from station, railway station: - airport: 15 km

PRICE STRUCTURE

**2 Bedrooms and
3 Apartments**
second floor – Duplex Les Violettes: bathroom with wc along corridor, single bed + room twin beds: FF200 (2 people) FF370 (3 people)
Suite – Les Muguets: lounge, television, kitchen, bathroom with wc along corridor, double bed, single bed: FF200 (2 people) FF300 (3 people)
ground floor – Les Myrtilles: lounge, television, kitchen, shower, bathroom, wc, double bed, single bed (child-size): FF250 (2 people) FF300 (3 people)
first floor – Myosotis: kitchen, bathroom with wc, double bed: FF200

Extra Bed: FF50

Reduction: groups

Capacity: 11 people

03.11 VICHY

You may think that you know Vichy well, but Marie-Claude will surprise you. She was born here, and loves her native town, famous for its spa waters, so passionately that she will be sure to show you something that is new to you. She has a talent for entertaining, and throws open her house with great enthusiasm. You will always feel at home here and, if you wish to discuss flying, she holds a pilot's licence.

PROPERTY

off-street parking, hosts have pets, telephone, kitchen, babies welcome, free cot, 1 shared bathroom with wc, hiking, cycling, sea or lake watersports, riversports, golf course 3km, gliding 5km, vineyard 30km, interesting flora 60km

Basic English spoken

——Telephone your hosts for directions.

Michèle & Alain LAFON

Le Bourg

15130 GIOU DE MAMOU

Tel: (0) 4 71 64 51 55

http://site.voila.fr/chlaf

Residence of
Outstanding Character

7 km - E -
AURILLAC
Giou de Mamou:
hosts can collect
from station, railway
station: 8km
airport: 8km
car essential

15.06 AURILLAC

This charming 19th century house with lots of character is near to the Cantal Mountains. There is a nice contrast between the rugged exterior stone walls and the bright pastel shades inside. The charm of the decor, the warm welcome and the mass of tourist information available, give you all you need for an excellent stay. Fleur de Soleil member.

PROPERTY

off-street parking, garden, pets not accepted, non-smoking, hiking, cycling, fishing, hunting, interesting flora, golf course 4km, sea or lake watersports 20km, winter sports 25km

Basic English spoken

——At Aurillac, take the N122 towards Murat. After 7 km, turn left towards Giou de Mamou. The house in the centre of the village (look for the B&B France sign).

PRICE STRUCTURE

4 Bedrooms
Campagne: bathroom with wc, double bed: FF270

Tilleul: shower room with wc, twin beds: FF290

Gentiane & Croix des Champs: shower room with wc, double bed, single bed:
FF290 (2 people)
FF370 (3 people)

Extra Bed: FF80

Reduction: 01/09–30/06 and 5 nights and groups

Capacity: 10 people

Jean-Louis WELSCH

'Château de Courbelimagne'

15800 RAULHAC

Tel: (0) 4 71 49 58 25

Fax: (0) 4 71 49 58 25

Château

AUVERGNE

AURILLAC

29 km - E - AURILLAC
Raulhac: hosts can collect from station, railway station: 25km
airport: 70km
car essential

PRICE STRUCTURE

3 Bedrooms and 2 Suites
first room & second room & Alsacienne: shower room with wc, double bed: FF480

Suite Henry II: shower room with wc, double bed + en-suite room single bed: FF680

Suite Bleue: bathroom with wc, double bed + en-suite room single bed: FF680

Extra Bed: FF100

Reduction: 4 nights and children

Capacity: 12 people

15.07 AURILLAC

A 16th-century château, 700m up amongst the trees. Jean-Louis and his wife will welcome you to their home with its cosy ambience and candle-lit dinners. You will be charmed by the helpfulness of your hosts, their beautiful house and all its facilities. Weddings can be held in the château's chapel.

PROPERTY

private parking, extensive grounds, tv lounge, hosts have pets, telephone, dinner available, packed lunch, babies welcome, free cot, closed: 30/09–15/04, hiking, cycling, hunting, mushroom-picking, fishing 2km, sea or lake watersports 10km, riversports 10km, gliding 15km, interesting flora 20km

Adequate English spoken

——From Aurillac, take the D990 towards Mur-de-Barrez. Go through Raulhac (still heading towards Mur-de-Barrez) on the D660. The château is situated 4km further on, on the left.

15.09 AURILLAC

In the heart of the country between Auvergne and Rouergue, at an altitude of 750m, the house is simple and very well designed. Claude will welcome you as a friend. He will be delighted to guide and advise you on your trips throughout the region, which he knows particularly well. Be sure to visit the town of Conques.

Claude BRUEL

Aubespeyre de Junhac

15120 MONTSALVY

Tel: (0) 4 71 49 22 70 /29 43

Private Home

PROPERTY

off-street parking, extensive grounds, tv lounge, pets not accepted, telephone, 1 shared shower room with wc, closed: 30/11–01/03, hiking, fishing, hunting, interesting flora, mushroom-picking, golf course 4km, sea or lake watersports 4km

PRICE STRUCTURE

6 Bedrooms

(1 room) shower, wc, double bed, single bed: FF260 (2 people) FF320 (3 people)

(3 rooms) shower room with wc, washbasin, double bed: FF260

(1 room) washbasin, 2 double beds: FF250 (2 people) FF320 (4 people)

(1 room) washbasin, double bed, single bed: FF240 (2 people) FF270 (3 people)

Reduction: 1/09–30/06 and groups

Capacity: 16 people

30 km - S - AURILLAC
Aubespeyre:
railway station: 40km
airport: 40km
car essential
——At Aurillac, take the D920 as far as Montsalvy, and then the D41 on the right towards Aubespeyre. In Aubespeyre, follow the signs.

Myriam
CAILLAUD de MAHE

'La Bastide Haute'

15800 THIEZAC

Tel: (0) 4 71 47 02 71

mahe53@yahoo.com

Private Home

30 km - E -
AURILLAC
Thiézac:
railway station: 7km
airport: 30km
car essential

PRICE STRUCTURE

2 Bedrooms and 1 Suite
Lavande: shower room with
wc, double bed + en-suite
room twin beds:
FF370 (2 people)
FF590 (4 people)

Gentiane: bathroom with
wc, double bed: FF370

Violette: shower room with
wc, single bed:
FF220 (1 person)

Extra Bed: FF110

Capacity: 7 people

15.14 AURILLAC

This impressive 13th-century country house is away from it all, up in the mountains at 1,000m altitude with superb views. There is so much to do here, particularly hiking along the waterfall route or the ancient volcano route, or visiting Roman churches. Spend your weekend picking mushrooms or wild berries, or photographing the wildlife. It is a good area for all types of skiing (35 slopes), and your hosts also specialise in yoga and Tai Chi. Otherwise, just relax and enjoy their traditional cooking using organic produce from their garden. Vegetarians are particularly welcome. Fleur de Soleil member.

PROPERTY

private parking, extensive grounds, dinner available, packed lunch, non-smoking, hiking, cycling, fishing, hunting, interesting flora, mushroom-picking, golf course 10km, winter sports 20km, sea or lake watersports 25km

——From Aurillac, take the N122 towards Murat. At Thiézac, take the D59 towards Raulhac and, after 5km, turn left (signposted).

Jacqueline CHAILLY

'La Jacquerolle'

Rue Maréchal

43160 LA CHAISE DIEU

Tel: (0) 4 71 00 07 52

Private Home

35 km - N W -
PUY-EN-VELAY
La Chaise Dieu:
railway station: 40km
airport: 40km
car essential

43.05 PUY-EN-VELAY

La Chaise Dieu is well-known for the wonderful atmosphere of its abbey and its famous sacred music festival at the end of August. Now we would add Jacqueline's hospitality, her delicious meals and her comfortable home as more good reasons to return here regularly. On sale: Local produce, honey.

PROPERTY

off-street parking, garden, lounge, pets not accepted, dinner available, hiking, cycling, interesting flora, mushroom-picking, winter sports, sea or lake watersports 2km, fishing 5km

——At Le Puy take the N102 for 8km. At Borne take the D906 for 27km. The house is situated below the abbey and below the square with the memorial.

PRICE STRUCTURE

5 Bedrooms

Bleue: shower room with wc along corridor, bathroom along corridor, double bed: FF320

Rose: shower room with wc, double bed, 2 single beds: FF320 (2 people)
FF480 (4 people)

Fleurs Rose & Jaune: shower room with wc, double bed, single bed:
FF320 (2 people)
FF410 (3 people)

Blanche: shower room with wc along corridor, twin beds: FF320

Extra Bed: FF100

Reduction: 01/09–01/06 and 7 nights

Capacity: 14 people

Marie-Louise BERTHUY

'Ferme de Vazerat'

15500 MASSIAC

Tel: (0) 4 71 23 03 05

Fax: (0) 4 71 23 03 05

Working Farm

30 km - S - ISSOIRE
Massiac: hosts can
collect from station,
railway station: 2km
airport: 70km

PRICE STRUCTURE

4 Bedrooms and 1 Suite
shower room with wc,
washbasin, double bed,
single bed: FF270 (2
people) FF350 (3 people)

shower room with wc,
washbasin, twin beds: FF270

(2 rooms) shower room
with wc, washbasin, double
bed, single bed: FF270 (2
people) FF310 (3 people)

Suite: shower room with wc,
washbasin, double bed +
en-suite room 2 single beds:
FF290 (2 people)
FF420 (4 people)

Extra Bed: FF50

Reduction: 15/09–15/04
and 4 nights and groups
and children

Capacity: 15 people

15.05 ISSOIRE

On the main north-south route via the pleasant A75, this is a good place to stop overnight in green countryside, off the beaten track. Marie-Louise is not far from the autoroute, and her magnificent ferme-auberge serves local specialities in a superb dining room. Overnight stops including dinner are FF385 per person.

PROPERTY

off-street parking, hosts have pets, telephone, dinner available, 3 nights minimum stay: (01/08–20/08), hiking, cycling, fishing, hunting, interesting flora, mushroom-picking, riversports 25km, bird-watching 40km, sea or lake watersports 40km, winter sports 40km

——On the A75 Exit number 23 or 24 towards Massiac. After the church, follow the signs.

Brigitte LAROYE

7, rue du 8 Mai

63590 CUNLHAT

Tel: (0) 4 73 72 20 87

Residence of
Outstanding Character

40 km - S - THIERS
Cunlhat:
airport: 53km
car essential

63.03 THIERS

Leave the beaten track and head for this large, very comfortable manor house, where you will enjoy the atmosphere of another era. It is in the village and all the rooms overlook the wooded garden.

PROPERTY

off-street parking, garden, lounge, hosts have pets, pets not accepted, dinner available, babies welcome, free cot, riding, hiking, cycling, fishing, interesting flora, sea or lake watersports, bird-watching 40km, golf course 50km, winter sports 50km

PRICE STRUCTURE

4 Bedrooms
ground floor – Louis XVI: shower room with wc, double bed, 2 single beds: FF330 (2 people) FF530 (4 people)

1930 & Fleurie: shower room with wc, double bed: FF280

Glycine: bathroom with wc, double bed: FF300

Extra Bed: FF100

Capacity: 10 people

——From the A72, Exit Thiers-Ouest, take the D906 towards Ambert. 11km after Courpière, turn right on to the D225 towards Cunlhat. The house is behind the church (signposted).

Elisabeth BEAUJARD

8 rue de la Limagne - Chaptes

63460 BEAUREGARD VENDON

Tel: (0) 4 73 63 35 62

Residence of Outstanding Character

25 km - N - CLERMONT-FERRAND
Chaptes:
railway station: 9km
airport: 25km
car essential

PRICE STRUCTURE

3 Bedrooms
shower room with wc, double bed: FF380

shower room with wc, double bed: FF330

shower room with wc, double bed: FF320

Extra Bed: FF110

Capacity: 6 people

63.05 CLERMONT-FERRAND

This 18th century home is only a few kilometres from the gentle and volcanic countryside of the Auvergne. It is surrounded by attractive buildings and a walled garden. Inside, a refined atmosphere is created by the antique furniture, paintings and artefacts on display. Your hosts ensure a lively welcome.

PROPERTY

private parking, extensive grounds, pets not accepted, hiking, interesting flora, mushroom-picking, fishing 6km, cycling 10km, riversports 15km, golf course 25km, bird-watching 25km, gliding 25km, winter sports 70km

Adequate English spoken

——A71, Exit Riom. After the autoroute 'péage' (toll), when you reach the first roundabout follow the sign 'toutes directions'. At the second roundabout, take the N144 towards Montluçon, and 2.5km after Davayat take the D122 on the right for Chaptes and follow the signs in the village.

Jacqueline VERLHAC

Belveyre

19600 NESPOULS

Tel: (0) 5 55 85 82 58

Working Farm

15 km - S - BRIVE-LA-GAILLARDE
Belveyre Nespouls:
railway station: 15km
airport: 15km
car essential

19.07 BRIVE-LA-GAILLARDE

This is an unusual village, in white stone. If Jacqueline is not in the house, you will probably find her on her tractor...She is restoring her farmhouse, and the bedrooms are very comfortable. Sit in the shade of the vine, and soak up the peace and quiet of this place.

PROPERTY

private parking, garden, pets not accepted, dinner available, babies welcome, free cot, hiking, bird-watching, sea or lake watersports 6km, golf course 10km, fishing 10km, riversports 20km

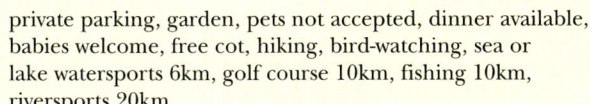

——From the A20, take Exit 53, 10km from Brive. Turn right on to the D19 towards Larche and right towards Belveyre. Follow the signs 'gîte de la ferme' and then look for the B&B (France) sign.

PRICE STRUCTURE

5 Bedrooms
Bleu: shower room with wc, washbasin, double bed:
FF220

Rose & Beige: shower room with wc, washbasin, double bed, single bed:
FF220 (2 people)
FF280 (3 people)

Attic – Rouge: bathroom with wc, washbasin, double bed, single bed:
FF220 (2 people)
FF280 (3 people)

Attic – Verte: bathroom with wc, washbasin, double bed, 2 single beds:
FF220 (2 people)
FF340 (4 people)

Capacity: 15 people

Sylvie & André
RICHARD SOUDANT

'Ferme Equestre de Leix'

Leix

19320 CLERGOUX

Tel: (0) 5 55 27 75 49

Fax: (0) 5 55 27 75 49

Working Farm

21 km - E - TULLE
Clergoux:
railway station: 21km
car essential
——At Tulle take the
D978 towards Mauriac
for 21km. At the hamlet
of Les Cambuzes turn
right on the C5 road and
follow the signs to
'chambres d'hôtes-ferme
équestre' for 3km

19.05 TULLE

Wonderful food. You are also in the middle of 20 hectares of fields and woods and, whether you are a beginner or an expert, your hosts will be pleased to accompany you to explore this area on horseback. Well worth a stop, even if only overnight.

PROPERTY

off-street parking, extensive grounds, hosts have pets, dinner available, packed lunch, babies welcome, free cot, riding, hiking, cycling, fishing, hunting, interesting flora, mushroom-picking, bird-watching, sea or lake watersports 8km, riversports 20km

Fluent English spoken

PRICE STRUCTURE
3 Bedrooms

Jaune: shower room with wc, washbasin, double bed: FF270

Vanille – Mezzanine: shower room with wc, washbasin, double bed, twin beds: FF270 (2 people) FF420 (4 people)

Saumon – Mezzanine: shower room with wc, washbasin, double bed, 2 single beds: FF270 (2 people) FF420 (4 people)

Extra Bed: FF80

Reduction: 5 nights and groups

Capacity: 10 people

Gisèle & Daniel BERTHE

21, rue Bouloux

87110 BOSMIE L'AIGUILLE

Tel: (0) 5 55 36 12 87

Fax: (0) 5 55 36 12 87

Private Home

11 km - S - LIMOGES
Bosmie l'Aiguille: hosts can collect from station, railway station: 11km airport: 11km car essential

87.09 LIMOGES

If you are making for Oradour or Lourdes, or intend to visit the Limoges Porcelain Museum, then be sure to stop chez Gisèle and Daniel. They are known for the comfort of their home, the swimming pool and their spontaneous friendly welcome, all in a calm setting surrounded by flowers. Daniel is mechanically-minded and collects old cars. Your breakfast will be served on Limoges porcelain, of course!

PROPERTY

private parking, garden, tv lounge, hosts have pets, dinner available, non-smoking, wheelchair access, swimming pool, hiking, cycling, fishing, mushroom-picking, sea or lake watersports 6km, riversports 6km, bird-watching 10km

Basic English spoken

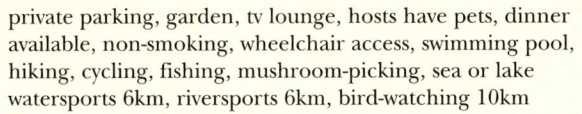

——From Limoges on the N21, head towards Périgueux for 10km. In Bosmie l'Aiguille, turn left on the bridge which crosses the river Vienne. Turn left and follow signs to 'chambres d'hôtes'. Head towards the sports stadium (Stade) and it is the second street on the right after the stadium.

PRICE STRUCTURE

2 Bedrooms and 1 Apartment

Isis & Rose: shower room with wc, double bed: FF240

Apartment: lounge, kitchen, shower room with wc, double bed, twin beds.
FF250 (2 people)
FF450 (4 people)

Extra Bed: FF100

Capacity: 8 people

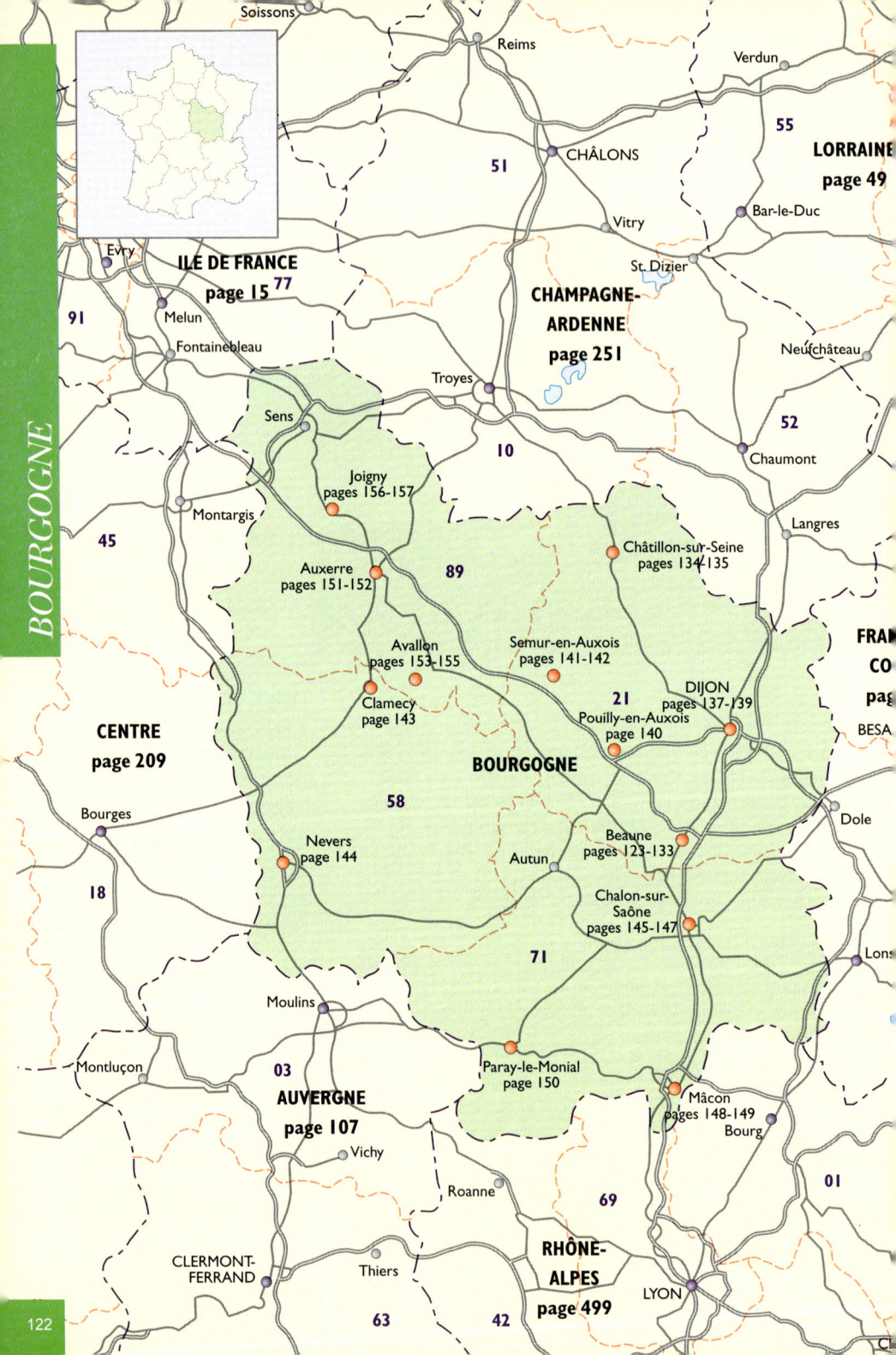

BOURGOGNE

Soissons

Reims

Verdun

CHÂLONS

51

55

Vitry

Bar-le-Duc

St. Dizier

LORRAINE
page 49

Evry

ILE DE FRANCE
page 15 77

91

Melun

Fontainebleau

CHAMPAGNE-
ARDENNE
page 251

Neufchâteau

Troyes

52

Chaumont

Sens

10

Langres

Joigny
pages 156-157

Montargis

45

89

Châtillon-sur-Seine
pages 134-135

Auxerre
pages 151-152

Avallon
pages 153-155

Semur-en-Auxois
pages 141-142

Clamecy
page 143

21

DIJON
pages 137-139

Pouilly-en-Auxois
page 140

FRANCHE-
CO
pag

BESA

CENTRE
page 209

BOURGOGNE

58

Bourges

Dole

18

Nevers
page 144

Autun

Beaune
pages 123-133

Chalon-sur-
Saône
pages 145-147

Lons

71

Moulins

Paray-le-Monial
page 150

Mâcon
pages 148-149

Montluçon

03

AUVERGNE
page 107

Vichy

Roanne

69

Bourg

01

RHÔNE-
ALPES
page 499

CLERMONT-
FERRAND

Thiers

63

42

LYON

Patrick & Françoise
ROCHET

'Château d'Ecutigny'

21360 ECUTIGNY

Tel: (0) 3 80 20 19 14

Fax: (0) 3 80 20 19 15

Château

20 km - N W -
BEAUNE
Ecutigny: hosts can
collect from station,
railway station: 25km
airport: 60km

21.04 BEAUNE

This château, dating from the 12th and 17th centuries, is a listed historic monument situated close to the vine slopes. The owners have restored the place beautifully and with very good taste. You will be offered a welcoming drink in a unique venue. Carriage rides and stabling for horses. On sale: Wine, home-baked bread.

PROPERTY

private parking, extensive grounds, tv lounge, hosts have pets, telephone, dinner available, packed lunch, babies welcome, free cot, tennis court, riding, hiking, fishing, golf course 25km

Fluent English spoken

——In Beaune, take the D970 towards Bligny-sur-Ouche then turn left on to the D33 towards Ecutigny.

PRICE STRUCTURE
5 Bedrooms and 1 Suite
au Parquet: television, bathroom with wc, double bed, single bed: FF700 (2 people) FF800 (3 people)
Jaune: television, bathroom with wc along corridor, double bed, single bed: FF600 (2 people) FF700 (3 people)
au Baldaquin: television, shower room with wc, double bed: FF800
Suite: television, shower room with wc, double bed, single bed + en-suite room double bed: FF600 (2 people) FF1100 (5 people)
du Four à Pain: television, bathroom with wc, double bed, single bed: FF700 (2 people) FF800 (3 people)
de la Tour: television, bathroom with wc, double bed: FF500
Extra Bed: FF100
Capacity: 18 people

Christiane de LOISY

'Domaine Comtesse Michel de Loisy'

21700 NUITS-ST-GEORGES

Tel: (0) 3 80 61 02 72

Fax: (0) 3 80 61 36 14

Residence of Outstanding Character

16 km - N E - BEAUNE
Nuits-St-Georges:
railway station: 1km
airport: 20km

PRICE STRUCTURE
3 Bedrooms and 2 Suites

Madame: bathroom with wc, double bed: FF850

Monsieur:bathroom with wc along corridor, double bed: FF600

Boudoir: bathroom with wc, twin beds: FF650

Suite Enfants bleus: bathroom with wc, double bed, twin beds + en-suite room 2 single beds: FF750 (2 people) FF990 (6 people)

Suite Mademoiselle: shower room with wc, double bed, twin beds + en-suite room 2 single beds: FF750 (2 people) FF990 (6 people)

Extra Bed: FF100

Reduction: 6 nights

Capacity: 18 people

21.05 BEAUNE

The Countess de Loisy, Master of Wine and a registered guide, welcomes you to her wonderful home, with comfy rooms furnished with antiques. The splendid salon and the dining room on the ground floor open on to indoor gardens. Please book ahead and do not arrive before 5 p.m.

PROPERTY

private parking, extensive grounds, tv lounge, hosts have pets, telephone, dinner available, packed lunch, babies welcome, free cot, tennis court, riding, hiking, fishing, golf course 25km

Fluent English spoken

——In Beaune, take the A31 towards Dijon. Take Exit Nuits-St-Georges. After the 4th roundabout, follow the signs to Beaune (N74). The street starts at the 2nd set of traffic lights. Continue for 120m towards Beaune.

Jeanne ESMONIN

Paquis de Rolanges

21700 ST-BERNARD

Tel: (0) 3 80 62 81 60
06 68 29 74 47

Fax: (0) 3 80 62 89 14

Private Home

20 km - N E - BEAUNE
St-Bernard:
railway station: 8km
airport: 23km
car essential

21.15 BEAUNE

A warm welcome from this couple in their spotlessly clean home. You are very close to the autoroute but this spot is completely quiet in the middle of the Nuits-St-Georges vineyards (only 5km from Clos Vougeot). A magical place for lovers of vintage Burgundy. On sale: Honey.

PROPERTY

Private parking, extensive grounds, lounge, hosts have pets, dinner available, non-smoking, 2 wc, 2 nights minimum stay, closed: 1/12–15/03, vineyard 5km, golf course 16km

Fluent English spoken

——From the A31 Exit Nuits-St-Georges and then take the D8 as far as Boncourt-le-Bois. In this village take the first on the left which is the D116b towards St-Bernard. Follow the signs.

PRICE STRUCTURE

5 Bedrooms

first room: shower room with wc, double bed: FF280

second room:bathroom with wc along corridor, twin beds: FF320

(2 rooms) shower room with wc, double bed: FF320

fifth room: shower room with wc, double bed: FF300

Extra Bed: FF65/100

Reduction: 01/11–31/03 and 7 nights and groups and children

Capacity: 10 people

François ISTACE

21700 VILLEBICHOT

Tel: (0) 3 80 61 22 07

Fax: (0) 3 80 61 22 07

Private Home

20 km - N E - BEAUNE
Villebichot: hosts can collect from station, railway station: 9km airport: 23km car essential

PRICE STRUCTURE

2 Bedrooms
first room: bathroom with wc, shower, double bed: FF270
second room: bathroom with wc, twin beds: FF270

Extra Bed: FF70
Reduction: 01/12–28/02 and 7 nights

Capacity: 4 people

21.17 BEAUNE

A large house in a small, quiet village near the famous vineyards. You will be captivated by the living room, with a mezzanine that leads to bedrooms with exposed beams. François has a wonderful collection of African artefacts that he has picked up during his travels there. Bedroom 2 will surprise you with its enormous elephant's tusks!

PROPERTY

private parking, garden, tv lounge, hosts have pets, telephone, non-smoking, wheelchair access, vineyard, fishing 1km, hiking 5km

——Take the Nuits-St-Georges Exit from the A31, and head towards Agencourt, Boncourt and Villebichot on the D8. With the town hall (Mairie) in front of you, head towards St-Bernard for 100m. The house is on the right.

Françoise MOINE

'La Monastelle'

21360 THOMIREY

Tel: (0) 3 80 20 00 80

Fax: (0) 3 80 20 00 80

Residence of
Outstanding Character

27 km - N W -
BEAUNE
Thomirey:
railway station: 25km
airport: 60km

PRICE STRUCTURE

4 Bedrooms
Bleu: shower room with wc,
double bed: FF350

Rose: shower room with wc,
twin beds, single bed: FF350
(2 pcople)
FF450 (3 people)

Verte: shower room with wc,
double bed, 2 single beds:
FF350 (2 people)
FF550 (4 people)

Jaune: shower room with
wc, double bed, single bed:
FF350 (2 people)
FF450 (3 people)

Extra Bed: FF100
Reduction: groups

Capacity: 12 people

21.18 BEAUNE

**Françoise is completely refurbishing this old farm building,
typical of the area, with comfortable, rustic bedrooms.
The old dining room centres around a large farmhouse
table and a beautiful fireplace. Genuine atmosphere and a
sincere welcome.**

PROPERTY

✹ ✹ ✹

off-street parking, garden, tv lounge, hosts have pets,
telephone, dinner available, packed lunch, cycling, vineyard,
hiking 1km, fishing 1km, hunting 1km, mushroom-picking
1km, golf course 26km

Basic English spoken

——From the A6, take Exit 24, Pouilly-en-Auxois. Take the
N81 towards Arnay-le-Duc and then the N6 towards La
Rochepot and Chagny for 10km. Turn left towards Thomirey.
The house is situated just as you leave the village, towards
Ecutigny.

Dominique PETIN

'La Closerie des Ormes'

21 rue de la Grand' Velle - Vosne-Romanée

21700 NUITS-ST-GEORGES

Tel: (0) 3 80 62 35 19

Fax: (0) 3 80 62 17 59

Residence of Outstanding Character

19 km - N - BEAUNE
Vosne-Romanée:
railway station: 2km
airport: DIJON 30km
car essential

BOURGOGNE

BEAUNE

PRICE STRUCTURE

5 Bedrooms

first room: telephone, shower room with wc along corridor, double bed, single bed: FF500 (2 people) FF700 (3 people)
second room: telephone, shower room with wc along corridor, double bed: FF500
third room: telephone, bathroom with wc, twin beds: FF550
fourth room: television, telephone, shower room with wc along corridor, double bed, single bed: FF450 (2 people) FF650 (3 people)
fifth room: television, telephone, shower room with wc along corridor, double bed: FF450
Extra Bed: FF200
Capacity: 12 people

21.19 BEAUNE

This delightful house, amongst the vines, welcomes you through its doors to a world of colour and charm. Dominique will give you invaluable tips on how to get the most out of your stay in this wonderful region, whose name is synonymous with gastronomy. This is a very special place, near to the N74 and close to Nuits-St-Georges.

PROPERTY

private parking, garden, tv lounge, hosts have pets, dinner available, packed lunch, babies welcome, free cot, wheelchair access, hiking, fishing, hunting, mushroom-picking, bird-watching, golf course 25km, interesting flora 70km, sea or lake watersports 70km

Adequate English spoken

——From the A31 towards Beaune, Exit Nuits-St-Georges. Then take the N74 towards Dijon, as far as Vosné-Romanée. As you leave the village, take the last street on the left. The house is 50m on the right.

Jean PROST

Grande Rue

21700 MEUILLY

Tel: 03 80 61 09 37/03
91-06 85 75 94 42

Private Home

25 km - N E -
BEAUNE
Meuilly:
railway station: 6 km
airport: 30 km
car essential

21.24 BEAUNE

Madame Picard will probably welcome you, and you will soon warm to this adorable grandmother. She will look after you, and is very good at explaining all you need to know about wine, coming from a wine-producing family. Ask for room No. 1, which is particularly pretty.

PRICE STRUCTURE

1 Suite
shower, bathroom, double bed: FF360

+ ensuite room: double bed: FF200

Extra Bed. FF100

Capacity: 4 people

PROPERTY

private parking, garden, tv lounge, telephone, dinner available, packed lunch, babies welcome, free cot, non-smoking, wheelchair access, hiking, cycling, vineyard, gliding 2km, fishing 3km, mushroom-picking 3km, sea or lake watersports 5km, interesting flora 10km, golf course 20km

Fluent English spoken

——From the A31 Exit Nuits-St-Georges. In Nuits-St-Georges, take the D25 to Meuilley. The house (with a green gate) is at the corner of the road to Arcenant and the main street.

Françoise & Alain
BERTHAUD

'La Saura'
Route de Beaune

21360 LUSIGNY-SUR-
OUCHE

Tel: 03 80 20 17 46/
06 10 32 68 87

Fax: (0) 3 80 20 07 73

la.saura@wanadoo.fr
www.douix.fr/la saura

Residence of
Outstanding Character

17 km - N W -
BEAUNE
Lusigny sur Ouche:
railway station: 15km
airport: 160km
car essential

BOURGOGNE

BEAUNE

PRICE STRUCTURE

6 Bedrooms
ground floor – Botanique:
bridal room, lounge, shower
room with wc, double bed,
single bed: FF410 (2
people) FF500 (3 people)
ground floor – Aux Fleurs:
wheelchair access, shower
room with wc, double bed:
FF410
first floor – Bleue &
Orientale: shower room
with wc, double bed (queen
size): FF410
first floor – Aux Chinois:
along corridor bathroom,
double bed: FF310
first floor – Aux Lys: shower
room with wc, twin beds:
FF310

Extra Bed: FF100

Capacity: 13 people

21.25 BEAUNE

**Françoise and Alain will give you a warm welcome to their
impressive detached house. The bedrooms are quiet,
comfortable, spacious and decorated with great taste.
A wonderful place to make your base for several days while
discovering and sampling the 'grands crus' of this famous
wine-producing region.**

PROPERTY

private parking, garden, non-smoking, wc, 6 years old
minimum age, hiking, vineyard, fishing 6km, golf course 20km

——On the D970, next to the church. It is the first house on
the right, when coming from Bligny-sur-Ouche, and the last
house on the left when coming from Beaune.

Sandrine & André LANAUD

'La Closerie de Gilly'

16, Av. Bouchard

21640 GILLY-LES-CITEAUX

Tel: 03 80 62 87 74/ 06 60 73 10 11

Fax: (0) 3 80 62 87 74

as.lanaud@wanadoo.fr

Residence of Outstanding Character

20 km - N E - BEAUNE
Gilly-les-Citeaux: hosts can collect from station, airport: 15 km

21.26 BEAUNE

This young couple have restored this beautiful house with great taste and enthusiasm. The bedrooms are very spacious, ideal for an enjoyable stay of several days. Remember, you are only 1km from Clos Vougeot, a name to quicken the pulse of any wine lover.

PROPERTY

off-street parking, garden, tv lounge, pets not accepted, babies welcome, free cot, wheelchair access, swimming pool, hiking, fishing, cycling 2km, vineyard 1km, golf course 15km, sea or lake watersports 20km

Adequate English spoken

——On the A31, Exit Nuits-St-Georges, take the N74 towards Dijon. At the Vougeot roundabout, head towards Gilly-Centre. After the railway bridge, take the first on the right and follow the signs.

PRICE STRUCTURE

4 Bedrooms

ground floor – Chambertin: shower room with wc, bathroom, double bed: FF450

first floor – Romanée: shower room with wc, bathroom, twin beds, single bed: FF550 (2 people) FF650 (3 people)

first floor – Vougeot: shower, bathroom, double bed, single bed: FF500 (2 people) FF600 (3 people)

second floor – Chambolle: shower room with wc, bathroom, twin beds: FF500

Extra Bed: FF100

Reduction: 10% and 5 nights

Capacity: 10 people

Andrée & Philippe
JEANJEAN

21700 VILLARS-
FONTAINE

Tel: 03 80 61 29 59

Fax: (0) 3 80 62 37 49

jeanjean.philippe
@wanadoo.fr

http://chambres.ifrance.
com

Private Home

20 km - N -
BEAUNE
Villars-Fontaine:
railway station: 5km
airport: 25km
car essential

PRICE STRUCTURE

4 Bedrooms
(2 rooms) shower room
with wc, washbasin, double
bed: FF230

shower room with wc,
washbasin, double bed,
single bed:
FF230 (2 people)
FF270 (3 people)

lounge, shower room with
wc, double bed, twin beds:
FF230 (2 people)
FF340 (4 people)

Extra Bed: FF70

Reduction: 2 nights

Capacity: 11 people

21.27 BEAUNE

This place is at the centre of a little village, on the slopes of Les Hautes Côtes de Nuits-St-Georges vineyards. A find that will really get you excited. Start with the jovial welcome from Philippe, followed by dinner in the cellar. He is very well versed in wine-making, particularly 'les grands crus', but can also talk about New York amongst other things! Be sure to ask him to demonstrate the workings of the amazing 'Robocop' shutters on the bedroom windows.

PROPERTY

off-street parking, extensive grounds, tv lounge, hosts have pets, pets not accepted, dinner available, babies welcome, free cot, non-smoking, hiking, cycling, fishing, vineyard, sea or lake watersports 20km, riversports 20km, golf course 25km, gliding 25km

——A31 towards Beaune, Exit Nuits-St-Georges. Then head towards Dijon as far as the traffic lights and take the D25 for Villars-Fontaine. You will find the house as you enter the v village, 20m after the restaurant.

Martine LYSSY

Champseuil

71350 ST-GERVAIS-EN-VALLIERE

Tel: 03 85 91 80 08

Fax: (0) 3 85 91 80 08

martineLYSSY.
chambrhotes@
wanadoo.fr

Private Home

15 km - S E -
BEAUNE
St-Gervais-en-
Vallière: hosts can
collect from station,
railway station: 14km
airport: 165km
car essential

71.17 BEAUNE

In true Burgundian style, take your time chez Martine and Jean-Marc. Martine is very talented and she has decorated the bedrooms with great skill and simplicity, adding lots of clever little touches. If you appreciate interior design, you will love this place. Their meals are great fun and should not be missed, as well as trips with Jean-Marc to taste some of the outstanding wines of this area or to the large flea markets. Fleur de Soleil member.

PROPERTY

off-street parking, lounge, hosts have pets, dinner available, kitchen, babies welcome, free cot, closed: 1/12–31/01, hiking, cycling, bird-watching, vineyard, fishing 1km, interesting flora 1km, mushroom-picking 1km, sea or lake watersports 5km, golf course 20km *Basic English spoken*

——A6, Exit 24-1 to Beaune. Take the D970 towards Verdun-sur-le-Doubs. At St-Loup-de-la-Salle, take the D183 for Champseuil and follow the signs to 'chambre d'hôte Champseuil'.

PRICE STRUCTURE

2 Bedrooms and 1 Suite
television, bathroom with wc, double bed: FF320

television, bathroom with wc, twin beds: FF320

television, bathroom with wc, shower, twin beds + en-suite room twin beds: FF320 (2 people)
FF640 (4 people)

Extra Bed: FF100
Capacity: 8 people

Pierre BAEHLER

'L'Oasis'

Porte de Chatillon

21400 POTHIERES

Tel: (0) 3 80 81 94 44

Fax: (0) 3 80 81 94 44

Private Home

6 km - N W -
CHATILLON-SUR-
SEINE
Pothières:
railway station: 28km
airport: 85km
car essential

PRICE STRUCTURE

3 Bedrooms
Coccinelle & Papillon:
television, double bed,
single bed:
FF248 (2 people)
FF298 (3 people)

Orchidée: television, shower
room with wc, double bed,
single bed:
FF290 (2 people)
FF350 (3 people)

Extra Bed: FF50

Reduction: 01/11–28/02
and 7 nights and groups

Capacity: 9 people

21.20 CHATILLON-SUR-SEINE

Pierre is Swiss, and his place near the main Troyes-Dijon road is a paradise for nature lovers. The wildlife in the forest is exceptional: stags, hinds, birds... ideal for eco-tourists. The area is also particularly well-known for shooting and fishing (it is excellent for fly-fishing). On sale: Hand-made wooden crafts.

PROPERTY

off-street parking, garden, tv lounge, hosts have pets, pets not accepted, dinner available, packed lunch, babies welcome, free cot, closed: 30/11–1/03, hiking, cycling, fishing, vineyard, golf course 8km

Basic English spoken

——At Tonnere, head for Châtillon-sur-Seine on the D965 and the N71 towards Troyes. Cross Montliot, and turn left towards Vix, then head towards Pothières. It is the first house on the right in the village.

Pierre
VANDENDRESSCHE

'Château de Courban'

21520 COURBAN

Tel: 03 80 93 78 69/
06 09 62 51 77

Fax: (0) 3 80 93 79 23

Residence of
Outstanding Character

18 km - N E -
CHATILLON-SUR-
SEINE
Courban: hosts can
collect from station,
ferry port: 45km
car essential

21.28 CHATILLON-SUR-SEINE

Pierre, who at the time was an interior designer in Lille,
discovered this house is 1998. Captivated by it, he decided to
create a large family home, and the result is very appealing.
There are five bedrooms decorated in perfect taste, a large
lounge with a piano, a beautiful dining room, a library for
relaxing and a French style garden with a lake in which the
dovecote is reflected. Pierre has a gift for providing perfect
hospitality complemented by delicious food and wine,
producing the perfect B & B experience.

PROPERTY

private parking, garden, tv lounge, hosts have pets, telephone,
dinner available, packed lunch, babies welcome, free cot,
swimming pool, hiking, cycling, hunting 1km, mushroom-
picking 1km, bird-watching 1km, golf course 2km, lake
watersports 4km, vineyard 15km *Fluent English spoken*

——A5, Exit 23 La Ferté-sur-Aube and Colombey-les-Deux-
Eglises. Take the D996 towards Montigny-sur-Aube. Go
through the village, as far as the D965 and then turn right and
continue to Courban. Follow signs to 'Château de Courban'.

PRICE STRUCTURE
6 Bedrooms

Beaurepaire: shower room
with wc, washbasin, double
bed: FF420

Beauregard: shower room
with wc, washbasin, double
bed: FF620

Les Muses: shower room
with wc, washbasin, double
bed (queen size): FF620

Manon: shower room with
wc, washbasin, twin beds:
FF620

Suite Bellevue: twin beds,
single bed: FF870

Bellecourt: shower room
with wc, washbasin, double
bed: FF620

Extra Bed: FF100

Reduction: groups

Capacity: 13 people

Bertrand BERGEROT

'Château de Rosières'

St-Seine-sur-Vingeanne

21610 FONTAINE-
FRANÇAISE

Tel: (0) 3 80 75 82 53

Fax: (0) 3 80 75 82 53

Château

40 km - N E - DIJON
St-Seine-sur-
Vingeanne:
railway station: 40km
airport: 40km
car essential

PRICE STRUCTURE

**2 Bedrooms and
1 Apartment**
Chambre du Puits:shower
room with wc along
corridor, twin beds: FF270

floor: bathroom with wc,
double bed: FF420

Apartment: lounge,
television, kitchen,
bathroom with wc, double
bed + en-suite room double
bed: FF600 (2 people)
FF740 (4 people)

Extra Bed: FF50
Reduction: 4 nights

Capacity: 8 people

21.07 DIJON

**This fortress, situated on the edge of Bourgogne,
Champagne and Franche-Comté is tastefully furnished. We
did not hesitate in giving this place 4 'suns' as it has so much
character, and dominates the Vingeanne valley in the heart of
an area steeped in history. Excellent for walking, cycling and
horse-riding. Fleur de Soleil member.**

PROPERTY

private parking, extensive grounds, hosts have pets, babies
welcome, free cot, riding, hiking, cycling, fishing

Basic English spoken

——On the A31 Dijon-Chaumont autoroute, take the
Til-Chatel Exit. Go toward Lux. After Lux, turn left towards
Bourberain and Fontaine-Française. Continue towards Gray
for 5km. St-Seine-sur-Vigeanne is on your right. Follow the
signs 'Château de Rosières' for 4km.

Laurence & Patrick
BERGER

'Le Vieux Moulin'

21610 FONTAINE-
FRANÇAISE

Tel: (0) 3 80 75 82 16

Fax: (0) 3 80 75 97 52

PATRICK.BERGER2
@wanadoo.fr
http://perso.wanadoo.fr
/le-vieux-moulin

Residence of
Outstanding Character

40 km - N E - DIJON
Fontaine-Française:
railway station: 37km
airport: 40km
car essential

21.08 DIJON

Patrick's passions are art, history and archaeology. His home is a beautiful 17th-century watermill, completely restored right down to the waterwheel and its associated machinery. You will have some great evenings here. Hikers are welcome.On sale: Home-made jam.

PROPERTY

off-street parking, extensive grounds, tv lounge, dinner available, packed lunch, non-smoking, swimming pool, closed: 23.12–31.12, riding, hiking, cycling, golf course, interesting flora, gliding

Basic English spoken

——On the A31 Dijon–Chaumont autoroute, Exit number 5 at Til-Chatel. Head towards Fontaine-Française via Orville and Chazeuil (15km). Follow the signs in the village.

PRICE STRUCTURE

**4 Bedrooms and
2 Apartments**

Jardin & Nénuphar: television, shower room with wc, double bed, 2 single beds: FF301 (2 people) FF445 (4 people)

Château: shower room with wc, double bed, 3 single beds: FF301 (2 people) FF517 (5 people)

Etang: bathroom with wc along corridor, double bed, single bed: FF301 (2 people) FF374 (3 people)

Piscine: shower room with wc, twin beds: FF301

Terrasse: shower room with wc, double bed: FF301

Extra Bed: FF72
Reduction: 4 nights and groups
Capacity: 22 people

Peter & Véréna
ZIMMERMANN

9 Grand Chemin

21310 RENÈVE

Tel: (0) 3 80 47 78 40

Fax: (0) 3 80 47 78 40

Private Home

BOURGOGNE

DIJON

30 km - E - DIJON
Renève:
airport: 30km
car essential

PRICE STRUCTURE

3 Bedrooms
ground floor – 1: shower,
wc, twin beds: FF270
ground floor – 2: shower,
wc, double bed: FF270
first floor – shower room
with wc, twin beds: FF270

Extra Bed: FF80

Capacity: 6 people

21.11 DIJON

**A lovely Swiss-German couple, Peter and Verena have
transformed this old post office into a charming little haven
of tranquility. There is a relaxing, uninterrupted view over
the valley, a pleasant swimming pool and many flowers. Near
to the A31, it is the ideal spot to spend your holidays,
particularly as Peter is a chef.**

PROPERTY

private parking, extensive grounds, tv lounge, hosts have pets,
pets not accepted, dinner available, swimming pool, 12 years
old minimum age, closed: 01/11–31/03, hiking, cycling,
fishing 1km

Fluent English spoken

——On the A31, take the Exit Dijon-Arc-sur-Til. Then take the
D70 towards Gray/Vesoul for 20km. At Renève, turn left
immediately after the bridge and continue for 1km. The
house is on the left at the crossroads.

Anne & François
BRUGERE

7 rue Jean Jaurès

21160 COUCHEY

Tel: 03 80 52 13 05

Fax: (0) 3 80 52 93 20

Private Home

8 km - S - DIJON
COUCHEY:
railway station: 8km
airport: 150km
car essential

21.23 DIJON

You are in the heart of the vine-growing country in deepest Burgundy. This old house, full of character, is on the 'Grand Crus' wine route that links Dijon and Nuits-St-George via Gevrey-Chambertin (4km away). Should you not be interested in wine, there are châteaux and churches nearby and this is a good area for hiking and cycling. On sale: Burgundy wine from their own cellar (wine tastings). Fleur de Soleil member.

PROPERTY ✳ ✳ ✳

Private parking, garden, hiking, cycling

——Contact your host for detailed directions.

PRICE STRUCTURE

4 Bedrooms

Nuptiale: double or twin room: shower room with wc, bathroom, double bed:
FF340

Verte: double or twin room: shower room with wc, double bed:
FF310

Jaune: shower room with wc, double bed, single bed: FF290 (2 people) FF370 (3 people)

Rose: shower room with wc, bathroom, double bed: FF290

Extra Bed: FF80

Capacity: 11 people

Michel & Chantal
RANCE

'La Rente d'Eguilly'

Eguilly

21320 POUILLY-EN-
AUXOIS

Tel: (0) 3 80 90 83 48/
06 62 39 35 20

Working Farm

8 km - N W -
POUILLY-EN-
AUXOIS
Eguilly: hosts can
collect from station,
airport: Dijon 12km
car essential

PRICE STRUCTURE

Bedrooms and 1 Suite
Four: bridal room, shower
room with wc, twin beds:
FF280

ground floor: bathroom
with wc along corridor,
washbasin, twin beds: FF280

second room: bathroom
with wc, double bed, twin
beds: FF350 (2 people)
FF600 (4 people)

Suite: lounge, bathroom
with wc, washbasin, 3 single
beds: FF350 (2 people)
FF450 (3 people)

double bed: FF350

Extra Bed: FF60

Reduction: 15/09–06/04
and 4 nights

Capacity: 16 people

21.12 POUILLY-EN-AUXOIS

Here you will find absolute peace and quiet, not far from the Exit from the A6 autoroute. A beautiful farmhouse in the middle of the countryside and pleasant surroundings. Chantal and Michel offer a warm welcome and, having stopped here once, theirs is an address you will hang on to.

PROPERTY

off-street parking, garden, hosts have pets, pets not accepted, dinner available, packed lunch, non-smoking, wheelchair access, closed: 01/10–15/10 & 01/12–15/01, hiking, cycling, hunting, interesting flora, mushroom-picking, fishing 2km, golf course 4km, bird-watching 10km, sea or lake watersports 10km, gliding 12km

———A6, Exit Pouilly-en-Auxois. To Pouilly and cross the village on the D970. After 4.5km, turn left towards Eguilly. Cross the A6 and turn left, then right towards Blancey. The farm is on the left.

Judith LEMOINE

'Couvent des Castafours'

21150 FLAVIGNY-SUR-OZERAIN

Tel: (0) 3 80 96 24 92

Private Home

17 km - E - SEMUR-EN-AUXOIS
Flavigny-sur-Ozerain: hosts can collect from station, railway station: 8km airport: 70km car essential

SEMUR-EN-AUXOIS

21.03 SEMUR-EN-AUXOIS

A superb location. Judith is English and a great cook. You will be surprised to find yourself going downstairs to the bedrooms – they are in a 17th century convent in the centre of what is considered to be one of the most beautiful medieval villages in France. The view of l'Auxois and the Valley of Alésia is also superb.

PROPERTY

off-street parking, garden, tv lounge, hosts have pets, pets not accepted, dinner available, babies welcome, free cot, hiking, cycling, fishing

Fluent English spoken

PRICE STRUCTURE

2 Bedrooms
Beige: shower room with wc along corridor, double bed: FF270

Rose: shower room with wc, twin beds: FF270

Extra Bed: FF60
Reduction: 7 nights

Capacity: 4 people

——On the A6, take the Exit Bierre-les-Semur towards Semur. Take the D9 towards Pouillenay and Flavigny. Go to the church and you can see the house below in the courtyard.

Elisabeth & Yves
DONOIS

'La Passerose'

Route d'Aisy

21500 ROUGEMONT

Tel: (0) 3 80 92 46 18
Fax: (0) 3 80 92 40 75

lapasserose@infonie.fr

Residence of
Outstanding Character

28 km - N W -
SEMUR-EN-
AUXOIS
Rougemont:
hosts can collect
from station,
railway station: 10km
airport: 90km
car essential

PRICE STRUCTURE

4 Bedrooms

Dauphin: shower room with
wc, 3 single beds:
FF250 (2 people)
FF320 (3 people)

Grenouille: shower room
with wc along corridor, twin
beds: FF250

Pinson: twin beds + en-suite
room Oie: 4 single beds:
FF250 (2 people)
FF540 (6 people)

Extra Bed: FF70

Reduction: 5 nights
and groups

Capacity: 11 people

21.16 SEMUR-EN-AUXOIS

Are you looking for a place where you can unwind, with a relaxed and friendly atmosphere and charming hosts? Elisabeth and Yves will welcome you to their 14th century home (which explains the steep staircase and low doorways!). You are close to one of the most beautiful villages in France. Fleur de Soleil member.

PROPERTY

private parking, garden, lounge, dinner available, babies welcome, free cot, non-smoking, 1 shared shower room with wc, hiking, fishing, sea or lake watersports 10km, golf course 24km

Fluent English spoken

——On the A6, take the Bierre-les-Semur Exit, and then head towards Semur-en-Auxois. Take the D980 to Montbard, then the D905 towards Tonnerre. Rougemont is situated 10km after Montbard. The house is in the centre of the town, 300m from the church towards Aisy. (If coming from Paris, take the Nitry Exit.)

Eliane & Jean-Marc
BAUTISTA

'Château de la Chaise'

58800 PAZY

Tel: (0) 3 86 20 28 25

Fax: (0) 3 86 20 28 25

E-mail:
chateau.de.la.chaise
@libertysurf.fr

Château

35 km - S -
CLAMECY
Pazy:
railway station: 3km
airport: 50km
car essential

58.07 CLAMECY

This rustic château is situated between the River Yonne and the Nivernais Canal, which give it that extra bit of charm. Eliane and Jean-Marc provide an excellent welcome. They certainly know what they are doing, and have brilliantly restored this building, particularly the tapestries. This is a great place in which to settle down and appreciate the delights of Burgundy.

PROPERTY

✸ ✸ ✸ ✸

private parking, extensive grounds, tv lounge, hosts have pets, telephone, dinner available, closed: 1/11–31/03, hiking, cycling, golf course, fishing, sea or lake watersports 5km, riversports 5km

Adequate English spoken

——From Clamecy, take the D951 towards Vézelay and the D985 on the right towards Corbigny. (From Avallon, take the D957 towards Vézelay and, at St-Père, take the D958 on the left as far as Corbigny.) At Corbigny, take the D985 towards St Saulge and turn left before the canal.

PRICE STRUCTURE

4 Bedrooms and 1 Suite
Romantique & Marine-Baldaquins: bathroom with wc, double bed: FF700

Chambre du Roi-Baldaquin: bridal room, bathroom with wc, double bed: FF800

Nuages-Baldaquin: bathroom with wc, double bed, single bed:
FF700 (2 people)
FF900 (3 people)

Suite: bathroom with wc, double bed + en-suite room twin beds: FF700 (2 people)
FF1200 (4 people)

Capacity: 13 people

Marie-France O'LEARY

'Le Beauvais'

58330 ST-SAULGE

Tel: (0) 3 86 58 29 98

Fax: (0) 3 86 58 29 97

eleonort@wanadoo.fr

Private Home

25 km - N E - NEVERS
St-Saulge:
airport: 35km
car essential

PRICE STRUCTURE

4 Bedrooms

Verte: telephone, shower room with wc, double bed: FF604

Bleue: lounge, telephone, bathroom, wc, double bed: FF604

Pêche: shower room with wc, washbasin along corridor, 2 single beds: FF304

Jaune: television, telephone, shower, wc, double bed: FF604

Reduction: 2 nights and groups and children

Capacity: 8 people

58.03 NEVERS

Marie-France is a writer. She opens her spacious country house to you, overlooking woodland gardens., and spares no effort to ensure you relax and feel good. Only 40km from the Magny-Cours motor-racing circuit. Well worth the detour. On sale: Books and CDs.

PROPERTY

off-street parking, extensive grounds, tv lounge, pets not accepted, dinner available, packed lunch, wheelchair access, closed: 01/01–31/01, hiking, cycling, sea or lake watersports 5km, fishing 12km

Fluent English spoken

——In Nevers, take the D978 towards Autun/Dijon, for 10km. Turn left on to the D958 towards St-Saulge, where you follow the signs.

Jacqueline DEVILLARD

Le Village - Rue Charcot

71590 GERGY

Tel: (0) 3 85 91 74 10

Residence of
Outstanding Character

13 km - N E -
CHALON-SUR-
SAONE
Gergy:
airport: 135km
car essential

71.04 CHALON-SUR-SAONE

We receive many compliments from our guests about Jacqueline's place. You will like this small ensemble of characterful, independent houses in attractive grounds, which slope gently down towards the River Saône. Make full use of the grounds, the swimming pool and barbecue, or visit the numerous Burgundy vineyards of the area.

PROPERTY

off-street parking, extensive grounds, lounge, hosts have pets, pets not accepted, babies welcome, free cot, wheelchair access, swimming pool, closed: 01/10–01/05, hiking, fishing, golf course 13km

——On the A6, take the Exit Châlon-Sud in the direction of Châlon-Centre. Do not cross the river Saône. Take the D5 towards Crissey, Sassenay. On entering Gergy bear right at the top of the hill (by the cross). Sign to 'Le Village'. The house is on your left.

PRICE STRUCTURE

1 Apartment, 1 Suite & 1 Bedroom
Verte: double bed + en-suite room Rose: bathroom with wc, twin beds:
FF300 (2 people)
FF550 (4 people)

Bleue: lounge, double bed: FF350

Apart-Chambre Rouge: lounge, kitchen, bathroom with wc, double bed: FF350

Reduction: 4 nights

Capacity: 10 people

Margrit & Peter KOLLER

'Le Monestier'

Le Bourg

71640 ST-DENIS-DE-VAUX

Tel: (0) 3 85 44 50 68

Fax: (0) 3 85 44 50 68

lemonestier@wanadoo.fr

Château

15 km - W - CHALON-SUR-SAONE
St Denis de Vaux: hosts can collect from station, railway station: 15km airport: 135km car essential

CHALON-SUR-SAONE

PRICE STRUCTURE

6 Bedrooms
first room: shower room with wc, washbasin, twin beds: FF600

second room: shower, wc, twin beds: FF450

(3 rooms) shower room with wc, twin beds: FF500

fourth room: bathroom with wc, twin beds: FF600

Extra Bed: FF120

Reduction: 3 nights and groups

Capacity: 12 people

71.15 CHALON-SUR-SAONE

This 17th-century house is in a quiet valley and offers beautiful, elegant rooms in traditional style, as well as a bar, a smoking room and a swimming pool. Do not be surprised to be welcomed by a Swiss cow, as Margrit and Peter, a charming couple, are from Switzerland. Bonhomie and elegance combined. Visa and Mastercard accepted.

PROPERTY

private parking, extensive grounds, tv lounge, dinner available, babies welcome, free cot, swimming pool, hiking, cycling, bird-watching, gliding 10km, golf course 15km, fishing 15km, sea or lake watersports 15km

Fluent English spoken

——From Châlon-sur-Saône, take the D978 towards Autun for 9km, until you reach the roundabout of La Côte Châlonnaise. Take the D48 on the left and, after 100m, turn right towards Mellecey and St-Denis-de-Vaux. 'Le Monestier' is in the centre of the village.

France & Jean-Pierre JOUVIN

'L'Arcane'

71240 LA-CHAPELLE-DE-BRAGNY

Tel: 03 85 92 25 31

jean-pierre.france.jouvin@wanadoo.fr

Private Home

20 km - S - CHALON-SUR-SAONE
La-Chapelle-de-Bragny:
railway station: 27km
airport: 80km

71.18 CHALON-SUR-SAONE

You are in the centre of this quiet old village between the church and the château. First, you will be welcomed by birdsong, then by two small dogs, then a larger one and finally by France, your Canadian host who is a translator and singer. She will lead you towards the walled garden, full of flowers and with a little pond. After a good night's sleep, let Jean-Pierre, philosopher and researcher, show you the secret paths only known to the disciples of witchcraft in the Middle Ages. Not at all scary and really interesting.

PROPERTY

Private parking, garden, tv lounge, hosts have pets, pets not accepted, dinner available, packed lunch, kitchen, babies welcome, free cot, non smoking, cycling, riversports, fishing 1km, mushroom picking 1km, hiking 5km, sea or lake watersports 5km, vineyard 8km *Fluent English spoken*

——A6, Exit Châlon-Sud. Then the N6 towards Macon, then the D6 on the right to La-Chapelle-de-Bragny. The house is 200m.s from the church.

PRICE STRUCTURE

1 Apartment
Chambre+mezzanine: lounge, television, kitchen, shower room with wc, double bed, twin beds, single bed:
FF250 (2 people)
FF400 (5 people)

Extra Bed: FF50
Reduction: 4 nights

Capacity: 5 people

Daniel & Colette GUYOT

'Domaine d'Entre les Roches'

71960 VERGISSON

Tel: (0) 3 85 35 84 55

Fax: (0) 3 85 35 87 15

Working Farm

BOURGOGNE

10 km - W - MACON
Vergisson:
railway station: 5km
car essential

MACON

PRICE STRUCTURE

**2 Bedrooms and
2 Apartments**
Studio 1: lounge, television,
kitchen, shower room with
wc, double bed: FF270

Studio 2: television, kitchen,
shower room with wc,
double bed, 2 single beds:
FF270 (2 people)
FF430 (4 people)

Saumon: shower room with
wc, double bed: FF250

Grande Chambre: shower
room with wc, double bed,
single bed:
FF250 (2 people)
FF330 (3 people)

Extra Bed: FF80

Capacity: 11 people

71.06 MACON

This house, with its typical balcony and stone staircase, is on a wine-producer's estate. It is situated between the famous 'Roches Maconnaises', Vergisson and Solutré, in the heart of the Pouilly-Fuissé wine region. For literary buffs, the Lamartine Trail is nearby. On sale: Their own wine.

PROPERTY

private parking, garden, hosts have pets, kitchen, hiking, vineyard, fishing 5km, sea or lake watersports 10km, gliding 10km

Basic English spoken

——On the A6, take the Exit 'Macon-Sud'. Turn right towards TGV Loché and then after the railway station turn right towards Prissé. By the restaurant 'La Patte d'Oie' turn left and continue towards Davayé, then on to Vergisson where you follow the signs.

Christopher BLACK

'La Tour de Bassy'

Bassy

71260 ST-GENGOUX-
DE-SCISSE

Tel: (0) 3 85 33 28 77

Fax: (0) 3 85 33 24 69

Château

25 km - N - MACON
St-Gengoux-de-
Scissé:
hosts can collect
from station,
railway station: 20km
airport: 90km
car essential

71.11 MACON

This is the old priory of La Tour de Bassy, and still bears witness to a time when the monks from the abbey of Cluny worked this land. The setting is attractive, quiet and charming. There are some excellent vineyards to be visited on the picturesque 'Route des Vins'. On sale: Wine.

PROPERTY ✹✹✹✹

off-street parking, garden, tv lounge, pets not accepted, telephone, 10 years old minimum age, hiking, hunting, mushroom-picking 2km, golf course 5km, fishing 7km, sea or lake watersports 20km

Fluent English spoken

PRICE STRUCTURE

2 Bedrooms
(2 rooms) bathroom with
wc, double bed: FF500

Capacity: 4 people

——At Macon, head towards Cluny. At La Roche Vineuse, take the D85 on the right towards Verzé, Igé then Bassy. La Tour de Bassy is situated in the hamlet of Bassy.

Caroline & Jacques
AMBERGER - REPOND

'Les Chevaux
du Grand Bois'
Le Bois Bouton
71800 OYE

Tel: (0) 3 85 25 82 42/
06 80 88 40 72
Fax: (0) 3 85 25 91 41

info@chevaux-du-grand-
bois.com
www.chevaux-du-grand-
bois.com

Private Home

20 km - S - PARAY
LE MONIAL
Oye: hosts can
collect from station,
railway station: 13km
airport: 100km
car essential

BOURGOGNE

PARAY-LE-MONIAL

PRICE STRUCTURE

1 Bedroom
kitchen, twin beds, single
bed, cot: FF270 (2 people)
FF340 (3 people)

Capacity: 3 people

71.16 PARAY-LE-MONIAL

Welcome to Burgundy, a region known for 'la bonne vie'. On this typical farm, which overlooks the countryside, they have just one bedroom with a kitchenette. Caroline and Jacques are simply wonderful, warm and full of energy. They also run their riding centre with great enthusiasm, and organise treks round the area. A gîte is also available for 7–9 people.

PROPERTY

off-street parking, garden, tv lounge, hosts have pets, pets not accepted, telephone, dinner available, babies welcome, free cot, riding, hiking, hunting, mushroom-picking, sea or lake watersports, hiking 6km, interesting flora 10km, cycling 13km, riversports 13km, golf course 15km *Basic English spoken*

——At Paray-le-Monial, take the D24 towards Poisson, Varenne and St-Christophe-en-Brionnais. At the hamlet of 'Le Bois Bouton', turn left. (If coming from Macon, head towards Paray-le-Monial and Charolles and on the D985, turn left towards La Clayette and continue for 8km. There, take the D20 on the right.)

Patricia & Eric
WILLOCQ

'les Tourterelles'

8, Allée du Bois Chazelles

89240 LINDRY

Tel: (0) 3 86 47 12 82

Fax: (0) 3 86 47 07 96

Private Home

13 km - W -
AUXERRE
Chazelles: hosts can
collect from station,
railway station: 13km
airport: 150km
car essential

89.02 AUXERRE

A quiet place to relax in la Puisaye. This old farmhouse has been beautifully restored, showing off to good effect its old beams and stonework. Michèle will always have something delicious cooking when you return from your visits to Auxerre, St Fargeau, Escolives and the Vallée de la Cure, and the potteries.

PRICE STRUCTURE

4 Bedrooms
first room: bathroom with wc, double bed: FF230

(2 rooms) bathroom with wc, twin beds: FF230

fourth room: bathroom with wc, double bed, 2 single beds: FF230 (2 people) FF370 (4 people)

Extra Bed: FF60

Reduction: 3 nights

Capacity: 10 people

PROPERTY

off-street parking, garden, tv lounge, hosts have pets, dinner available, packed lunch, kitchen, babies welcome, free cot, cycling, hiking 2km, mushroom-picking 3km, fishing 6km, golf course 20km, sea or lake watersports 35km

Adequate English spoken

——On the A6, take the Exit Auxerre-Sud, then go towards Auxerre, to take the D965 towards St-Fargeau. In Pourrain, go towards Lindry. In Chazelles, take the small lane on the right.

Daniel & Jeannette
CHAUMET

'La Posterle'

2, Place Aristide Briand

89110 ST-AUBIN-
CHATEAU-NEUF

Tel: (0) 3 86 73 64 09

Fax: (0) 3 86 73 64 09

Private Home

20 km - W -
AUXERRE
St-Aubin-
Chateau-Neuf:
hosts can collect
from station, railway
station: 20km
airport: 150km

PRICE STRUCTURE

4 Bedrooms
Bouton d'Or & Bleuet:
bathroom with wc, double
bed: FF370

Eglantine: bathroom with
wc, 2 double beds:
FF370 (2 people)
FF570 (4 people)

Violette: television,
bathroom with wc, double
bed: FF420

Extra Bed: FF80

Reduction: 15/10–15/12 &
15/01–15/03 and 3 nights
and groups and children

Capacity: 10 people

89.05 AUXERRE

This house was a café at the start of the 20th century, in a village with many beautiful houses. Daniel and Jeannette have made it extremely welcoming, and decorated it with impeccable taste, which make it excellent value for money. It is next to the bell tower... but the bells sleep at night too!

PROPERTY

private parking, garden, tv lounge, pets not accepted, telephone, dinner available, packed lunch, babies welcome, free cot, non-smoking, hiking, cycling, hunting, interesting flora, mushroom-picking 2km, golf course 3km, fishing 3km, sea or lake watersports 30km

——A6, Exit Joigny. Then D943 towards Montargis, and turn left on to the D3 towards Toucy. Turn left on to the D955 towards Les Placeaux and right to St-Aubin-Chateau-Neuf. The house is in the upper part of the village, on the square next to the church.

89.15 AVALLON

We have wished for a long time to include an entry for Vézelay, so that you could experience this magnificent place. It is a World Heritage Site, full of religious and spiritual significance, from which many of the Crusades set off. We have at last come up trumps – Sylvie and Bernard's place is few steps away from the basilica, and they combine their artistic talents with such a sincere and warm welcome. Be sure to visit the amazing 12th-century Pilgrim's Room in the crypt of the house, which never fails to impress.

PROPERTY

hosts have pets, non-smoking, wc, hiking, cycling, interesting flora, bird-watching, vineyard, mushroom-picking 2km, riversports 2km, fishing 4km, sea or lake watersports 15km

Basic English spoken

PRICE STRUCTURE

4 Bedrooms

Marie-Madeleine & St-Bernard: shower room with wc, double bed: FF342
Berthe: shower, twin beds: FF342
shower along corridor, double bed: FF292

Capacity: 8 people

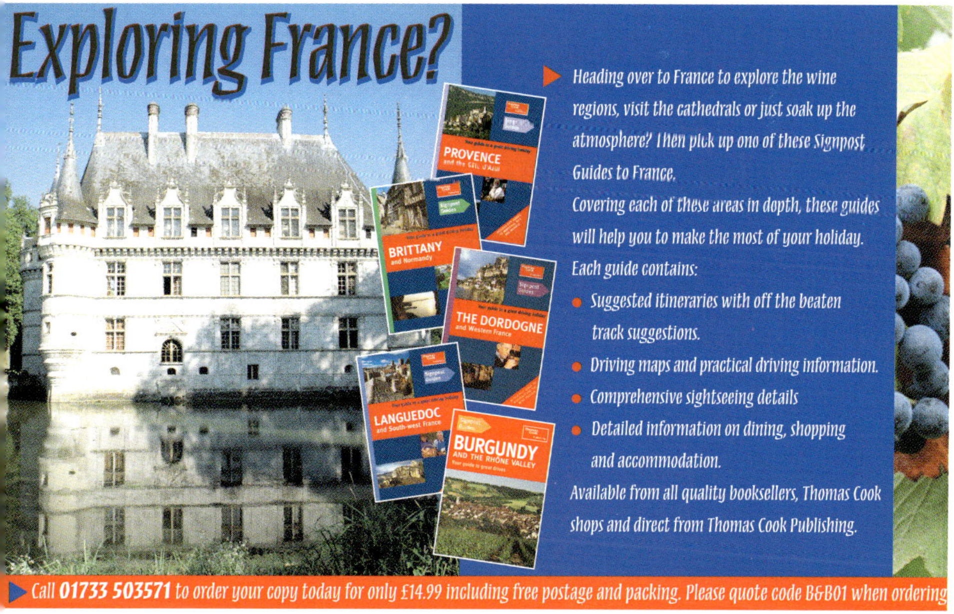

Sylvie & Bernard VAN DEN BOSSCHE

'Le Porc Epic'

80, rue St-Pierre

89450 VEZELAY

Tel: 03 86 33 32 16

Residence of Outstanding Character

14 km - W - AVALLON
Vézelay:
railway station: 10km
car essential
—— In Vézelay, take the main street which goes up to the basilica. The house is number 80. Enter through the sculpture gallery.

Martine COSTAILLE

'Château Jaquot'

N6

89420 STE-MAGNANCE

Tel: (0) 3 86 33 00 22

Château

13 km - E -
AVALLON
Ste Magnance:
car essential

PRICE STRUCTURE

1 Bedroom
shower room with wc,
bathroom, double bed, twin
beds: FF550 (2 people)
FF950 (4 people)

Capacity: 4 people

89.04 AVALLON

If you had any doubts that Burgundy was a region famed for its gastronomy and wine, a stay at this 12th-century château, restored with loving care and great attention to originality, will leave you in no doubt. Well worth the price and a detour. Their dinners use mostly organic produce.

PROPERTY

off-street parking, extensive grounds, tv lounge, telephone, dinner available, 8 years old minimum age, vineyard, hiking 2km, interesting flora 2km, mushroom-picking 2km, fishing 10km, hunting 10km, riversports 10km, cycling 15km, sea or lake watersports 20km

Basic English spoken

——From the A6, take the exit to Avallon. Then join the N6 and turn left towards Saulieu. You can see the château as you arrive at Ste-Magnance.

Marie & Yves CLAVERIE

'Château d'Island'

Island

89200 AVALLON

Tel: 03 86 34 22 03/
06 86 96 48 12
Fax: (0) 3 86 34 22 03

island@hotmail.com
www.lafrancetouristique.
com/89/chateaudisland

Château

BOURGOGNE

AVALLON

7 km - S W -
AVALLON
Island: hosts can
collect from station,
railway station: 5km
airport: 230km
car essential

89.16 AVALLON

Marie and Yves run this château for the pleasure of their guests. It is situated in the Morvan National Park, between the historic towns of Vézelay and Avallon. Marie produces wonderful dishes, inspired mainly by her Vietnamese origin, and also serves delicious home-made pastries for breakfast. The lounge is particularly pleasant.

PROPERTY

private parking, extensive grounds, lounge, pets not accepted, telephone, dinner available, babies welcome, free cot, hiking, cycling, fishing, hunting, interesting flora, mushroom-picking, sea or lake watersports 4km, riversports 5km, gliding 5km, vineyard 10km

—— From the A6, Exit Avallon. Then take the D957 towards Vézelay. At Pontaubert, take the D53 on the left towards Island. The château is on this road on the left.

PRICE STRUCTURE

6 Bedrooms
Claire: television, telephone, shower room with wc, bathroom, double bed: FF400
Agathe: television, telephone, shower room with wc, bathroom, double bed: FF470
Hortensia: television, telephone, shower room with wc, bathroom, double bed: FF430
Or: television, telephone, shower room with wc, bathroom, double bed: FF550
Suite Cosmos: lounge, shower room with wc, bathroom, double bed: FF900
Billiard room: television, telephone, shower room with wc, bathroom, twin beds: FF700
Extra Bed: FF150; Reduction: 1/11–31/03 and 7 nights and group; Capacity: 12 people

Dominique & Daniel
ACKERMANN

'Ferme de Plénoise'

Plénoise

89120 CHARNY

Tel: (0) 3 86 63 63 53

Working Farm

30 km - S W -
JOIGNY
Plénoise:
railway station: 30km
car essential

PRICE STRUCTURE

4 Bedrooms

Saumon: bathroom with wc,
double bed: FF280

Rose: bathroom with wc,
twin beds, cot: FF280

Verte: bathroom with wc,
double bed (queen size),
single bed:
FF280 (2 people)
FF350 (3 people)

Bleu: bathroom with wc,
twin beds, 2 single beds:
FF280 (2 people)
FF420 (4 people)

Extra Bed: FF70

Reduction: 2 nights

Capacity: 11 people

89.11 JOIGNY

This is a working beef and dairy farm in the Puisaye, and this lovely couple and their two young children will be delighted to show you around. It is in a super setting, right out in the country beside a river. You can learn everything you ever wanted to know about dairy farming, thanks to the workshop 'Traite des Vaches'! On sale: Milk, cider, and top quality home-made patisserie.

PROPERTY

off-street parking, garden, tv lounge, hosts have pets, pets not accepted, telephone, dinner available, babies welcome, free cot, hiking, cycling, fishing, mushroom-picking, golf course 20km, sea or lake watersports 30km, gliding 30km

Basic English spoken

——From the A6, Exit Joigny. D943 towards Montargis, then left on to the D16 towards Charny. Head towards the covered market and continue on the D16, towards Chatillon-Coligny. Go over the bridge and up the hill as you leave the village. At the top, turn right, signposted 'Plénoise-Chambres d'hôtes'.

Aldine BENINI

'L'Ecole Buissonnière'

9, Grande Rue

89120 CHARNY

Tel: (0) 3 86 63 65 65

Fax: (0) 3 86 63 64 02

Residence of
Outstanding Character

25 km - S W -
JOIGNY
Charny: hosts can
collect from station,
railway station: 30km
airport: 50km

89.14 JOIGNY

This old priory and its 18th-century church school are in a quiet location in this small town. The priest's garden is full of flowers, and there is also a barbecue. If you are not too keen on climbing spiral stairs, then ask for the apartment by the old school playground. Aldine is always ready with an enthusiastic welcome, and you are likely to be served their own poultry for dinner. On sale: eggs, honey. A house is also available to rent for weekends or holidays (100m2).

PROPERTY

garden, tv lounge, hosts have pets, pets not accepted, dinner available, kitchen, babies welcome, free cot, wc, cycling, bird-watching, hiking 1km, fishing 1km, hunting 1km, interesting flora 2km, mushroom-picking 2km, golf course 20km

Fluent English spoken

From the A6, Exit 17 at Courtenay. D34, then D950 towards Charny. 'L'Ecole Buissonière' is in the centre of the village, near the church. (If coming from the south, take Exit 18 Charny-Châteaurenard to the D943 then the D16.)

PRICE STRUCTURE

5 Bedrooms and 1 Suite
Marine: shower, double bed: FF280
bathroom along corridor, double bed: FF230
Maison Indépendante –
Style: television, kitchen, shower room with wc, double bed + en-suite room 3 single beds (child-size): FF280 (2 people) FF505 (5 people)
Rustique: shower room with wc along corridor, double bed: FF280
La Buissonnière: shower room with wc, double bed, single bed (child-size): FF280 (2 people) FF355 (3 people)
L'Outeau: lounge, kitchen, shower room with wc, double bed, 2 single beds (child-size): FF300 (2 people) FF450 (4 people)
Extra Bed: FF150; Reduction: 7 nights; Capacity: 18 people

ENGLISH CHANNEL

Guernsey
(to UK)

Jersey
(to UK)

Cherbourg

50

NORMA
page

BRETAGNE

Perros-Guirec
page 168

Roscoff
page 176

Lannion

St. Malo
pages 187-194

Cancale
pages 178-180

Mont-St-Michel

Morlaix
page 173

Guingamp

Lamballe
pages 166-167

Dinard
pages 181-183

Dol
pages 184-185

St-Thegonnec
page 177

St. Brieuc
page 169

Brest

29

22

Châteaulin

Dinan
pages 159-165

BRETAGNE

35

Douarnenez
pages 171-172

Pontivy

Quimper
pages 174-175

56

RENNES
page 186

Concarneau
page 170

Ploërmel
page 200

Lorient
page 199

Vannes
pages 201-208

Redon

Châte

Ile de Groix
pages 196-198

PAYS DE
LA LOIRE
page 384

44

Belle Ile
page 195

St. Nazaire

ATLANTIC
OCEAN

NANTES

La Roche

85

les Sables-d'Olonne

Anne COLLINET

'La Chênevière'

35270 MEILLAC

Tel: (0) 2 99 73 04 25

Château

17 km - S E - DINAN
Meillac: hosts can
collect from station,
railway station: 8km
airport: 50km
car essential

35.37 DINAN

Anne is a charming lady, and will give you a courteous
welcome to her 350-year-old manor house (which explains the
rather steep staircase). The place exudes an ambience of the
good life, French-style. She has also accumulated souvenirs of
her travels, particularly from the Polynesian Islands, and
these are part of the decor throughout the house. The
grounds are very romantic.

PROPERTY

private parking, extensive grounds, lounge, hosts have pets,
pets not accepted, telephone, dinner available, hiking, cycling
5km, golf course 15km, riversports 20km, sea or lake
watersports 30km

Adequate English spoken

——From Dinan take the D794 towards Rennes. Meillac is
then 5km further on. Before the church, heading towards
Bonnemain, take the second lane on the left, and there is a
sign to 'La Chenevière'. Go along this lane for 500m, and you
will come to a large house with three white gates. Ring the bell
on the large gate.

PRICE STRUCTURE

1 Bedroom and 1 Suite
Suite: shower room with wc,
double bed + en-suite room
2 single beds:
FF320 (2 people)
FF570 (4 people)
shower room with wc along
corridor, double bed: FF320

Extra Bed: FF100

Capacity: 6 people

Sylvie RONSSERAY

'Le Logis de Jerzual'

25-27, rue du Petit Fort

22100 DINAN

Tel: (0) 2 96 85 46 54

Fax: (0) 2 96 39 46 94

Residence of
Outstanding Character

DINAN:
railway station: 1km
airport: 12km

BRETAGNE

DINAN

PRICE STRUCTURE

**5 Bedrooms and
1 Apartment**
Baldaquin: television,
shower room with wc,
double bed: FF436

Husbeck: shower room with
wc, double bed, twin beds:
FF396 (2 people)
FF562 (4 people)

Perse: shower room with wc,
2 double beds: FF354 (2
people) FF538 (4 people)

Pastorale: shower room with
wc, double bed: FF304

La Halte: kitchen, shower
room with wc, double bed:
FF406

Jardin: shower, wc, single
bed: FF206 (1 person)

Extra Bed: FF80/100

Capacity: 15 people

22.02 DINAN

A real gem. This house has been featured in many magazines. Although the architecture is impressive and rooted in local history, your welcoming hosts, who work for the Ministry of Historic Monuments, are even more interesting. The house is near the yacht harbour, in the heart of the old town, which is a preservation area. There are 5,000 m² of terraced gardens, with an outstanding view over the old harbour.

PROPERTY

garden, tv lounge, hosts have pets, telephone, kitchen, golf course 15km, sea or lake watersports 15km

Fluent English spoken

——From the port of Dinan, the street is opposite the old bridge. The car park is 150m higher up on the right. The rue du Petit Fort is accessible by car in both directions. Stop by the sign, in front of the steps.

Pierre & Yvonne JOUFFE

'Le Chesnay-Chel'

22980 LA LANDEC

Tel: (0) 2 96 27 65 89

Working Farm

10 km - W - DINAN
La Landec:
airport: 20km
car essential

22.05 DINAN

On the way from Dinan to St-Brieuc, near a lake, this is an old stone farm with lots of character. Quiet and rural but handy for Dinan. Beautifully decorated with hanging flower baskets. There is a riding centre nearby. A great place to relax, and less than 30 mins. from the Mont-St-Michel and St-Malo.

PROPERTY

off-street parking, garden, lounge, hosts have pets, dinner available, kitchen, non-smoking, hiking, cycling, golf course 5km, sea or lake watersports 15km

PRICE STRUCTURE

3 Bedrooms
first room: shower room with wc, double bed, single bed: FF200 (2 people) FF250 (3 people)

second room: shower room with wc, double bed: FF200

third room: bathroom with wc, double bed, single bed: FF200 (2 people) FF250 (3 people)

Extra Bed: FF50
Capacity: 8 people

——In Dinan take the N176 towards St Brieuc. At the crossroads, do not follow the sign 'La Landec', but take the opposite direction. After 1km you will see a sign to the farm.

Jean POMMERET

'La Gravelle'

22690 PLEUDIHEN-SUR-RANCE

Tel: (0) 2 96 83 20 82

Private Home

10 km - N E - DINAN
Pleudihen-sur-Rance:
railway station: 10km
airport: 10km
car essential
——Go through the cen-
tre of Dinan
following signs for
Rennes-Caen. Continue
for 6km then turn left on
to the D29 towards
Pleudihen. Go past the
church and the ceme-
tery. Turn right at the
crossroads and follow the
signs for 'Camping
La Vilger'.

22.09 DINAN

A stone farmhouse in a pretty hamlet in pleasant surroundings with lots of flowers. Friendly Madame Pommeret will give you a warm welcome and ensure you are well looked-after in her clean rooms. Ideal for an overnight stop or a longer stay to explore this part of Brittany.

PROPERTY

off-street parking, garden, tv lounge, pets not accepted,
1 shared bathroom, wc, 2 years old minimum age, golf course
5km, sea or lake watersports 15km

PRICE STRUCTURE
4 Bedrooms

first room: washbasin, double bed: FF210

second room: wc, washbasin, double bed: FF230

third room: shower room with wc, double bed, 2 single beds: FF240 (2 people) FF320 (4 people)

fourth room: shower room with wc, double bed: FF240

Extra Bed: FF50

Capacity: 10 people

Bernard & Déborah
KERKHOF

'La Tarais'

Calorguen

22100 DINAN

Tel: (0) 2 96 83 50 59

Fax: (0) 2 96 83 50 59

tarais@worldonline.fr
http://perso.
worldonline.fr/tarais/
index.htm

Private Home

7 km - S - DINAN
Calorguen:
railway station: 7km
airport: 20km
car essential

22.27 DINAN

In this quiet little hamlet close to Dinan, you are ideally placed for excursions to Les Cotes d'Armor. All year round there is a warm welcome from this Anglo-Dutch couple in their gaily decorated old farmhouse.

PROPERTY

off-street parking, garden, tv lounge, hosts have pets, pets not accepted, non-smoking, wheelchair access, 4 years old minimum age, 3 nights minimum stay: (10/07–10/09), closed: 01/12–28/02, hiking, fishing, hunting, riversports 7km, golf course 20km, sea or lake watersports 20km

Fluent English spoken

PRICE STRUCTURE

4 Bedrooms and 1 Suite
ground floor: shower room with wc, double bed, single bed: FF275 (2 people) FF350 (3 people)

(3 rooms) shower room with wc, double bed: FF275

Suite: shower room with wc, double bed + en-suite room 4 single beds:
FF275 (2 people)
FF650 (6 people)

Extra Bed: FF75

Reduction: 3 nights

Capacity: 14 people

——In Dinan, take the D12 towards Léhon then Calorguen. Just before Calorguen, turn left and follow the signs 'La Tarais'.

Claudine GUERIN

'Les Colverts'

12, rue de Bel Air

22490 TREMEREUC

Tel: (0) 2 96 27 17 65

Private Home

10 km - N - DINAN
Trémereuc:
airport: 5km
car essential
——At Dinan, take the
D766 towards Dinard.
The house is in the
centre of Trémereuc.

22.34 DINAN

Claudine welcomes you to her restored old stone farmhouse in the centre of Trémereuc. You are only 15 minutes from St-Malo and Dinard. The breakfast room and the salon are spacious, the latter having a particularly attractive fireplace.

PROPERTY

off-street parking, garden, tv lounge, hosts have pets, golf course 15km, sea or lake watersports 15km

PRICE STRUCTURE
4 Bedrooms

first room: shower, bathroom, wc, double bed, twin beds: FF250 (2 people) FF430 (4 people)

second room: shower room with wc along corridor, double bed: FF230

third room: shower room with wc along corridor, twin beds: FF230

fourth room: bathroom with wc, double bed, single bed: FF230 (2 people) FF320 (3 people)

Extra Bed: FF65

Capacity: 11 people

Helen & Joe GOODMAN

'La Ville Gout'

22130 CORSEUL

Tel: (0) 2 96 27 99 33

Fax: (0) 2 96 82 77 56

Private Home

10 km - N W -
DINAN
Corseul:
railway station: 8km
airport: 10km
car essential

22.39 DINAN

Helen and Joe, of English origin, gave up their restaurant in Australia to settle in this little, old Breton farmhouse, between Dinan and the sea. It is quaint and charming, just like an English doll's house! They even have a 'barbie'.

PROPERTY

private parking, garden, tv lounge, hosts have pets, telephone, dinner available, packed lunch, babies welcome, free cot, 1 shared shower room, cycling, mushroom-picking, hiking 1km, interesting flora 6km, fishing 10km, sea or lake watersports 10km, golf course 15km, riversports 15km

PRICE STRUCTURE

3 Bedrooms
first room: shower room with wc, double bed, 2 single beds:
FF270 (2 people)
FF470 (4 people)

shower room with wc, double bed, single bed:
FF270 (2 people)
FF370 (3 people)

third room: twin beds:
FF220

Extra Bed: FF75

Reduction: 01/10–31/05 and 3 nights

Capacity: 9 people

——From Dinan, take the D794 towards Plancoët. After 12 km, enter Corseul and take the first road on the right towards Ville Gout (B & B signs).

Colette SOHIER

'La Maison de Coellée'

22270 PLEDELIAC

Tel: (0) 2 96 34 14 08-06
85 44 71 79

Private Home

10 km - E -
LAMBALLE
Pledeliac:
railway station: 8km
airport: 35km
car essential

PRICE STRUCTURE

4 Bedrooms
Famille:bathroom with wc
along corridor , twin beds +
room double bed:
FF200 (2 people)
FF400 (4 people)

Hunaudaye: television,
shower, washbasin, double
bed: FF200

Broceliande: television,
kitchen, shower room with
wc, double bed, single bed
(child-size):
FF250 (2 people)
FF280 (3 people)

Extra Bed: FF70

Capacity: 9 people

22.41 LAMBALLE

Even if you arrive a bit earlier than planned, do not worry as Colette has thought of everything. She has a little summer house, in the shade in her flower garden, where you can relax and enjoy a cup of tea or coffee and read up on the local tourist information. Some clients, from China, come back again and again just to taste her wonderful crêpes for breakfast.

PROPERTY

off-street parking, garden, tv lounge, pets not accepted, kitchen, babies welcome, free cot, hunting, hiking 2km, mushroom-picking 2km, fishing 5km, golf course 15km, sea or lake watersports 22km

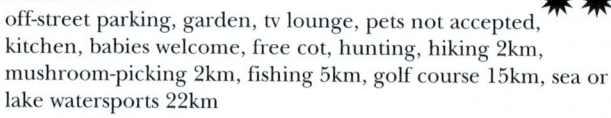

——From Lamballe, take the N176 towards Dinan. Turn off for St-Rieul and the D55. At St-Rieul, follow the signs to 'La Maison de Coellée'.

Yannick & Annick
LE TENO

14, rue Notre Dame

22400 LAMBALLE

Tel: (0) 2 96 31 00 41

Fax: (0) 2 96 31 00 41

Residence of
Outstanding Character

LAMBALLE:
railway station: 500m
airport: 30km

22.11 LAMBALLE

The setting and your welcoming hosts will together create the mood for an unforgettable stay. The painter Méheut was born in this attractive 18th-century townhouse, which is furnished with antiques and is just 10 minutes from the beach. Outstanding value for money and well worth a detour.

PROPERTY

✹ ✹ ✹

garden, tv lounge, telephone, kitchen, babies welcome, free cot, wheelchair access, wc, closed: 15/12–31/01, hiking, golf course 15km, sea or lake watersports 15km

English spoken

PRICE STRUCTURE

5 Bedrooms
Armelle: bridal room, shower, double bed: FF225

Nicolas & Isabelle: shower room with wc, double bed, single bed:
FF280 (2 people)
FF380 (3 people)

Bleu: bathroom along corridor, double bed: FF225

Rouge: bathroom with wc, twin beds: FF250

Extra Bed: FF60

Capacity: 12 people

—Go in to the centre of Lamballe. The street is close to the place du Marché.

Katerine CHABOUD

'Ker'ever'

1 chemin de
Kertanouarn

22620 PLOUBAZLANEC

Tel: 02 96 55 82 76   06
14 59 56 96

Private Home

BRETAGNE

PERROS GUIREC

35 km - E - PERROS-
GUIREC
Ploubazlanec:
hosts can collect
from station,
railway station: 5km
airport: 40km
car essential

PRICE STRUCTURE

3 Bedrooms
Jaune Double or twin room:
television, shower room
with wc, bathroom, double
bed (queen size): FF330

Lin: television, shower room
with wc, bathroom, double
bed: FF300

Vert Anglais: television,
shower room with wc, bathroom, twin beds: FF330

Reduction: 4 nights

Capacity: 6 people

22.42 PERROS GUIREC

**This green region, with its hidden villages, is near Paimpol
and the coast, a place much loved by Pierre and Marie Curie.
Here, Katherine will ensure that you get to know and love the
real rural Brittany. She will be delighted to take you along the
coast on a sailing boat or motor boat (you need to book). The
Ile de Bréhat (only 6 minutes crossing) is well worth the trip.**

PROPERTY

off-street parking, garden, tv lounge, pets not accepted, dinner
available, babies welcome, free cot, closed: 30/11–15/03,
hiking, cycling, fishing, sea or lake watersports
Adequate English spoken

———From Paimpol, head towards Loguivy-de-la-Mer on the
D15 for 1km. At the top of the hill, turn right towards
Ker'ever. Then follow the signs.

Lucien & Marie-Hélène CHOUPAUX

11, rue du Tertre de la Motte

22440 PLOUFRAGAN

Tel: (0) 2 96 78 65 81

Fax: (0) 2 96 76 60 91

Private Home

2 km - S W - ST-BRIEUC Ploufragan: hosts can collect from station, railway station: 3km airport: 8km car essential

22.35 ST-BRIEUC

Marie-Hélène and Lucien are retired, and welcome you to their modern house in a large garden. They will go out of their way to ensure that you feel at home. Marie-Hélène practices yoga. You have use of a barbecue, lounge and kitchenette.

PROPERTY

off-street parking, garden, tv lounge, pets not accepted, telephone, kitchen, non-smoking, wc, closed: 1/09–30/06, hiking, cycling, fishing 2km, sea or lake watersports 2km, riversports 2km

Adequate English spoken

——From the suburbs of St-Brieuc go in the direction of Loudéac. When you get to the village of Ploufragan, follow signs to Plédran and then signs to 'Chambre des Métiers'. Continue for 1km and then turn left about 300m after the Hotel Beaucemaine.

PRICE STRUCTURE

5 Bedrooms
first room: shower, washbasin, double bed: FF254

second room: shower, washbasin, double bed: FF244

third room: shower room with wc, washbasin, double bed: FF244

fourth room: bathroom with wc, shower, double bed: FF264

ground floor: television, shower room with wc, double bed (queen size): FF264

Extra Bed: FF100

Reduction: 4 nights and groups and children

Capacity: 10 people

Michèle LESCOAT

'La Maison d'Hippolyte'

2, quai Surcouf

29300 QUIMPERLE

Tel: (0) 2 98 39 09 11 06
62 57 09 11

Residence of
Outstanding Character

28 km - E -
CONCARNEAU
Quimperlé:
hosts can collect
from station,
railway station: 2km
airport: 18km

BRETAGNE

CONCARNEAU

PRICE STRUCTURE

4 Bedrooms

first room: television, shower, double bed: FF277

second room: bridal room, television, shower room with wc, double bed: FF277

third room: television, shower room with wc, double bed: FF277

fourth room: television, shower, double bed: FF277

Extra Bed: FF100

Capacity: 8 people

29.08 CONCARNEAU

Just 15km from Pont-Aven, this was the home of Hippolyte, the 'World's greatest salmon fisherman'. His charming daughter has dedicated the house to his memory and it overlooks the river with its salmon ladder. Hippolyte's fishing rods are on display. Well worth a detour. On sale: Watercolours, photos.

PROPERTY

garden, tv lounge, hosts have pets, babies welcome, free cot, wc, fishing, riversports, sea or lake watersports 12km, golf course 15km

Fluent English spoken

——From Concarneau, go to Pont-Aven, then Quimperlé. (In Lorient, take the N165 towards Quimper. Take the Exit Quimperlé.) The house is on the bank of the river Laïta, 50m from the tourist office.

'Kérantun'

Mahalon

29790 PONT-CROIX

Tel: (0) 2 98 74 51 93

Fax: (0) 2 98 74 51 93

Working Farm

10 km - S W -
DOUARNENEZ
Mahalon:
airport: 18km
car essential

29.12 DOUARNENEZ

A typical stone farm with all modern comforts. They have three spacious and comfortable rooms with separate entrances. Close to Pont-Croix, a town of great character, and La Pointe-du-Raz. There is an excellent, reasonably priced restaurant nearby. On sale: Eggs, vegetables.

PROPERTY

off-street parking, garden, lounge, hosts have pets, kitchen, babies welcome, free cot, hiking, cycling, fishing, interesting flora 8km, golf course 10km, sea or lake watersports 10km, bird-watching 15km

Basic English spoken

PRICE STRUCTURE

3 Bedrooms
shower room with wc,
double bed, single bed:
FF260 (2 people)
FF350 (3 people)

shower room with wc,
double bed; FF260

shower room with wc, twin
beds: FF260

Extra Bed: FF70

Reduction: 1/10–30/04 and
2 nights

Capacity: 7 people

——In Douarnenez, take the D765 towards Pont-Croix. As you enter Confort-Meilars, 200m after the Renault garage on your right, turn left on to the first road and follow the signs for 2.5km.

Claudine BROSSARD

'Rose Marine'

17, rue d'Estienne
d'Orves

29100 DOUARNENEZ

Tel: 02 98 92 85 08/
06 87 25 49 63

Private Home

DOUARNENEZ:
railway station: 25km
airport: 18km
——Coming from
Quimper, at
Douarnenez head
for the Centre-Ville
and then the
harbour (le port).
Rue Estienne
d'Orves is a little
street that runs
along by the Sacré-
Coeur church.

29.37 DOUARNENEZ

This grand house, dating from the end of the 19th century, is situated in a quiet street in the heart of the town, where the church bells will set the tempo of your stay. It is mid-way between the fishing harbour and the second harbour, with its museum of old boats. From Claudine's place, you can wander the small streets, visit the harbours, the beautiful beaches and the crêperies, or take in a Celtic music concert. This is the real Breton lifestyle!

PROPERTY

off-street parking, garden, tv lounge, babies welcome, free cot, hiking, cycling, fishing, sea or lake watersports, riversports, bird-watching 15km

Fluent English spoken

PRICE STRUCTURE
2 Bedrooms

shower room with wc, twin beds: FF280

shower room with wc, double bed, cot: FF280

Reduction: 1/09–30/06

Capacity: 4 people

Yves & Hervelina
BERTHOU

'La Ferme de Porz Kloz'

Trédudon-le-Moine

29690 BERRIEN

Tel: (0) 2 98 99 61 65

Fax: (0) 2 98 99 67 36

Residence of
Outstanding Character

20 km - S -
MORLAIX
Trédudon-le-Moine:
railway station: 20km
airport: 20km
car essential

29.30 MORLAIX

In this pretty, Breton hamlet, there are three charming maisonettes, each named after Breton dances. The garden is beautiful and the ambiance is romantic. In the evening, your host will entertain you by playing the bombarde and the bagpipes around the fire, after a delicious dinner. On sale: Honey, goat's cheese, cider.

PROPERTY

private parking, garden, lounge, hosts have pets, pets not accepted, telephone, dinner available, packed lunch, babies welcome, free cot, wheelchair access, 3 nights minimum stay: (1/07–31/08), closed: 01/12–01/03, hiking, interesting flora, mushroom-picking, bird-watching, fishing 1km, hunting 1km, sea or lake watersports 10km, riversports 10km, golf course 15km, gliding 40km

Fluent English spoken

——At Morlaix, take the D769 towards Huelgoat. At Le Plessis, turn right on to the D111, and then turn left towards Trédudon.

PRICE STRUCTURE

7 Bedrooms

Each room: television, telephone

first House: ground floor – Andro: shower room with wc, twin beds, single bed: FF480 (2 people) FF580 (3 people); First floor – Laridée: bathroom with wc, twin beds: FF400; First floor – Gavotte: bathroom with wc, twin beds, single bed: FF400 (2 people) FF500 (3 people)

second House: Jabadao: bathroom with wc, twin beds, single bed: FF480 (2 people) FF580 (3 people)

third House: Pach-Pi: bathroom with wc, twin beds, single bed: FF420 (2 people) FF520 (3 people); Kost Ar'hoad: bathroom with wc, twin beds: FF400; Piler Lann: bathroom with wc, 2 single beds: FF340

Extra Bed: FF60; Reduction: 3 nights and groups and children; Capacity: 18 people

Annick QUILFEN

'Kerjaouen'

23, route de Kerouter -
Clohars-Fouesnant

29950 BENODET

Tel: (0) 2 98 57 01 86

Private Home

12 km - S -
QUIMPER
Clohars-Fouesnant
Bénodet: hosts can
collect from station,
railway station: 13km
airport: 14km
——In Quimper,
take the D34
towards Bénodet.
Take the 2nd road
on the right towards
Gouesnac'h (at
Bénéteau boats)
then left into the
'Rue de Kerouter'

29.11 QUIMPER

Dynamic, generous, happy, pleasant, natural: this is the way in which past guests have described Annick. Two rooms in a large modern house, furnished with every comfort. This house is situated 2km from Bénodet, a charming fishing port with many restaurants. On sale: Honey, mead, cider.

PROPERTY

off-street parking, garden, tv lounge, kitchen, babies welcome, free cot, golf course 2km, sea or lake watersports 2km

PRICE STRUCTURE
2 Bedrooms

shower room with wc, double bed: FF300

bathroom with wc, double bed: FF300

Extra Bed: FF80

Capacity: 4 people

Philippe DAVY

'Château du Guilguiffin'

29710 LANDUDEC

Tel: (0) 2 98 91 52 11

Fax: (0) 2 98 91 52 52

www.guilguiffin.com

Château

13 km - W - QUIMPER
Landudec: hosts can collect from station, railway station: 16km airport: 8km car essential

29.35 QUIMPER

This luxurious, listed 18th-century château in Finistère offers space, peace and quiet and is totally authentic. It is a family property, surrounded by vast grounds which contain areas full of wild flowers, as well as magnificent gardens planted with 350,000 daffodils and 3,800 hydrangeas. You will find your host's enthusiasm for this place irresistible.

PROPERTY

off-street parking, extensive grounds, tv lounge, hosts have pets, telephone, babies welcome, free cot, 3 nights minimum stay, closed: 15/11–31/03, hiking, sea or lake watersports 11km, cycling 15km, fishing 15km, golf course 20km, interesting flora 25km

Fluent English spoken

——At Quimper, go towards Audierne on the D784. 13km from Quimper and 3km before Landudec, you will see the entrance to the estate on the left. Follow the signs.

PRICE STRUCTURE

4 Bedrooms and 2 Suites

rooms Bleue & Rose: television, bathroom with wc, twin beds: FF650
room Jaune: television, shower room with wc, double bed: FF650
room Chapelle: television, bathroom with wc, double bed: FF650
Suite Bleue: television, bathroom with wc, twin beds + en-suite room twin beds: FF800 (2 people) FF1100 (4 people)
Suite Jaune: television, bathroom with wc, twin beds + en-suite room twin beds: FF800 (2 people) FF1100 (4 people)

Extra Bed: FF150
Reduction: 01/04–15/06 & 16/09–15/11 and 3 nights
Capacity: 16 people

Marceline GRALL

'Ferme de Kernevez'

29233 CLEDER

Tel: (0) 2 98 69 41 14

Working Farm

13 km - S W - ROSCOFF
Cléder: hosts can collect from station,
railway station: 30km
airport: 40km
car essential

PRICE STRUCTURE

3 Bedrooms

Lit fermeau: shower room with wc, washbasin, twin beds: FF250

Rose: shower room with wc along corridor, double bed, single bed:
FF250 (2 people)
FF350 (3 people)

ground floor: shower room with wc, double bed: FF250

Extra Bed: FF75

Reduction: 01/10–30/06

Capacity: 7 people

29.32 ROSCOFF

What a sight! Just past an impressive cross, you will see this beautiful farmhouse surrounded by fields of cauliflowers and artichokes. Marceline is a retired farmer and will invite you to make full use of her garden and its barbecue. You are only 2.5km from the beach and there are Breton manor houses and parish enclosures to visit.

PROPERTY

off-street parking, garden, tv lounge, kitchen, babies welcome, free cot, 2 nights minimum stay: (01/07–1/08), hiking 2km, cycling 2km, fishing 2km, sea or lake watersports 2km, golf course 15km, interesting flora 30km

Basic English spoken

——From Roscoff, head to St-Pol-de-Léon and take the D10 towards Plouescat and Cléder. There, turn right towards the 'An Amied' beaches, and follow the signs to 'Ferme de Kernevez'.

Jean & Annie MARTIN

'Ty-Dreux'

29410 LOC-EGUINER-ST-THEGONNEC

Tel: (0) 2 98 78 08 21

Fax: (0) 2 98 78 01 69

Working Farm

8 km - S - ST-THEGONNEC
Loc-Eguiner-St-Thégonnec:
airport: 40km
car essential

29.05 ST-THEGONNEC

Well worth a detour. This farm is furnished in authentic style in an 18th-century weaving village. Your hosts are proud of their Breton traditions and language and will help you discover the nearby Parish Enclosures. They have a beautiful collection of antiques and Breton costumes. On sale: Farm produce.

PROPERTY

off-street parking, garden, tv lounge, hosts have pets, kitchen, hiking, cycling, fishing, sea or lake watersports 5km, golf course 10km

Adequate English spoken

——In St-Thégonnec, go towards Loc-Eguiner-St-Thégonnec (D118 then D18). In the village, continue on to the D111 towards Plonéour-Ménez.

PRICE STRUCTURE

5 Bedrooms

(1 room) shower room with wc, double bed, single bed:
FF270 (2 people)
FF350 (3 people)

Baldaquin: shower room with wc, double bed: FF270

(2 rooms) shower room with wc, double bed: FF270

Suite: shower room with wc, double bed + en-suite room single bed:
FF270 (2 people)
FF350 (3 people)

Extra Bed: FF100

Capacity: 12 people

Pierre & Nicole
HUBERT

'La Margriette'

34, Avenue Pasteur

35260 CANCALE

Tel: (0) 2 99 89 73 27-06
81 49 71 04

Fax: (0) 2 99 89 55 41

Private Home

CANCALE:
hosts can collect
from station,
railway station: 14km
airport: 30km

PRICE STRUCTURE

3 Bedrooms
ground floor – Blanche-
Bordeaux: television,
bathroom with wc, shower,
double bed: FF320

Baldaquin Bleu-Blanc:
double bed: FF270

Verte-Rose: twin beds: FF270

Extra Bed: FF105
Reduction: 1/10–30/03

Capacity: 6 people

35.14 CANCALE

Here you will find an attentive hostess in a very attractive, modern house, which is beautifully furnished and in a peaceful location. The bedrooms are pretty. Close to tennis courts and several art and regional history museums. Cancale is a charming fishing port, well known for its oysters.

PROPERTY

off-street parking, garden, tv lounge, hosts have pets, pets not accepted, babies welcome, free cot, 1 shared shower room, wc, 3 nights minimum stay: (11/11–28/02), hiking, cycling, sea or lake watersports 3km, bird-watching 5km, golf course 25km

Adequate English spoken

——In Cancale, the street is to the south of the town, parallel to the sea front, heading towards Rennes.

35.22 CANCALE

This lovely, tranquil house has beautiful bathrooms, a piano, relaxing chairs in the garden and private parking. Believe it or not, you are in the town centre, 500m from the port of Cancale, where you must taste their famous oysters. The bedrooms have mini-bars.

PROPERTY

✸ ✸

private parking, garden, pets not accepted, non smoking, 2 years old minimum age, closed: 1/10–01/04, hiking, cycling, sea or lake watersports, bird-watching 5km, golf course 25km

Basic English spoken

PRICE STRUCTURE
2 Bedrooms

La Rose: lounge, television, bathroom with wc, twin beds: FF380

Le Bleuet: lounge, television, shower room with wc, double bed, twin beds: FF360 (2 people) FF460 (4 people)

Extra Bed: FF100

Capacity: 6 people

Eugène & Marie-Thérèse Le SAULNIER

20, Avenue Pasteur

35260 CANCALE

Tel: (0) 2 99 89 66 07/ 06 82 50 17 90

Fax: (0) 2 99 89 66 07

Private Home

CANCALE:
hosts can collect from station,
railway station: 15km
airport: 20km

——From the port, take the main street towards the centre of the town. Then take the first on the left towards Rennes, and the first on the left again.

BRETAGNE

CANCALE

Marie-France SIMON

'Auberge de la Motte Jean'

35350 ST-COULOMB

Tel: (0) 2 99 89 41 99

Fax: (0) 2 99 89 92 22

Private Home

2 km - W - **CANCALE**
St-Coulomb:
railway station: 18km
airport: 25km
car essential

PRICE STRUCTURE

10 Bedrooms and 1 Apartment

Each room: television, telephone:

Rose Elisabeth: bathroom with wc, double bed: FF570

Jonquille & Genêts & Tulipes: shower room with wc, double bed: FF570

Glycines: shower room with wc, twin beds: FF570

Bleuets: shower room with wc, double bed: FF540

Capucines: bathroom with wc, double bed: FF540

Little House: lounge, kitchen, shower room with wc, double bed: FF560

Hortensias: bathroom with wc, double bed (queen size): FF570

Camélias: bathroom with wc, 2 single beds: FF570

Extra Bed: FF100

Reduction: 01/10–31/03

Capacity: 20 people

35.33 CANCALE

Madame Simon's place is very quiet and near the beaches. It has its own lake, so you will not be surprised to learn that she collects ornamental ducks. She also runs a restaurant nearby, at which duck is off the menu! Be sure to try her mother's famous jam: apple jelly from la Motte Jean.

PROPERTY

off-street parking, garden, hosts have pets, pets not accepted, telephone, packed lunch, kitchen, hiking 1km, gliding 2km, cycling 3km, fishing 3km, mushroom-picking 3km, sea or lake watersports 3km, bird-watching 5km, golf course 15km

Basic English spoken

——From Cancale, head towards St-Malo on the D355. Turn left after 2km following the large sign 'Auberge de la Motte Jean'.

Yvonnick LE MIRE

'Château de la Villerobert'

22130 ST-LORMEL

Tel: (0) 2 96 84 12 88

Fax: (0) 2 96 84 03 27

Château

20 km - S W - DINARD
St-Lormel:
railway station: 30km
airport: 4km
car essential

22.23 DINARD

Monsieur and Madame Le Mire will receive you like old friends in their 17th-century château, quietly situated in its own grounds. It is furnished with antiques and only 5km from the sea. Ideal base for the 'Emerald Coast'. Fleur de Soleil member.

PROPERTY

★ ★ ★ ★

private parking, extensive grounds, tv lounge, babies welcome, free cot, golf course 8km, sea or lake watersports 8km

Adequate English spoken

PRICE STRUCTURE

3 Bedrooms
Bleue: shower, wc, double bed, single bed:
FF425 (2 people)
FF525 (3 people)

Rose: bathroom along corridor, wc, twin beds:
FF425

Jaune: shower room with wc, double bed, single bed:
FF425 (2 people)
FF525 (3 people)

Extra Bed: FF60

Capacity: 8 people

——In Dinard, go towards Ploubalay, Plancoët. After Créhen, turn right towards St-Lormel. Cross St-Lormel then, 50m after the sign as you exit the village, the château is on the left.

Jean-François STENOU

'Manoir de la Duchée'

ST-BRIAC-SUR-MER

35800 DINARD

Tel: (0) 9 88 00 02

Fax: (0) 2 99 88 92 57

http://pro.wanadoo.fr/
manoir.duchee/

Residence of
Outstanding Character

7 km - W - DINARD
St-Briac-sur-mer:
railway station: 13km
airport: 3km
car essential

PRICE STRUCTURE

4 Bedrooms and 2 Suites

Suite Rose: lounge, television, bathroom with wc, double bed + en-suite room single bed: FF500 (2 people) FF600 (3 people)
Lilas: bridal room, television, shower room with wc, double bed: FF500
Bleuet: television, bathroom with wc, double bed: FF400
Coquelicot: television, bathroom with wc, single bed: FF350 (1 person)
Camélia: television, bathroom with wc, double bed (queen size): FF500
Pivoine – Duplex: television, bathroom with wc, double bed + en-suite room twin beds: FF500 (2 people) FF600 (4 people)
Extra Bed: FF100
Capacity: 14 people

35.28 DINARD

Jean-François's house is meant to be fun. When you enter this 16th-century manor house, you could quite easily shake the hand of the lady in Breton folk costume, who turns out to be a statue! You will be captivated. On sale: Paintings.

PROPERTY

private parking, extensive grounds, lounge, hosts have pets, pets not accepted, telephone, hiking, cycling, fishing 1km, golf course 3km, sea or lake watersports 3km

——At Dinard take the D786 coast road, Exit St-Briac. Go towards the Camping Municipal and follow the signs.

BRETAGNE

DINARD

Hugues & Marie-Christine BARBERE

'La Sauvageais'

35730 PLEURTUIT

Tel: (0) 2 99 88 82 47/
06 07 70 73 09

Fax: (0) 2 99 88 82 47

Private Home

4 km - S - DINARD
Pleurtuit: hosts can
collect from station,
railway station: 15km
airport: 6km
car essential

35.35 DINARD

You will be warmly welcomed to a recently-built house with a large garden, situated in the village of Pleurtuit. It is an ideal base for visiting this part of Brittany, renowned for its tourist towns: Dinard (4km), St-Malo (8km) and Cancale (20km). The Blue and Green rooms are self-contained. Don't miss the Breton crêpes and galettes.

PROPERTY

private parking, garden, lounge, hosts have pets, dinner available, non-smoking, hiking, cycling, fishing 2km, interesting flora 2km, sea or lake watersports 2km, gliding 2km, golf course 8km, riversports 15km

Adequate English spoken

——From Dinard, take the D266 to Pleurtuit. Turn left just as you enter the village, towards 'Les Sauvageais'. Continue for 800m to the 'Stop' sign, then turn right. Continue for another 50m.

PRICE STRUCTURE

4 Bedrooms

Rose: shower room with wc, double bed: FF255

Marron: shower room with wc, double bed, 2 single beds: FF255 (2 people) FF335 (4 people)

Bleue: kitchen, shower room with wc, twin beds, 2 single beds: FF315 (2 people) FF425 (4 people)

Verte: kitchen, shower room with wc, double bed, 2 single beds: FF315 (2 people) FF425 (4 people)

Extra Bed: FF55

Capacity: 14 people

Andy ANDREWS

'La Higourdais'

Parc de la Higourdais

35120 EPINIAC

Tel: (0) 2 99 80 01 46

Fax: (0) 2 99 80 01 46

Private Home

BRETAGNE

10 km - S - DOL-DE-BRETAGNE
Epiniac: hosts can collect from station, ferry port: 10km airport: 50km

DOL-DE-BRETAGNE

PRICE STRUCTURE
6 Bedrooms
Senteurs du jardin: wc, double bed, single bed:
FF225 (2 people)
FF300 (3 people)
Lake view: wc, twin beds:
FF225
Petit Nid: twin beds: FF225
Blue Moon: wc, washbasin, double bed, 2 single beds:
FF225 (2 people)
FF400 (4 people)
Crystal room: television, wc, double bed, 2 single beds:
FF225 (2 people)
FF325 (4 people)
Tudor room: shower room with wc along corridor, 2 double beds: FF225 (2 people) FF400 (4 people)

Extra Bed: FF100
Reduction: groups and children; Capacity: 19 people

35.07 DOL-DE-BRETAGNE

Andy and his small Franco-British family clearly know how to create a cosy atmosphere, a very warm welcome and friendly ambiance. In this rustic and relaxing house, in the heart of a protected nature park, you will share their family life.

PROPERTY

off-street parking, extensive grounds, tv lounge, hosts have pets, telephone, dinner available, packed lunch, kitchen, babies welcome, free cot, non-smoking, 1 shared bathroom with wc, 3 shared shower rooms with wc, fishing, golf course 7km, sea or lake watersports 15km

Fluent English spoken

——In Dol-de- Bretagne, take the D795 towards Combourg then the D4 towards Epiniac. Near the church, head in the direction of Cuguen for 4km. Turn left and follow the signs for 'La Higourdais'.

Marga MULLER

'La Morière'

La Morière

35120 MONT-DOL

Tel: 02 99 48 92 88

Fax: (0) 2 99 48 92 88

lamoriere.muller
@wanadoo.fr

Private Home

2 km - N - DOL-DE-BRETAGNE
Mont-Dol: hosts can collect from station, ferry port: 20km airport: 25km car essential

35.43 DOL-DE-BRETAGNE

This house is in the middle of the marshlands, near to Mont-Dol, a place of pilgrimage for the Druids. Marga and Hans have restored this typical, old Breton farmhouse in a sober and traditional style. Everything adds up to a warm and convivial welcome, in an attractive setting. There is a covered terrace with a barbecue, a bedroom suitable for handicapped visitors and an artist's studio.

PROPERTY

off-street parking, garden, tv lounge, hosts have pets, dinner available, packed lunch, babies welcome, free cot, wheelchair access, hiking, cycling, hunting, bird-watching, mushroom-picking 1km, fishing 3km, sea or lake watersports 3km, golf course 7km, interesting flora 10km

PRICE STRUCTURE

5 Bedrooms

Double or twin room: bridal room, along corridor shower room with wc, double bed: FF300

(2 rooms) along corridor shower room with wc, twin beds: FF300

single bed: FF150 (1 person)

wheelchair access, shower room with wc, twin beds: FF300

Capacity: 9 people

——From St Malo take the D4 to Mont Dol. Take the D123 and then the D282 towards Le Vivier-sur-Mer for 2km.

Odile & Alain
LE CLAINCHE

'Le Logis du
Bonamenec'h'

Bonnemanay

35380 PAIMPONT

Tel: (0) 2 99 06 82 13
Fax: (0) 2 99 06 82 13

logisbo@club-internet.fr

Residence of
Outstanding Character

30 km - W -
RENNES
Bonamenay:
hosts can collect
from station,
railway station: 17km
airport: 30km
car essential

PRICE STRUCTURE

35.30 RENNES

3 Bedrooms
first room: shower room
with wc, washbasin, double
bed: FF320

second room: shower room
with wc, washbasin, twin
beds: FF320

third room: double bed:
FF300

Extra Bed: FF100/120

Capacity: 6 people

If you enjoy mystery and the legends of knights and their ladies, then this is the place for you – you are right by the enchanted forest of Brocéliande. Your host, who is an architect, has restored the interior of this 16th century Breton house with great taste and skill. Fleur de Soleil member.

PROPERTY

private parking, garden, lounge, dinner available, hiking, cycling, fishing 5km, hunting 5km, mushroom-picking 5km, bird-watching 5km, sea or lake watersports 10km

Basic English spoken

——At Rennes take the dual-carriageway towards Lorient. Take the Exit at Plelan-Le-Grand and then turn right off the slip road. Cross the N24 and follow the D61 for 3km. Then take the gravel road on the left, 500m after Bonamenay-le-Breuil.

ROUXEVILLE

'Parc Ombragé'

rue de St-Ideuc

35400 ST-MALO

Tel: (0) 2 99 40 09 41

Fax: (0) 2 99 40 09 41

Private Home

ST-MALO:
hosts can collect
from station,
railway station: 1km
airport: 12km

BRETAGNE

ST-MALO

35.20 ST-MALO

St-Malo is a town steeped in the history of the seafarers and merchant adventurers who conquered the new territories in past centuries. Be sure to try the seafood, for which St-Malo is famous. Your hosts are newly retired, and will give you a classy welcome in their villa in a residential area near to the main roads. What a great idea to open their house to visitors in such an outstanding position in St-Malo. Their 3 'suns' are well deserved. Fleur de Soleil member.

PROPERTY

off-street parking, extensive grounds, tv lounge, pets not accepted, non-smoking, 3 wc, hiking, cycling, fishing, sea or lake watersports, golf course 15km, bird watching 30km

Basic English spoken

——Coming from Rennes, at St-Malo take the D301 towards Cancale and 'Centre-Ville'. At the 4th roundabout go towards 'Stade Lemarié' At the set of traffic lights, take the road in front of you as far as the roundabout. and again in front of you, enter the courtyard of the 'beige château'. It is the last house on your left. (white gate).

PRICE STRUCTURE

3 Bedrooms
Yann: shower room with wc along corridor, double bed + room Pascal: double bed:
FF300 (2 people)
FF560 (4 people)

Frédérique: along corridor bathroom, double bed, single bed:
FF300 (2 people)
FF500 (3 people)

Extra Bed: FF120

Capacity: 7 people

Martine MONSIMET

La Rimbaudais

35350 ST-MELOIR-DES-ONDES

Tel: (0) 2 99 89 19 75-06
62 29 70 31

Private Home

BRETAGNE

ST-MALO

7 km - E - ST MALO
St-Méloir-des-Ondes:
airport: 16km
car essential

PRICE STRUCTURE

2 Bedrooms
first room: shower room
with wc, double bed, single
bed: FF235 (2 people)
FF300 (3 people)

second room: shower room
with wc along corridor,
double bed: FF235

Extra Bed: FF50

Capacity: 5 people

35.24 ST-MALO

Martine is a charming person. Her house is very well situated, 5km from Cancale and 7km from St-Malo. The barbecue, dishwasher and fridge are available for your use. There are many restaurants and crêperies nearby and, of course you are in the land of oysters and mussels. On sale: Oysters, mussels, honey, cider, Calvados….

PROPERTY

private parking, garden, hosts have pets, pets not accepted, babies welcome, free cot, hiking 5km, cycling 5km, fishing 5km, bird-watching 5km, sea or lake watersports 5km, riversports 5km, golf course 10km, gliding 10km

Basic English spoken

——At St-Malo, head in the direction of Mont-St-Michel via the D155, and then turn right towards St-Méloir. At the Mairie (town hall), take the D2 towards St-Servan for 1.5km as far as La Rimbaudais.

Peter SOBEK

'La Goëlette'

2, rue Besnier

35430 ST SULIAC

Tel: (0) 2 99 58 47 03/ 06 68 10 97 99

Fax: (0) 2 99 58 47 03

http://perso. worldonline.fr./goelette/ index.htm

Residence of Outstanding Character

10 km - S - ST-MALO
St-Suliac: hosts can collect from station, ferry port: 10km airport: 20km

35.27 ST-MALO

This Franco-German couple will welcome you to their 17th-century stone house, in the heart of one of the most beautiful fishing villages in Brittany. The bedrooms have been tastefully modernised. You will love the courtyard and the garden. Large breakfast.

PROPERTY

garden, tv lounge, pets not accepted, dinner available, babies welcome, free cot, hiking, cycling, fishing, sea or lake watersports, bird-watching 2km, golf course 15km

Adequate English spoken

——On the N137 dual carriageway (Rennes to St-Malo road) turn off between the N137 and the N176 at the exit to St-Suliac. 50m before the church on the square, in front of the post office (PTT), you will see the large white gates on your left.

PRICE STRUCTURE

3 Bedrooms
bathroom with wc, double bed (queen size): FF290

shower room with wc, double bed (queen size), 2 single beds:
FF350 (2 people)
FF510 (4 people)

shower room with wc, double bed (queen size), single bed:
FF290 (2 people)
FF370 (3 people)

Extra Bed: FF80

Reduction: 1/11–30/04 and 4 nights

Capacity: 9 people

Marie Paule LEAUSTIC

'Les Ajoncs d'Or'

11b, rue des Ajoncs d'Or

35540 MINIAC-MORVAN

Tel: (0) 2 99 58 55 08

Residence of
Outstanding Character

15 km - S -
ST-MALO
Miniac-Morvan:
hosts can collect
from station,
ferry port: 15km
airport: 25km

PRICE STRUCTURE

5 Bedrooms

Ti Koad: shower room with
wc, washbasin, twin beds:
FF210

Amzerz'o: shower room
with wc along corridor,
washbasin, double bed:
FF160

Karantez ar mor: shower
room with wc along
corridor, washbasin,
double bed: FF210

Extra Bed: FF70

Capacity: 6 people

35.02 ST-MALO

**A modern house in its own grounds, great for picnics. A
pleasant spot not far from the main St-Malo–Rennes road.
Tennis, golf and riding are available nearby. Marie-Paule is
very keen on ancestor-tracing. Fleur de Soleil member.**

PROPERTY

off-street parking, extensive grounds, tv lounge, hosts have
pets, pets not accepted, kitchen, babies welcome, free cot, golf
course 3km, sea or lake watersports 15km

Basic English spoken

——Go in to the centre of Dinan, go through the centre and
follow the signs to Rennes–Caen. On the viaduct go straight
on towards Caen. After 13km, turn left on to the D73 towards
Miniac-Morvan. Near to the church, go towards Pleudihen for
300m then turn right and follow the signs for 300m. The
house is on the left (private lane).

Jean-Paul RAUX

'Maison de Quokelunde'

41, rue du Bord-de-Mer

35120 HIREL

Tel: (0) 2 99 48 80 12

Fax: (0) 2 99 48 80 12

Private Home

17 km - S E -
ST-MALO
Hirel:
ferry port: 17km
airport: 25km
car essential

35.31 ST-MALO

This is a restored Breton house. The rooms are spacious, well-equipped, and some have a view over the bay. An ideal and practical base for visiting this area. Your host is an expert on Canada.

PROPERTY

off-street parking, garden, lounge, pets not accepted, kitchen, babies welcome, free cot, wheelchair access, 7 nights minimum stay: (4/07–2/09), hiking, bird-watching, golf course 12km, sea or lake watersports 12km, fishing 15km

Basic English spoken

PRICE STRUCTURE

**2 Bedrooms and
3 Apartments**

All rooms: shower room with wc, washbasin, lounge, television, kitchen

Opale: double bed: FF200

Améthyste: double bed, 3 single beds: FF200 (2 people) FF400 (5 people)

Emeraude: double bed, 2 single beds: FF250 (2 people) FF400 (4 people)

Saphir: twin beds, 2 single beds: FF250 (2 people) FF400 (4 people)

Topaze: double bed, 2 single beds: FF250 (2 people) FF400 (4 people)

Extra Bed: FF80

Reduction: 1/09–30/06

Capacity: 19 people

——When coming from St-Malo take the D155 coast road towards Mont-St-Michel. Hirel is situated on this road at number 41 on the sea front.

Beryl & Raymond
FROUD

Mont-Servin

35270 BONNEMAIN

Tel: (0) 2 99 73 70 62

Fax: (0) 2 99 73 70 62

Private Home

30 km - S E -
ST-MALO
Mont-Servin:
railway station: 4km
airport: 40km
car essential

PRICE STRUCTURE

2 Bedrooms
first room: washbasin,
double bed: FF250

second room: washbasin,
double bed: FF250

Capacity: 4 people

35.40 ST-MALO

You may not want to play cricket in Brittany but, if you do, Beryl and Ray, this friendly, retired English couple, can arrange it. If not, they can also show you wonderful walks through the medieval forest and by the enchanting lakes of this area. The lawn is immaculate and tea is always served.

PROPERTY

private parking, garden, tv lounge, hosts have pets, pets not accepted, babies welcome, free cot, non-smoking, 1 shared shower room with wc, fishing 3km, hunting 3km, golf course 8km, sea or lake watersports 21km

Fluent English spoken

——From St-Malo, take the N137 towards Rennes. Turn off at Miniac-Morvan and take the D73 towards Combourg. At Lanhélin, take the D12 on the left towards Bonnemain. Just after the exit sign 'Lanhélin', turn left to Mont-Servin, then first on the left.

Chantal & Jean-Pierre
JENOUVRIER

'La Grande Bellevue'

8, Impasse Bellevue

35400 ST-MALO

Tel: 02 99 82 41 29/
06 12 66 32 91

Fax: (0) 2 99 82 41 29

RSURCOUF
@club-internet.fr

Residence of
Outstanding Character

ST MALO:
hosts can collect
from station,
railway station: 2km
airport: 4km
car essential

35.41 ST-MALO

This is the place to savour the atmosphere of St-Malo. This small manor house is furnished in the style of the town and was built by the Surcouf family, a legendary dynasty of wealthy, seafaring adventurers. The house is only 300m from the large aquarium and near the town centre, yet its garden is a haven of peace.

PROPERTY

private parking, garden, tv lounge, kitchen, babies welcome, free cot, cycling 1km, interesting flora 1km, hiking 2km, fishing 2km, sea or lake watersports 2km, gliding 2km, bird-watching 3km, golf course 4km, mushroom-picking 5km, hunting 10km

Adequate English spoken

——From the large Aquarium at St-Malo, head towards the Centre-Ville. When you have reached the cemetery, turn right in to the rue du Tertre-Belot and then left into rue Descartes. Then turn right in to rue de Bellevue and the impasse Bellevue is on the right.

PRICE STRUCTURE

3 Bedrooms
double or twin room: television, bathroom with wc, double bed (queen size), single bed: FF300

(2 rooms) television, shower room with wc, double bed, single bed: FF300

Extra Bed: FF50

Reduction: 3 nights and groups

Capacity: 6 people

William & Catherine
CALAIS

8, route du Groussay

35120 HIREL

Tel: 02 99 48 86 54/
06 70 83 32 70

Private Home

17 km - S E - ST-
MALO
Hirel:
ferry port: 17km
airport: 20km

PRICE STRUCTURE

35.42 ST-MALO

3 Bedrooms
Danone: bathroom with wc,
double bed + extra room
Groseille: double bed:
FF200 (2 people) FF400 (4
people)

Flèche: shower room with
wc, double bed: FF200 (2
people)

Extra Bed: FF50

Capacity: 6 people

This place is near the coast but away from the crowds, and the pace of life is set by the two majestic horses, Danone and Groseille, who regularly pull carriages or caravans through the countryside. William is a professional coachman, and Catherine takes care of everything else. Their simple stone house offers a warm and friendly welcome. Stabling is also available.

PROPERTY

off-street parking, garden, hosts have pets, dinner available, hiking, fishing 2km, interesting flora 2km, sea or lake watersports 10km, riversports 10km, golf course 15km

Basic English spoken

——From St-Malo, d155 to St-Benoit-des-Ondes and Hirel. From the village, head for the campsite and continue for 2km. It is the fourth road on the right.

56.24 BELLE-ILE-EN-MER

Guests describe Anne as 'very motherly, full of kindness...', and we agree that you will be overwhelmed by the warmth of the welcome in this little house in the country, not far from the beaches and fortifications of Belle-Ile. If you are only familiar with the magical world of the small islands of Brittany through song, then this is the chance to take the boat experience the real thing.

PROPERTY

off-street parking, garden, tv lounge, pets not accepted, babies welcome, free cot, 1 shared shower room, 2 wc, closed: 01/01–31/01, hiking, cycling, golf course, fishing, hunting, interesting flora, mushroom-picking, bird-watching, sea or lake watersports, riversports

Basic English spoken

PRICE STRUCTURE
3 Bedrooms

Mer & Soleil: double bed: FF280

Sable: twin beds: FF280

Extra Bed: FF70

Reduction: 01/10–31/03 & 01/06–30/06

Capacity: 6 people

Anne OLIERO

'TI MENOU'

Village de Nanscol - Le Palais

56360 BELLE-ILE-EN-MER

Tel: (0) 2 97 31 85 53

Private Home

BELLE-ILE-EN-MER
Le Palais: hosts can collect from station, ferry port: 2,5km
——Take the ferry at Quiberon. From the harbour, go up the hill and turn left before you reach the vaulted arcade and then right, after the Maison de la Nature. Continue along by the Ramonette beach and then take the only road which climbs up steeply. Take the first tarmac road, which is a cul-de-sac, on the right. There is a sign for 'Ti Menou'.

Solange GUILLOUX

'La Dame de Nage'

13, rue de Bellevue -
Loc Maria

56590 ILE-DE-GROIX

Tel: (0) 2 97 86 55 90/
06 81 68 37 96

Fax: (0) 2 97 86 55 90

Private Home

ILE-DE-GROIX
Loc Maria:
ferry port: 1km

PRICE STRUCTURE

3 Bedrooms
Primiture & Piwisi: shower
room with wc, double bed:
FF330

Thoniers: television,
bathroom with wc, twin
beds, 2 single beds, cot:
FF330 (2 people)
FF580 (4 people)

Extra Bed: FF75
Reduction: 2 nights

Capacity: 8 people

56.19 ILE-DE-GROIX

Tie up and enjoy and the magic of of l'Ile de Groix, with its nature reserve and its beach of white sand. Solange welcomes you to her house, typical of the island. From the shade of the garden, you can see the sea only 100m away. The charm of this enchanting place is enhanced by nauticalia, old chests and wood carvings.

PROPERTY

off-street parking, garden, tv lounge, hosts have pets, kitchen, closed: 01/10–15/03, hiking, cycling, fishing, interesting flora, bird-watching, sea or lake watersports

Basic English spoken

——From Lorient, head towards l'Ile-de-Groix. There is a free car park opposite the jetty (a car is not essential on the island). The crossing takes 45 minutes and, as you leave the boat at Port Tudy, go up to the village and follow the signs (on the ground) to 'Locmaria'. The house is at the top of the village. If you do not bring your car, there is a regular taxi service (FF15 per person), that goes all round the island.

Monique POUPEE

'La Christe Marine'

Locqueltas

56590 ILE-DE-GROIX

Tel: (0) 2 97 86 83 04

Fax: (0) 2 97 86 83 04

la-christe-
marine@wanadoo.fr

Private Home

ILE-DE-GROIX
Locqueltas:
ferry port: 1km

56.20 ILE-DE-GROIX

You will be captivated by the l'Ile de Groix, and even more so by your stay chez Monique. This is a modern house, constructed of old building materials, in a verdant spot. From the garden, your bedroom window or the terrace, there is an interrupted view of the sea (100m away). A very special place, particularly for nature-lovers.

PROPERTY

off-street parking, garden, tv lounge, hosts have pets, pets not accepted, babies welcome, free cot, closed: 21/12–11/01, hiking, cycling, fishing, interesting flora, bird-watching, sea or lake watersports

Basic English spoken

——From Lorient, head towards l'Ile de Groix. There is a free car park opposite the jetty (a car is not essential on the island), and the crossing takes 45 minutes. As you leave the boat at Port Tudy, go up to the village and follow the signs (on the ground) to 'Lomener, Locqueltas'. Otherwise there is a regular taxi service (FF15 per person), that goes round the whole island.

PRICE STRUCTURE

2 Bedrooms
Pimprenelle: bathroom with wc, double bed: FF380

Grandmère: bathroom with wc along corridor, double bed: FF380

Extra Bed: FF125

Capacity: 4 people

Brigitte LE PRIOL

'Les Cormorans'

rue du Chalutier les '2 Anges' - Port Tudy

56590 ILE-DE-GROIX

Tel: 02 97 86 57 67

Fax: (0) 2 97 86 50 04

aubergedu pecheur @aol.fr

Private Home

ILE-DE-GROIX
Port Tudy:
ferry port: 1 km

PRICE STRUCTURE

1 Bedroom and 2 Apartments

Les Sables & Les Vignes: kitchen, shower room with wc, double bed: FF440

Les Algues: shower room with wc, twin beds: FF340

Extra Bed: FF55

Capacity: 6 people

56.28 ILE-DE-GROIX

Now that Brigitte has arrived, there is no longer any excuse for not making the crossing to the island, so charmingly Breton. This is the third excellent address, and this charming, traditional little house is only 5 minutes walk from the harbour. This is a little corner of heaven, where the colours of the sea are enlivened by Bridget's boundless energy. She also runs the 'Auberge du Pêcheur' near the harbour. You can take breakfast at the Auberge or in your bedroom, whichever you prefer.

PROPERTY

off-street parking, garden, hosts have pets, hiking, cycling, fishing, hunting, interesting flora, bird-watching, sea or lake watersports

Adequate English spoken

——From Lorient, head towards l'Ile-de-Groix. There is a free car park opposite the jetty (a car is not essential on the island), and the crossing takes 45 minutes. As you leave the boat at Port Tudy, go up rue du Général de Gaulle, then first left.

Marie-Lise & Jean
LORGEOUX

5 rue Fontaine de
Kerlavret

56270 PLOEMEUR

Tel: (0) 2 97 82 85 59

Fax: (0) 2 97 82 85 59

chambrehote@free.fr

Private Home

10 km - S W -
LORIENT
Ploemeur:
railway station: 10km
airport: 4km
car essential

56.30 LORIENT

Jean and Marie-Lise are delighted to welcome you to their Breton-style house, situated 500m from Lomener beach, opposite the Isle-de-Groix in Southern Brittany. This is a village where the countryside meets the sea. The area is famous for hiking, Breton dancing and the International Celtic Festival in August. Be sure to visit the standing stones of Carnac and Concarneau.

PRICE STRUCTURE

1 Bedroom and 1 Suite
shower room with wc, double bed: FF250

shower room with wc, double bed + en-suite room double bed:
FF230 (2 people)
FF400 (4 people)

PROPERTY

Private parking, garden

Capacity: 6 people

——On the N165, head towards Ploemeur and Lomener. At the traffic lights at the Lomener crossroads, continue straight on for 1km, then take the first on the left. Follow the signs to the village of Kerlavret and turn left in front of number 20, and it is the first house on the right.

Madeleine & Jean GRU

Evas - St-Laurent-sur-Oust

56140 MALESTROIT

Tel: (0) 2 97 75 02 62

Private Home

18 km - S -
PLOERMEL
St-Laurent-sur-Oust:
railway station: 30km
airport: 65km
car essential

PRICE STRUCTURE

3 Bedrooms

Les Roses: television, shower
room with wc, double bed:
FF210

Bleuet: twin beds: FF210

Blé d'Or: television, double
bed: FF210

Extra Bed: FF70

Capacity: 6 people

56.11 PLOERMEL

Madeleine and Jean's cosy home, in the centre of a small village, has a beautiful garden. The bright bedrooms have rural views, and little extras like a home-made aperitif and the Breton breakfast with home-made jam, add to the enjoyment of your stay here.

PROPERTY

off-street parking, extensive grounds, tv lounge, hosts have pets, pets not accepted, kitchen, babies welcome, free cot, non-smoking, 1 shared shower room with wc, hiking, fishing, hunting, mushroom-picking, cycling 4km, riversports 4km, golf course 15km, interesting flora 20km, gliding 20km

——At Ploërmel, N166 towards Vannes. Take the Exit Malestroit. In Malestroit head towards Ruffiac for 4km. Then turn right to St-Laurent-sur-Oust and follow the signs.

Daniel & Monique le DOUARAN

Guerlan - Plougoumelen

56400 AURAY

Tel: (0) 2 97 57 65 50/ 06 15 71 19 49

Fax: (0) 2 97 57 65 50

Working Farm

15 km - W - VANNES
Guerlan:
airport: 40km
car essential

56.05 VANNES

Monique and Daniel, a friendly young farming couple, welcome you with a smile into their imposing house. Much of the typical Breton furniture has been restored by Monique as a labour of love. The Bay of Morbihan is 10km away.

PROPERTY

off-street parking, garden, tv lounge, hosts have pets, kitchen, babies welcome, free cot, wheelchair access, sea or lake watersports 30km

Adequate English spoken

——In Vannes, take the N165 towards Lorient. After Vannes, take the first exit Ploeren/Meriadec and take the D127 towards Meriadec for 3.5km. 2nd farm on the left (after the level-crossing).

PRICE STRUCTURE

5 Bedrooms and 1 Suite
Chambre au balcon: shower room with wc, double bed: FF220

Verte: shower room with wc, twin beds: FF220

Ground floor – Berder: shower room with wc, double bed: FF260; Gaur'Iwiz: shower room with wc, double bed + en-suite room Er Lannic: double bed: FF260 (2 people) FF520 (4 people)

First floor: – Logodew: shower room with wc, double bed, single bed: FF260 (2 people) FF360 (3 people); Irus: shower, wc, 3 single beds: FF260 (2 people) FF360 (3 people)

Extra Bed: FF40

Capacity: 16 people

Patrick & Marie COSSÉ

'Auberge du Château de Castellan'

Castellan

56200 ST-MARTIN-SUR-OUST

Tel: (0) 2 99 91 51 69/ 06 87 44 41 76

Fax: (0) 2 99 91 57 41

Château

40 km - E - VANNES
Castellan: hosts can collect from station, railway station: 23km airport: 65km car essential

PRICE STRUCTURE

5 Bedrooms

Saumon: shower room with wc, double bed, single bed:
FF500 (2 people)
FF620 (3 people)

Verte: shower room with wc, twin beds: FF500

Médaillon: bathroom with wc, double bed, twin beds:
FF650 (2 people)
FF890 (4 people)

Roland: bathroom with wc, double bed: FF500

Dormitory: shower room with wc, double bed, twin beds: FF550 (2 people)
FF790 (4 people)

Extra Bed: FF120

Capacity: 15 people

56.10 VANNES

This 18th-century château is in superb surroundings, and one bedroom is listed as an historic monument. This is a farmhouse inn, run by a family famous for their 'pâté en croute' as well as other excellent traditional Breton dishes. On sale: Jam, gingerbread, terrines, local produce.

PROPERTY

off-street parking, extensive grounds, pets not accepted, dinner available, babies welcome, free cot, hiking, cycling, fishing 2km, interesting flora 18km, sea or lake watersports 40km, bird-watching 45km

——At Vannes, N166 towards Rennes. D776 towards Malestroit. In Malestroit, D764 towards St-Congard. D149 towards St-Martin. Sign 'Auberge', on the left, before you reach St-Martin.

Maria FLOHIC

7 rue Er Vammenn - Kerguillé

56470 LA-TRINITE-SUR-MER

Tel: (0) 2 97 55 76 74

Private Home

30 km - S W - VANNES
La-Trinité-sur-Mer:
railway station: 12km
airport: 50km

56.14 VANNES

A world famous port, La-Trinité is a rendezvous for lovers of the sea, and famous skippers. Close to the port and its restaurants, the beaches and menhirs, a peaceful, white-painted house awaits you. Breathe in the sea air and dream of distant horizons.... Fleur de Soleil member.

PROPERTY

✸ ✸ ✸ ✸

private parking, garden, babies welcome, free cot, fishing, bird-watching 1km, hiking 2km, cycling 15km

PRICE STRUCTURE

3 Bedrooms
shower room with wc, double bed: FF270

shower room with wc, twin beds: FF270

shower room with wc along corridor, double bed, single bed: FF270 (2 people) FF345 (3 people)

Extra Bed: FF70

Capacity: 7 people

——At Vannes, take the N165 to Auray, where you will take the D28 to La-Trinité. From the port, head towards Auray (D186). 300m after leaving the town, turn left towards Kerguillé. Rue Er Vammen is the first on the right.

Maria & Eric
DE MAGALHAES

Kerbissac de Lesnoyal

56230 QUESTEMBERT

Tel: (0) 2 97 26 65 89/
06 07 21 19 08

Residence of
Outstanding Character

27 km - E - VANNES
Questembert:
hosts can collect
from station,
railway station: 2km
airport: 100km
car essential

PRICE STRUCTURE

2 Bedrooms
Jaune: television, shower
room with wc, washbasin,
double bed, 2 single beds:
FF280 (2 people)
FF380 (4 people)

Rose: television, telephone,
bathroom with wc,
washbasin, double bed:
FF270

Extra Bed: FF50
Reduction: 1/10–1/04
and groups

Capacity: 6 people

56.16 VANNES

Maria, who used to be a flight-attendant, has brought a knowledge of many foreign languages and the art of the perfect welcome, back from her travels. Her longhouse, marvellously constructed (even if the staircase is a little steep), boasts excellent facilities and a swimming pool. Be sure to try Eric's honey. This place is a real find! On sale: Embroidery, hand-painted earthenware.

PROPERTY

private parking, garden, tv lounge, hosts have pets, telephone, packed lunch, babies welcome, free cot, swimming pool, hiking, mushroom-picking 1km, cycling 5km, fishing 5km, sea or lake watersports 11km, golf course 18km, interesting flora 30km, bird-watching 30km, gliding 30km

Fluent English spoken

——At Vannes, take the N166 towards Ploërmel, then the D775 towards Redon. At the Bel-Air roundabout, head towards the racecourse. After the stands, take the 3rd left, and then the 1st left. The house is at the end of the small lane.

Jeanne CHEILLETZ-MAIGNAN

'Chaumière de Kérisac'

56390 LOCQUELTAS

Tel: (0) 2 97 66 60 13

Fax: (0) 2 97 66 67 57

chaumierekerisac
@minitel.net.

Residence of
Outstanding Character

12 km - N - VANNES
Locqueltas:
railway station: 12km
airport: 100km
car essential

56.22 VANNES

Jeanne has finished travelling, and now she loves welcoming and making a fuss of her guests in this thatched cottage, dating from 1750, which is full of life and warmth. She serves you a hearty breakfast in a dining room decorated with souvenirs from the colonies. There is also the peaceful garden in which to relax.

PRICE STRUCTURE

3 Bedrooms
Blé-noir: shower room with wc, double bed: FF380

Chanvre: bathroom, wc, double bed, single bed: FF400 (2 people)
FF480 (3 people)

Seigle: bathroom with wc, twin beds: FF400

Capacity: 7 people

PROPERTY

off-street parking, garden, tv lounge, hosts have pets, pets not accepted, babies welcome, free cot, closed: 05/01–05/02, hiking, fishing 1km, mushroom-picking 6km, bird-watching 15km, sea or lake watersports 15km, golf course 25km

Fluent English spoken

——From Vannes, head in the direction of Pontivy-St-Brieuc on the D767 as far as the dual carriageway. Take the third Exit, Locqueltas. Go through the village and, as you exit the village, after 500m turn left at the first crossroads. This is the chemin de Kerisac. Then follow the signs.

Marie Madeleine
BOCANDÉ

32, rue Châteaubriand

56450 THEIX

Tel: (0) 2 97 43 12 37

Private Home

8 km - S E - VANNES
Theix:
railway station: 10km
car essential

PRICE STRUCTURE

3 Bedrooms
(2 rooms) shower room
with wc, double bed, single
bed: FF230 (2 people)
FF290 (3 people)

third room: bathroom with
wc along corridor, double
bed: FF210

Extra Bed: FF60

Capacity: 8 people

56.23 VANNES

This detached house is on the edge of the village and the countryside, 6km from Vannes. It is easy to find, and very convenient for the sea, only 3km away. Do not worry about the fox on the lounge table – he is stuffed. On the other hand, Marie-Madeleine is full of life and joie-de-vivre.

PROPERTY

off-street parking, garden, tv lounge, fishing km, bird-watching 3km, sea or lake watersports 3km, golf course 12km

——From the Vannes–Nantes dual carriageway, take Exit Theix. At Theix, by the post office, head towards Noyalo. At the second roundabout, turn right towards the 'Z.A. du Landy'. Continue straight on, and then take the last street on the left before leaving the village (rue Lesage), which leads to the rue Châteaubriand on the right.

Marie Joe & Gilbert LE PORT

'Les Hauts de Ker Dréan'

St-Philibert

56470 LA-TRINITE-SUR-MER

Tel: (0) 2 97 55 02 57

Fax: (0) 2 97 55 16 66

Private Home

25 km - S W - VANNES
St-Philibert:
railway station: 12km
airport: 25km
car essential

56.27 VANNES

This modern house is 1km from the beaches, between the famous standing-stone sites at Carnac and Locmariaquer. It is set in spacious grounds, where horses, sheep, goats and peacocks roam. Each bedroom has its own private terrace. There are great walks to trendy La-Trinité. On sale: Honey.

PROPERTY

off-street parking, garden, lounge, hosts have pets, babies welcome, free cot, riding, hiking, sea or lake watersports 1km, fishing 2km, bird-watching 8km

PRICE STRUCTURE

2 Bedrooms
first room: shower, wc, twin beds: FF290

second room: shower room with wc along corridor, double bed: FF290

Extra Bed: FF50
Reduction: 01/09–15/06

Capacity: 4 people

——Leave the N165 dual-carriageway at Auray and head towards Locmariaquer via the D28. After Crach, turn right on to the D781 towards la-Trinité-sur-Mer. At St-Philibert, take the first road on the left, then the second on the right. Follow the signs.

Elisabeth MALHERBE

'Kerimel'

Kerimel

56400 PLOEMEL

Tel: 02 97 56 84 72

Fax: (0) 2 97 56 84 72

elisabeth.malherbe
@wanadoo.fr

http://kerimel.free.fr

Private Home

25 km - W - VANNES
Ploemel:
railway station: 6km
airport: 40km
car essential

BRETAGNE

VANNES

PRICE STRUCTURE

56.29 VANNES

This beautiful and impressive farmhouse, dating from the 18th century, is near to the beaches at Carnac and the trendy sailing harbour of La-Trinité, and not far from the Quiberon peninsula. Your kindly hosts will make sure that your stay is quiet and relaxing.

5 Bedrooms
Roi Arthur & Merlin &
Lancelot – twin or king size
rooms: television, shower
room with wc, twin beds,
single bed:
FF350 (2 people)
FF450 (3 people)

Mélusine & Tristan – twin
or king size rooms:
television, shower room
with wc, twin beds: FF300

PROPERTY

off-street parking, garden, tv lounge, hosts have pets, pets not accepted, babies welcome, free cot, closed: 15/11–1/02, hiking, mushroom-picking, golf course 2km, sea or lake watersports 6km, fishing 7km

Fluent English spoken

Capacity: 13 people

———On the N165,when you reach Auray, Exit Carnac/Quiberon. At the first roundabout, take the D22 towards Etel-Belz. After about 3km, turn left on to the D105 towards Ploërmel-Erveden. Go through the town and after about 1km, turn right towards Kerimel.

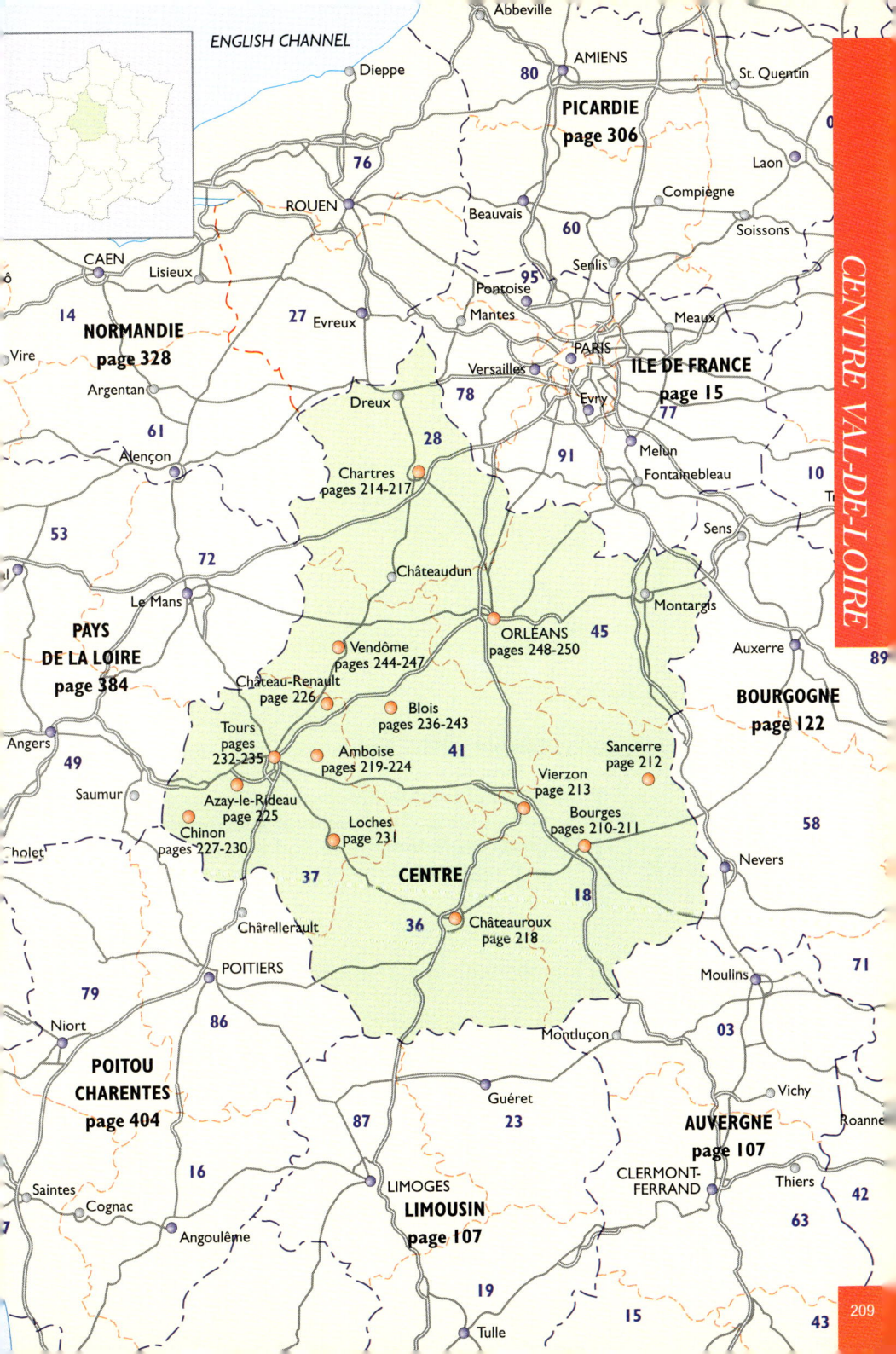

ENGLISH CHANNEL

Abbeville

Dieppe

PICARDIE
page 306

AMIENS
80

St. Quentin
0

Laon

76

ROUEN

Beauvais

Compiègne

Soissons

60

CAEN
Lisieux

14

NORMANDIE
page 328

Vire

Argentan

61

Alençon

53

72

Le Mans

Pontoise
95

Mantes

Senlis

Meaux

27
Evreux

PARIS

Versailles

Evry

ILE DE FRANCE
page 15

77

Melun

Fontainebleau

10

Dreux

78

28

Chartres
pages 214-217

91

Châteaudun

Sens

Montargis

Auxerre

89

ORLÉANS
pages 248-250

45

BOURGOGNE
page 122

PAYS
DE LA LOIRE
page 384

Angers

49

Saumur

Vendôme
pages 244-247

Château-Renault
page 226

Tours
pages
232-235

Azay-le-Rideau
page 225

Chinon
pages 227-230

cholet

Blois
pages 236-243

41

Amboise
pages 219-224

Loches
page 231

37

CENTRE

36

Châteauroux
page 218

Vierzon
page 213

Sancerre
page 212

Bourges
pages 210-211

18

58

Nevers

71

Châtellerault

POITIERS

POITOU
CHARENTES
page 404

79

Niort

86

16

Saintes

Cognac

7

Angoulême

87

LIMOGES

LIMOUSIN
page 107

Guéret

23

Montluçon

Moulins

03

Vichy

AUVERGNE
page 107

CLERMONT-
FERRAND

Roanne

Thiers

42

63

19

15

Tulle

43

Robert ROY

'Relais des Gaillards'

Route de
Neuvy/Barangeon

18110 ALLOGNY

Tel: (0) 2 48 64 00 84/
06 80 58 16 83

Fax: (0) 2 48 70 52 50

Private Home

18 km - N W -
BOURGES
Allogny:
railway station: 20km
airport: 20km
car essential

PRICE STRUCTURE

8 Bedrooms
(5 rooms) television, shower
room with wc, double bed:
FF300

television, shower room
with wc, double bed: FF275

television, shower room
with wc, 3 single beds:
FF300 (2 people)
FF375 (3 people)

television, shower room
with wc, 2 double beds:
FF375 (2 people)
FF430 (4 people)

Extra Bed: FF50

Capacity: 19 people

18.04 BOURGES

**This old working farm has now been modernised and makes
an ideal overnight stop. Another bonus is that it is situated in
110 ha of grounds, in Sologne du Cher, near to the Route
Jacques Coeur. There are many wild animals (nothing
dangerous) in the grounds, and you can also fish in the lakes
on the property. Golf and riding can also be arranged nearby.**

PROPERTY

off-street parking, extensive grounds, tv lounge, hosts have
pets, kitchen, babies welcome, free cot, wheelchair access,
hiking, cycling, fishing, hunting, golf course 10km

Adequate English spoken

——In Bourges, take the D944 towards Orléans. The house is
3km on the right, after Allogny. From the A71, take the Salbris
exit. In Salbris, take the D944 towards Bourges. The farm is
7km on the left after Neuvy-sur-Barangeon.

Olivier & Nathalie
LLOPIS

'Les Bonnets Rouges'

3 rue de la Thaumassière

18000 BOURGES

Tel: (0) 2 48 65 79 92

Fax: (0) 2 48 69 82 05

Private Home

BOURGES
railway station: 1km
airport: 2km

18.18 BOURGES

This 15th-century home is located in the heart of medieval Bourges, in the old antique dealers' district. It is a charming and gently welcoming place. Your hosts can tell you more about its fascinating history. Fleur de Soleil member.

PROPERTY ✹ ✹ ✹

off-street parking, garden, lounge, non smoking

PRICE STRUCTURE

2 Bedrooms and 2 Suites
bathroom with wc, twin beds + en-suite room double bed: FF380 (2 people) FF580 (4 people)

bathroom with wc, double bed + en-suite room double bed: FF380 (2 people) FF580 (4 people)

bathroom with wc, double bed: FF350

shower room with wc, double bed: FF380

Capacity: 12 people

——In the centre of Bourges, close to the cathedral.

Wilfrid de POMMEREAU

'Château de Beaujeu'

18300 SENS-BEAUJEU

Tel: (0) 2 48 79 07 95/
06 88 32 24 98

Fax: (0) 2 48 79 05 07

info@
chateau-de-beaujeu.com
www.chateau-de-
beaujeu.com

Château

10 km - W -
SANCERRE
Sens-Beaujeu: hosts
can collect from sta-
tion, railway station:
20km
airport: 200km
car essential

PRICE STRUCTURE

5 Bedrooms and 1 Suite
La Tour: bathroom with wc,
double bed, single bed:
FF750 (2 people)
FF900 (3 people)

Louis XVI: bathroom with
wc, double bed: FF700

Bleue: bathroom with wc,
twin beds: FF700

Pigeonnier: bathroom with
wc, double bed: FF700

des Communs: shower
room with wc, 2 single beds:
FF650

Suite Bleue: bathroom with
wc, 4 single beds:
FF950 (4 people)

Capacity: 15 people

18.13 SANCERRE

**You will enjoy the relaxed atmosphere and the warm welcome
in this 16th-century family château, situated in large grounds
through which a river flows. For wine lovers, you are in the
heart of the Sancerre vineyards.**

PROPERTY

off-street parking, extensive grounds, hosts have pets, dinner
available, babies welcome, free cot, closed: 15/11–1/03,
fishing, vineyard, hiking 3km, cycling 10km, bird-watching
10km, gliding 12km, golf course 15km, riversports 15km
Adequate English spoken

——At Sancerre take the D7 towards Sens-Beaujeu. In this
village then take the D74 towards Neuilly.

Pierre & Colette
PARENT

'Les Caillotières'

54, Chemin Blanc

18120 MEREAU

Tel: (0) 2 48 71 11 56

Fax: (0) 2 48 71 89 58

Private Home

2 km - S - VIERZON
Méreau: hosts can
collect from station,
railway station: 2km
airport: 55km

18.16 VIERZON

Pierre is a pastry cook, and you will enjoy the delicious results of his skills at breakfast. Each bedroom has its own personality: one with soft pastel colours, a rustic room with a piano and another with a gaming table. The family welcome is warm and relaxing. On sale: Honey, wine.

PROPERTY

private parking, garden, tv lounge, hosts have pets, telephone, dinner available, packed lunch, kitchen, babies welcome, free cot, fishing 2km, riversports 2km, hiking 4km, cycling 4km, golf course 5km, mushroom-picking 5km, sea or lake watersports 10km, interesting flora 20km, hunting 30km

Basic English spoken

——On the A20, Exit 7 to Vierzon heading towards Mereau/Issoudun via the D320. On this road, look out on the right for the signs 'Chambres d'hôtes' (do not go as far as Mereau, as the house is nearer to the autoroute Exit at Vierzon).

PRICE STRUCTURE

4 Bedrooms

Serin & Rouge-Gorge:
television, single bed:
FF160 (1 person)

Mésange: double bed,
2 single beds (child-size):
FF190 (2 people)
FF300 (4 people)

Pivert: double bed, single
bed (child-size):
FF190 (2 people)
FF300 (3 people)

Extra Bed: FF60

Capacity: 9 people

Roger PARMENTIER

2, rue des Champarts

28170 BLEVY

Tel: (0) 2 37 48 01 21/
06 70 49 69 12

Fax: (0) 2 37 48 01 80

parti@club-internet.fr

Private Home

35 km - N W -
CHARTRES
Blévy: hosts can
collect from station,
railway station: 20km

PRICE STRUCTURE

1 Bedroom and 1 Suite
Blévy: television, bathroom
with wc along corridor,
double bed: FF280

Paris: lounge, television,
shower room with wc,
double bed: FF330

Extra Bed: FF150/180

Capacity: 4 people

28.03 CHARTRES

Dagmar and Roger, an adorable couple whom our clients always praise highly, offer a warm welcome. Dagmar is German and Roger is a retired chef, so, make sure you try his cooking. The bedrooms are very pretty, and the breakfast plentiful. Well worth a detour.

PROPERTY

private parking, garden, tv lounge, dinner available, packed lunch, closed: 1/02–28/02, hiking, cycling, golf course 8km

Fluent English spoken

——Exit Chartres on the A11. In Chartres, take the D939 towards Verneuil-sur-Avre. In Maillebois, turn right on to the D20 towards Blévy and Dreux. In Blévy go towards Laons and, as you leave the village, the house is the first on the right.

Géraldine NIVET

8, rue de Chanzy

28140 LOIGNY-LA-BATAILLE

Tel: (0) 2 37 99 70 71

Working Farm

40 km - S E - CHARTRES
Loigny-La-Bataille:
car essential

28.06 CHARTRES

This is a really handy stop on the way south, spotlessly clean and quiet. You can park your car in the interior courtyard in complete safety. They have earned their third 'sun' because of their meticulously high standards. On sale: Home-made jam, eggs, fruit and vegetables.

PROPERTY ✸ ✸ ✸

private parking, garden, tv lounge, hosts have pets, dinner available, hiking 5km, cycling 5km, fishing 5km

PRICE STRUCTURE

3 Bedrooms
ground floor (2 rooms)
shower room with wc,
double bed, twin beds:
FF210 (2 people)
FF310 (4 people)

first floor: shower room with wc, double bed + room single bed:
FF210 (2 people)
FF260 (3 people)

Extra Bed: FF50

Capacity: 11 people

——From the A10, Exit Artenay, then the D10 towards Poupry and then the D3-9 towards Loigny-la-Bataille.

BARRACHIM Philippe &
KAPPS Jacques

'La Grange du Bois'

34, la Grange du Bois

28190 PONTGOUIN

Tel: (0) 2 37 37 44 00
Fax: (0) 2 37 37 44 00

barraka@club-internet.fr
perso.club-
internet.fr//barraka

Private Home

26 km - W -
CHARTRES
Pontgouin: hosts
can collect from
station,
railway station: 3km
airport: 110km
car essential

PRICE STRUCTURE

1 Bedroom and 1 Suite

Thymerais: bathroom with
wc along corridor, double
bed + en-suite room Perche:
double bed:
FF300 (2 people)
FF540 (4 people)

Loft: lounge, bathroom with
wc, twin beds, single bed:
FF350 (2 people)
FF450 (3 people)

Extra Bed: FF100
Reduction: 3 nights

Capacity: 7 people

28.10 CHARTRES

In the Vallée de l'Eure, this restored 19th-century thatched
cottage is a great place to recharge your batteries and
discover the region. You will enjoy the company of Jacques
and Philippe, who are nature-lovers and experts on
architecture. This place is both simple and refined, with a
warm and friendly ambience.

PROPERTY

private parking, extensive grounds, lounge, 14 years old
minimum age, hiking, cycling, fishing, mushroom-picking,
interesting flora 4km, bird-watching 12km, gliding 14km, golf
course 15km

Fluent English spoken

——From Chartres, take the N23 towards Le Mans for 19km.
At Courville-sur-Eure, take the D920 towards La Loupe, and at
Pontgouin take the D155 towards Senonches for 3km.

Catherine & Jean-Marc
SIMON

'Les Chandelles'

19, rue des Sablons -
Chandelles

28130 VILLIERS-LE-
MORHIER

Tel: (0) 2 37 82 71 59
Fax: (0) 2 37 82 71 59
chandellesgolf@aol.com
www.chandelles-golf.com

Working Farm

30 km- N -
CHARTRES
Chandelles: hosts
can collect from
station,
railway station: 5km
airport: 70km
car essential

28.11 CHARTRES

This restored old farmhouse (watch out for the steep staircase!), far from the stress of the big city, allows you to make the most of its beautiful, peaceful location surrounded by woods. Jean-Marc is a professional golf instructor and will be delighted to give you some coaching. There are stables for horses and plenty for the children to do.

PROPERTY

private parking, extensive grounds, hosts have pets, riding, hiking, cycling, golf course, fishing, interesting flora, mushroom-picking, bird-watching, sea or lake watersports 5km, riversports 5km

Adequate English spoken

——From Chartres, take the D906 towards Rambouillet for 25km. At Maintenon, take the D116 towards Villiers-le-Morhier, and Chandelles is the next village. The rue des Sablons is the main street of Chandelles.

PRICE STRUCTURE

3 Bedrooms
first room: television, bathroom with wc, double bed: FF350

(2 rooms) television, bathroom with wc, twin beds: FF350

Extra Bed:FF100

Reduction: 3 nights

Capacity: 6 people

Danièle SCHOLL

'Moulin Foulon'

36200 TENDU

Tel: (0) 2 54 24 31 66

Private Home

23 km - S -
CHATEAUROUX
Tendu:
airport: 100km
car essential

PRICE STRUCTURE

1 Bedroom
television, shower room
with wc, washbasin, double
bed, single bed:
FF245 (2 people)
FF275 (3 people)

Reduction: 7 nights

Capacity: 3 people

36.04 CHATEAUROUX

A warm welcome from this couple in their little country house beside the river. The house has a conservatory and a view over the river, and the one bedroom is in the main house. If staying for a week, you will have use of the kitchen, but otherwise there is a good restaurant nearby.

PROPERTY

off-street parking, garden, hosts have pets, dinner available, fishing, sea or lake watersports 15km, interesting flora 25km, bird-watching 35km, riversports 40km, golf course 45km

——At Châteauroux, take the A20 (Exit 16, Tendu) towards Limoges. At Tendu, go behind the church and follow the signs 'Vallée de la Bouzanne'. The house, which is 3.5km from the village, adjoins the restaurant 'Le Moulin des Eaux Vives'.

37.31 AMBOISE

Although the bedrooms are small, this typical 19th-century house, 300m from the Château d'Amboise beside the River Loire, is in a wonderful position. You will really appreciate the town of Amboise and the magic of La Loire. Monsieur Durand has now retired from flying, and has plenty of time to chat to his guests. An excellent choice of restaurants is less than 30m away.

Bernadette DURAND

24, rue de l'Entrepont

37400 AMBOISE

Tel: (0) 2 47 57 00 54

Private Home

PROPERTY ✸

private parking, garden, hosts have pets, babies welcome, free cot, hiking, cycling, fishing, interesting flora, bird-watching, riversports, sea or lake watersports 1km, mushroom-picking 2km, golf course 10km, gliding 10km

Fluent English spoken

PRICE STRUCTURE

3 Bedrooms
Bleue: shower room with wc, double bed, single bed: FF270 (2 people) FF350 (3 people)

Rose & Jaune: shower room with wc, double bed: FF270

Capacity: 7 people

AMBOISE
hosts can collect from station,
railway station: 1km
airport: 30km
——On the Ile d'Or between two branches of the river Loire (in front of La Salamandre). At the traffic lights it is down below on the right (look for the signs).

Claude FOURSAC

3, Rue de l'Europe

37150 CHISSEAUX

Tel: (0) 2 47 23 90 87

Residence of
Outstanding Character

20 km - S -
AMBOISE
Chisseaux:
railway station: 1km

PRICE STRUCTURE

2 Suites
first room: shower room
with wc, bathroom, double
bed, single bed + en-suite
room 2 single beds:
FF400 (2 people)
FF750 (5 people)

second room: bathroom
with wc along corridor,
double bed + en-suite room
2 single beds:
FF300 (2 people)
FF600 (4 people)

Reduction: 3 nights

Capacity: 9 people

37.35 AMBOISE

The same family have lived in this impressive house for the last 150 years. With a bit of luck you will meet all four generations, all extremely likeable. It is 1km from Chenonceaux and near some of the most famous of the Loire Valley châteaux. On sale: Wine from their vineyard.

PROPERTY

private parking, garden, tv lounge, pets not accepted, dinner available, packed lunch, riding, hiking, cycling, fishing, mushroom-picking, riversports, vineyard

Fluent English spoken

——At Amboise take the D31 towards Bleré as far as La-Croix-en-Touraine where you should take the D40 on the left towards Chenonceaux. The house is on the D40 going towards Montrichard.

Caroline MANIE

'Auberge Forestière Marcheroux'

Route de Chenonceaux
D81
37400 FORET
D'AMBOISE

Tel: (0) 2 47 57 27 57/
06 13 61 72 21
Fax: (0) 2 47 30 28 29

Residence of
Outstanding Character

2 km - S - AMBOISE
Forêt d'amboise:
railway station: 5km
airport: 30km
car essential

37.38 AMBOISE

A former 17th-century hunting lodge, this inn in the heart of the Amboise forest is an ideal base for day trips (2km from Amboise and 4km from Chenonceaux). Off the beaten track, with simple rooms. Try some classic old-fashioned dishes in the restaurant. Helicopter trips over the châteaux can be arranged.

PROPERTY

private parking, extensive grounds, tv lounge, hosts have pets, dinner available, swimming pool, hiking, mushroom-picking, hunting 1km, cycling 2km, fishing 4km, riversports 4km, golf course 10km

Adequate English spoken

——From Paris, take the A10, then the N18 Exit to Amboise. Near Amboise, on the D751, head towards Chenonceaux (D81). Take the first right after 2km. Follow the signs.

PRICE STRUCTURE

5 Bedrooms
room1 & room 3: television, shower room with wc, washbasin, double bed, single bed:
FF320 (2 people)
FF400 (3 people)

room 2 & room 4 & room 5: television, shower room with wc, washbasin, double bed: FF320

Reduction: 15/10–30/03 and 3 nights and groups

Capacity: 12 people

Michèle DUVIVIER

'Relais de la Herserie'

Château de la Herserie

37150 LA CROIX EN
TOURAINE

Tel: (0) 2 47 23 54 36/
06 80 07 01 33

Fax: (0) 2 47 64 56 85

Château

10 km - S -
AMBOISE
La-Croix-de-
Touraine: hosts can
collect from station,
railway station: 3km
airport: 30km
car essential

PRICE STRUCTURE

23 Bedrooms and 1 Suite
(5 rooms) shower room
with wc, double bed: FF300;
Bayard: washbasin, single
bed: FF150 (1 person);
shower room with wc,
double bed, twin beds: FF460
(4 people); La Palice: washbasin, double bed: FF250;
double bed: FF250; (2 rooms)
double bed, single bed: FF300
(3 people); twin beds: FF300;
Château – (4 rooms) shower,
double bed: FF300; (3 rooms)
shower, twin beds: FF300;
bathroom, double bed:
FF300; shower room with
wc, 4 single beds or double
bed+twin beds: FF460
(4 people); Suite – bathroom
with wc, double bed + en-
suite room (2 rooms) FF750
(4 people). Extra Bed: FF80;
Reduction: 01/10–01/04 and
7 nights and groups;
Capacity: 58 people

37.39 AMBOISE

**This château overlooks a superb estate with a lake and 3 ha
of undulating grounds, containing a wildlife park with over
130 animals. Do not be surprised to see a kangaroo, a llama,
deer or peacocks... a magical experience. The rooms are
quite basic, but it is ideal for a group of friends.**

PROPERTY

private parking, extensive grounds, lounge, hosts have pets,
telephone, babies welcome, free cot, 3 shared shower rooms
with wc, 2 wc, riding, hiking, hunting, interesting flora, cycling
5km, fishing 10km, bird-watching 10km, sea or lake
watersports 25km *Basic English spoken*

——At Amboise, take the D31 towards La-Croix-de-Touraine
(from Tours, take the D140 towards Chenonceaux). From the
centre of La-Croix-de-Touraine, head in the direction of
Chenonceaux, then take the second road on the left. The
chateau is 700m further on, on the right.

Ann & Roger MASON

'Moulin du Fief Gentil'

3, rue de Culoison

37150 BLERE

Tel: (0) 2 47 30 32 51

Fax: (0) 2 47 30 22 38

fiefgentil@wanadoo.fr
www.fiefgentil.fr.fm

Residence of
Outstanding Character

10 km - S -
AMBOISE
Bléré:
railway station: 20km
airport: 150km
car essential

37.41 AMBOISE

This is a first-class address. Situated near Chenonceaux, this superb 16th-century watermill is set in beautiful grounds with a lake. We particularly liked the large lounge and, above all, the dining room with its bay window and an amazing view of the mill race. Ann is a gifted and inventive cook, using regional produce.

PROPERTY

private parking, extensive grounds, tv lounge, hosts have pets, pets not accepted, dinner available, 12 years old minimum age, closed: 1/12–31/01, hiking, cycling, fishing, sea or lake watersports, riversports, gliding 8km, golf course 30km

Fluent English spoken

——At Amboise, take the D31 as far as Bléré. (Coming from Tours, take the N76 towards Bléré and Chenonceaux.) At Bléré, take the D52 towards Luzillé. The mill is on this road, 700m from the centre of the village, on the right.

PRICE STRUCTURE

4 Bedrooms
Clémentine: shower room with wc, bathroom, double bed: FF500

Séraphine: shower room with wc, bathroom, twin beds: FF500

Primevère: shower room with wc, twin beds: FF450

Camélia: shower room with wc, bathroom, double bed: FF550

Extra Bed: FF100
Reduction: 3 nights

Capacity: 8 people

Dominique & Jean-
Renaud GUILLEMOT

24, rue des Déportés

37150 BLERE

Tel: (0) 2 47 30 30 25-06
85 65 61 92

Fax: (0) 2 47 30 30 25

jr.guillemot@wanadoo.fr

Château

10 km - S -
AMBOISE
Bléré: hosts can
collect from station,
railway station: 2km
airport: 5km
car essential

PRICE STRUCTURE

1 Bedroom and 1 Suite
Chambre des Dames:
shower room with wc,
double bed: FF400

Bleue: shower room with
wc, twin beds + en-suite
room Rose: double bed:
FF400 (2 people)
FF600 (4 people)

Extra Bed: FF100

Capacity: 6 people

37.47 AMBOISE

Dominique and Jean-Renaud, a former flight attendant and airline pilot, welcome you to their listed house near the châteaux of Amboise and Chenonceaux. Their welcome is kind and courteous and they are antiques collectors, as reflected in the excellent decor of their home. Breakfast is served under a charming arbour.

PROPERTY

private parking, garden, lounge, hosts have pets, pets not accepted, hiking, cycling, fishing, riversports, hunting 8km, interesting flora 15km, bird-watching 15km

Fluent English spoken

——At Amboise, take the D31 as far as Bléré. (From Tours, take the N76 towards Bléré and Chenonceaux.) The house is in the centre of Bléré, in the street opposite the bridge over the River Cher.

Mme SALLES

'Château du Gerfaut'

Le Gerfaut

37190 AZAY-LE-RIDEAU

Tel: (0) 2 47 45 40 16

Fax: (0) 2 47 45 20 15

Château

AZAY-LE-RIDEAU
Azay-le-Rideau:
railway station: 4km
airport: 30km
car essential

37.03 AZAY-LE-RIDEAU

A hunting lodge of the Kings of France, particularly favoured by Louis XI for falconry. The château was built at the beginning of the 20th century. The rooms are rather sober but the location is so wonderful. Deer roam in the grounds. On sale: Honey, pâté.

PROPERTY

off-street parking, extensive grounds, lounge, hosts have pets, pets not accepted, telephone, packed lunch, babies welcome, free cot, tennis court, closed: 1/11–31/03, hiking, cycling, golf course 12km

Fluent English spoken

——In Azay-le-Rideau, take the D751 towards Tours. At the 'Gendarmerie' and the supermarket, turn left towards Villandry then take the first road on the right.

PRICE STRUCTURE

7 Bedrooms

Verte: bathroom with wc, double bed, single bed: FF650 (2 people) FF790 (3 people)

Rouge: bathroom with wc, shower, twin beds: FF600

Jaune & Rose: bathroom with wc, double bed, single bed: FF560 (2 people) FF700 (3 people)

Blanche: shower, wc, double bed: FF460

Bleue: bathroom with wc, shower, double bed: FF635

Lilas: shower room with wc, twin beds: FF560

Extra Bed: FF140

Reduction: 4 nights and children

Capacity: 17 people

Jacky & Michèle
COCHEREAU

'Ferme de La Persillerie'

37110 LES HERMITES

Tel: (0) 2 47 56 32 04

Private Home

16 km - N W -
CHATEAU-
RENAULT
Les Hermites:
airport: 30km
car essential

PRICE STRUCTURE

3 Bedrooms

Aliénor: shower, wc, double
bed: FF200

Adélaïde: double bed:
FF200

Alyssia: bathroom, wc,
double bed, single bed:
FF200 (2 people)
FF250 (3 people)

Extra Bed: FF50

Reduction: 4 nights

Capacity: 7 people

37.19 CHATEAU-RENAULT

This is just as you imagine a farm should be, in the middle of the fields, and you will love the warm accent of Michèle and Jacky. You are mid-way between two rival tourist areas: the listed villages of the beautiful Loir valley and the châteaux of the Loire Valley. The choice is yours!

PROPERTY

off-street parking, garden, hosts have pets, dinner available, babies welcome, free cot, hiking, cycling, fishing 5km, interesting flora 15km, sea or lake watersports 20km, golf course 23km, gliding 30km

——In Château-Renault, take the D766 towards Angers for 1km. Turn right towards Le Boulay. As you leave the village, turn right on to the D72 towards Monthodon, then Les Hermites. The farm is on the left, 4km after Monthodon.

Michel & Claudette
BODET

'la Butte de l'Epine'

37340 CONTINVOIR

Tel: (0) 2 47 96 62 25

Fax: (0) 2 47 96 07 36

Residence of
Outstanding Character

30 km - N -
CHINON
Continvoir:
railway station: 20km
airport: 40km
car essential

37.05 CHINON

This is really a fantastic address. Be sure to stay with Claudette and Michel in their 17th-century-style house, which is absolutely charming. It is set back in the woods, with spacious, English-style grounds. Come in the Spring, when the game birds abound, or in the Autumn, when the colours are at their best. Whenever you arrive, Michel will show you around his garden and his roses, and will ensure that you try the Bourgueil wine that he knows so well.

PRICE STRUCTURE

3 Bedrooms
first room: shower room
with wc, washbasin, twin
beds: FF350

second room & Pigeonnier:
shower room with wc, twin
beds: FF350

Extra Bed: FF120
Reduction: 5 nights

Capacity: 6 people

PROPERTY

private parking, extensive grounds, lounge, hosts have pets, pets not accepted, telephone, babies welcome, free cot, non-smoking, closed: 24/12–2/01, hiking, cycling, interesting flora, bird-watching, vineyard, mushroom-picking 1km, fishing 2km, hunting 2km, sea or lake watersports 6km, golf course 15km *Basic English spoken*

——At Chinon, take the D749 towards Bourgeuil and then to Gizeux, where you turn right for Continvoir, then follow the signs.

Anne BUREAU

'Le Clos de l'Ormeau'

4, rue du Presbytère

37420 HUISMES

Tel: (0) 2 47 95 41 54

Fax: (0) 2 47 95 41 54

Residence of
Outstanding Character

10 km - N -
CHINON
Huismes: hosts can
collect from station,
railway station: 7km
airport: 40km

PRICE STRUCTURE

37.08 CHINON

This substantial house really does have character. Anne produces wonderful breakfasts and Jean-Marc will take you into his cellar and talk Loire Valley wine. Once you have tried their swimming pool, who cares about châteaux? Anne and Jean-Marc, a delightful couple, will advise you on the best vineyards to visit, as well as places off the beaten track.

3 Bedrooms
Tante Angèle: shower, bathroom, double bed: FF260

Oncle Vincent: shower, 2 single beds: FF240

Jardin Secret: shower along corridor, bathroom along corridor, double bed, single bed: FF300 (2 people) FF380 (3 people)

Extra Bed: FF80
Reduction: 15/09–01/06 and 5 nights

Capacity: 7 people

PROPERTY

private parking, extensive grounds, lounge, hosts have pets, pets not accepted, babies welcome, free cot, wc, swimming pool, closed: 25/12, hiking, vineyard, fishing 3km, sea or lake watersports 7km

Adequate English spoken

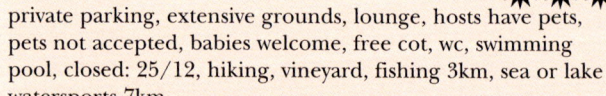

——In Chinon, take the D751 towards Tours, turn left on to the D16 towards Huismes. In the village, go to the church, go through the arch close by the church then take the first street on the left and it is the second house on the right.

Martine DESCAMPS

'Le Clos de Ligré'

22, rue du Rouilly

37500 LIGRE

Tel: (0) 2 47 93 95 59

Residence of
Outstanding Character

5 km - S E -
CHINON
Ligré: hosts can
collect from station,
railway station: 6km
airport: 40km
car essential

37.42 CHINON

**Martine will welcome you to her authentic Touraine
farmhouse, dating from the 19th century. The old wine press
sets off these ancient surroundings beautifully. The garden is
quiet, and there is a music room available to you. Bedroom
'Fruitier' is totally authentic, but mind the low ceiling!**

PROPERTY

private parking, garden, lounge, hosts have pets, dinner
available, babies welcome, free cot, swimming pool, hiking,
cycling, bird-watching, fishing 5km, hunting 5km, mushroom-
picking 6km, interesting flora 15km, golf course 20km, sea or
lake watersports 40km

Fluent English spoken

——At Chinon, cross the River Vienne and take the D749
towards l'Ile Bouchard. Turn right towards Ligré, and
continue for 5km. Turn left at the hamlet of 'Le Rouilly'.
'Le Clos de Ligré' is signposted.

PRICE STRUCTURE

3 Bedrooms
Pressoir: bathroom with wc,
double bed: FF480

Treille: bathroom with wc,
double bed, single bed:
FF480 (2 people)
FF610 (3 people)

Fruitier: lounge, television,
bathroom with wc, twin
beds, single bed:
FF480 (2 people)
FF610 (3 people)

Extra Bed: FF130

Capacity: 8 people

Hilaire Le ROUX de LENS

'Château du Puy d'Arçay'

Arçay

86200 LOUDUN

Tel: (0) 5 49 98 29 11

Château

30 km - S W - CHINON
Arçay: hosts can collect from station, railway station: 50km airport: 70km car essential

PRICE STRUCTURE

3 Bedrooms

Ménage: shower room with wc, washbasin, double bed: FF240

second room: shower room with wc, washbasin, double bed, single bed: FF240 (2 people) FF280 (3 people)

third room: bathroom along corridor, washbasin, single bed: FF160 (1 person)

Reduction: groups and children

Capacity: 6 people

86.17 CHINON

Old-world charm in a superb setting. This 17th-century house contains furniture and a dining room in the style of the period. Your hostess loves to spoil her guests and, along with her husband, will fill you in on all the local legends. This area contains many attractive villages.

PROPERTY

private parking, extensive grounds, tv lounge, hosts have pets, telephone, dinner available, babies welcome, free cot, closed: 01/12–01/02, hiking, mushroom-picking, fishing 4km, sea or lake watersports 12km, riversports 12km, golf course 30km

Fluent English spoken

——At Chinon take the D759 towards Loudun. Continue towards Thouars for 7km and then turn left on to the D19 towards Arçay. It is the first house on the right.

Malvina & Olivier
MASSELOT

'La Capitainerie'

37600 VERNEUIL-SUR-INDRE

Tel: 02 47 94 88 15

Fax: (0) 2 47 94 70 75

captain@creaweb.fr

Private Home

7 km - S - LOCHES
Verneuil-sur-Indre:
railway station: 7km
airport: 35km
car essential

CENTRE VAL-DE-LOIRE

LOCHES

37.43 LOCHES

Right in the heart of the Loire Valley castles and vineyards, Malvina welcomes you to her 18th-century property, surrounded by 8 ha of fields.It is 7km from the quiet, small town of Loches, with its citadel, 11th-century keep and 14th-century château, bearing witness to 1,000 years of history. The three attic rooms have been tastefully restored, and they have a pleasant, cool garden with a swimming pool. Fleur de Soleil member.

PROPERTY

private parking, garden, pets not accepted, dinner available, non-smoking, swimming pool, hiking, cycling, fishing

PRICE STRUCTURE

4 Bedrooms

Jaune: shower room with wc, twin beds: FF310

Bleue: shower room with wc, twin beds: FF290

Verte: shower room with wc, double bed, single bed: FF310 (2 people)
FF370 (3 people)

Rouge: shower room with wc, twin beds, single bed: FF310 (2 people)
FF370 (3 people)

Capacity: 10 people

——South of Loches, N143 towards Chateauroux then D41 to Verneuil sur Indre. On the village square,opposite the 'Salle Communale', turn left and the Capitainerie is 400m further on.

Jacqueline GAY

'Les Hautes Gatinières'

7, chemin de Bois Soleil

37210 ROCHECORBON

Tel: (0) 2 47 52 88 08

Fax: (0) 2 47 52 85 90

jacquelinegay
@minitel.net

Private Home

3 km - N E - TOURS
Rochecorbon: hosts
can collect from
station,
railway station: 7km
airport: 8km
car essential

PRICE STRUCTURE

2 Bedrooms and 1 Suite
first room: television,
bathroom with wc, double
bed + en-suite room 2 single
beds: FF295 (2 people)
FF480 (4 people)

second room: television,
bathroom with wc, double
bed, single bed:
FF295 (2 people)
FF380 (3 people)

third room: television,
bathroom with wc, double
bed: FF295

Extra Bed: FF85

Reduction: 01/10–30/04
and 6 nights and groups
and children

Capacity: 9 people

37.24 TOURS

A new Touraine-style house, on the hillside overlooking the village. All the rooms are spotlessly clean and have a beautiful view. You will be able to taste Vouvray wine as Jacqueline lives beside a vineyard. Fleur de Soleil member.

PROPERTY

private parking, garden, lounge, hosts have pets, telephone, babies welcome, free cot, closed: 15/01–15/02, hiking, cycling, fishing, riversports, vineyard, mushroom-picking 4km, interesting flora 6km, golf course 10km, hunting 10km

Adequate English spoken

——In Tours, take the N152 towards Vouvray. At the set of traffic lights, just after the information point 'l'observatoire', turn left into the 'rue des Clouets', then follow the signs 'chambres d'hôtes'.

Françoise CHAINEAU

'Relais de la Martinière'

37, route de la Martinière

37510 SAVONNIERES

Tel: (0) 2 47 50 04 46

Fax: (0) 2 47 50 11 57

Residence of
Outstanding Character

10 km - W - TOURS
Savonnières:
airport: 20km
car essential

37.25 TOURS

A marvellous setting for this 17th-century farmhouse, which has been superbly restored. Here are peace and quiet, relaxation, simplicity and a convivial atmosphere. Plus a swimming pool, tennis courts, a large conservatory, cycling and visits to the châteaux. Well worth a detour.

PROPERTY

✳ ✳ ✳

off-street parking, garden, lounge, hosts have pets, kitchen, 1 shared shower room with wc, swimming pool, tennis court, closed: 01/10–01/05, hiking, cycling, fishing, riversports 2km, golf course 6km

Adequate English spoken

In Tours, take the D7 towards Villandry. In Savonnières, take the road towards Ballan, by the 'Hotel du Faisan'. As you go up the hill, take the road on the right.

PRICE STRUCTURE

6 Bedrooms

Villandry & Azay: shower room with wc, twin beds: FF350

Langeais: shower room with wc, double bed: FF350

Amboise: shower room with wc, double bed, 2 single beds (1 child-size): FF350 (2 people) FF450 (4 people)

New Forest: bridal room, washbasin, double bed: FF250

Connemara: washbasin, double bed, single bed: FF250 (2 people) FF310 (3 people)

Capacity: 14 people

Anne-Marie LARIÉ

'Le Clos du Paradis'

46, rue Descartes

37130 LANGEAIS

Tel: (0) 2 47 96 65 37

Fax: (0) 2 47 96 65 37

Private Home

25 km - W - TOURS
Langeais:
railway station: -
airport: 30km

PRICE STRUCTURE

3 Bedrooms and 1 Suite
Peintre: washbasin, double
bed, cot: FF240

Vue: twin beds: FF240

third room: twin beds:
FF240

ground floor: shower room
with wc, twin beds + en-suite
room shower room with wc,
twin beds: FF280 (2 people)
FF420 (4 people)

Extra Bed: FF70

Capacity: 10 people

37.30 TOURS

This house is in quiet grounds, in the centre of the town with a view over the Château de Langeais, where Charles VIII and Anne de Bretagne were married. Many artists come to Le Clos in order to paint the view of the château from the bedroom called 'Peintre'.

PROPERTY

private parking, extensive grounds, tv lounge, hosts have pets, babies welcome, free cot, wheelchair access, 1 shared bathroom, 1 shared shower room, wc, hiking, cycling, fishing, bird-watching, hunting 5km, interesting flora 5km, mushroom-picking 5km, golf course 10km, riversports 10km

Basic English spoken

——At Tours, take the N152 towards Saumur. In the town, turn right at the château. The street is immediately on the left after the church.

Jean Pierre SCHWEIZER

'Ferme de Launay'

37210 CHANCAY

Tel: (0) 2 47 52 28 21

Fax: (0) 2 47 52 28 21

Working Farm

15 km- E - TOURS
Chançay:
railway station: 15km
airport: 15km
car essential

37.45 TOURS

You will fall for this place straight away, in the heart of the Loire Valley and the vineyards of Vouvray. It is an 18th-century farmhouse, completely restored. Jean-Pierre, who is Swiss, has mastered the art of entertaining to perfection, thanks to his international hotel experience. Relax by the typical Touraine fireplace and make sure you try his cordon bleu cuisine.

PROPERTY

off-street parking, garden, lounge, hosts have pets, telephone, dinner available, non-smoking, 2 nights minimum stay: (01/05–31/10), fishing, hunting, interesting flora, mushroom-picking, bird-watching, vineyard, cycling 5km, riversports 5km, golf course 15km, gliding 40km

Fluent English spoken

——When coming from Tours, take the N152 as far as Vouvray. Turn left at the traffic lights in the direction of Château-Renault and the D46 (third on the right). Pass Vernou and then 2km further on, the house is on the left on a big bend.

PRICE STRUCTURE

3 Bedrooms

Saule: shower room with wc, double bed: FF400

Vigne: shower room with wc, twin beds: FF400

Rose: shower room with wc, bathroom, double bed, single bed:
FF500 (2 people)
FF600 (3 people)

Reduction: 3 nights

Capacity: 7 people

Marie-Claude
DENICHERE

'Manoir du Vieux Cèdre'

5, rue Basse des Grouëts

41000 BLOIS

Tel: (0) 2 54 78 24 29/
06 15 15 40 86

Fax: (0) 2 54 78 24 29

Residence of
Outstanding Character

BLOIS:
hosts can collect
from station,
railway station: 3km
airport: 180km

PRICE STRUCTURE

4 Bedrooms and 2 Suites

Bleue: television, bathroom with wc, double bed, single bed: FF300 (2 people) FF380 (3 people)
Boiserie: television, shower room with wc, double bed, single bed: FF300 (2 people) FF380 (3 people)
Verte: bathroom with wc, double bed: FF260
Tourelle: shower, wc, double bed: FF300
Suite – second floor: bathroom with wc, 2 double beds, single bed: FF300 (2 people) FF580 (5 people)
Suite – Jardin: television, bathroom with wc, 2 double beds, single bed: FF300 (2 people) FF580 (5 people)

Extra Bed: FF60; Reduction: groups and children
Capacity: 20 people

41.06 BLOIS

This is a pleasant, family-run guesthouse in an 18th-century manor, once an old post house. Surrounded by flowery and shady gardens, this place is very easy to find, being on the N152. Blois, with its restaurants and places of interest, is very close.

PROPERTY

private parking, garden, tv lounge, hosts have pets, dinner available, packed lunch, babies welcome, free cot, swimming pool, closed: 15/11–15/02, hiking, fishing, golf course 4km, sea or lake watersports 7km

Adequate English spoken

——From the centre of Blois, take the N152 towards Tours. Follow the river Loire for 4km. The manor is on the right.

Bernard & Micheline POHU

5, Place de l'Eglise - Villeneuve-Frouville

41290 OUCQUES

Tel: (0) 2 54 23 22 06

Working Farm

20 km - N - BLOIS
Villeneuve-Frouville:
airport: 180km
car essential

41.12 BLOIS

This simple farm is very clean and has a lovely courtyard (the stairs are quite steep). Situated in a quiet, charming and attractive village, it is equidistant from Blois and Vendome. You can visit both the châteaux of the Val de Loire and the romantic Vallée du Loir. On sale: Honey, cheese, wine.

PROPERTY

private parking, garden, tv lounge, hosts have pets, pets not accepted, wc, closed: 15/01–31/01, hiking 4km, cycling 4km, hunting 4km, sea or lake watersports 4km, golf course 6km, fishing 15km, bird-watching 15km, gliding 18km, interesting flora 20km, riversports 20km

Basic English spoken

——In Blois take the D924 towards Châteaudun-Chartres. In the village of Villeneuve-Frouville, the farm is near to the church.

PRICE STRUCTURE

3 Bedrooms

Ecossaise: shower along corridor, washbasin, twin beds: FF250

Clémentine: shower along corridor, washbasin, double bed, cot: FF250 (2 people) FF300 (2 people)

Pervenche: shower, washbasin, twin beds, 2 single beds:
FF270 (2 people)
FF350 (4 people)

Extra Bed: FF70

Capacity: 8 people

Marie Claude
NAVAR-DENICHERE

'Les Chercherelles'

1, Voie du Petit Moulin

41700 COUR-
CHEVERNY

Tel: (0) 2 54 79 93 63

Fax: (0) 2 54 78 24 29

Private Home

14 km - S E - BLOIS
Cour-Cheverny:
airport: 180km
car essential

BLOIS

PRICE STRUCTURE

5 Bedrooms
1 & 2 & 3: bathroom with
wc, washbasin, double bed:
FF270

4 & 5: bathroom with wc,
washbasin, double bed:
FF250

Extra Bed: FF50

Reduction: groups
and children

Capacity: 10 people

41.25 BLOIS

Cécile will welcome you to her sparkling new detached house in the country. This is a nice, comfortable stop, quiet and relaxing in the heart of Sologne, yet also near to the Loire Valley château of Cheverny. A very handy overnight stop.

PROPERTY

off-street parking, garden, lounge, hosts have pets, kitchen, babies welcome, free cot, wheelchair access, closed: 3/11–25/03, hiking, fishing, hunting, interesting flora, cycling 1km, golf course 1km

Adequate English spoken

——At Blois, take the D765 towards Romorantin-Vierzon. As you leave Cour-Cheverny, take Les Chercherelles on the left, then follow the signs.

Jocelyne
BRUMEL-JOUAN

'La Guibruyère'

7, rue de la Croix

41220 THOURY-EN-SOLOGNE

Tel: (0) 2 54 87 01 32

Residence of
Outstanding Character

23 km - E - BLOIS
Thoury-en-Sologne:
railway station: 12km
airport: 180km
car essential

41.26 BLOIS

Typical, pleasant Sologne farmhouse. A friendly home, where Jocelyne's love of entertaining shines through. Add the charm of the garden, the walking and bike rides: theirs is a life dedicated to the outdoors and the history of France. On sale: Honey, asparagus, wine, cheese.

PROPERTY

private parking, extensive grounds, tv lounge, hosts have pets, pets not accepted, telephone, dinner available, babies welcome, free cot, hiking, cycling, mushroom-picking, fishing 4km, bird-watching 6km, hunting 10km, sea or lake watersports 18km, gliding 20km

Fluent English spoken

——From Blois, take the D33 to Thoury. Once you reach the village, turn right at the 'Stop' sign and head towards Dhuizon, then take the first left. This is rue de la Croix (in the centre of the village).

PRICE STRUCTURE

4 Bedrooms

first room: television, telephone, bathroom with wc along corridor, double bed (queen size): FF290

second room: television, shower room with wc along corridor, double bed: FF290

third room: television, bathroom with wc along corridor, double bed: FF290

Chambre des Enfants: single bed (child-size), cot: FF250

Capacity: 7 people

Jean-Pierre & Inge
TARTIERE

'Château du Bois Minhy'

Chèmery

41700 CONTRES

Tel: (0) 2 54 79 51 01

Fax: (0) 2 54 79 06 26

Château

27 km - S - BLOIS
Chemery:
railway station: 25km
airport: 180km
car essential

PRICE STRUCTURE

**3 Bedrooms and
1 Apartment**

bathroom with wc, double
bed, twin beds, single bed:
FF300 (2 people)
FF570 (5 people)

bathroom with wc, double
bed, single bed: FF300 (2
people) FF390 (3 people)

shower room with wc,
double bed, single bed:
FF280 (2 people)
FF350 (3 people)

Grande Suite: lounge,
television, kitchen, shower
room with wc, 2 double
beds, single bed: FF450 (2
people) FF720 (5 people)

Extra Bed: FF90

Capacity: 16 people

41.27 BLOIS

This charming little château in Renaissance style is on a 7 ha estate, with a swimming pool, a large terrace and a barbecue. Here, you will find perfect peace and quiet. This is the ideal spot to visit the Loire Valley châteaux, only between 15km and 40km away. It is possible to rent the whole château if required.

PROPERTY ✹ ✹ ✹

private parking, extensive grounds, tv lounge, hosts have pets, dinner available, kitchen, babies welcome, free cot, swimming pool, hiking, cycling, mushroom-picking, fishing 5km, riversports 12km, golf course 15km, sea or lake watersports 25km

Fluent English spoken

——At Blois, take the D956 towards Contres, then Selles-sur-Cher. The château is just before Chèmery.

Agnès & Jacques
MASQUILIER

'Le Retour'

8, route de la Chaussée
St-Victor

41000 VILLEBAROU

Tel: (0) 2 54 78 40 24

Fax: (0) 2 54 56 12 36

Residence of
Outstanding Character

5 km - N - BLOIS
Villebarou: hosts can
collect from station,
railway station: 5km
airport: 180km
car essential

41.30 BLOIS

This is a farm in its own grounds, near to Blois. They come
from all over the world to enjoy the company of Agnès and
Jacques in their family home – their attention to detail, the
quality of the bedrooms and their love of children (they have
eight, all now grown up). Even Baloo, the gentle labrador,
does his bit to maintain the warm, welcoming atmosphere
about this place.

PROPERTY

private parking, extensive grounds, tv lounge, hosts have pets,
kitchen, wheelchair access, hiking, cycling, fishing 3km,
hunting 4km, interesting flora 4km, bird-watching 4km, sea or
lake watersports 7km, gliding 15km, golf course 20km

Fluent English spoken

PRICE STRUCTURE

3 Bedrooms
Les Amandiers & Les
Bouleaux: shower room
with wc, 2 double beds:
FF280 (2 people)
FF440 (4 people)

Les Genets: wheelchair
access, shower room with
wc, 2 double beds:
FF280 (2 people)
FF440 (4 people)

Extra Bed: FF70

Capacity: 12 people

——From Blois, take the N924 towards Chartres and
Châteaudun for 4km. At the traffic lights at the crossroads in
Villebarou, turn right towards Francillon. The house is 1km
further on, on the right (follow the signs 'chambre d'hôtes').

Marie-Thérèse & Remi
BELLETESTE

'Les Fondières'

20, route de Muides

41220 THOURY-EN-
SOLOGNE

Tel: (0) 2 54 87 08 62

Fax: (0) 2 54 87 08 63

Private Home

23 km - E - BLOIS
Thoury-en-Sologne:
hosts can collect
from station,
railway station: 12km
airport: 180km
car essential

PRICE STRUCTURE

1 Bedroom and 1 Suite
Erable: shower room with
wc, double bed: FF380

Chinoise: along corridor
shower, wc, washbasin, double bed: FF340 (2 people)
FF650 (2 people)

+ Napoléon: shower room
with wc, double bed: FF380

Reduction: 5 nights

Capacity: 6 people

41.31 BLOIS

Only 1.5km from the Château de Chambord, this former
hunting lodge dates from the beginning of the 19th century. The
atmosphere is rustic, the food is good, the welcome is warm and
relaxed and they have a conservatory and a barbecue. Your
hosts, Marie-Thérèse and Rémi, organise shooting trips into the
Sologne forest. On sale: The paintings which are on display.

PROPERTY

private parking, extensive grounds, tv lounge, hosts have pets,
dinner available, packed lunch, closed: 10/09–1/10, hiking,
cycling, fishing, mushroom-picking 4km, bird-watching 6km,
golf course 10km, sea or lake watersports 18km, hunting
20km, interesting flora 30km

Fluent English spoken

——From Blois, D956 towards Cheverny for 3km then left on
to the D33 for 20km towards Chambord. In the village of
Thoury, head towards Muides. Number 20 is on the right.

Claude MOREAU

'Le Patis des Bouleaux'

41220 DHUIZON

Tel: 02 54 98 30 32

Working Farm

29 km - E - BLOIS
Dhuizon:
railway station: 25km
airport: 180km

41.33 BLOIS

'And just one more thing...' says Claude, because he always has something interesting to tell you. He is a retired goat farmer, and will explain all about goat's milk and cheese, as well as telling you about the Château de Chambord and the walks and hiking routes through the forest. The welcome here is sincere, down to earth and full of local colour. The bedrooms overlook the lake.

PROPERTY

private parking, garden, lounge, hosts have pets, pets not accepted, babies welcome, free cot, wheelchair access, hiking, cycling, fishing 3km, hunting 4km, golf course 20km, vineyard 25km, sea or lake watersports 30km, riversports 30km

——Leave Blois on the D765 towards Romorantin, and then take the D923 as far as Neuvy, then the D18 as far as Dhuizon. In this village, head towards Villeny for 3km. Le Patis des Bouleaux is on the right. Go through the gates and, if no-one is about, continue as far as the 'fromagerie'.

PRICE STRUCTURE

2 Bedrooms
first room: shower room with wc, double bed, single bed: FF300 (2 people) FF380 (3 people)

second room: shower room with wc, 3 single beds: FF300 (2 people) FF380 (3 people)

Extra Bed: FF80

Reduction: 3 nights

Capacity: 6 people

Claudine & François
BREDON

9, rue de la Plaine -
Chanteloup

41100 VILLERABLE

Tel: (0) 2 54 77 48 67-06
13 07 88 31

homere41@aol.com

Private Home

7 km - S -
VENDOME
Chanteloup:
hosts can collect
from station,
railway station: 7km
airport: 150km
car essential

PRICE STRUCTURE

2 Bedrooms
first room: double bed:
FF200
second room: twin beds:
FF200

Reduction: 8 nights

Capacity: 4 people

41.29 VENDOME

This modern house is on the road to the châteaux of the Loire Valley, out in the country of mushroom cellars, and ancient troglodyte villages. You reach the bedrooms via the mezzanine floor with a small games corner. François, a former chef, uses all his talent to bring out the very best of his beloved local cuisine.

PROPERTY

private parking, garden, tv lounge, hosts have pets, dinner available, packed lunch, 1 shared shower room with wc, fishing, hunting, bird-watching, hiking 3km, cycling 3km, sea or lake watersports 10km, interesting flora 20km
Adequate English spoken

——At Vendôme, N10 towards Tours and, as you leave Vendôme by the 'BUT' store, head towards Villerable, then Chanteloup. In Chanteloup, turn left at the 'Stop' sign in the direction of Marcilly-en-Beauce. The house is on the right, just before the edge of the village of Chanteloup.

Stéphanie & Frédéric
GINISTY

'Le Moulin Frabault'

116bis, rue du Faubourg
St-Bienheuré

41100 VENDOME

Tel: (0) 4 54 73 16 58
Fax: (0) 1 53 69 06 85

quantis@calva.net

Residence of
Outstanding Character

VENDOME
Vendôme:
railway station: 3km
airport: 170km
car essential

41.34 VENDOME

This is a 14th-century mill by the château, on a small island in a mass of vegetation, in the heart of Vendôme. Stéphane will lend you a rowing boat to go in to town the romantic way. From your bedroom window you can watch the sunset over the River Loir with its carpet of water lilies. As you cross the little wooden bridge, lean over and admire the frogs – one of them may be a handsome prince. Magic!

PRICE STRUCTURE

1 Suite
bathroom with wc, double bed, single bed + en-suite room bathroom with wc, single bed:
FF350 (2 people)
FF600 (4 people)

Capacity: 4 people

PROPERTY

off-street parking, tv lounge, hosts have pets, telephone, dinner available, cycling, fishing, mushroom-picking, riversports, vineyard, golf course 15km

——In Vendôme, head towards the town centre as far as the abbey. Continue in front of the abbey as far as the Pizzeria. Dipsi, turn left. You should then be in the Faubourg St-Bienheure. Leave your car at number 116 bis and cross the bridge to reach the island.

Brigitte BECQUELIN

'Château de la Volonière'

72340 PONCE-SUR-LE-LOIR

Tel: (0) 2 43 79 68 16

Fax: (0) 2 43 79 68 18

Château

35 km - W - VENDOME
Poncé-sur-le-Loir:
airport: 45km
car essential

PRICE STRUCTURE

3 Bedrooms and 1 Suite and 2 Apartments

Roméo: lounge, television, kitchen, shower room with wc, twin beds: FF480 & Juliette: shower room with wc, double bed: FF370
Louis XIII: shower room with wc, twin beds: FF370
Barbe Bleue: bathroom with wc, double bed: FF370
Mille et une nuits: 2 single beds + en-suite room bathroom with wc, 2 single beds (child-size): FF370 (2 people) FF570 (4 people)
Roi Arthur: lounge, television, kitchen, bathroom with wc, twin beds + en-suite room 2 single beds: FF600 (2 people) FF800 (4 people)
Extra Bed: FF100
Reduction: 2 nights and children
Capacity: 16 people

72.08 VENDOME

This 15th-century château is in a village of craftsmen. Each bedroom has a different theme. The restoration has been done so skillfully that you would expect the poet Ronsard to appear at any moment. Superb lake. Very good value for money. There is an inn nearby. On sale: Paintings and sculptures.

PROPERTY

off-street parking, extensive grounds, tv lounge, hosts have pets, telephone, packed lunch, babies welcome, free cot, closed: 1/12–15/03, hiking, cycling, fishing, sea or lake watersports 7km

Basic English spoken

——In Vendôme, take the D917 towards Montoire-sur-Loir, Troo and Poncé-sur-le-Loir.

Monique DEAGE

'Les Patis du Vergas'

72310 LAVENAY

Tel: (0) 2 43 35 38 18/
06 85 92 01 07

Fax: (0) 2 43 35 38 18

Private Home

35 km - W -
VENDOME
Lavenay:
railway station: 25km
airport: 40km
car essential

72.09 VENDOME

Chez Monique, you are surrounded by beauty. The rooms are in a separate house, with many facilities (barbecue, games room, sauna, billiard table), in beautiful grounds with a private lake, well stocked with fish. The Loir region is known for its tranquility, the inspiration of poets.

PROPERTY

off-street parking, extensive grounds, tv lounge, dinner available, packed lunch, kitchen, wheelchair access, closed: 1/12–1/03, fishing, riversports, hiking 3km, lake watersports 15km
Fluent English spoken

——At Vendôme, take the D917 towards Montoire-sur-Loir, Troo and Pont-de-Braye, where you turn right on to the D303 towards St-Calais. Then turn left towards Lavenay.

PRICE STRUCTURE

5 Bedrooms
Paquerette: television, shower room with wc, double bed: FF330

Iris: shower room with wc, twin beds: FF270

Bleuet: shower room with wc, double bed: FF270

Primevère & Jasmin: shower room with wc, double bed, single bed:
FF270 (2 people)
FF330 (3 people)

Extra Bed: free
Reduction: 2 nights

Capacity: 12 people

Denise & Pierre DURIN

9, Chemin du Pleu

45730 ST-BENOIT-SUR-
LOIRE

Tel: (0) 2 38 35 72 68/
06 80 68 05 76

Fax: (0) 2 38 35 72 68

durin.pierre@wanadoo.fr

Residence of
Outstanding Character

30 km - S E -
ORLEANS
St-Benoit-sur-Loire:
railway station: 25km
airport: 150km
car essential

PRICE STRUCTURE

1 Bedroom and 1 Suite
Suite: bathroom with wc
along corridor, shower,
double bed + en-suite room
twin beds: FF280 (2 people)
FF480 (4 people)

Mansardée: shower, wc,
double bed, 2 single beds:
FF280 (2 people)
FF420 (4 people)

Extra Bed: FF70
Reduction: 3 nights

Capacity: 8 people

45.09 ORLEANS

This couple took early retirement and have put their hearts into renovating their farmhouse without losing any of its character. You may think you are going to stay for just one night but, by the time Denise has served you her delicious meals, you may well extend your stay much longer. On sale: Watercolour courses.

PROPERTY

off-street parking, garden, tv lounge, hosts have pets, pets not accepted, dinner available, babies welcome, free cot, closed: 01/10–01/04, cycling, fishing, riversports, hiking 5km, golf course 10km, interesting flora 10km, mushroom-picking 10km, hunting 15km, sea or lake watersports 20km

——At Orléans on A11 Exit Orléans-Nord, take the N60 towards Montargis as far as Châteauneuf-sur-Loire. There, take D60 towards St-Benoit. The house is midway between St-Benoit and St-Père in hamlet of Les Places (head towards ULM and enter on garden side).

Muguette BERNARD

4, route de Clémont

45620 ISDES

Tel: (0) 2 38 29 12 10/
10 89-06 72 36 39 41

Fax: (0) 2 38 29 10 00

Residence of
Outstanding Character

35 km - S E -
ORLEANS
Isdes:
railway station: 20km
car essential

45.11 ORLEANS

A romantic atmosphere fills this manor house. Relax and chat in the lounge, or enjoy the cool of the garden. On summer evenings you will dine under the arbour, with its attractive coloured lights. Your hostess is distinguished, charming and cultured. There is also a semi-detached lodge, independent from the main house.

PRICE STRUCTURE

3 Bedrooms

Jaune: bathroom with wc, double bed: FF340

Rose: bathroom with wc along corridor, washbasin, double bed: FF340

Petit pavillon: kitchen, shower room with wc, double bed: FF340

Capacity: 6 people

PROPERTY

off-street parking, garden, tv lounge, pets not accepted, dinner available, non-smoking, hiking, fishing, golf course 12km, hunting 12km, sea or lake watersports 12km

Fluent English spoken

——Exit 3 on the A71 (Lamotte-Beuvron). Head towards Vouzon, Souvigny and Isdes on the D101. The house is in centre of the village.

James FALCK

'Bagatelle'

45510 VANNES-SUR-COSSON

Tel: 02 38 58 15 10

Fax: (0) 2 38 58 15 10

Private Home

30 km - S - ORLEANS
Vannes-sur-Cosson:
railway station: 35km
airport: 140km
car essential
——From Orleans, take
the 'Voie Express' N60
towards Gien. At
Châteauneuf-sur-Loire,
take the D11 as far as
Vannes. When you are in
the village, it is the first
street on the right.

45.12 ORLEANS

This French couple, with Swedish ancestry, welcome you like long-lost friends to their large red-brick house in the heart of La Sologne. Their English-style breakfasts will set you up for the day. Perhaps you will try your luck at fishing in the neighbouring lake, or just relax on the large terrace beside the pool.

PROPERTY

off-street parking, extensive grounds, hosts have pets, telephone, dinner available, babies welcome, free cot, non-smoking, 1 shared bathroom with wc, swimming pool, fishing, golf course 10km

Adequate English spoken

PRICE STRUCTURE
5 Bedrooms

Bleue: bathroom with wc along corridor, double bed: FF260

Rose: shower room with wc, double bed, single bed: FF260 (2 people) FF360 (3 people)

(2 rooms) single bed: FF230 (1 person)

Blanche: single bed: FF260 (1 person)

Extra Bed: FF100

Reduction: 7 nights

Capacity: 8 people

BELGIUM

GERMA

LUXEMBOURG

Valenciennes
Douai

NORD PAS-DE-CALAIS
page 306

59

St. Quentin

02

PICARDIE
page 306

Laon

Compiègne

Soissons

Charleville-Mézières   Sedan

08

Rethel
page 252

Reims
pages 254-255

Epernay
page 253

51

CHÂLONS

Sézanne
page 256

Vitry
page 257

Verdun

METZ

57

LORRAINE
page 49

55

Bar-le-Duc

Nancy

Lunéville

54

Thionville

Meaux

DE FRANCE
page 15

77

St. Dizier

CHAMPAGNE-ARDENNE

Neufchâteau

88

Èpinal

ainebleau

Troyes

10

Chaumont

52

Langres

Sens

ontargis

Auxerre

89

BOURGOGNE
page 122

21

FRANCHE-COMTE
page 49

70   Vesoul

58

DIJON

251

Sylvie & Régis
GOULDEN

'Les Sources'

Route de Saulces aux
Tournelles

08270 SAULCES-
MONCLIN

Tel: (0) 3 24 38 59 71
Fax: (0) 3 24 72 74 60

sources@club-internet.fr

Private Home

12 km - N E -
RETHEL
Saulces-Monclin:
hosts can collect
from station,
railway station: 12km

PRICE STRUCTURE

8 Bedrooms
Rose & Pervenche &
Rossignol: bathroom with
wc, washbasin, 3 single beds:
FF270 (2 people)
FF340 (3 people)

Anémone: bathroom with
wc, washbasin, 4 single beds:
FF270 (2 people)
FF420 (4 people)

Pinson: bathroom, 3 single
beds: FF270 (2 people)
FF340 (3 people)

Bleuet & Jonquille &
Coquelicot: shower,
washbasin, 2 single beds:
FF270

Reduction: 2 nights and
children
Capacity: 22 people

08.01 RETHEL

This place used to be an old people's home in the middle of extensive grounds with a river, a lake, and a waterfall. Sylvie and Régis are most friendly. Be sure to try their apple juice which is excellent, and they will introduce you to organic food, yoga and even the Internet!

PROPERTY

off-street parking, extensive grounds, tv lounge, hosts have pets, telephone, dinner available, packed lunch, 1 shared bathroom, 2 wc, fishing

Adequate English spoken

——From Rethel take the N51 Reims–Charleville road, towards Charleville-Mézières. At Saulces-Monclin follow the signs to Les Sources.

Anne-Laure
GUILLEPAIN

'Le Domaine du Village'

14, rue René Baudet

51160 CHAMPILLON

Tel: (0) 3 26 51 65 75/
    06 81 20 08 63

Fax: (0) 3 26 52 84 94

Residence of
Outstanding Character

8 km - N - EPERNAY
Champillon:
railway station: 5km
airport: 25km
car essential

51.16 EPERNAY

This is a wine-producing estate, in a prestigious area: from the terrace of this beautiful property, refurbished in typical regional style, you can admire the view over Epernay – the home of Champagne. Near the vineyard, have a look at the 19th-century wine press, capable of handling 4 tons of grapes and manually operated. On sale: Local wine.

PROPERTY

private parking, extensive grounds, tv lounge, hosts have pets, pets not accepted, hiking, cycling, interesting flora, vineyard, mushroom-picking 1km, fishing 3km, hunting 3km, golf course 20km

Basic English spoken

PRICE STRUCTURE

2 Bedrooms
Vignoble: television, shower room with wc, bathroom, double bed: FF500

Village: television, shower room with wc, bathroom, twin beds: FF400

Capacity: 4 people

——From Epernay, take the N51 towards Reims until you get to Dizy. From there, take the scenic route (N2051) as far as Champillon.

Annie-France
MALISSART

9, rue Thiers

51500 MAILLY-
CHAMPAGNE

Tel: (0) 3 26 49 43 47
06 83 13 97 87

Fax: (0) 3 26 49 43 47

Working Farm

10 km - S - REIMS
Mailly-Champagne:
airport: 10km
car essential

PRICE STRUCTURE

51.06 REIMS

2 Bedrooms
(2 rooms) washbasin,
double bed: FF200

Extra Bed: FF100
Capacity: 4 people

Here they produce 'Grand Cru' Champagne. There is also
plenty to do in this beautiful part of the 'Montagne de
Reims': forest-walking, hiking (GR14), visits to sulphur
quarries, the River Marne, 'Les Faux de Verzy' and the
'Route du Champagne'. On sale: Their own Champagne
(Grand Cru classé 100%).

PROPERTY

garden, tv lounge, hosts have pets, 1 shared shower room,
2 wc, hiking

Fluent English spoken

——At Reims, on the A4, take the Exit 26 to Cormentreuil. In
Cormentreuil, take the D9 towards Louvois. There, turn left
on to the D26 towards Mailly-Champagne.

Michel & Chantal
LE VARLET

'Ferme du Temple'

51700 PASSY-GRIGNY

Tel: (0) 3 26 52 90 01

Fax: (0) 3 26 52 18 86

m.levarlet@online.fr

Working Farm

30 km - S W - REIMS
Passy-Grigny:
railway station: 10km
airport: 110km
car essential

51.11 REIMS

This is a cereal growing farm, but there are still remnants from the time of the Knights Templar here. It is very well situated, convenient to an exit from the A4 (without any of the noise), 1 hour from Disneyland and near to the 'Route de Champagne'.

PROPERTY

off-street parking, garden, tv lounge, hosts have pets, pets not accepted, dinner available, babies welcome, free cot, golf course km, hiking 8km, cycling 8km, fishing 10km

Adequate English spoken

——On the A4 Reims–Paris, take Exit 21 towards Dormans. Then take the D980 on the right, and continue for 1km towards Dormans. Then take the second unmade road, which descends on the right, lined with walnut trees.

PRICE STRUCTURE

4 Bedrooms
Bleu: shower room with wc, twin beds: FF300

Rose & Jaune: shower room with wc, double bed, cot: FF300

ground floor – Abricot: shower room with wc, double bed, single bed, cot: FF300 (2 people) FF400 (3 people)

Capacity: 9 people

Christine MALARD

17, Grande Rue

51230 CONNANTRE

Tel: (0) 3 26 81 07 42

Private Home

18 km - E -
SEZANNE
Connantre:
airport: 70km
car essential

PRICE STRUCTURE

2 Bedrooms
first room: television,
washbasin, twin beds: FF280

second room: television,
twin beds, single bed:
FF200 (2 people)
FF290 (3 people)

Extra Bed: FF45

Capacity: 5 people

51.12 SEZANNE

Very easy to find from the N4. This is a restored barn, with two self-contained rooms above the doctor's surgery. They have billiards and table-tennis, etc. It is near to the famous Lac du Der, about 1 hour from Disneyland Paris and on the doorstep of Champagne country. On sale: Champagne.

PROPERTY

off-street parking, extensive grounds, tv lounge, hosts have pets, kitchen, babies welcome, free cot, hiking, hunting, sea or lake watersports, fishing 15km

Fluent English spoken

——At Sézanne, take the N4 towards Vitry-le-François as far as Connantre. Turn right 1.5km from the main road, and take the D5. Pass the sugar factory and the house is in the centre of the village, near to the shops.

Denis & Michelle GEOFFROY

16, rue de Hancourt

51290 MARGERIE-HANCOURT

Tel: (0) 3 26 72 48 47

Fax: (0) 3 26 72 48 47

Working Farm

20 km - S - VITRY-LE-FRANÇOIS
Margerie-Hancourt: hosts can collect from station, railway station: 20km

51.05 VITRY-LE-FRANÇOIS

A working farm, with pigeons everywhere. An excellent overnight stop with a warm and friendly welcome. Only 15km from the Der lake, famous for its migratory birds and fishing. Do not miss the unusual wooden churches of the region.

PROPERTY

off-street parking, garden, tv lounge, hosts have pets, dinner available, kitchen, babies welcome, free cot, closed: 15/12–15/01, fishing 2km, bird-watching 15km, sea or lake watersports 15km

 In Vitry, take the D396 towards Brienne-le-Château. Just before Margerie, turn left, then right. Follow the sign 'Ferme de Hancourt'.

PRICE STRUCTURE

3 Bedrooms
ground floor: shower room with wc, washbasin, double bed: FF200

first floor – first room: shower room with wc, 2 double beds:
FF200 (2 people)
FF270 (4 people)

first floor – third room: shower room with wc, double bed, single bed:
FF200 (2 people)
FF250 (3 people)

Extra Bed: FF50

Capacity: 9 people

MEDITERRAN
SEA

Bastia

Calvi

2B

Corte

CORSE

AJACCIO

2A

Propriano

Sartène
page 259

Porto Vecchio

MEDITERRANEAN
SEA

Bonifacio

Christian & Claudine
PERRIER

'Domaine de Croccano'

Km 3 route de Granace

20100 SARTENE

Tel: (0) 4 95 77 11 37
Fax: (0) 4 95 73 42 89

christian.perrier
@wanadoo.fr
www.corsenature.com

Residence of
Outstanding Character

SARTENE:
hosts can collect
from station,
ferry port: 15km
airport: 40km
car essential

20.06 SARTENE

This exceptional spot is ideal for riding and romantic hiking excursions. Spend wonderful evenings in this old house, off the beaten track, but with a view over the sea. This is the real Corsica ... 'Heaven on Earth'! Room 2 has bath & WC in the room. On sale: Home-made jam. Fleur de Soleil member.

PROPERTY

private parking, extensive grounds, hosts have pets, telephone, dinner available, babies welcome, free cot, non-smoking, 1 shared bathroom with wc, closed: 1/12–31/12, riding, hiking, cycling, fishing, hunting, interesting flora, mushroom-picking, bird-watching, sea or lake watersports 10km, riversports 20km *Fluent English spoken*

——On the square by the church in Sartène, turn left towards the 'Maison de l'Artisanat'. At the intersection, take the road on the right towards Granace for 3km. The entrance is on the left and the house is 300m further down, at the end of the unmade road.

PRICE STRUCTURE

4 Bedrooms
Bonifacio & Côte Sauvage:
twin beds, single bed:
FF440 (2 people)
FF570 (3 people)

Campo Moro: bathroom
with wc, washbasin, twin
beds: FF440

Alta Rocca: bathroom with
wc, washbasin, 2 single beds:
FF440

Reduction: 01/09–30/06
and groups and children

Capacity: 10 people

Roanne

69

CLERMONT-FERRAND

Thiers

RHÔNE-ALPES
page 499

LYON

63

42

St.-Etienne

AUVERGNE
page 107

19

Tulle

LIMOUSIN
page 107

Brive

15

43

le Puy

Valence

07

Privas

46

Aurillac

Cahors

Mende
pages 278-279

48

Rodez

12

Millau

Alès
page 268

8

82

Le Vigan
page 267

Ca

30

Avignon

MIDI-PYRÉNÉES
page 283

Nîmes
pages 269-272

LANGUEDOC-
ROUSSILLON

Albi

81

13

Arles

TOULOUSE

Castres

Béziers
pages 273-276

34

MONTPELLIER
page 277

PROVENCE-AL
CÔTE D'AZU
page 421

31

Castelnaudary
page 266

Carcassonne
pages 261-264

11

Narbonne
page 265

MEDITERRANEAN
SEA

Foix

09

Perpignan
pages 280-282

66

ANDORRA

S P A I N

Sarah WORTHINGTON

'Le Vieux Relais'

1, rue de l'Etang

11700 PEPIEUX

Tel: (0) 4 68 91 69 29
Fax: (0) 4 68 91 45 49

sally.worthington
@wanadoo.fr

http://perso.wanadoo.fr
/carrefourbedbreakfast

Residence of
Outstanding Character

26 km - E -
CARCASSONNE
Pépieux:
railway station: 40km
airport: 40km
car essential

11.30 CARCASSONNE

Your hostess is English and welcomes you to her home, in what was formerly a 17th-century coaching inn. It is 25 mins. From Carcassonne and 5 mins. from the Canal du Midi, between the Montagne Noire and Les Corbières. There is so much to see in this area.

PROPERTY

off-street parking, garden, tv lounge, pets not accepted, telephone, dinner available, packed lunch, non-smoking, 12 years old minimum age, cycling, sea or lake watersports 2km, hiking 5km, fishing 8km, mushroom-picking 8km, interesting flora 15km, golf course 20km, riversports 20km, gliding 70km *Fluent English spoken*

PRICE STRUCTURE

3 Bedrooms and 1 Suite
Jaune: bathroom with wc, shower, double bed: FF400

Bleu: bathroom with wc, shower, double bed: FF400

Vert: bathroom with wc, shower, double bed + en-suite room twin beds: FF400 (2 people) FF800 (4 people)

Reduction: 7 nights

Capacity: 8 people

——At Carcassonne, take the N113 towards Narbonne. Then turn left on to the D610 towards Trèbes-Puichéric, Olonzac on the left and then Pépieux. The house is to the left of the church.

Nicole GALINIER

'La Maison sur la Colline'

Mas de Ste-Croix

11000 CARCASSONNE

Tel: (0) 4 68 47 57 94

Private Home

CARCASSONNE:
hosts can collect
from station,
railway station: 3km
airport: 6km
car essential

PRICE STRUCTURE

5 Bedrooms

Bleue: bridal room, television, bathroom with wc, shower, double bed, 2 single beds: FF450 (2 people) FF520 (4 people)

Jaune: shower room with wc, double bed: FF330

Beige: television, shower room with wc along corridor, double bed, single bed: FF450 (3 people)

Rez de jardin – Blanche: television, shower room with wc, double bed: FF350

Coquelicot: lounge, shower room with wc, double bed, 3 single beds: FF400 (2 people) FF650 (5 people)

Extra Bed: FF80

Reduction: 4 nights

Capacity: 16 people

11.13 CARCASSONNE

This house is peacefully situated amongst the vines, 1km from the medieval city of Carcassonne. Your hosts are retired gardeners and Nicole loves plants. The interior of the house has a great deal of character and you will be well looked after.

PROPERTY

off-street parking, garden, tv lounge, hosts have pets, dinner available, packed lunch, babies welcome, free cot, swimming pool, hiking, cycling, fishing, interesting flora, sea or lake watersports, vineyard, golf course 3km, mushroom-picking 15km

——In Carcassonne, head for the cemetery which is on the left of the entrance to the place du Prado. Follow it round, keeping on the left, and DO NOT take the chemin des Anglais, which descends. The house is 1km further on, after you have gone under the bridge.

Vanessa, Jérôme YAGER
& Nathalie, Alain
GRANDIN

'Domaine de la Bonde'

11390 CUXAC-
CABARDÈS

Tel: (0) 4 68 26 57 16

Fax: (0) 4 68 26 59 94

www.labonde-cuxac.com

Residence of
Outstanding Character

25 km - N -
CARCASSONNE
Cuxac-Cabardès:
hosts can collect
from station,
railway station: 25km
airport: 25km
car essential

11.23 CARCASSONNE

Vanessa, Jérome, Nathalie and Alain have taken over this establishment and receive their guests with great enthusiasm. The setting is really pleasant and the rooms spacious, with large bathrooms. A lovely village – you will have an excellent holiday here.

PROPERTY

off-street parking, extensive grounds, lounge, hosts have pets, pets not accepted, dinner available, packed lunch, kitchen, babies welcome, free cot, swimming pool, closed: 01/11–01/03, hiking, mushroom-picking, fishing 1km, cycling 4km, golf course 25km, sea or lake watersports 25km

Fluent English spoken

PRICE STRUCTURE

5 Bedrooms
first room: bridal room, shower room with wc, double bed, 2 single beds:
FF380 (2 people)
FF540 (4 people)
(4 rooms) shower room with wc, double bed: FF350

Extra Bed: FF80
Reduction: 7 nights

Capacity: 12 people

——At Carcassonne, take the D118 towards Castres and Mazamet. At Cuxac-Cabardés, follow the signs 'chambres d'hôtes'.

Jérôme & Olivia JOSEPH

'La Bastide Saint Louis'

42, rue Barbès

11000 CARCASSONNE

Tel: (0) 4 68 72 34 81 06
13 42 89 14

Fax: (0) 4 68 72 09 88

Residence of
Outstanding Character

CARCASSONNE:
hosts can collect
from station, railway
station:
airport: 3km

PRICE STRUCTURE

2 Bedrooms and 1 Suite

Grise: television, bathroom
with wc, shower, washbasin,
double bed, single bed:
FF350 (2 people)
FF430 (3 people)

Bleue: television, shower
room with wc along
corridor, double bed, single
bed: FF300 (2 people)
FF380 (3 people)

Suite Ocre: television,
bathroom with wc, shower,
washbasin, double bed +
en-suite room 2 single beds:
FF300 (2 people)
FF500 (4 people)

Extra Bed: FF80

Reduction: 15/10–15/02
and 7 nights

Capacity: 10 people

11.28 CARCASSONNE

In the town centre, near to the medieval cité, this home has
an interesting history. It is an ancient convent dating from the
Middle Ages, which was destroyed by the Black Prince and
re-built as a 'hotel particulier' in the 18th century. Your hosts
manage to combine the traditional building with modern
decor. On sale: Wine.

PROPERTY

lounge, hosts have pets, telephone, babies welcome, free cot,
golf course 2km, fishing 5km, hunting 5km, hiking 10km,
cycling 10km, mushroom-picking 15km, bird-watching 50km,
sea or lake watersports 50km, riversports 50km

——At Carcassonne, head towards the 'Centre-Ville' and place
Carnot. The rue Barbès is a one-way street and is a
continuation of the rue Victor Hugo, parallel to the rue
Verdun. It crosses the only pedestrianised street. At the end,
park in one of the many free parking spaces.

This is an old vine-grower's house in the process of being restored. Serge and Marie offer a warm welcome, and you must try their delicious cooking in the magnificent dining room decorated with wine vats. This place really has the atmosphere of a typical old farmhouse.

PROPERTY

✺ ✺ ✺

off-street parking, garden, lounge, pets not accepted, dinner available, packed lunch, babies welcome, free cot, fishing, golf course 2km, hiking 15km, interesting flora 15km, mushroom-picking 15km, sea or lake watersports 15km

Basic English spoken

PRICE STRUCTURE
3 Bedrooms and 1 Suite

shower room with wc, double bed: FF200

shower room with wc, double bed: FF220

shower room with wc, 2 single beds: FF220

Suite: shower room with wc, double bed + en-suite room 2 single beds: FF330 (2 people) FF440 (4 people)

Reduction: 16/09–30/05

Capacity: 10 people

Serge MAYEN

'Domaine du Petit Fidèle'

Ancienne route de Coursan

11100 NARBONNE

Tel: (0) 4 68 32 18 12-06 71 46 49 85

Private Home

NARBONNE:
railway station: 5km
airport: 30km
car essential
——Take the Exit Narbonne-Sud on the A9. Go straight on along the bypass. At the fourth round-about turn right, turn left immediately and left again (the old road to Coursan). Continue for 2.5km. The house is a red-dish-ochre colour.

Philippe & Martine
DUPRESSOIR

'Château de Gandels'

81700 GARREVAQUES

Tel: (0) 5 63 70 27 67/
06 07 14 11 55

Fax: (0) 5 63 70 27 67

www.chateau-de-
gandels.com

Château

23 km - N -
CASTELNAUDARY
Garrevaques:
airport: 50km
car essential

PRICE STRUCTURE

**4 Bedrooms and 1 Suite
and 1 Apartment**

Rétro: television, bathroom
with wc, double bed: FF650

Tour & Baldaquin:
television, bathroom with
wc, double bed: FF700

Terrasse : television,
bathroom with wc, twin
beds: FF690

Suite Eugénie: television,
bathroom with wc, double
bed + en-suite room double
bed: FF1,200 (4 people)

Empereur: television,
kitchen, bathroom with wc,
double bed, twin beds:
FF1200 (4 people)

Séquoïa: double bed: FF700

Extra Bed: FF100

Reduction: groups

Capacity: 18 people

81.06 CASTELNAUDARY

Martine knows all about quality, and this is reflected in the large salons and stylish bedrooms. She also loves cooking and bakes her own bread. The landscaped gardens were designed by the famous architect Le Notre, with fountains, and pools full of waterlilies.

PROPERTY

off-street parking, extensive grounds, tv lounge, hosts have pets, dinner available, babies welcome, free cot, swimming pool, riding, hiking, fishing, hunting, bird-watching, mushroom-picking 1km, cycling 5km, sea or lake watersports 5km, riversports 5km

English spoken

——From the A61, Exit Castelnaudary. Take the D624 and then the D622 as far as Revel. Then go towards Castres and, as you leave the town, at the roundabout, turn left towards Garrevaques, and continue for 2.4km. The château is on the right.

Maryvonne & Richard
ROUDIER-VILLARD

'Château d'Isis'

30440 ST-JULIEN-DE-
LA-NEF

Tel: 04 67 73 56 22

Fax: (0) 4 67 73 56 22

castelisis@free.fr

Château

13 km - S E -
LE VIGAN
St-Julien-de-la-Nef:
airport: 50km

30.22 LE VIGAN

The château is is the process of being restored, but you will love the peace and quiet that pervades this place, along with the cool shade of the trees and the babbling brook. What an ideal spot to relax! Be sure to ask to see the trout farm. On sale: Vegetables, jam, wine, vinegar.

PROPERTY

private parking, extensive grounds, lounge, hosts have pets, dinner available, closed: 10/01–31/01, hiking, hunting, interesting flora, mushroom-picking, bird-watching, cycling 5km, riversports 5km, golf course 20km, fishing 50km

Fluent English spoken

——At Le Vigan take the D999 towards Montpellier. At St-Julien-de-la-Nef follow the signs for 1km along by the river Hérault.

PRICE STRUCTURE

4 Bedrooms and
2 Apartments

Bleu: bathroom with wc, double bed: FF300

Rose: bathroom with wc, twin beds: FF340

Verte: bathroom with wc, 2 double beds, 2 single beds: FF400 (2 people) FF780 (6 people)

Suite: lounge, bathroom with wc, double bed: FF340

St-Bresson & Thaurac: kitchen, shower room with wc, 2 double beds, 2 single beds: FF360 (2 people) FF540 (6 people)

Capacity: 24 people

Françoise & Yves
GANGE - MENARD

'L'Endroune'

Grande Rue

30360 VEZENOBRES

Tel: (0) 4 66 83 76 03

Fax: (0) 4 66 83 76 21

Private Home

7 km - S - ALES
Vézenobres:
hosts can collect
from station,
railway station: 7km
airport: 50km
car essential

PRICE STRUCTURE

4 Bedrooms

Terrasse: shower room with wc, twin beds: FF340

Liberty: shower room with wc, twin beds, single bed: FF340 (2 people) FF440 (3 people)

Vendée: double bed: FF240

Berger: twin beds: FF240

Extra Bed: FF100
Reduction: 4 nights

Capacity: 9 people

30.33 ALES

There are three main attractions in this area. First, the medieval fortress town of Vézenobres; second, the 12th-century residence 'L'Endroune' and, third, your hosts. Françoise is a writer who lectures on the mythology of Sumer, the Greeks and the Egyptians. Yves is a qualified architect. There will be no shortage of subjects for conversation.

PROPERTY

tv lounge, hosts have pets, pets not accepted, dinner available, 1 shared shower room with wc, hiking, golf course 5km, interesting flora 7km, riversports 20km, sea or lake watersports 60km

Fluent English spoken

——From Alès, take the N106 towards Nîmes for 7km. Turn left in Vézenobres towards the 'Mairie' (Town Hall). 'L'Endroune' is almost opposite the tourist office.

Nathalie de VILLARS

'La Portalade'

15, rue de la Portalade

30111 CONGENIES

Tel: (0) 4 66 80 79 36

Fax: (0) 4 66 80 79 36

la.portalade@wanadoo.fr

Residence of
Outstanding Character

17 km - S W -
NIMES
Congenies:
railway station: 17km
airport: 30km
car essential

PRICE STRUCTURE

3 Bedrooms
Jaune: wc, twin beds: FF220

second room: television,
shower room with wc,
double bed, single bed:
FF350 (2 people)
FF380 (3 people)

third room: television,
shower room with wc,
double bed: FF350

Extra Bed: FF80
Reduction: 5 nights

Capacity: 7 people

30.32 NIMES

This is a very old house, typical of this vine-growing village, in the land of bullfights, fiestas, asparagus and olive oil. Nathalie is great company, and she also runs cookery courses. There is a peaceful walled garden with a swimming pool. (The 'Jaune' bedroom shares a bathroom with your hostess).

PROPERTY

private parking, garden, tv lounge, hosts have pets, telephone, dinner available, wheelchair access, 1 shared bathroom, 1 shared shower room, swimming pool, 12 years old minimum age, 2 nights minimum stay, closed: 1/11–30/11, hiking, hunting, vineyard, fishing 5km, cycling 10km, golf course 20km, sea or lake watersports 25km, bird-watching 30km, interesting flora 40km *Fluent English spoken*

——From Nîmes, D40 towards Calvisson and Sommières, continue for 20km as far as Congénies. Pass the town hall (mairie), the post office and the school, then turn right into la rue du Clos. When you reach the cross, take the street furthest on the right. Continue as far as the next junction and the house is on the corner, on your right.

Eliette COUSTON

'La Mazade'

12, rue de la Mazade

30730 ST-MAMERT

Tel: (0) 4 66 81 17 56

Fax: (0) 4 66 81 17 56

Residence of
Outstanding Character

14 km - N W - NIMES
St-Mamert: hosts can
collect from station,
railway station: 14km
airport: 20km
——On the A9, Exit
Nîmes-Ouest. Go towards
Alès and turn left on to
the D999 towards Le
Vigan for 10km. Turn
right on to the D1
towards St-Mamert for
4km. In the village, the
house is on the corner
by the 'coiffeur'.

Eliette is an artist and her studio is part of the house. She has cleverly combined modern art and the charms of this 19th-century house. She is a mine of information on places to visit, festivals and local artists and exhibitions. On sale: Hand-made leather garments.

PROPERTY

off-street parking, extensive grounds, tv lounge, pets not accepted, dinner available, babies welcome, free cot, wheelchair access, hiking, fishing 18km, riversports 25km, bird-watching 40km

Basic English spoken

PRICE STRUCTURE
3 Bedrooms
shower room with wc, twin beds: FF300

(2 rooms) shower room with wc, double bed: FF300

Extra Bed: FF70

Reduction: 8 nights

Capacity: 6 people

Eric & Mercédes
BREL-THIANGE

'Le Clos de Vic'

2, rue du Temple

30260 VIC-LE-FESQ

Tel: (0) 4 66 80 52 01
Fax: (0) 4 66 80 59 77

clos.de.vic@wanadoo.fr
http://perso.wanadoo.fr
/clos.de.vic

Private Home

24 km - W - NIMES
Vic-le-Fesq: hosts
can collect from
station,
railway station: 25km
airport: 30km
car essential

30.26 NIMES

Mercédes is a retired antique dealer. She provides a really warm welcome in the heart of this quiet village, and puts great emphasis on giving each room a style of its own. Here, you are on the edge of the Cévennes, near to numerous interesting towns and historic sites which are well worth a visit. The Cévennes are among the most spectacular parts of France, with a mass of activities and sports to choose from.

PROPERTY

garden, lounge, hosts have pets, dinner available, packed lunch, non-smoking, swimming pool, 2 nights minimum stay (01/07–31/08), riding, cycling, fishing, hunting, hiking 1km, golf course 25km, sea or lake watersports 40km, mushroom-picking 60km, winter sports 60km *Fluent English spoken*

——From Nîmes, take the D999 towards Guissac. Then take the second Exit for Vic-le-Fesq. In the village, take the first road on the left, and it is the last house on the right, with a wall with railings on top and a sign 'Clos de Vic'.

PRICE STRUCTURE

4 Bedrooms

Pagnol: television, shower room with wc, double bed: FF380

Mistral: television, shower room with wc, twin beds: FF380

Daudet: television, bathroom with wc, double bed: FF380

Giono: television, shower room with wc along corridor, double bed: FF380

Extra Bed: FF50/100

Capacity: 8 people

John KARAVIAS

'Les Marronniers'

Place de la Mairie

30580 LA BRUGUIERE

Tel: (0) 4 66 72 84 77-06
14 98 76 93

Fax: (0) 4 66 72 85 78

les.marronniers@hello.to

Residence of
Outstanding Character

39 km - N - NIMES
La Bruguière:
railway station: 39km
airport: 50km
car essential

LANGUEDOC-ROUSSILLON

NIMES

PRICE STRUCTURE

30.29 NIMES

4 Bedrooms

television, shower room
with wc, double bed: FF500

television, shower room
with wc, twin beds: FF500

television, shower room
with wc, bathroom, twin
beds: FF600

television, shower room
with wc, double bed: FF500

Capacity: 8 people

This large and imposing 19th-century house, with well-decorated, comfortable rooms, is situated near Uzès. This is the Midi with its little villages, vineyards and châteaux. You will stay on for the beauty of the surroundings as well as the genuine welcome of your hosts, Michel and John.

PROPERTY ✳ ✳ ✳

garden, lounge, pets not accepted, telephone, dinner available, swimming pool, 15 years old minimum age, 3 nights minimum stay, hiking, cycling, mushroom-picking, vineyard, golf course 11km, riversports 15km

Fluent English spoken

——From Nîmes, take the D979 to Uzès. Continue towards Lussan for 8km. Turn right on to the D238 as far as La Bruguière. The house can be found in the main village square, next to the town hall and the château.

Margaret & Martin
HASKINS

'La Vigneronne'

15, av Pierre Sirven

34530 MONTAGNAC

Tel: (0) 4 67 24 14 36

Fax: (0) 4 67 24 03 59

mhaskins@wanadoo.fr

Residence of
Outstanding Character

25 km - N E -
BEZIERS
Montagnac:
railway station: 20km
airport: 40km
car essential

34.23 BEZIERS

Margaret and Martin (a lively rugby player) have filled this house with wooden masks and sculptures brought back from their travels in Africa. Here there is an irresistible 'joie de vivre', and you will have great evenings in the charming interior courtyard with its informal, Mediterranean-style garden, where breakfast is also served.

PROPERTY

private parking, garden, tv lounge, hosts have pets, pets not accepted, dinner available, non-smoking, swimming pool, cycling, fishing 3km, golf course 12km, riversports 20km, sea or lake watersports 36km

Fluent English spoken

PRICE STRUCTURE

2 Bedrooms
first room: shower room
with wc, double bed: FF250

second room: shower room
with wc, double bed, single
bed: FF250 (2 people)
FF330 (3 people)

Extra Bed: FF80
Capacity: 5 people

——From Béziers, take the N9 towards Pézenas, which you by-pass, and then turn right on to the N113 towards Montagnac. 'La Vigneronne' is on this road in the centre of the village, on the right.

Andrew & Jennifer
VINER

7, rue de la Fontaine

34420 VILLENEUVE-LES-
BEZIERS

Tel: (0) 4 67 39 87 15

Fax: (0) 4 67 32 00 95

anges-gardiens
@wanadoo.fr

Residence of
Outstanding Character

5 km - S - BEZIERS
Villeneuve-les-
Beziers: hosts can
collect from station,
railway station: 5km
airport: 65km

PRICE STRUCTURE

34.06 BEZIERS

4 Bedrooms

Pois de Senteur: shower
room with wc, twin beds:
FF280

Baldaquin: bathroom with
wc, double bed: FF280

Provençale: bathroom with
wc, shower, double bed:
FF280

Rose: bathroom with wc,
shower, 2 single beds: FF280

Extra Bed: FF70

Reduction: 01/10–31/05
and 7 nights and groups
and children

Capacity: 8 people

Jennifer is Australian and her passion is her guests. She will introduce you to her wonderful 15th-century home, in the heart of a peaceful village, with its beautiful staircase, comfortable rooms and remarkable frescoes. Near to the beaches.

PROPERTY

lounge, hosts have pets, pets not accepted, dinner available, packed lunch, babies welcome, free cot, hiking, cycling, fishing 2km, bird-watching 5km, sea or lake watersports 5km, golf course 15km

Fluent English spoken

——On the A9, take the Exit Béziers-Est. Go towards Sérignan. The house is opposite the 'Mairie' (Town Hall), in the centre of Villeneuve.

Ann Marie HIGGINS

5, rue René Soulette

34490 THÉZAN-LES-BÉZIERS

Tel: (0) 4 67 37 05 65

Fax: (0) 4 67 37 05 65

Private Home

12 km - N - BEZIERS
Thézan-Les-Beziers:
railway station: 10km
airport: 25km
car essential

34.09 BEZIERS

Overlooking the Vallée de l'Orb, in the heart of the Béziers vineyards, this place has a superb view. Relax beside the pool or on the beach, or visit Cathar castles and vineyards.

PROPERTY

private parking, garden, lounge, hosts have pets, pets not accepted, dinner available, kitchen, swimming pool, tennis court, 5 years old minimum age, hiking, cycling, vineyard, fishing 3km, riversports 10km, golf course 15km, sea or lake watersports 25km

Fluent English spoken

PRICE STRUCTURE

3 Bedrooms
Bleu: shower room with wc along corridor, double bed: FF290

Vert: bathroom with wc along corridor, twin beds: FF290

Jaune: shower room with wc, double bed: FF290

Extra Bed: FF75

Capacity: 6 people

——Take Exit Béziers-Est from the A9, then the D909 towards Bédarieux. Then, left on to the D33 towards Pailhès-Thézan.

André & Jeanne CRISIAS

'Résidence Le Clôt'

111, 113, Quai Cornu

La Tamarissière

34300 AGDE

Tel: (0) 4 67 94 21 78

Fax: (0) 4 67 94 19 32

CRISIAS.LECLOT
@wanadoo.fr

Private Home

20 km - S E -
BEZIERS
Agde: hosts can
collect from station,
railway station: 3km
airport: 6km
car essential
——At Béziers take
the N112 towards
Agde then turn
right on to the N32
towards Sète. Then
right towards La
Tamarissière.
Le Clot is on the
right-hand side of
the road.

Here the accommodation is in very basic studio-cabins which are 100m from the river Hérault and 1km from the sea. You are free to explore the 10 ha wooded estate and there are many games provided for children.

PROPERTY

off-street parking, garden, hosts have pets, swimming pool, closed: 1/10-31/03, hiking, fishing, sea or lake watersports, golf course 4km, bird-watching 6km

Basic English spoken

PRICE STRUCTURE

3 Apartments

Le Coquillage & l'Etoile de Mer & l'Hippocampe: kitchen, shower room with wc, double bed, 2 single beds (child-size): FF230 (2 people) FF330 (4 people)

Capacity: 12 people

Marie Claude DEMAILLY

2, rue du Vieux Pont

34670 ST-BRES

Tel: (0) 4 67 70 62 75

Fax: (0) 4 67 70 62 75

mcdemail@mnet.fr

Residence of
Outstanding Character

15 km - E -
MONTPELLIER
St-Brès:
railway station: 15km
airport: 14km
car essential

34.19 MONTPELLIER

This was originally a 17th-century coaching inn, in this village between the famous towns of Montpellier and Nîmes. You will be captivated immediately. The setting is magnificent and the bedrooms comfortable. There is an indoor swimming pool and you are only 30 mins. from the beaches. You are also near to the Camargue and the Cévennes. Fleur de Soleil member.

PROPERTY

off-street parking, garden, lounge, hosts have pets, babies welcome, free cot, swimming pool, 6 years old minimum age, golf course 3km, bird-watching 20km, sea or lake watersports 20km

Fluent English spoken

—— From the A9, take Exit 28. Head towards Nîmes on the N113. After Baillargues, go towards St-Brès on the left. The house is just after the little bridge, No. 2.

PRICE STRUCTURE

2 Bedrooms and 1 Suite
Suite: lounge, kitchen, bathroom along corridor, wc, double bed, twin beds + en-suite room twin beds:
FF400 (2 people)
FF800 (6 people)

Jaune & Bleue: shower room with wc, double bed:
FF350

Extra Bed: FF100
Reduction: 7 nights

Capacity: 10 people

Danielle & Pierre
MEJEAN PARENTINI

'La Maison de Marius'

8, rue du Pontet

48320 QUEZAC

Tel: 04 66 44 25 05

Private Home

30 km - S - MENDE
Quézac:
railway station: 40km
airport: 100 km
car essential

PRICE STRUCTURE

3 Bedrooms and 1 Suite
Rivière & Pontet & Moulin:
shower room with wc,
double bed: FF300

Le Toit: shower room with
wc, bathroom, twin beds +
en-suite room Lucarne:
single bed:
FF400 (2 people)
FF500 (3 people)

Extra Bed: FF100

Capacity: 9 people

48.06 MENDE

This typical Languedoc village house is in the Cevennes National Park, at the beginning of the Gorges du Tarn. The welcome is warm and attentive, the decor refined and the local food healthy and colourful. The region offers a wealth of sporting activities. Fleur de Soleil member.

PROPERTY

private parking, garden, dinner available, swimming pool, hiking

——From the A75, Exit Marvejols. Then take the N88 to Monde and the N106 towards Alès. Turn right on to the D907bis to Isparnac and Quénac.

This old house is unforgettably situated almost at the world's end, at the heart of the Cévennes National Park. The facilities are basic but practical. It is a long way to the nearest restaurant so take good advantage of Marie-Claude's dinners, using farm produce. Totally natural!

PROPERTY

off-street parking, garden, lounge, hosts have pets, pets not accepted, dinner available, packed lunch, non-smoking, 1shared shower room with wc, closed: 15/11–31/01, hiking, interesting flora, mushroom-picking

Basic English spoken

PRICE STRUCTURE

3 Bedrooms

Miel: washbasin, double bed: FF172

Claire: washbasin, double bed, twin beds: FF172 (2 people) FF324 (4 people)

Rustique: washbasin, double bed, cot: FF162

Capacity: 8 people

Marie Claude & Corine CHARBONNIER & Fabrice MAUGE

'La Devèze'

48110 STE-CROIX-VALLEE-FRANCAISE

Tel: (0) 4 66 44 74 41

Working Farm

70 km - S E - MENDE
Ste-Croix-Vallée-Française:
car essential
——At Mende, take the N88 and the N106 towards Alès. At Florac, take the D907 towards La Corniche des Cévennes. At Le Pompidou, turn left towards Ste-Croix-Vallée-Française as far as Pont Ravager. Then turn left and take the small road for 5km, keeping right on until the end of the road, as far as La Devèze.

Helena-Shelagh MICHIE

'La Belle Auriole'

66600 OPOUL

Tel: (0) 4 68 29 19 26

Fax: (0) 4 68 29 19 26

labelleauriole
@wanadoo.fr

Private Home

35 km - N -
PERPIGNAN
Opoul: hosts can
collect from station,
railway station: 30km
airport: 30km
car essential

PRICE STRUCTURE

66.01 PERPIGNAN

2 Suites
Mezzanine – 1: double bed
+ en-suite room twin beds,
2 single beds:
FF250 (2 people)
FF840 (6 people)

Mezzanine – 2: lounge,
double bed + en-suite room
3 single beds:
FF250 (2 people)
FF690 (5 people)

Extra Bed: FF75

Reduction: 4 nights

Capacity: 11 people

Helena, who is English, loves this region, where she put down her roots many years ago. Her mas is typical of the Roussillon area. Here you are surrounded by vines and the garrigues – wilderness all around you. Helena organises themed stays, and hiking trips.

PROPERTY

off-street parking, garden, hosts have pets, pets not accepted, dinner available, packed lunch, 2 shared shower rooms, 2 wc, closed: 30/10–15/04, hiking, cycling, vineyard, sea or lake watersports 25km, gliding 25km, interesting flora 30km, mushroom-picking 30km, bird-watching 30km, winter sports 50km *Fluent English spoken*

——From the A9, Exit Perpignan Nord. Then take the D12 towards Vingrau and turn right on to the D9 towards Opoul. Go through Opoul and follow the signs to 'Château de Périllos' and, after 1.5km, turn left on to a small tarmac road (C7), which slopes downwards.

Annie & Paul FAVIER

'Mas Bazan'

66200 ALENYA

Tel: 04 68 22 98 26

Fax: (0) 4 68 22 97 37

masbazan@wanadoo.fr

Residence of
Outstanding Character

9 km - S E -
PERPIGNAN
Alénya: hosts can
collect from station,
railway station: 10km
airport: 15km
car essential

66.11 PERPIGNAN

This imposing Catalan mas is set amongst the vineyards and orchards of Le Roussillon, a short distance from the beaches. Set on a vine-growing domain, the house is covered with wisteria, climbing roses and jasmine. Ancient trees provide the shade for the vast courtyard, which is almost like a second living room. Everything contributes to the holiday mood: the spacious living room, the large swimming pool and the enthusiastic welcome of Annie and Paul. They will certainly introduce you to the secrets of their local wine 'Côtes de Roussillon'. On sale: Wine from their vineyard.

PROPERTY

off-street parking, extensive grounds, lounge, hosts have pets, dinner available, babies welcome, free cot, swimming pool, closed: 15/12–15/01, hiking, vineyard, golf course 3km, sea or lake watersports 4km

——Exit Perpignan-Sud from the A9. Take the N114 towards Argelès-sur-Mer. Take Exit 3 towards Saleille, then the D25 towards Alenya. The mas is situated before the village. Turn on the left in to a road through the vines and continue to the end.

PRICE STRUCTURE

**4 Bedrooms and
1 Apartment**

Bleue: television, shower room with wc, bathroom, double bed: FF330

(3 rooms) shower room with wc, bathroom, double bed, single bed: FF330 (2 people) FF380 (3 people)

Suite campagnarde: lounge, kitchen, shower room with wc, bathroom, double bed + en-suite room 2 single beds: FF330 (2 people) FF430 (4 people)

Capacity: 15 people

Jacques & Michelle
ARNAL

'Mas Arnal'

66130 ST-MICHEL-DE-
LLOTES

Tel: (0) 4 68 84 84 79
Fax: (0) 4 68 84 84 79

http://
perso.club-internet.fr
/mvilar

Private Home

30 km - W -
PERPIGNAN
St-Michel-de-Llotes:
hosts can collect
from station,
railway station: 2km
airport: 25km
car essential

66.09 PERPIGNAN

Wonderful countryside, in which this old Catalan mas blends beautifully with the abundant vegetation – oaks, pines, box and rosemary. The village is listed as a 'Ville d'Art et d'Histoire' and Michelle and Jacques know their region in depth, in particular the scenic footpaths through the mountains, the orchards and the vineyards.

PRICE STRUCTURE

1 Bedroom
lounge, shower room with
wc, double bed: FF320

Extra Bed: FF90

Capacity: 2 people

PROPERTY

off-street parking, garden, lounge, pets not accepted, babies welcome, free cot, swimming pool, hiking, cycling, hunting, interesting flora, mushroom-picking, sea or lake watersports 10km, riversports 15km, winter sports 15km, golf course 20km

Basic English spoken

——At Perpignan, take the N116 towards Prades and Andorra, as far as Ille-sur-Têt. Then turn left towards St-Michel-de-Llotes. The 'Mas Arnal' is on the right, just as you enter St-Michel.

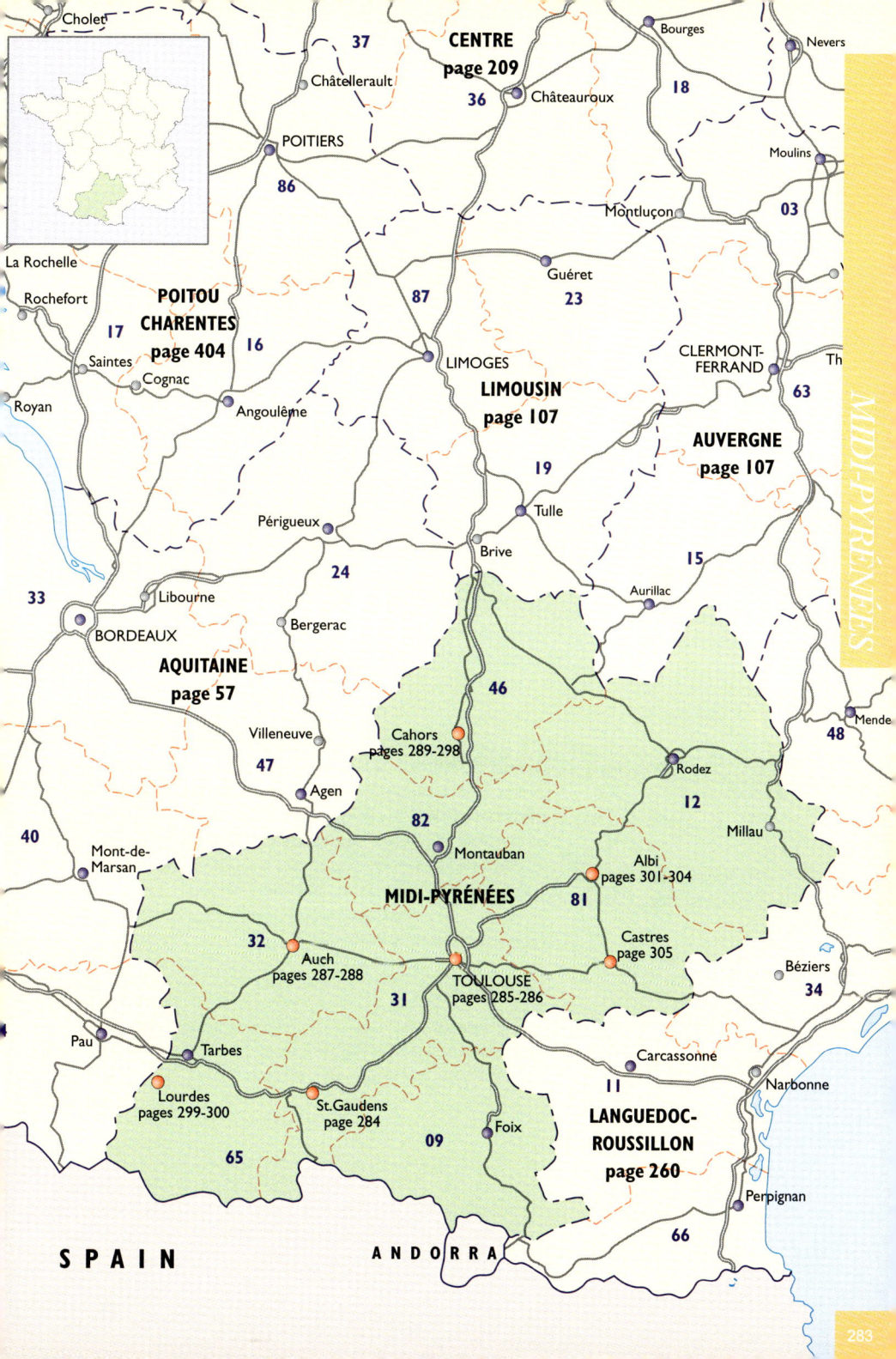

Cholet

CENTRE
page 209

Bourges

Nevers

37

Châtellerault

36   Châteauroux

18

POITIERS

86

Moulins

Montluçon

03

POITOU
CHARENTES
page 404

87

Guéret

23

CLERMONT-
FERRAND

La Rochelle

Rochefort

17   16

Saintes

Cognac

LIMOGES

LIMOUSIN
page 107

AUVERGNE
page 107

63   Th

Royan

Angoulême

19   Tulle

33

Libourne

Périgueux

24   Brive

Aurillac

15

Mende

BORDEAUX

Bergerac

46

Rodez

48

AQUITAINE
page 57

Villeneuve

Cahors
pages 289-298

12

Millau

47

Agen

82

MIDI-PYRÉNÉES

40

Mont-de-
Marsan

Montauban

Albi
pages 301-304

81

Rodez

32   Auch
pages 287-288

MIDI-PYRÉNÉES

TOULOUSE
pages 285-286

Castres
page 305

Béziers

31

34

Pau

Tarbes

Carcassonne

Narbonne

Lourdes
pages 299-300

St.Gaudens
page 284

11

LANGUEDOC-
ROUSSILLON
page 260

65

09   Foix

66

Perpignan

S P A I N

A N D O R R A

Rosina de PÈIRA

'Les Estivades'

Peyre

09230 FABAS

Tel: 05 61 96 40 16

Fax: (0) 5 61 96 42 36

www.ariege.com/
les.estivades/

Private Home

35 km - E - ST-
GAUDENS
Peyre:
railway station: 70km
airport 70km
car essential

PRICE STRUCTURE

6 Bedrooms
(5 rooms) shower room
with wc, twin beds: FF300

(1 room) shower room with
wc, 2 single beds: FF300

Reduction: groups

Capacity: 12 people

09.04 ST-GAUDENS

**Rosina de Pèira is a real ambassador for Languedoc culture
and is also a Languedoc singer of international repute.
Because of this, it easily deserves 3 'suns'. If you are
interested in her art and culture, try to be there on a Sunday
afternoon. 'When they arrive, we shake hands, but when they
leave, we kiss,' proclaims Rosina with glee. The terrace is a
haven of quiet and cool shade, from which there is a superb
view over the mountains of the Piémont Pyrénéen.**

PROPERTY

off-street parking, extensive grounds, lounge, pets not
accepted, telephone, dinner available, swimming pool,
12 years old minimum age, hiking, fishing 4km

——From the A64 Toulouse–St-Gaudens, take Exit 23 at
Cazeres. Then take the D6 as far as St-Croix-Volvestre, and
then follow the D35 towards Fabas for 4km. Les Estivades are
signposted on the right. Go right to the very end of the
tarmac road, into the courtyard of the farm.

Valérie BALANSA

'La Manufacture'

2, rue des Docteurs Basset

31190 AUTERIVE

Tel: (0) 5 61 50 08 50

Fax: (0) 5 61 50 08 50

Residence of Outstanding Character

30 km - S - TOULOUSE
Auterive:
railway station: 1km
airport 35km

31.05 TOULOUSE

This magnificent building has been in the same family for five generations. It was originally a small 18th-century sheet factory, right in the centre of the village. Now you can enjoy the swimming pool and the large pleasant garden.

PROPERTY

✳ ✳ ✳

private parking, extensive grounds, tv lounge, hosts have pets, dinner available, kitchen, babies welcome, free cot, swimming pool, hiking, cycling, fishing, hunting 5km, sea or lake watersports 15km, golf course 30km

English spoken

PRICE STRUCTURE

5 Bedrooms

Noire: bathroom with wc, double bed, single bed:
FF380 (2 people)
FF490 (3 people)

Empire: shower room with wc, twin beds: FF380

de Claude: bathroom with wc, double bed: FF380

du Parc: bathroom with wc, twin beds, single bed:
FF380 (2 people)
FF490 (3 people)

aux Oiseaux: shower room with wc, double bed: FF380

Extra Bed: FF100

Reduction: 7 nights

Capacity: 12 people

In Toulouse take the N20 towards Foix. At Auterive turn left at the second traffic lights towards the Centre-Ville. Cross the river Ariège and the canal, and it is the first street on the left opposite the Post Office. First house on the right.

Geneviève LANSIAUX

Le Village

31290 MONTGAILLARD-
LAURAGAIS

Tel: (0) 5 61 27 27 90

Private Home

31.07 TOULOUSE

This charming residence is in a very quiet village amongst the undulating hills of the Cathar country, 30 mins. from Carcassonne and Toulouse. There is a swimming pool to cool off in, the private terrace of the charterhouse, plus Genevi's boundless enthusiasm for the history of art.

PROPERTY

private parking, garden, tv lounge, hosts have pets, pets not accepted, babies welcome, free cot, swimming pool, closed: 01/10–30/04 & 01/07–31/07, riding, hiking, cycling, cycling, fishing, interesting flora, gliding 5km, golf course 10km, sea or lake watersports 10km, winter sports 80km

Basic English spoken

30 km - S E -
TOULOUSE
Montgaillard:
railway station: 5km
airport 40km
car essential
——On the A61, Exit
Villefranche-de-
Lauragais. Then take the
N113 towards Toulouse,
and after 3km turn right.
The village of
Montgaillard is on top of
a hill, and the house is
on the square with the
war memorial.

PRICE STRUCTURE

1 Bedroom and 1 Suite and 1 Apartment

Glycine: shower room with wc along corridor, washbasin, double bed: FF250

Chartreuse: lounge, television, kitchen, shower room with wc, double bed, 2 single beds: FF400 (2 people) FF700 (4 people)

Perroquet: bathroom with wc, double bed + en-suite room bathroom with wc, 2 single beds: FF300 (2 people) FF550 (4 people)

Extra Bed: FF100

Reduction: 3 nights

Capacity: 10 people

Frédérique & Thierry ALBERT

'Au Cardenau'

32390 STE-CHRISTIE

Tel: (0) 5 62 64 33 33

Fax: (0) 5 62 64 30 17

Residence of Outstanding Character

13 km - N - AUCH
Ste Christie: hosts can collect from station,
railway station: 12km
airport: 70km
car essential

32.04 AUCH

This vast 18th-century pile is typical of Gascony, d'Artagnan country! It combines peace and quiet with a respect for tradition. Peacocks roam in the 2 ha of grounds, and the enormous rooms contain beautiful furniture. The welcome is warm, and numerous music festivals are held in the area.

PROPERTY

private parking, extensive grounds, lounge, hosts have pets, babies welcome, free cot, swimming pool, hiking, fishing, hunting, interesting flora, mushroom-picking, gliding 5km, cycling 10km, sea or lake watersports 10km, golf course 12km

Basic English spoken

——At Auch take the N21 towards Agen for 12.5km, then turn right on to the D172 towards Ste-Christie.

PRICE STRUCTURE
3 Bedrooms

La Belle Matinée: shower room with wc, double bed, 2 single beds (1child-size): FF280 (2 people) FF375 (4 people)

Le Cardenau: lounge, television, bathroom with wc, double bed, single bed, cot: FF310 (2 people) FF405 (3 people)

Les Voiles de la Liberté: bathroom with wc, shower, washbasin, double bed, twin beds, cot: FF310 (2 people) FF500 (4 people)

Extra Bed: FF95

Reduction: 5 nights and children

Capacity: 10 people

Marie-Thérèse KOVACS

'Maison de la Porte
Fortifiée'

32320 MONTESQUIOU

Tel: (0) 5 62 70 97 59/
06 87 89 31 02

Fax: (0) 5 62 70 97 59

Residence of
Outstanding Character

27 km - S W - AUCH
Montesquiou:
railway station: 27km
airport: 90km
car essential

PRICE STRUCTURE

4 Bedrooms

Gris manet: lounge,
kitchen, shower room with
wc, twin beds: FF400

Baldaquin: shower room
with wc, double bed (queen
size): FF290

Verte: shower room with wc,
double bed, single bed:
FF270 (2 people)
FF490 (3 people)

Crème: bathroom with wc,
twin beds: FF350

Reduction: 5 nights and
children

Capacity: 9 people

32.08 AUCH

This house is built on to the walls of a 13th-century fortified gate, in a quiet village full of flowers, on the 'Route des Bastides'. There is a wonderful panoramic view from the terrace. Marie-Thérèse is a mine of information on this region, making this an outstanding address. You should also remember that you are in the Gers region, famous for its traditional foie-gras and many arts festivals.

PROPERTY ✹ ✹ ✹

garden, lounge, hosts have pets, pets not accepted, packed lunch, babies welcome, free cot, closed: 06/01–06/02, bird-watching, hiking 1km, fishing 1km, hunting 1km, mushroom-picking 5km, sea or lake watersports 5km, golf course 10km, riversports 20km

Fluent English spoken

——From Auch, go to Mirande on the N21 where you join the D137 for Montesquiou. In the village, follow the signs for 'chambres d'hotes'/ 'Porte Fortifiée'.

Ferme Auberge
'Aux Délices de La Serpt'

46250 FRAYSSINET-LE-GELAT

Tel: (0) 5 65 36 66 15

Fax: (0) 5 65 36 60 34

Working Farm

35 km - N W - CAHORS
Frayssinet-Le-Gelat:
railway station: 35km
airport: 150km
car essential

46.04 CAHORS

You are sure of a friendly, family welcome from Annick and Marie-France in this 18th-century 'ferme-auberge', typical of le Quercy, in the middle of a countryside filled with flowers. Admire their beautiful old dovecot and taste the local produce. On sale: Foie-gras, confits, rillettes, pâtés.

PROPERTY ✹✹✹

off-street parking, garden, lounge, hosts have pets, dinner available, packed lunch, hiking, cycling, mushroom-picking, fishing 4km, riversports 30km

Adequate English spoken

PRICE STRUCTURE

1 Bedroom
shower room with wc, double bed, single bed:
FF200 (2 people)
FF240 (3 people)

Extra Bed: FF50

Capacity. 3 people

——At Cahors, take the D911 towards Villeneuve-sur-Lot for 15.5km as far as Rostassac. Turn right on to the D660 towards Frayssinet. At the roundabout, go towards Villefranche, Périgueux. Follow the signs.

Mireille PINATEL

'La Grange de Marcillac'

MARCILLAC

46800 ST-CYPRIEN

Tel: (0) 5 65 22 90 73
(0) 5 65 22 90 42

Fax: (0) 5 65 24 91 05

Working Farm

24 km - S W -
CAHORS
Marcillac: hosts can
collect from station,
railway station: 25km
airport: 100km

PRICE STRUCTURE

**5 Bedrooms and 1 Suite and
3 Apartments**
Each room: shower room
with wc
1st room: double bed FF280
2nd room: 3 single beds
FF350 (3 people)
3rd room: 2 single beds
FF280
Le Cellier : 3 single beds:
FF370 (3 people)
5th room: double bed,
single bed: FF370 (3 people)
La Métairie: kitchen, double
bed, twin beds: FF550 (2
people) FF700 (4 people)
Suite: double bed + en-suite
twin room: FF300 (2
people) FF440 (4 people)
Le Verger: kitchen, double
bed, single bed: FF450 (2
people) FF550 (3 people)

Extra Bed: FF70
Reduction: 3 nights and
groups; Capacity: 24 people

46.07 CAHORS

**Mireille's kindness will overwhelm you, as she welcomes you
to her stone house, typical of the Quercy Blanc. She will
invite you to sample and enjoy music, flowers and wildlife, as
well as truffles, foie-gras and other local cuisine. However
tempting, try and drag yourself away from the swimming pool
some of the time. Be sure to book in advance. On sale: Duck
preserves, jam.**

PROPERTY

off-street parking, garden, lounge, hosts have pets, telephone,
dinner available, packed lunch, babies welcome, free cot,
1 shared bathroom with wc, swimming pool, closed: 20/12–
28/12, hiking, cycling, fishing 3km, golf course 5km, sea or
lake watersports 7km, riversports 40km

Basic English spoken

——At Cahors, N20 towards Caussade (3km). Right on to
D653 then left on to D7 towards Lascabanes. Cross St-Cyprien
towards Montcuq. As you leave the village, left towards
Marcillac (2.5km, signposted).

Marcelle HOURRIEZ

'Château de Roussillon'

46090 ST-PIERRE-LAFEUILLE

Tel: (0) 5 65 36 87 05

Fax: (0) 5 65 36 82 34

Château

12 km - N - CAHORS
St-Pierre-Lafeuille:
railway station: 10km
airport: 120km
car essential

46.15 CAHORS

A madly romantic, authentic feudal château in completely peaceful surroundings. The ideal place for a relaxing holiday and a complete change of scene. Here, originality is the by-word and the atmosphere is quite unique. Marcel started restoring this place 40 years ago and the interior contrasts strongly with the style of the exterior. Why not stay for a week and and book the 'Barbacane' apartment?

PROPERTY

off-street parking, extensive grounds, pets not accepted, telephone, closed: 01/11–31/03, hiking, fishing 10km, riversports 10km

Basic English spoken

PRICE STRUCTURE

1 Bedroom
Chapelle: lounge, television, telephone, shower room with wc, double bed, 2 single beds:
FF450 (2 people)
FF650 (4 people)

Extra Bed: FF100

Reduction: 2 nights

Capacity: 4 people

——At Cahors, take the N20 towards Brive for 12km. The château is at St-Pierre-Lafeuille, on the right after the church.

Dominique BRUN

'Château d'Uzech'

46310 ST-GERMAIN-DU-BEL-AIR

Tel: (0) 5 65 22 75 80

Fax: (0) 5 65 22 75 80

Château

25 km - N - CAHORS
St-Germain-du-Bel-Air:
railway station: 20km
airport: 110km
car essential

PRICE STRUCTURE

1 Bedroom and 3 Apartments

Bergerie: lounge, television, kitchen, shower room with wc, double bed, single bed:
FF500 (2 people)
FF600 (3 people)

Remparts: lounge, television, kitchen, bathroom with wc, double bed, single bed:
FF500 (2 people)
FF600 (3 people)

Tour: lounge, television, kitchen, bathroom with wc, double bed: FF500

Petite Tour: shower room with wc, single bed: FF300 (1 person)

Capacity: 9 people

46.16 CAHORS

In this ancient castle, you will be enthralled by the welcome of your hosts, their sense of style and their inventive cooking, both pleasant to the eye and even more delicious. You will have an unforgettable stay. Also a visit to Rocamadour and Sarlat should not be missed.

PROPERTY

off-street parking, extensive grounds, tv lounge, hosts have pets, dinner available, kitchen, babies welcome, free cot, swimming pool, closed: 30/11–30/01, hiking, mushroom-picking, sea or lake watersports 7km, golf course 20km, riversports 30km

Fluent English spoken

——At Cahors, take the D911 towards Villeneuve-sur-Lot. At Espère, turn right on to the D12 towards Nuzejouls, St-Denis Catus and Uzech.

Barbara SZILÀGYI

'La Charrue'

Engrange

46090 FRANCOULÈS

Tel: (0) 5 65 36 84 21

Fax: (0) 5 65 36 84 21

Residence of
Outstanding Character

15 km - N -
CAHORS
Engrange:
railway station: 17km
airport: 160km
car essential

46.18 CAHORS

This ancient stone farmhouse is typical of the Dordogne. It has been restored by a very friendly English couple, who know this area very well. They cook with great enthusiasm, and really love receiving their guests. Special weekly half-board rates.

PRICE STRUCTURE

4 Bedrooms
(4 rooms) shower room with wc, washbasin, double bed: FF260

Reduction: 01/09–30/06 and 7 nights

Capacity: 8 people

PROPERTY

off-street parking, garden, tv lounge, hosts have pets, pets not accepted, dinner available, 15 years old minimum age, closed: 01/11–01/03, hiking, sea or lake watersports 8km, fishing 17km, golf course 50km

Fluent English spoken

——Take the N20 towards Limoges. Engrange is on the right, 1km after Pelacoy.

Christian MONCOUTIÉ

'Les Graves'

46090 ST-PIERRE-
LAFEUILLE

Tel: (0) 5 65 36 83 12

Private Home

12 km - N - CAHORS
St-Pierre-Lafeuille:
railway station: 12km
airport: 110km
car essential
——At Cahors, take the
N20 towards Brive. Then
take the Exit Nord for
St-Pierre-Lafeuille.

46.20 CAHORS

Near the main road, this old farmhouse also has a campsite.
The rooms have independent entrances, and are simple with
basic bathrooms. The welcome is warm and a kitchenette is
available, but you will also be tempted by the village inn.

PROPERTY

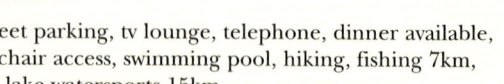

off-street parking, tv lounge, telephone, dinner available,
wheelchair access, swimming pool, hiking, fishing 7km,
sea or lake watersports 15km

Adequate English spoken

PRICE STRUCTURE
3 Bedrooms

(2 rooms) shower room with wc, washbasin, double bed: FF254

third room: bathroom with wc, washbasin, double bed, 2 single
beds: FF254 (2 people) FF358 (4 people)

Reduction: 01/09–30/06; Capacity: 8 people

Carmen & Pierre
NOUYRIT

'Les Mazuts'

46090 ARCAMBAL

Tel: (0) 5 65 23 95 29

Fax: (0) 5 65 53 04 96

Residence of
Outstanding Character

11 km - E - CAHORS
Arcambal:
railway station: 11km
airport: 100km
car essential

46.24 CAHORS

This old farm has 3 ha of land, a little pond and a beautiful view over the Lot Valley. Pierre and Carmen are retired, and their genuine welcome is complemented by the charm of this farm: little beamed corridors, narrow staircases, pigeon loft.... Fleur de Soleil member.

PROPERTY

private parking, garden, hosts have pets, dinner available, packed lunch, babies welcome, free cot, 1 shared bathroom with wc, 1 shared shower room with wc, hiking, fishing 4km, riversports 6km, cycling 11km, golf course 20km

——From Cahors, take the D911 as far as Arcambal and then head towards St-Cirq-Lapopie. Follow the signs as far as Les Mazuts.

PRICE STRUCTURE

4 Bedrooms

Bleu: double bed, single bed: FF200 (2 people) FF250 (3 people)

Rose: 3 single beds: FF200 (2 people) FF250 (3 people)

Vert: double bed: FF200

Méditerranée: shower room with wc along corridor, double bed, 2 single beds: FF250 (2 people) FF350 (4 people)

Extra Bed: FF50

Reduction: 6 nights

Capacity: 12 people

Caroline & Knud
KRISTOFFERSEN

'Domaine Lapèze'

46800 MONTCUQ

Tel: (0) 5 65 24 91 97

Fax: (0) 5 65 24 91 98

Private Home

28 km - S W -
CAHORS
Montcuq:
railway station: 24km
airport: 100km
car essential

PRICE STRUCTURE

3 Bedrooms

Les Pruniers: bathroom with wc, shower, twin beds: FF400

Les Vignes & Le Jardin: shower room with wc, double bed: FF350

Studio: kitchen, shower room with wc, twin beds: FF450

Extra Bed: FF100

Capacity: 8 people

46.25 CAHORS

Eat your heart out Peter Mayle! Caroline and Knud, a delightful Anglo-Danish couple, have cracked it. Recently settled in this wonderful area, they have tastefully renovated this impressive stone house on the slopes, overlooking their vines and fruit trees. Peace and quiet, and a swimming pool on the terrace. Don't miss the Sunday market in the village.

PROPERTY

off-street parking, extensive grounds, hosts have pets, dinner available, babies welcome, free cot, swimming pool, hiking, cycling, fishing, lake watersports 2km, golf course 15km

Fluent English spoken

——From Cahors, follow the signs from Montauban and Toulouse. At the second roundabout, follow the D653 signed Montcuq, a small, winding road for about 25km. After passing the Montcuq village sign, pass 'Shopi' on the right. Exactly on the pedestrian crossing, turn right signed 'Lapeze', and carry on, keeping right, up the hill. After the plum orchards, Domaine Lapeze is on the left.

Carin & Occo
BINNENDIJK

'La Cabane'

Poudens

46340 DEGAGNAC

Tel: 05 65 41 49 74

Fax: (0) 5 65 41 49 74

lacabanez@wanadoo.fr

Private Home

25 km - N -
CAHORS
DEGAGNAC:
railway station: 6 km
airport: 80 km

46.28 CAHORS

Your Dutch hosts, Carin and Occo, welcome you to their 18th-century residence, which has been completely restored. In the summer they serve a varied and interesting breakfast on the beautiful terrace, with its panoramic view over the Céou valley. This place is quiet and rural and has a swimming pool, as well as spacious, comfortable bedrooms. You can just relax here, or enjoy visiting the numerous places of interest in the area. Fleur de Soleil member.

PROPERTY

private parking, extensive grounds, hosts have pets, swimming pool, fishing, cycling 6km, riversports 12km, golf course 20km

Fluent English spoken

PRICE STRUCTURE

3 Bedrooms
first room: lounge, bathroom with wc, shower, double bed (queen size): FF395

second room: shower room with wc, double bed (queen size): FF280

third room: lounge, shower room with wc, twin beds: FF360

Extra Bed: FF50/100
Reduction: 1/09–30/06

Capacity: 6 people

——On the N20 Brive–Gourdon road, Exit Gourdon. Head towards Cahors on the D12 and, after 6km, at the bridge over the river, look for the signs 'La Cabane'.

Ria & Henri
VAN CITTERT

'Domaine La Grèze'

46240 LABASTIDE-
MURAT

Tel: (0) 5 65 24 52 97
Fax: (0) 5 65 25 52 97

henri.van-citter
t@wanadoo.fr

Residence of
Outstanding Character

30 km - N E -
CAHORS
La-Bastide-Murat:
hosts can collect
from station,
railway station: 24km
airport: 95km
car essential
——From Cahors,
take the N20
towards Brive for
25km, then turn
right on to the D677
towards Labastide-
Murat. As you enter
this village, follow
the signs.

46.29 CAHORS

Ria and Henry, a Dutch couple, are keen on sport, so do not be surprised to find a fully-equipped fitness room, sauna, swimming pool and solarium all available to you. The hearty breakfast will get your strength up for a day of sport or just sightseeing. You'll leave 'Le Domaine la Grèze' on top form.

PROPERTY

off-street parking, extensive grounds, tv lounge, hosts have pets, pets not accepted, non-smoking, wheelchair access, swimming pool, 8 years old minimum age, hiking, cycling, golf course 2km, fishing 10km

Fluent English spoken

PRICE STRUCTURE
3 Bedrooms

first room: television, shower room with wc, twin beds: FF300

second room: television, bathroom with wc, twin beds: FF300

third room: lounge, television, shower room with wc, twin beds: FF300

Reduction: 01/09–30/06 and 7 nights

Capacity: 6 people

Bernadette & Bruno
HAURINE ALBERT

'La Grange'

65120 VIZOS

Tel: (0) 5 62 92 87 41

Private Home

32 km - S -
LOURDES
Vizos: hosts can
collect from station,
railway station: 30km
airport: 35km
car essential

65.06 LOURDES

This little barn is 830m up in the hills, in a village of only 37 inhabitants, with a wonderful view over the route of the Tour de France. The location, the warm welcome and the reasonable price will tempt you to spend a lot of time here. Enjoy mountain treks on which you can learn about the shepherd's way of life, as well as skiing and spa treatments. On sale: Rabbits, chickens, cheese, eggs.

PROPERTY

off-street parking, garden, tv lounge, hosts have pets, dinner available, packed lunch, babies welcome, free cot, 1 shared shower room with wc, hiking, cycling, interesting flora, mushroom-picking, fishing 2km, winter sports 7km, gliding 9km, riversports 12km, golf course 30km

——From Lourdes, go to Luz-St-Saveur (N21 to Argelès then the D921 to Luz). From here, turn left on to the D172 towards Vizos and continue for 2km. The house is at the beginning of the village (slightly down the mountainside).

PRICE STRUCTURE

2 Bedrooms
(2 rooms) double bed:
FF180

Extra Bed: FF60
Reduction: 7 nights

Capacity: 4 people

Nadine & Jean-Marc
VIVES

28, route des Bartres

65100 LOUBAJAC

Tel: 05 62 94 44 17/
06 08 57 38 95

Fax: (0) 5 62 42 38 58

nadine.VIVES
@wanadoo.fr

Working Farm

5 km - N W -
LOURDES
Loubajac:
airport: 15km

PRICE STRUCTURE

6 Bedrooms
(2 rooms) bathroom with
wc, double bed: FF220

bathroom with wc, double
bed, single bed:
FF220 (2 people)
FF340 (3 people)

bathroom with wc, 2 double
beds: FF220 (2 people)
FF340 (4 people)

(2 rooms) shower room
with wc, 2 double beds:
FF220 (2 people)
FF340 (4 people)

Extra Bed: FF50

Capacity: 19 people

65.08 LOURDES

This haven of peace and quiet is only 5km from Lourdes and
ideal for a walking holiday. Nadine and Jean-Marc rear
chickens, ducks, guinea fowl and turkeys in the meadows at
the foot of the Pyrénées. Follow Eros the dog, and he will
lead you towards the country park. Do not miss dinner, using
their own farm produce. On sale: Duck conserve, free-range
chickens and turkeys.

PROPERTY

private parking, extensive grounds, tv lounge, hosts have pets,
pets not accepted, dinner available, packed lunch, hiking,
fishing, hunting, mushroom-picking, cycling 5km, golf course
5km, sea or lake watersports 5km, riversports 8km, winter
sports 50km

Adequate English spoken

——At Lourdes, take the D940 towards Pau. Then at
Loubajac, take the D3 towards Bartres. The farm is number 28
on this road.

Olivier FOUCHIER

'Le Rivatou'

81140 VAOUR

Tel: (0) 5 63 56 28 34

Fax: (0) 5 63 56 28 34

Residence of
Outstanding Character

45 km - N W - ALBI
Vaour: hosts can
collect from station,
railway station: 12km
airport: 90km
car essential

81.11 ALBI

This restored 18th-century farmhouse is in the middle of the countryside and near Les Gorges de l'Aveyron, in a region that combines charm and pleasure. The comfort and discreet welcome of your hosts is another plus. An ideal place to 'recharge your batteries'. Numerous summer festivals.

PRICE STRUCTURE

3 Bedrooms
first room: washbasin,
double bed: FF170

(2 rooms) washbasin, twin
beds: FF170

Extra Bed: FF70
Reduction: 3 nights

Capacity: 6 people

PROPERTY

off-street parking, extensive grounds, hosts have pets, pets not accepted, dinner available, babies welcome, free cot, non-smoking, 1 shared bathroom, 2 shared shower rooms, wc, closed: 01/11–31/03, hiking, cycling, mushroom-picking 1km, interesting flora 3km, fishing 13km, riversports 13km, golf course 25km

Fluent English spoken

——At Albi, take the D600 towards Cordes. 5km after Cordes, take the D91 then the D15 as far as Vaour. Le Rivatou is 500m along the small road, opposite the Gendarmerie.

Monique, Raymond ZIDI
& Christiane AIRAUDO

'Villa Akwaba'

81140 LE VERDIER

Tel: (0) 5 63 33 94 72-06
07 24 46 78

Fax: (0) 5 63 33 96 58

Private Home

30 km - W - ALBI
Le Verdier: hosts
can collect from
station,
railway station: 14km
airport: 75km
car essential

PRICE STRUCTURE

3 Bedrooms

Verdi: lounge, television,
telephone, bathroom with
wc, shower, double bed,
single bed:
FF670 (2 people)
FF790 (3 people)

Chopin: television,
telephone, bathroom with
wc, double bed, single bed:
FF570 (2 people)
FF690 (3 people)

Mozart: television,
telephone, shower room
with wc, double bed: FF470

Extra Bed: FF120

Reduction: 01/10–31/03
and 7 nights and children

Capacity: 8 people

81.12 ALBI

**Raymond and Monique have travelled the world and, in their
very comfortable, modern villa, display their collection of
African sculptures and other souvenirs beautifully. Good
cooking. It is quiet here, with a beautiful view, and the two
donkeys are just waiting for you to make a fuss of them.**

PROPERTY

private parking, extensive grounds, tv lounge, hosts have pets,
pets not accepted, telephone, dinner available, packed lunch,
babies welcome, free cot, swimming pool, closed: 15/12–
15/01, hiking, cycling, fishing 1km, hunting 2km, mushroom-
picking 3km, lake watersports 3km, riversports 20km, golf
course 25km *Fluent English spoken*

——At Albi, head towards Toulouse. N2088 for Gaillac. Join
the D964 towards Castelnau-de-Montmirail. D15 towards Le
Verdier for 4km. At the bottom of the village, left towards
Castelnau-de-Montmirail (300m), First little road on the right
towards Ste-Cécile-Dne-des-Trois-Moineaux for 1.5km. Straight
on, as far as the modern house with the swimming pool.

Lyne & Denis SOULIE

'Domaine de Gradille'

Route de Montauban

81310 LISLE-SUR-TARN

Tel: (0) 5 63 41 01 57

Fax: (0) 5 63 57 43 73

lynesoulie@wanadoo.fr

Working Farm

27 km - W - ALBI
Lisle-sur-Tarn:
railway station: 5km
airport: 55km
car essential

81.13 ALBI

This impressive large house is in pastoral surroundings near Albi and Cordes. Perfectly quiet, your sleep will be undisturbed. During the day, relax under the trees in the grounds, or walk through the vineyards to the lake and have a go at fishing. Alternatively, make use of the swimming pool – what a choice! Be sure to try the Vin de Gaillac. On sale: Their own wine.

PROPERTY

off-street parking, extensive grounds, tv lounge, hosts have pets, pets not accepted, telephone, dinner available, wc, swimming pool, riding, hiking, fishing, hunting, mushroom-picking, lake watersports, vineyard, cycling 5km, golf course 25km, riversports 25km

Adequate English spoken

——At Albi, head towards Toulouse. N2088 for Gaillac. At Gaillac, D999 towards Montauban. Continue for 5km as far as the crossroads. The house is opposite 'La Grouillère', near to the bus stop. Follow the signs.

PRICE STRUCTURE

5 Bedrooms
first room: bathroom with wc, double bed: FF250

2 & 3: shower, double bed, single bed:
FF200 (2 people)
FF280 (3 people)

4 & 5: bathroom with wc, double bed, single bed:
FF250 (2 people)
FF330 (3 people)

Extra Bed: FF50

Capacity: 14 people

Claude & Alain TIZIOLI

'Restaurant Les Ormeaux'

3, rue Saint-Michel

81170 CORDES-SUR-CIEL

Tel: (0) 5 63 56 19 50

Fax: (0) 5 63 56 23 37

Private Home

25 km - N W - ALBI
Cordes-sur-Ciel:
railway station: 20km
airport: 80km
car essential

81.14 ALBI

PRICE STRUCTURE

4 Bedrooms

(2 rooms) shower room with wc, washbasin, double bed: FF340

(2 rooms) shower room with wc, washbasin, double bed, single bed: FF340 (2 people) FF420 (3 people)

Extra Bed: FF50

Capacity: 10 people

This charming couple have their home in the heart of the medieval town centre, which has been beautifully preserved since 1222. The bedrooms, which are above the restaurant, are brand new and spotlessly clean. You have a separate entrance via the beautiful, quiet courtyard. This is a place for lovers of ancient buildings and history, as well as the delights of foie-gras, cassoulet and the sweet products of the Sugar Art Museum.

PROPERTY

off-street parking, garden, hosts have pets, dinner available, wheelchair access, closed: 22/12–31/01, hiking, golf course 20km, riversports 20km, interesting flora 60km

English spoken

——At Albi, take the D600 as far as Cordes-sur-Ciel. In Cordes, the 'Les Ormeaux' restaurant is at the top of the medieval citadel by the Porte des Ormeaux.

Erika & Jean TRICON

'Les Pierres Bleues'

3 bis, rue de la
République

81200 MAZAMET

Tel: 05 63 98 88 62
Fax: (0) 5 63 98 88 62

www.chez.com/
pierresbleues/

Residence of
Outstanding Character

20 km - S -
CASTRES
Mazamet:
airport: 45km
car essential

81.17 CASTRES

You will love the charm of this 19th-century residence and its grounds. Erica and Jean, a retired Franco-Swiss couple, love the countryside and are mad about art. 'Les Pierres Bleues' are, in fact, modern mini standing stones, which dominate the grounds by the ancient trees. The house is situated in the centre of this flower-filled town, at the foot of the Montagne Noire, famous for its lakes and forests. The plentiful breakfast includes cheese and local charcuterie.

PROPERTY

private parking, extensive grounds, tv lounge, babies welcome, free cot, hiking, golf course 3km, fishing 4km, sea or lake watersports 4km, riversports 12km, vineyard 20km

——At Castres, take the N112 towards Mazamet. In the centre of Mazamet, follow signs to 'Centre-Ville' and 'Office de Tourisme'. When facing the Office de Tourisme, go left around the square, then take the first on the right, then turn left in to the rue de la République. The house is number 3 bis.

PRICE STRUCTURE

3 Bedrooms

Baldaquin: shower room with wc, double bed (king size): FF350

second room: lounge, television, shower room with wc, twin beds, single bed: FF350 (2 people) FF460 (3 people)

third room: television, bathroom with wc, double bed (queen size): FF350

Extra Bed: FF110
Reduction: 7 nights

Capacity: 7 people

NETHERLA

BELGIUM

ENGLISH CHANNEL

Calais
pages 312-315

Dunkerque

St. Omer
pages 320-321

Boulogne
page 311

NORD
PAS-DE-
CALAIS

Béthune
page 310

LILLE
pages 307-308

Le Touquet
pages 316-319

62

59

Douai

Valenciennes

Abbeville
pages 325-327

Arras
page 309

Dieppe

80

AMIENS

St. Quentin
page 322

Charleville-Mézières

Sed

PICARDIE

02

Le Havre

76

Compiègne
pages 323-324

Laon

08

Rethel

ROUEN

Beauvais

60

Soissons

Reims

Lisieux

Senlis

95

Pontoise

NORMANDIE
page 328

27

Evreux

Mantes

Meaux

51

CHÂLONS

93

92

PARIS

75

Ba

Versailles

ILE DE FRANCE
page 15

Vitry

78

94

Dreux

Evry

77

St. Di

61

28

Chartres

91

Melun

CHAMPAGNE-
ARDENNE
page 251

Fontainebleau

Troyes

CENTRE
page 209

Sens

Ch

Le Mans

72

Châteaudun

10

Montargis

21

Vendôme

ORLÉANS

45

Auxerre

89

BOURGOGNE
page 122

59.01 LILLE

This place is about 90 mins. drive from Calais on the road to Brussels, yet you are in a village only 6 minutes by metro from the centre of Lille. Your charming hostess has given up teaching English in order to look after her guests and her beloved association of 'Aides Volontaires'.

Yves & Chantal LE BOT

59, Rue Faidherbe

59139 WATTIGNIES

Tel: (0) 3 20 60 24 51

PROPERTY

off-street parking, garden, hosts have pets, dinner available, kitchen, wc, cycling, hiking 2km, fishing 10km, interesting flora 10km, mushroom-picking 10km, golf course 15km, sea or lake watersports 50km

Fluent English spoken

Private Home

PRICE STRUCTURE
3 Bedrooms

(2 rooms) shower room with wc, double bed: FF260

third room: bathroom with wc, 2 single beds: FF230

Extra Bed: FF50

Reduction: 5 nights

Capacity: 6 people

3 km - S - LILLE
Wattignies: hosts can collect from station, railway station: 8km airport 10km
——Take Exit 19 off the A1. Take the D549 towards Wattignies (7km). At the chemist (pharmacie), turn left towards the centre. The house is on the left just before the church.

Jeannine HULIN

28, rue des Hannetons

59000 LILLE

Tel: (0) 3 20 53 46 12

Fax: (0) 3 20 53 46 12

Private Home

LILLE: hosts can collect from station,
railway station: 3km
airport: 5km
——From the place de la Garde, take the rue Nationale, and turn left into rue Solférino, then rue de Douai, and then Armand Caret as far as a bridge which crosses the road. Turn right under the bridge, then second on the left, left again and then left once more into the rue des Hannetons.

59.07 LILLE

This charming little house is in a quiet street, 10 mins. from the centre of Lille. The conservatory is full of light, full of class and the paintings and period furniture add a cosy, warm feeling to this place. Jeannine is full of life. The beds are a bit small – not for giants!

PROPERTY

off-street parking, garden, lounge, hosts have pets, pets not accepted, dinner available, 1 shared bathroom, wc, 3 years old minimum age, golf course, gliding 70km

English spoken

PRICE STRUCTURE
1 Bedroom
2 single beds (child-size): FF260
Extra Bed: FF60

Capacity: 2 people

Chantal de SAULIEU

'Chateau de Grand-Rullecourt'

62810 GRAND-RULLECOURT

Tel: (0) 3 21 58 06 37

Château

24 km - S W - ARRAS
Grand-Rullecourt: hosts can collect from station, railway station: 24km airport: 70km

62.07 ARRAS

The Viscount makes the jam and his wife brings you your breakfast. You will really enjoy their company and their sense of humour. They need it because, for 10 years, they have been restoring this château, where a lady-in-waiting of Mary, Queen of Scots, was born.

PROPERTY

✹ ✹ ✹

private parking, extensive grounds, lounge, pets not accepted, packed lunch, non-smoking, hiking, interesting flora, mushroom-picking, fishing 7km, hunting 8km, golf course 20km, golf course 20km, gliding 24km, bird-watching 40km

Adequate English spoken

——At Arras, take the N39 towards Le-Touquet. Turn left on to the D75 towards Avesnes-le-Château, and continue for 4km to Doullens. The château is on the square, in the centre of the village.

PRICE STRUCTURE

4 Bedrooms and 1 Suite

Polonaise: bridal room, lounge, shower room with wc, double bed: FF500

second room: lounge, bathroom with wc, twin beds: FF500

Baldaquin: bathroom with wc, 2 double beds: FF500 (2 people) FF900 (4 people)

Suite: bathroom with wc, double bed, single bed + e n-suite room twin beds: FF500 (2 people) FF1100 (5 people)

No 5: lounge, bathroom with wc, double bed: FF500

Extra Bed: FF50/200

Reduction: children

Capacity: 15 people

Gina BULOT

'Les Cohettes'

28, rue de Pernes

62190 AUCHY-AU-BOIS

Tel: (0) 3 21 02 09 47

Fax: (0) 3 21 02 81 68

temps-libre-evasion
@wanadoo.fr

Residence of
Outstanding Character

25 km - W -
BETHUNE
Auchy-Au-Bois: hosts
can collect from
station,
railway station: 8km
airport: 75km
car essential

PRICE STRUCTURE

5 Bedrooms

Rose & Verte: shower room
with wc, double bed: FF270

Bleue: shower room with
wc, double bed, 2 single
beds: FF300 (2 people)
FF420 (4 people)

Jonquille: bathroom with
wc, double bed: FF270

Lilas: bathroom with wc,
double bed, 2 single beds:
FF270 (2 people)
FF390 (4 people)

Extra Bed: FF70

Capacity: 14 people

62.08 BETHUNE

**Here you are only 45 mins. from Calais. This restored
farmhouse is full of flowers, which are Gina's great passion.
She and her children guarantee you a kind, smiling welcome,
and you will enjoy her traditional French cuisine. The British
and Canadian military cemetery at Vimy is 20km away.**

PROPERTY

off-street parking, extensive grounds, tv lounge, hosts have
pets, pets not accepted, dinner available, kitchen, babies
welcome, free cot, hiking, cycling, fishing 10km, golf course
20km, sea or lake watersports 45km

Adequate English spoken

——From the A26, take exit No. 4 (Thérouanne). At
Thérouanne take the D341 towards Arras. 1km after Rely, turn
right towards Auchy. Then take the first on the left (rue des
Pernes) and continue for 1km.

62.19 BOULOGNE-SUR-MER

A peaceful location only 2 mins. from the A16 autoroute, convenient for Calais, Boulogne and St-Omer. Your host is a musician and you may be lucky enough to be present at one of his local musical events.

PROPERTY

off-street parking, extensive grounds, lounge, hosts have pets, pets not accepted, telephone, babies welcome, free cot, wheelchair access, hiking, cycling, bird-watching, hunting 3km, fishing 5km, sea or lake watersports 7km, golf course 15km, riversports 17km

Fluent English spoken

PRICE STRUCTURE

6 Bedrooms

(3 rooms) shower room with wc, double bed: FF260

wheelchair access, shower room with wc, double bed, 2 single beds: FF260 (2 people) FF520 (4 people)

shower room with wc, double bed, single bed: FF260 (2 people) FF390 (3 people)

shower room with wc, double bed, 2 single beds: FF260 (2 people) FF520 (4 people)

Extra Bed: FF45

Reduction: groups

Capacity: 17 people

DEVREESE & RAVERDY

'Calypso'

Hameau du Ledquent

62250 MARQUISE

Tel: (0) 3 21 92 68 12

Fax: (0) 3 21 92 68 12

www.gite.calypso.com

Private Home

11 km - N E - BOULOGNE-SUR-MER
Marquise: hosts can collect from station, ferry port: 1km airport: 80km car essential
——Exit 7 on the A16, at roundabout follow signs to Marquise centre. You will then see signs for Calypso which will direct you to the hamlet of Lequent.

Marie-Lou
VANDEWALLE

25 rue des Martyrs de la
Résistance

59630 BOURBOURG

Tel: (0) 3 28 22 21 41

Residence of
Outstanding Character

30 km - E - CALAIS
Bourbourg: hosts
can collect from
station,
railway station: 18km
airport: 20km
car essential

PRICE STRUCTURE

2 Bedrooms

Louis XV-Rose: television,
shower room with wc,
double bed: FF270

Campagnarde bleue:
television, shower room
with wc, double bed:
FF270 (2 people)
FF350 (2 people)

Extra Bed: FF100

Reduction: 3 nights and
groups and children

Capacity: 4 people

59.02 CALAIS

Marie-Lou knows what the word welcome means! Her 18th-century house is decorated in a half-Flemish, half-British style, and is right in the middle of this little town, 7km from the sea. The garden is full of flowers and a real oasis. An excellent address.

PROPERTY

private parking, garden, lounge, pets not accepted, kitchen, babies welcome, free cot, fishing km, hiking 7km, interesting flora 7km, sea or lake watersports 7km, riversports 7km

Basic English spoken

——On the A16 going towards Dunkerque take Exit number 23b to Bourbourg. Follow signs to Bourbourg-Centre and take the rue de la Mairie (rue des Martyrs de la Résistance). Look for the B&B France sign on the door (No.25).

Jean-Jacques BEHAGHEL

'La Ferme de Wolphus'

No 39 RN43 - Wolphus

62890 ZOUAFQUES

Tel: (0) 3 21 35 61 61

Fax: (0) 3 21 35 61 61

ferme.de.wolphus
@wanadoo.fr

Private Home

15 km - S E -
CALAIS
Zouafques:
railway station: 9km
airport: 80km

62.02 CALAIS

You will feel at home in their modernised, old farmhouse. Jean-Jacques does not hesitate to travel 10km to make sure you have fresh baguettes for breakfast. You will be captivated by the good humour of his wife, a school teacher. We have added a 2nd 'sun', as recommended by past guests.

PROPERTY

off-street parking, extensive grounds, hosts have pets, pets not accepted, kitchen, babies welcome, free cot, wc, hiking, fishing, golf course 5km, sea or lake watersports 5km, interesting flora 18km, bird-watching 18km

Adequate English spoken

PRICE STRUCTURE

3 Bedrooms
Grande: shower room with wc, washbasin, double bed, 2 single beds (child-size):
FF230 (2 people)
FF370 (4 people)

Mansardes 1 & 2: shower, washbasin, double bed, single bed:
FF210 (2 people)
FF280 (3 people)

Extra Bed: FF50

Capacity: 10 people

——On the A26, take Exit 2. At the first 'Stop', turn right towards Calais for 500m. At the 2nd 'Stop', turn left on to the N43 for 1km. The house is on the left (20 mins. from Eurotunnel).

Thérèse de
LAMARLIÈRE

693, Rue du Parc

62890 AUDREHEM

Tel: (0) 3 21 35 06 30

Fax: (0) 3 21 35 06 30

Private Home

27 km - S E -
CALAIS
Audrehem: hosts
can collect from
station,
railway station: 15km
airport: 25km
car essential

PRICE STRUCTURE

3 Bedrooms

first room: shower room
with wc, double bed: FF210

second room: shower,
washbasin, double bed:
FF180

third room: shower,
washbasin, double bed:
FF180

Extra Bed: FF50
Reduction: groups

Capacity: 6 people

62.12 CALAIS

They are experts on the history of the Channel Tunnel and this friendly couple love to make friends. There are hiking (GR168) and mountain-bike trails nearby. A washing machine and tumble dryer are available for serious walkers. Here you will find peace and quiet in the heart of the country. On sale: Honey, foie-gras, poultry, bread.

PROPERTY

off-street parking, garden, lounge, telephone, dinner available, packed lunch, kitchen, babies welcome, free cot, non-smoking, wc, fishing, hiking 1km, cycling 1km, golf course 17km, bird-watching 20km, sea or lake watersports 20km

Basic English spoken

——Take Exit 2, Ardres, from the A26. Follow the D217 towards Licques, Zouafques, Tournehem and Bonningues-les-Ardres. As you leave the village on the D223 towards Audrehem, it is the first road on the right.

Christine & François
BOREL

'Les Draps d'Or'

152, rue Lambert
d'Ardres

62610 ARDRES

Tel: (0) 3 21 82 20 44

Fax: (0) 3 21 82 20 44

Private Home

10 km - S E -
CALAIS
Ardres:
ferry port: 2km
airport: 100km
car essential

CALAIS

62.21 CALAIS

Christine and François have finished renovating their lovely old house, close to the church in the charming, historic centre of Ardres. Convenient for the Eurotunnel where they work. Delightful bright and airy rooms, some overlooking the garden. Great for weekend breaks!

PROPERTY

private parking, garden, tv lounge, hosts have pets, babies welcome, free cot, wc, hiking, cycling, fishing, sea or lake watersports, interesting flora 10km, mushroom-picking 10km, golf course 15km, bird-watching 20km

Fluent English spoken

——From Calais, take Exit 17 on the A16, towards Ardres/St-Omer (17 kms). From Reims and Paris take Exit 2 on the A26 (Calais–Paris) then follow signs to Ardres (7 kms). When in Ardres follow signs to the 'Centre-Ville' and Les Draps D'or is behind the church. The entrance is on rue Léon Delacre where you will see a sign.

PRICE STRUCTURE

3 Bedrooms
along corridor shower, twin beds: FF310

shower, double bed: FF310

shower, wc, double bed (queen size) + room twin beds: FF310 (2 people) FF490 (4 people)

Extra Bed: FF110

Capacity: 8 people

Elena DESPREZ

'Villa La Crête des Dunes'

Av. Blériot

62520 LE-TOUQUET

Tel: (0) 3 21 05 04 98

Fax: (0) 3 21 05 04 98

www..bnbletouquet.com

Private Home

LE-TOUQUET-PARIS-PLAGE: hosts can collect from station, railway station: 5km airport: 2km

NORD

LE-TOUQUET-PARIS-PLAGE

PRICE STRUCTURE

4 Bedrooms

Ecoute triple: shower, washbasin, double bed, single bed:
FF330 (2 people)
FF360 (3 people)

Capelage: bathroom with wc along corridor, double bed:
FF330 (2 people)
FF330 (2 people)

Cabestan 1: twin beds:
FF290

Cabestan 2: double bed:
FF290

Reduction: 31/10–31/03 and 6 nights and groups

Capacity: 9 people

62.15 LE-TOUQUET-PARIS-PLAGE

Elena and Fred are a really enthusiastic and welcoming young couple, who will welcome you to this special place, from which you can enjoy all the attractions of Le-Touquet. They serve a hearty breakfast, either in the garden or in the conservatory with its panoramic view. You are only a few steps from the sand dunes and the sea.

PROPERTY

off-street parking, garden, tv lounge, hosts have pets, pets not accepted, kitchen, babies welcome, free cot, 1 shared bathroom, wc, hiking, cycling, golf course, interesting flora, sea watersports, gliding 2km, fishing 6km, riversports 10km

Fluent English spoken

——On the A16, as you enter Le Touquet, follow the signs to 'Base nautique Sud–chars à voiles'. Just before you reach the sea front, take the rue de Paris on the left. Continue straight on, heading towards the sand dunes. 'La Crête des Dunes' is at the top of the hill.

62.18 LE-TOUQUET-PARIS-PLAGE

A lovely retired couple. Pierre used to be a language teacher and enjoys the chance to chat with his guests. Cecile will do her utmost to make you feel at home and provides everything you need to enjoy your stay. A delightful room with French windows that open out onto the garden. For a long stay enquire about their charming chalet with its own kitchen, veranda and log fire; perfect for a family. Only 8km from the beaches and an excellent base for Montreuil and Le Touquet. Easy access to the A16 autoroute.

PROPERTY

off-street parking, garden, pets not accepted, babies welcome, free cot, closed: 16/09–8/10 & 22/12–2/01, hiking, fishing 5km, riversports 5km, golf course 10km, sea or lake watersports 10km, bird-watching 30km

Fluent English spoken

PRICE STRUCTURE

1 Bedroom

shower room with wc, double bed: FF256

Extra Bed: FF50

Reduction: 3 nights

Capacity: 2 people

Cécile & Pierre
CACHERA

723, Grande Rue

62170 SORRUS

Tel: (0) 3 21 06 23 28

Private Home

15 km - S E - LE-TOUQUET-PARIS-PLAGE
Sorrus:
railway station: 5km
airport: 140km
car essential
——Take Exit 25 on the A16 indicated Berck. Follow signs to Montreuil and take the D144 and then the D145 to Sorrus.On the N1 take the D144 at the round-about south of Montreuil and then the D145 towards Sorrus. Number 723 is on the right hand side of La Grande Rue. The number is indicated on the letter box by their steep driveway. Be sure to ask your hosts about the village's unique house-numbering system!

Monique & Jean-Michel
MELCHIOR

49, Rue de la Ballastière

62170 RECQUES-SUR-
COURSE

Tel: (0) 3 21 90 78 94

Fax: (0) 3 21 90 78 94

Private Home

16 km - E -
LE-TOUQUET-
PARIS-PLAGE
Recques-sur-Course:
railway station: 5km
car essential

PRICE STRUCTURE

3 Bedrooms
shower room with wc,
double bed: FF250

shower room with wc,
double bed, single bed:
FF250 (2 people)
FF330 (3 people)

along corridor shower room
with wc, double bed, single
bed: FF250 (2 people)
FF330 (3 people)

Extra Bed: FF80

Capacity: 8 people

62.20 LE-TOUQUET-PARIS-PLAGE

Monique and Michel's front garden is full of flowers. Here you will be a part of the family and will admire Michel's dedication as he continues to improve the house for your comfort. This pretty 'village fleuri' is convenient for Le-Touquet and Montreuil.

PROPERTY

off-street parking, garden, tv lounge, hosts have pets, pets not accepted, babies welcome, free cot, non-smoking, cycling 1km, hiking 5km, fishing 5km, riversports 5km, golf course 15km, sea or lake watersports 15km, bird-watching 30km

——From Montreuil on the N1 towards Boulogne, take the turning on the right after the factory, signposted Estrée and Estrelles/La Vallée de la Course. Continue along this road (follow the signs) until you reach Recques-sur-Course. Number 49 is the first white house in the village on the right. You cannot miss the front garden full of flowers.

62.22 LE-TOUQUET-PARIS-PLAGE

Your charming room is separate from the main house where Madame Saelens lives and where breakfast is served. Her renovated farmhouse is full of character and tastefully decorated in traditional French style. In a pretty village near the forest of Hesdin.

PROPERTY

private parking, garden, hosts have pets, babies welcome, free cot, non-smoking, closed: 1/11–28/02, hiking 2km, mushroom-picking 3km, fishing 5km, riversports 10km, golf course 30km, bird-watching 40km, sea or lake watersports 40km

PRICE STRUCTURE

1 Bedroom

Television, shower room with wc, double bed: FF200

Capacity: 2 people

Micheline SAELENS

'Le Collet Vert'

rue d'en Haut

62770 WAMIN

Tel: 03 21 04 81 40
06 80 05 34 08

jeanlouis.saelens@free.fr

Residence of
Outstanding Character

38 km - E -
LE-TOUQUET-
PARIS-PLAGE
Wamin:
railway station: 5km
airport: 100km
car essential
——From Le-Touquet
head for Montreuil, then
Hesdin. Turn left on to
the D928 towards St-
Omer. Wamin is on your
right. Le Collet Vert is at
the start of the rue d'en
Haut, on the left hand
side when coming from
the D928. The name is
carved into the wooden
gate.

Yves & Josiane
FRAMMERY

'Ferme-Auberge du
Moulin'

5, Bout de la Ville

62650 CAMPAGNE-LES-
BOULONNAIS

Tel: (0) 3 21 86 55 20
Fax: (0) 3 21 86 55 20

Residence of
Outstanding Character

20 km - S W -
ST-OMER
Campagne-les-
Boulonnais:
hosts can collect
from station,
railway station: 30km
airport: 80km
car essential

PRICE STRUCTURE

1 Bedroom
television, shower room
with wc, double bed,
2 single beds:
FF270 (2 people)
FF430 (4 people)

Extra Bed: FF80
Reduction: 4 nights

Capacity: 4 people

62.11 ST-OMER

Josiane is full of kindness and Yves quite simply loves life. This farmhouse is enchantingly furnished. Here you are in the country in a typical family, where at the same time you can taste the local gastronomic specialities. For sale: Milk, cream, eggs, vegetables, pastries.

PROPERTY

private parking, extensive grounds, tv lounge, hosts have pets, dinner available, packed lunch, babies welcome, free cot, hiking, cycling, hunting, fishing 3km, mushroom-picking 3km, interesting flora 10km, golf course 12km, bird-watching 30km, sea or lake watersports 30km, riversports 30km

——Take the A16 to Boulogne-sur-Mer then take the D341 towards Desvres and Thérouanne. After the village of Senlecques, turn right and continue for 3km.

Béatrice & Gérard
TILLIETTE

'Aux Campagnes'

18, rue du Flot

62570 PIHEM

Tel: 03 21 93 81 53/
06 07 49 89 45

Fax: (0) 3 21 39 59 60

www.auxcampagnes.com

Private Home

10 km - S W -
ST-OMER
Pihem:
railway station: 7km

62.23 ST-OMER

Sporty Béatrice and Gérard will be happy to organise activities for you and your family, especially mountain-biking and canoeing. They regularly take their bikes to Britain, being so close to the A26 and Calais. They cater for groups and large families but, even if you are just passing by, you will be welcomed with a smile by this wonderful family. Two minutes from the La Coupole museum at St-Omer.

PROPERTY

private parking, garden, tv lounge, hosts have pets, pets not accepted, dinner available, packed lunch, kitchen, babies welcome, free cot, hiking, cycling, hunting, sea or lake watersports, riversports, interesting flora 7km, bird-watching 7km, fishing 8km, golf course 11km

Fluent English spoken

——Exit 4 off the A26, Thérouanne. Turn right at the next three roundabouts following signs to Desvres or Pihem (5 km). From St-Omer follow signs to Wizernes and then Pihem on the D928. Follow signs to 'Aux Compagnes'.

PRICE STRUCTURE

7 Bedrooms
Ananas & Pêche & Pomme & Pastèque: shower room with wc, double bed,
2 single beds:
FF230 (2 people)
FF450 (4 people)

Banane & Orange & Mangue: shower room with wc, 4 single beds:
FF230 (2 people)
FF450 (4 people)

Extra Bed: FF45

Capacity: 28 people

Geneviève GYSELINCK

'Ferme Auberge du Vieux Puits'

5 bis, Rue de L'Abbaye

02420 BONY

Tel: (0) 3 23 66 22 33

Fax: (0) 3 23 66 25 27

Working Farm

15 km - N - ST-QUENTIN
Bony:
airport: 100km
car essential

PRICE STRUCTURE

5 Bedrooms
Auberge – first room: television, telephone, shower room with wc, double bed, 2 single beds (1 child-size): FF310 (2 people) FF420 (4 people)

Auberge – second room: television, telephone, shower room with wc, twin beds: FF310

Auberge – third room: television, telephone, kitchen, bathroom with wc, double bed, single bed: FF310 (2 people) FF420 (3 people)

(2 rooms) television, telephone, shower room with wc, double bed: FF310

Extra Bed:FF110

Capacity: 13 people

02.01 ST-QUENTIN

You eat well chez Geneviève. This is a relaxing stop in a beautiful area, convenient for the A26 autoroute. The World War I American military cemetery is only 1km away. On sale: Regional farm produce.

PROPERTY

private parking, extensive grounds, tv lounge, pets not accepted, dinner available, kitchen, babies welcome, free cot, swimming pool, tennis court, hiking, cycling, fishing 5km, golf course 15km, hunting 15km

Basic English spoken

——In St-Quentin, take the N44 towards Cambrai. Bony is on the left, 1km from the N44. (From A26, Exit 9; from A1, Exit 13.)

Pauline BRUNGER

'Ferme-Hôtel de Bellerive'

492, Rue de Bellerive

60170 CAMBRONNE-LES-RIBECOURT

Tel: (0) 3 44 75 02 13/
06 80 62 68 35
Fax: (0) 3 44 76 10 34

bellerive@minitel.net

Residence of Outstanding Character

15 km - N - COMPIEGNE
Cambronne-les-Ribécourt: hosts can collect from station, railway station: 2km airport: 50km

60.03 COMPIEGNE

This old farmhouse near the A1 has been restored with great charm. It is on the edge of the forest and the rooms have a delightful view over the canal. This is also a restaurant, and Pauline is a very good chef. Dishes to take away.

PROPERTY

off-street parking, garden, tv lounge, hosts have pets, dinner available, packed lunch, babies welcome, free cot, hiking, cycling, fishing, hunting, interesting flora, mushroom-picking, golf course 5km, sea or lake watersports 5km, riversports 5km

Fluent English spoken

——In Compiègne, take the N32 towards Noyon. In Ribécourt, turn right on to the D66. (From Calais: A1, Exit 12 Roye then follow directions for Noyon. Then take the N32 towards Compiègne. After Ribécourt turn left on to D66.) Cross the canal, and the house is immediately on the right after the bridge.

PRICE STRUCTURE

5 Bedrooms
(3 rooms) shower room with wc, double bed: FF295

second room: shower room with wc, twin beds: FF295

third room: bathroom with wc, twin beds: FF295

Extra Bed: FF100
Reduction: 4 nights

Capacity: 10 people

Françoise GAXOTTE

'La Gaxottière'

363, rue du Champ du Mont - Hameau de Varanval

60880 JAUX

Tel: 03 44 83 22 41

Fax: (0) 3 44 83 22 41

Private Home

6 km - S - **COMPIEGNE**
Jaux:
railway station: 7km
airport: 55km
car essential

PRICE STRUCTURE

2 Bedrooms
bathroom, double bed: FF300

shower, double bed (king size): FF300

Capacity: 4 people

60.07 COMPIEGNE

The two guest rooms, full of character and with their own fireplaces, are in the old house. Your charming hostess, Françoise, is a retired chemist who lives in the converted barn next door. Enjoy breakfast outside in the lovely, peaceful garden. Françoise will make you feel very welcome, as will her dogs.

PROPERTY

private parking, garden, hosts have pets, pets not accepted, babies welcome, free cot, wc, hiking 6km, cycling 6km, golf course 6km, mushroom-picking 6km, sea or lake watersports 6km

——Take Exit 10 on the A1 signposted to Compiegne (4 km) Follow signs to Jaux (1.2 km from the N31 turning).When you reach the hamlet of Varanval, La Gaxottière is on the right opposite an impressive metal gate.

René & Christiane
AUGUSTIN

'Chateau de Drucas'

Beauvoir-Wavans

62390 AUXI-LE-
CHATEAU

Tel: (0) 3 21 04 01 11

Château

25 km - N E -
ABBEVILLE
Beauvoir-Wavans:
airport: 150km
car essential

62.06 ABBEVILLE

This small château is about 200 years old. It is reached via an avenue of lime trees, leading to magnificent grounds, through which a river flows. Madame's welcome is charming. The decor is simple, unpretentious Rococo-style.

PROPERTY

private parking, extensive grounds, lounge, hosts have pets, telephone, babies welcome, free cot, 1 shared bathroom with wc, riding, hiking, cycling, fishing, mushroom-picking, interesting flora 2km, sea or lake watersports 2km, golf course 25km, bird-watching 25km, gliding 40km

Basic English spoken

——In Abbeville, take the D925 towards St-Riquier and the D941 towards Auxi-le-Château. In Auxi, turn right on to the D938.

PRICE STRUCTURE

2 Bedrooms and 1 Suite
first room: double bed,
single bed (child-size):
FF220 (2 people)
FF300 (3 people)

second room: double bed:
FF220

suite: kitchen, bathroom
with wc, double bed
+ en-suite room double bed
+ en-suite room single bed:
FF250 (2 people)
FF500 (5 people)

Extra Bed: FF50

Capacity: 10 people

Yves & Geneviève
MALIVET

'Le château'

2, rue de Fouilly

80150 MAISON-
PONTHIEU

Tel: (0) 3 22 29 03 01

Fax: (0) 3 22 29 05 62

Château

20 km - N E -
ABBEVILLE
Maison-Ponthieu:
railway station: 20km
airport: 60km
car essential

PRICE STRUCTURE

4 Bedrooms

Primevert: bathroom with wc, twin beds: FF380

Suite Jonquilles: shower room with wc, twin beds:
FF380 (2 people)
FF600 (4 people)

Conciergerie-La Rose: shower room with wc, double bed: FF380

les Bleuets: shower room with wc, twin beds:
FF400 (2 people)
FF600 (4 people)

Extra Bed:FF100

Reduction: 4 nights

Capacity: 12 people

80.10 ABBEVILLE

Near to the forest of Crécy and its famous battlefield, this 17th-century château, in white stone, offers a warm and simple welcome. Ideal for a weekend by the sea, or for exploring the multitude of attractions in this area, including the Baie de la Somme and the Abbaye de St-Riquier. You will be served home-made pastries for breakfast.

PROPERTY

private parking, extensive grounds, tv lounge, hosts have pets, pets not accepted, packed lunch, babies welcome, free cot, non-smoking, wheelchair access, 3 nights minimum stay: (01/07–30/08), closed: 15/11–15/02, hiking, cycling, fishing 6km, riversports 6km, interesting flora 12km, mushroom-picking 12km, golf course 22km, hunting 25km, bird-watching 30km, sea watersports 30km *Basic English spoken*

——At Abbeville, D925 towards Arras. As you leave St-Riquier, D941 on the left towards Auxi-le-Château; continue for 10km. Left on to the D56 towards Maison-Ponthieu. Pass in front of the village church and you will reach the rue de Fouilly. The château is on your left.

Norbert JEAN

'Château Gaillard'

1, route Nationale

80120 FOREST-
MONTIERS

Tel: 03 22 23 97 33/
06 11 63 51 95

Fax: (0) 3 22 23 97 33

Château

17 km - N W -
ABBEVILLE
Forest-Montiers:
railway station: 5km
car essential

80.11 ABBEVILLE

Very warm welcome. Norbert is charming, very helpful and accommodating. His goal was to create the perfect place for a relaxed family holiday, which he has achieved. Château Gaillard is a building of character with large grounds. The rooms are pleasant and well-maintained. There are lots of facilities: heated swimming pool, exercise machines, table-tennis, and a room with an impressive fireplace for barbecues.

PROPERTY

private parking, extensive grounds, tv lounge, hosts have pets, telephone, babies welcome, free cot, non-smoking, swimming pool, hiking, interesting flora, mushroom-picking, bird-watching, fishing 2km, cycling 3km, golf course 5km, gliding 10km, sea or lake watersports 12km

Adequate English spoken

——2 minutes from Exit 24 on the A16. Take the N1 to Forest-Montiers. The entrance is off the N1, on the right.

PRICE STRUCTURE

1 Bedroom and 2 Suites
(2 rooms) shower room
with wc, double bed + room
double bed:
FF300 (2 people)
FF600 (4 people)

first floor: shower room with
wc, bathroom, double bed:
FF380

Extra Bed: FF100

Capacity: 10 people

ENGLISH CHANNEL

Dunkerque

Calais

Boulogne

St.

NORD PAS-DE-CALAIS
page 306

62

Abbeville

80

AMIENS

PICARDIE
page 306

Beauvais

60

Dieppe
pages 374-376

Etretat
pages 377-378

Cherbourg
pages 350-356

76

ROUEN
pages 379-383

Le Havre

Bayeux
pages 329-336

Cabourg
page 337

Deauville
pages 340-341

Pont-Audemer
pages 344-346

Pontoise

95

Mantes

9

92 P.
7

50

St. Lô

CAEN
pages 338-339

Lisieux
page 343

27

Evreux

Jersey
(to UK)

Coutances
page 357

14

NORMANDIE

Granville
page 358

Villedieu-les-Poêles
pages 368-370

Falaise
page 342

78

ILE DE FRANCE
page 15

Evry

St. Malo

Mont-St-Michel
pages 359-367

Avranches
pages 347-349

Argentan

Dreux

91

Dinan

Alençon
page 371

61

Mortagne-au-Perche
pages 372-373

Chartres

28

22

BRETAGNE
page 158

RENNES

Fougères

53

72

Châteaudun

45

35

Laval

Le Mans

ORLÉANS

56

Redon

Châteaubriant

Vendôme

41

Blois

CENTRE
page 209

44

Angers

49

Tours

37

Vierzon

St. Nazaire

NANTES

Saumur

Bourges

Cholet

Châtellerault

18

La Roche

Cécile GRENIER &
Thérèse DESSEAUX

'Le Vallon'

Hottot-les-Bagues

14250 TILLY-SUR-
SEULLES

Tel: (0) 2 31 08 11 85

Fax: (0) 2 31 08 11 85

Private Home

12 km - S - BAYEUX
Hottot-les-Bagues:
hosts can collect
from station,
railway station: 15km
airport: 15km

14.04 BAYEUX

**A renovated farmhouse in a quiet spot, near to the sea and
the Normandy beaches. The ideal place to recharge your
batteries! They even run yoga and massage courses. On sale:
Honey, vegetables, cider.**

PROPERTY

off-street parking, extensive grounds, tv lounge, babies
welcome, free cot, non-smoking, fishing

Basic English spoken

——At Bayeux, take the D6 towards Tilly-sur-Seulles. Turn
right on to the D9 towards Caumont. At Hottot-les-Bagues,
after the 'Mairie' (Town Hall) and opposite the school
(école), turn left. The house is on the left, just before the
château.

PRICE STRUCTURE

5 Bedrooms
shower room with wc,
double bed: FF220

shower room with wc, twin
beds: FF220

shower room with wc,
4 single beds: FF220 (2
people) FF380 (4 people)

shower room with wc,
3 single beds: FF220 (2
people) FF300 (3 people)

shower room with wc, single
bed: FF140 (1 people)

Extra Bed: FF60
Reduction: groups
Capacity: 12 people

Catherine GUY

'Le Clos St Jean'

Route de la Mer

14520 STE-HONORINE-
DES-PERTES

Tel: (0) 2 31 21 79 34/
06 85 83 28 72

Fax: (0) 2 31 34 60 51

Private Home

13 km - N W -
BAYEUX
Ste-Honorine-des-
Pertes:
car essential

PRICE STRUCTURE

**1 Bedroom and
2 Apartments**

Bleue: television, shower
room with wc, double bed,
single bed: FF290 (2
people) FF340 (3 people)

Verte – Apartment: shower
room with wc, double bed +
en-suite room twin beds:
FF270 (2 people)
FF470 (4 people)

Apartment: lounge,
television, shower room
with wc, double bed +
en-suite room twin beds:
FF280 (2 people)
FF500 (4 people)

Extra Bed: FF50

Capacity: 11 people

14.16 BAYEUX

**This large, modern, elegant stone house is only 300m from
the sea and the D-Day landing beaches. The garden has views
over the large lawn to the sea. The bedrooms lead out on to
the balcony. The American military cemetery at Omaha
Beach is 2km away, and Bayeux is also well worth a visit.**

PROPERTY

off-street parking, extensive grounds, babies welcome, free cot,
wheelchair access, hiking, fishing, sea or lake watersports,
cycling 2km, golf course 2km, interesting flora 10km,
bird-watching 40km

English spoken

——At Bayeux, take the D6 for Port-en-Bessin. Then turn left
on to the D514. Ste-Honorine is just after Huppain
(signposted).

Bertrand & Catherine
GIRARD

'Le Relais de la Vignette'

Route de Crouay
Tour en Bessin
14400 BAYEUX

Tel: (0) 2 31 21 52 83
Fax: (0) 2 31 21 52 83

Relais.Vignette
@wanadoo.fr
http://perso.wanadoo.fr
/Relais.Vignette/

Residence of
Outstanding Character

5 km N W - BAYEUX
Tour-en-Bessin:hosts
can collect from
railway station: 6km
airport: 30km
car essential

14.25 BAYEUX

This farmhouse, typical of the area, has been restored to a good standard with excellent taste. A pleasant family air reigns and Catherine is a good cook. Near the D-Day beaches and Bayeux, an excellent base for visiting Normandy.

PROPERTY

✳ ✳ ✳

off-street parking, garden, tv lounge, hosts have pets, dinner available, babies welcome, free cot, hiking, cycling, hunting, fishing 3km, golf course 6km, sea or lake watersports 6km, interesting flora 10km, mushroom-picking 10km, bird-watching 10km

English spoken

From Bayeux head towards Cherbourg on N13 for 6km, as far as the village of Tour-en-Bessin. As you leave the village turn left on the road towards Crouay. Continue for 1.5km and follow the signs.

PRICE STRUCTURE

4 Bedrooms

Rose: lounge, television, shower room with wc, double bed, 2 single beds: FF260 (2 people) FF410 (4 people)

Ground floor – Verte: bridal room, television, shower room with wc, double bed, single bed: FF260 (2 people) FF360 (3 people)

Blanche: television, shower room with wc along corridor, double bed, 2 single beds: FF260 (2 people) FF410 (4 people)

Ecossaise: television, bathroom with wc, 2 double beds, single bed: FF260 (2 people) FF490 (5 people)

Extra Bed: FF80

Capacity: 16 people

Odile & Jean-Claude
LENOURICHEL

'Ferme du Mouchel'

14710 FORMIGNY

Tel: (0) 2 31 22 53 79

Fax: (0) 2 31 21 56 55

Working Farm

NORMANDIE

15 km - N W -
BAYEUX
Formigny:
railway station: 15km
airport: 45km
car essential

BAYEUX

PRICE STRUCTURE

3 Bedrooms and 1 Suite
(2 rooms) shower room
with wc, double bed, single
bed: FF260 (2 people)
FF320 (3 people)

along corridor bathroom
with wc, double bed: FF260

Indépendante: shower room
with wc, double bed +
en-suite room twin beds:
FF270 (2 people)
FF540 (4 people)

Extra Bed: FF50

Capacity: 14 people

14.29 BAYEUX

This restored stone farmhouse offers good standards of comfort on a working farm. Odile is your lively hostess, full of enthusiasm for the area and attentive to all details that make your stay that extra bit enjoyable.

PROPERTY

off-street parking, garden, hosts have pets, pets not accepted, telephone, sea or lake watersports 5km

——From the N13 from Bayeux towards Cherbourg turn right after about 15km to Formigny (D517). Turn right after the church and then left, following signs to Ferme du Mouchel.

Chantal KLEIN

'Ferme de la Houlotte'

14400 NONANT

Tel: (0) 2 31 92 50 29/
06 13 13 58 97

Fax: (0) 2 31 92 50 29

Working Farm

4 km - S E - BAYEUX
Nonant:
railway station: 6km
airport: 20km
car essential

14.30 BAYEUX

Let Chantal's exuberant 'joie de vivre' sweep you into her farmhouse, full of character, in this quiet village close to the sea. On returning from sightseeing or swimming, try the regional dishes cooked with local farm produce. On sale: Farm produce, jam.

PROPERTY

off-street parking, extensive grounds, lounge, hosts have pets, dinner available, babies welcome, free cot, 1 shared shower room, 2 wc, cycling

Fluent English spoken

——In Bayeux, take the N13 towards Caen, then the D33 towards Nonant. Turn right at the church and go under the bridge. The farm is situated 1.6km further down the road. Follow the signs.

PRICE STRUCTURE

4 Bedrooms
Orme: shower along corridor, wc, double bed: FF250

Hêtre: double bed, single bed: FF250 (2 people) FF350 (3 people)

Merisier: double bed, 3 single beds: FF250 (2 people) FF500 (5 people)

Noyer: shower, double bed, single bed: FF250 (2 people) FF350 (3 people)

Extra Bed: FF100

Reduction: 3 nights and groups and children

Capacity: 13 people

Annick SIMONIN

'Ferme Mahyas'

14330 STE-MARGUERITE-D'ELLE

Tel: (0) 2 31 92 98 15

Working Farm

25 km - S W - BAYEUX
Ste-Marguerite-d'Elle:
railway station: 7km
airport: 60km

PRICE STRUCTURE

3 Bedrooms
(2 rooms) double bed: FF220

shower room with wc, washbasin, 2 double beds: FF280 (4 people)

Extra Bed: FF80

Capacity: 8 people

14.36 BAYEUX

This former coaching inn, over 300 years old, has been transformed into a farmhouse of great character on a 37-ha property. They produce their own fresh milk, veal and pork. This is the real rural experience, in the country with the river nearby. Add to this their Pommeau and Calvados, and you have the complete image of picture-postcard Normandy.

PROPERTY

off-street parking, garden, lounge, hosts have pets, 1 shared shower room with wc, closed: 01/10–01/04, fishing, hunting, hiking 5km, cycling 7km, sea or lake watersports 25km, golf course 30km

Basic English spoken

——At Bayeux, take the D752 towards St-Lô. In the forest, when you reach the roundabout, turn right and go as far as Cerisay-la-Forêt. At the 'Stop' sign, turn right and 200m further on turn left. At the crossroads, head in the direction of St-Jean-de-Savigny on the left and the farm is 300m further on, on the left.

Dominique & Alain
MARION

Le Chateau

14450 GRANDCAMP-
MAISY

Tel: 02 31 22 66 22

Fax: (0) 2 31 22 66 22

Private Home

30 km - N W -
BAYEUX
Grandcamp-Maisy:
railway station: 30km
car essential

14.37 BAYEUX

Ideally located among the D-Day landing beaches, and 30km from the old town Bayeux with its famous tapestry. You'll be welcomed to this XVII century farmhouse by Alain and Dominique and their family. Fleur de Soleil member.

PROPERTY

private parking, garden, dinner available, closed:
01/11–31/03, sea or lake watersports

English spoken

PRICE STRUCTURE

3 Bedrooms
Camélia & Jonquille: shower room with wc, double bed: FF300

Glycine: shower room with wc, 2 single beds: FF300

Extra Bed: FF100

Capacity: 6 people

——Contact your host for detailed directions.

Isabelle & Gérard
LEHARIVEL

'Manoir de la Rivière'

Gefosse-Fontenay

14230 ISIGNY-SUR-MER

Tel: (0) 2 31 22 64 45

Fax: (0) 2 31 22 01 18

g.leharivel@mageos.com

Château

30 km - W - BAYEUX
Gefosse-Fontenay:
railway station: 22km
airport: 60km
car essential

PRICE STRUCTURE

3 Bedrooms
Louis-Philippe: shower
room with wc, double bed,
single bed (child-size):
FF285 (2 people)
FF365 (3 people)

Louis XV: shower room with
wc, double bed, single bed:
FF285 (2 people)
FF365 (3 people)

Tour: shower room with wc,
double bed: FF285

Reduction: 3 nights

Capacity: 8 people

14.38 BAYEUX

This fortified farm/manor house dates from medieval times and is situated in the Regional National Park, near to the D-Day landing beaches. Ask for the bedroom in the square tower, complete with arrow-slits. Isabelle's warm welcome complements the cosy atmosphere. Also available to rent: a gîte for 2 people and an apartment for 4 people.

PROPERTY

private parking, garden, lounge, hosts have pets, pets not accepted, dinner available, packed lunch, hiking, fishing, interesting flora, bird-watching, sea or lake watersports 4km, cycling 5km, golf course 25km

Adequate English spoken

——At Bayeux, take the N13 towards Cherbourg for 29km and turn off at Osmanville. Cross the village and at the round-about, take the D514 towards Grandcamp-Maisy for 4km. Then turn left towards Géfosse-Fontenay. Continue for 800m and the manor is on the left, just before the church and with the lake by its entrance.

Michel & Dany
BERNARD

'Le Clos de St-Laurent'

St-Laurent-du-Mont

14340 CAMBREMER

Tel: (0) 2 31 63 47 04/
06 03 46 32 26

Fax: (0) 2 31 63 46 92

Residence of
Outstanding Character

22 km - S E -
CABOURG
St-Laurent-du-Mont:
hosts can collect
from station,
railway station: 12km
airport: 28km

14.12 CABOURG

A comfortable 18th century house, furnished with exquisite taste, 20 mins. from Deauville. From the garden there is a panoramic view over the valley and 'la Suisse Normande'. Excursions, delicious home-made jam, and pleasant hours spent at the table with Michel and Dany will add to your enjoyment.

PROPERTY

off-street parking, extensive grounds, tv lounge, hosts have pets, pets not accepted, dinner available, babies welcome, free cot, 2 nights minimum stay: (01/07–31/08), golf course 25km, sea or lake watersports 25km

Basic English spoken

——Exit Cabourg, on the A13. Take the D49 towards Carrefour St-Jean (N13) where you turn left on to the D50 towards Cambremer. The house is on the bend as you go up the hill, on the right.

PRICE STRUCTURE

2 Bedrooms and 1 Suite and 1 Apartment

Jaune: television, bathroom with wc, double bed: FF280

Orange: television, bathroom with wc along corridor, double bed + en-suite room Rose: double bed, single bed: FF280 (2 people) FF660 (5 people)

Bleuet: television, shower room with wc, double bed: FF280

La Maison de José: bridal room, lounge, television, kitchen, shower room with wc, double bed + en-suite room twin beds + en-suite room single bed: FF380 (2 people) FF700 (5 people)

Extra Bed: FF100

Capacity: 14 people

Samantha ACRES

'La Caillerie'

14240 CAHAGNES

Tel: 02 31 25 27 37

lacaillerie@aol.com

Residence of
Outstanding Character

32 km - S W - CAEN
Cahagnes:
railway station: 20km
airport: 15km
car essential

PRICE STRUCTURE

4 Bedrooms

shower room with wc,
double bed: FF370

shower room with wc,
double bed, single bed:
FF370 (2 people)
FF500 (3 people)

Suite familiale: shower
room with wc, bathroom,
double bed, 2 single beds:
FF400 (2 people)
FF550 (4 people)

Mezzanine: lounge,
television, shower room
with wc, bathroom, double
bed, 2 single beds: FF400 (2
people) FF550 (4 people)

Extra Bed: FF80

Reduction: 3 nights and
groups

Capacity: 13 people

14.39 CAEN

This place is in the heart of lush countryside of hedges, apple trees and meadow grass. Samantha is English and will welcome you with a lovely smile to her large, restored farmhouse dating from the 18th century. In the grounds there is a stream, a children's play area and a remarkable little house. An ideal base for visiting Normandy.

PROPERTY

private parking, garden, tv lounge, hosts have pets, babies welcome, free cot, non-smoking, hiking 3km, cycling 3km, fishing 4km, sea or lake watersports 13km, golf course 15km, interesting flora 15km, riversports 15km, gliding 15km, bird-watching 20km

Fluent English spoken

——From Caen, take the N175 towards Villedieu-les-Poêles and Mont-St-Michel. At Villers-Bocage, turn right on to the D71 towards Caumont-l'Eventé. After you have gone through the village of Amayé-sur-Seulles, take the third road on the left and, after 100m, left again into their road.

Martine & Boris
BEAUCUSE-FEREY

'Le Nid'

3, rue Jean Mermoz

14150 OUISTREHAM

Tel: 02 31 36 09 09

Fax: (0) 2 31 36 09 09

Private Home

15 km - N - CAEN
Ouistreham:
ferry port: 1km
airport: 20km

CAEN

14.40 CAEN

Our regular readers will remember Martine and Boris. They have now moved from their house at Le Havre and have finished settling in to their new home near to Caen. This large house is wonderful, in the centre of a resort, mid-way between the medieval village, the beach and the harbour. Book early.

PROPERTY ✹✹✹

private parking, garden, tv lounge, hosts have pets, pets not accepted, 15 years old minimum age, hiking, cycling, sea or lake watersports, golf course 10km, bird-watching 10km, interesting flora 20km

Fluent English spoken

—Contact your hosts in advance for detailed directions.

PRICE STRUCTURE

**2 Bedrooms and
1 Apartment**
Chez Nous – Bleue: lounge, television, shower room with wc, double bed: FF450

Chez Nous – Rose: shower room with wc, double bed: FF350

Studio (30m2): lounge, television, telephone, kitchen, shower room with wc, bathroom, double bed: FF600

Capacity: 6 people

Françoise VALLE

'Le Clos St Hymer'

Chemin des Toutains -
Le Torquesne

14130 PONT L'EVEQUE

Tel: (0) 2 31 61 99 15

Fax: (0) 2 31 61 99 36

Private Home

15 km - S -
DEAUVILLE
Le Torquesne: hosts
can collect from
station,
railway station: 3km
airport: 14km

PRICE STRUCTURE

3 Bedrooms
(2 rooms) shower room
with wc, double bed: FF320

third room: bathroom with
wc, double bed, single bed:
FF400

Studio: 2 nights minimum
stay, television, kitchen,
shower room with wc,
double bed, single bed:
FF400

Extra Bed: FF100

Capacity: 6 people

14.09 DEAUVILLE

Françoise used to own the Moulin at St-Hymer. She still loves the Pays d'Auge, with its manor houses and stud farms, and her new home is just as good and the welcome just as warm as before. On sale: Home-made jam. For bookings between 15 November and 15 February, it is essential to write in advance.

PROPERTY

off-street parking, extensive grounds, tv lounge, hosts have pets, pets not accepted, dinner available, babies welcome, free cot, hiking, cycling, golf course 4km, sea or lake watersports 5km

Adequate English spoken

——From Deauville, take the A13 and then the N117 as far as Pont-l'Evêque. Then take the D48 towards Lisieux. At the Breuil-en-Auge junction, turn right on to the D264 as far as Le Torquesne. Turn right after the church and go right to the end of the chemin des Toutains.

Pascal & Janneke MARIE

'Manoir de la Plane'

14130 ST-GATIEN-DES-BOIS

Tel: (0) 2 31 89 08 47/
06 85 92 46 05

Château

11 km - E -
DEAUVILLE
St-Gatien-des-Bois:
hosts can collect
from station,
railway station: 10km
airport: 5km

14.34 DEAUVILLE

Janneke and Pascal, a Franco-Dutch couple, welcome you to
their large manor house, dating from the turn of the 20th
century, between Honfleur and Deauville. The setting is quite
special, and you will enjoy the space, quiet and relaxing
atmosphere of this place, which is set in 2 ha of ancient
woodland and fruit trees. A collection of watercolours has
been used to decorate the bedroom walls. On sale: Paintings.

PROPERTY

private parking, extensive grounds, babies welcome, free cot,
1 shared shower room with wc, hiking, cycling, hunting, golf
course 4km, fishing 4km, sea or lake watersports 4km

——From the A13, Exit Deauville - Honfleur. Head towards
'Honfleur Hôpital' for 8km. The manor is the first property
on the left before the hospital.

PRICE STRUCTURE

**4 Bedrooms and
1 Apartment**
first room: bathroom with
wc, double bed: FF350

second room: bathroom
with wc, double bed, single
bed: FF400 (2 people)
FF450 (3 people)

third room: lounge,
bathroom with wc, double
bed: FF400

fourth room: bathroom with
wc, double bed: FF400

Apartment: lounge, kitchen,
bathroom with wc, double
bed + en-suite room shower
room with wc, double bed +
en-suite room 5 single beds:
FF600 (2 people)
FF1200 (9 people)

Extra Bed: FF50

Reduction: 3 nights

Capacity: 18 people

Patricia WALLIS

'Domaine de la Hamberie'

Fresné-la-Mère

14700 FALAISE

Tel: (0) 2 31 90 34 61

Fax: (0) 2 31 90 34 61

Private Home

NORMANDIE

FALAISE

5 km - E - FALAISE
Fresné-la-Mère:
airport: 45km
car essential

PRICE STRUCTURE

2 Bedrooms and 1 Suite
Double room: shower room
with wc, double bed: FF300

Twin room: shower room
with wc, twin beds: FF300

Family Suite: shower room
with wc, twin beds + en-suite
room twin beds:
FF480 (4 people)

Extra Bed: FF50
Reduction: groups

Capacity: 8 people

14.20 FALAISE

Here, a very friendly English couple from Yorkshire welcome you to their restored farmhouse. You will spend pleasant hours around their dinner table. They have a large swimming pool and sand-pit for children, plus 4 gîtes on the farm.

PROPERTY

off-street parking, garden, lounge, hosts have pets, dinner available, babies welcome, free cot, hiking 3km, fishing 6km, golf course 25km, riversports 35km, sea or lake watersports 40km

Fluent English spoken

——At Falaise, take the D63 towards Trun. As you enter Fresné-la-Mère, turn right before the level-crossing, and then take the second on the left. Cross over the level-crossing, and continue right to the end.

Henri & Betty
REVIGNAS

'La Tortue et le Tamaris'

10 rue du Chanoine
Porée

27300 BERNAY

Tel: 02 32 44 25 65/
06 12 87 58 66

Residence of
Outstanding Character

30 km - E - LISIEUX
Bernay:
railway station: -
airport: 150km

27.10 LISIEUX

'La Tortue et le Tamaris'… just the name is the start of a fairytale. This house is on the holiday route, in a sunny town on the edge of green slopes. Betty and Henri's welcome is what you always hope to find: warm, jolly, friendly and genuine. There is a good choice of restaurants nearby and your hosts can organise cycle tours on request.

PROPERTY

private parking, garden, tv lounge, pets not accepted, babies welcome, free cot, non-smoking, 1 shared shower room with wc, hiking, cycling, fishing, golf course 30km

Adequate English spoken

PRICE STRUCTURE

2 Bedrooms
Tamaris: double bed,
2 single beds, cot:
FF280 (2 people)
FF380 (4 people)

Tortue: double bed: FF220

Capacity: 6 people

——Head for the station at Bernay and then follow the signs to 'Centre-Ville', La Poste, then towards Thiberville and take the first on the right. Then take a sharp turn left, then right and follow the signs.

Jacques & Marie-Hélène
DECARSIN

'Le Prieuré des
Fontaines'

les Préaux

27500 PONT-AUDEMER

Tel: (0) 2 32 56 07 78
Fax: (0) 2 32 57 45 83

www.prieure-des-
fontaines.fr

Residence of
Outstanding Character

5 km - S W - PONT-
AUDEMER
LES PREAUX:
airport: 25km

PRICE STRUCTURE

4 Bedrooms and 1 Suite

Each room: telephone,
bathroom with wc

ground floor – Nénuphar:
bridal room, lounge, double
bed, single bed: FF650 (2
people) FF750 (3 people)

Capucine: twin beds: FF420

Marmotte: double bed,
single bed: FF390 (2
people) FF490 (3 people)

Cendrillon: double bed:
FF390

Familiale: shower,
washbasin, double bed,
2 single beds + en-suite
room washbasin, 2 single
beds: FF690 (6 people)

Extra Bed: FF40/100

Reduction: 1/10–1/05 and
4 nights

Capacity: 14 people

27.05 PONT-AUDEMER

**Jacques has wonderfully restored this 17th-century building,
with its ground floor that opens on to a swimming pool and a
garden, landscaped with great skill. A great place to stop in
Normandy.**

PROPERTY

private parking, extensive grounds, tv lounge, hosts have pets,
pets not accepted, telephone, dinner available, packed lunch,
non-smoking, swimming pool, cycling, mushroom-picking,
fishing 5km, sea or lake watersports 5km, golf course 20km

Basic English spoken

——In Pont Audemer, take the D139 towards Lisieux. The
house is on this road (signposted).

Michel & Françoise
LETELLIER

le Village

27350 ROUGEMONTIER

Tel: (0) 2 32 56 84 80

Fax: (0) 2 32 56 84 80

Residence of
Outstanding Character

20 km - E - PONT-
AUDEMER
Rougemontier:
airport: 40km
car essential

27.06 PONT-AUDEMER

A lovely welcome awaits in this substantial house with antique furniture, in very pleasant grounds. It is on the edge of the forest of Brotonne, where you can go hiking or riding. Easy to find on the N175. Enjoy their home-made jam and cakes. On sale: Home-made jam.

PROPERTY

private parking, extensive grounds, tv lounge, hosts have pets, pets not accepted, dinner available, babies welcome, free cot, closed: 25/12 & 1/01, hiking, fishing 3km, golf course 18km

Adequate English spoken

PRICE STRUCTURE

3 Bedrooms
Rose: shower room with wc, double bed: FF300

Verte: bathroom with wc, double bed: FF300

Bleue: bathroom with wc, double bed: FF300

Extra Bed: FF70
Reduction: 1/10–31/03 and 5 nights

Capacity: 6 people

——In Pont-Audemer, take the N175 towards Rouen for 15km. In the village, the house is on the left.

Jacqueline MESNIL

'Le Château'

27230 ST-AUBIN-DE-
SCELLON

Tel: (0) 2 32 46 85 41

Château

25 km - S -
PONT-AUDEMER
St-Aubin-de-Scellon:
airport: 25km
car essential

PRICE STRUCTURE

2 Bedrooms
Abricot: bridal room,
bathroom with wc, double
bed: FF330

Soleil Levant: shower, wc,
double bed: FF300

Extra Bed: FF50

Capacity: 4 people

27.07 PONT-AUDEMER

A small, 19th-century château, surrounded by delightfully verdant grounds, situated in a small village. Ideal for a stopover to and from Britain. There are also plenty of historic places, manors and châteaux to be visited.

PROPERTY

private parking, extensive grounds, tv lounge, babies welcome, free cot, closed: 15/09–01/04, sea or lake watersports 15km, golf course 20km

Basic English spoken

――――In Pont-Audemer, take the D810 towards Bernay. In Lieurey, take the D28 towards Thiberville. In St-Aubin-de-Scellon, the château is near to the church, opposite the D41.

Marilyn & Richard
TUBBS

'La Basse Grézilière'

St-Georges-de-
Reintembault

35420 LOUVIGNÉ-DU-
DESERT

Tel: (0) 2 99 97 10 19

Fax: (0) 2 99 97 10 19

Residence of
Outstanding Character

27 km - S -
AVRANCHES
St-Georges-de-
Reintembault:
railway station: 20km
airport: 80km
car essential

35.34 AVRANCHES

On the border between Brittany and Normandy, this is a beautiful 17th-century farmhouse which your English hosts have renovated with good taste. They have preserved the original oak beams, the fireplace and the bread oven. Take a good road map so that you are sure to find it, as it really is a wonderful place to stay! Your hosts only accept reservations for two or up to four guests travelling together.

PROPERTY

private parking, garden, tv lounge, hosts have pets, pets not accepted, non-smoking, 5 years old minimum age, hunting 2km, fishing 10km, sea or lake watersports 10km, interesting flora 14km, golf course 70km

Fluent English spoken

——A84, Exit 32 St-James. Then take the D30 towards St-Hilaire-du-Harcourt. As you leave St-James, take the D230 towards St-Georges-de-Reintembault. Near to the centre of this town, turn left on to the D115 towards Hamelin. Take the second road on the left, signposted to La Basse Grézilière.

PRICE STRUCTURE

2 Bedrooms
bathroom with wc along corridor, double bed + room twin beds:
FF275 (2 people)
FF550 (4 people)

Capacity: 4 people

Claude & Patrice
WAGNER

'Manoir de la Croix'

Le Gros Chêne

50530 MONTVIRON

Tel: (0) 2 33 60 68 30

Fax: (0) 2 33 60 69 21

Residence of
Outstanding Character

8 km - N W -
AVRANCHES
Montviron:
railway station: 9km
airport: 35km
car essential

NORMANDIE

AVRANCHES (Mont-St-Michel)

PRICE STRUCTURE

2 Bedrooms and 2 Suites
Rebecca: lounge, television,
bathroom with wc, shower,
double bed (queen size) +
en-suite room single bed:
FF430 (2 people)
FF520 (3 people)

Marie-Louise: lounge,
television, bathroom with
wc, shower, double bed +
en-suite room single bed:
FF430 (2 people)
FF520 (3 people)

Eugénie & Pauline:
television, bathroom with
wc, shower, double bed:
FF320

Extra Bed: FF80
Capacity: 10 people

50.26 AVRANCHES

Claude and Patrice have finished restoring their manor
house, dating from the 19th century, to the highest standards,
with flair and excellent taste. The bedrooms are spacious and
most have individual sun terraces. This manor is uniquely
situated in the bay of Mont-St-Michel, which makes it the
ideal base for enjoying the beaches and the sea, as well as
for visiting the outstanding historic sites in this area.

PROPERTY

off-street parking, extensive grounds, tv lounge, hosts have
pets, pets not accepted, non-smoking, hiking 8km, sea or lake
watersports 8km

Fluent English spoken

——From Avranches, take the D973 towards Granville. From
the village of Montviron cross the level-crossing, and after 1km
the 'manoir' is at the crossroads. Take the road to the left of
the property and turn right into the car park.

Geneviève & Jean PICOT

'La Ramade'

2, Route de la Côte - Marcey-les-Grèves

50300 AVRANCHES

Tel: (0) 2 33 58 27 40

Private Home

3 km - N W - AVRANCHES Marcey-les-Grèves: hosts can collect from station, railway station: 1km airport: 70km car essential

50.28 AVRANCHES

This large house in pink granite is situated between the Normandy beaches and Mont-St-Michel. It is easy to find (on the main road). The beautiful rooms have been completely renovated and are all sound-proofed. Geneviève is an attentive hostess.

PROPERTY

private parking, extensive grounds, tv lounge, pets not accepted, telephone, babies welcome, free cot, wc, closed: 3/11–1/03, hiking, cycling, fishing 10km, interesting flora 10km, mushroom-picking 10km, bird-watching 10km, gliding 18km, sea or lake watersports 20km

Adequate English spoken

——In Avranches head towards Granville. Just after the bridge take the CD911 towards Jullouville. The property is on the right.

PRICE STRUCTURE

5 Bedrooms
first room: shower, bathroom, wc, double bed, twin beds: FF340 (2 people) FF440 (4 people)

second room: shower room with wc, twin beds: FF340

third room: shower, wc, double bed. FF300

fourth room: shower room with wc, double bed, single bed: FF340 (2 people) FF400 (3 people)

fifth room: shower room with wc, double bed: FF340

Extra Bed: FF70
Reduction: 5 nights
Capacity: 13 people

Charles & Jacqueline
RENET

Le Bourg - Biville

50440 BEAUMONT-LA-
HAGUE

Tel: (0) 2 33 52 76 62

Private Home

18 km - W -
CHERBOURG
Biville: hosts can
collect from station,
railway station: 18km
airport: 30km
——At Cherbourg,
take the D901
towards Beaumont.
Turn left on to the
D37 towards
Vasteville then right
on to the D118
towards Biville. The
house is on the left,
opposite the school
(signposted).

50.04 CHERBOURG

Here at Jacqueline's place, you will find the atmosphere of the nice little family guesthouses of old. Biville is a small town, known for its beautiful sandy beaches. Public tennis courts are opposite the house.

PROPERTY

private parking, garden, tv lounge, hosts have pets, dinner available, packed lunch, kitchen, babies welcome, free cot, 1shared shower room, tennis court, hiking, sea or lake watersports

Adequate English spoken

PRICE STRUCTURE
6 Bedrooms

shower, wc, washbasin, double bed: FF220

washbasin, double bed: FF200

shower, wc, washbasin, double bed: FF250

shower, wc, washbasin, double bed, single bed: FF250 (2 people) FF350 (3 people)

shower, washbasin, double bed: FF220

shower, wc, washbasin, twin beds: FF250

Extra Bed: FF80

Reduction: 10 nights and groups

Capacity: 13 people

Marie-France CAILLET

'Le Manoir de la Fèverie'

Ste-Geneviève

50760 BARFLEUR

Tel: (0) 2 33 54 33 53

Fax: (0) 2 33 22 12 50

Château

CHERBOURG
Barfleur:
ferry port: 25km
airport: 15km
car essential

50.17 CHERBOURG

If you are going to Normandy, be sure to do whatever it takes to spend a few days chez Marie-France. This old manor will live up to your wildest dreams. The bedrooms are fantastic, Marie-France is charming and, if you love horses, there is a bonus as they are horse breeders.

PROPERTY

private parking, garden, tv lounge, hosts have pets, babies welcome, free cot, hiking, cycling, mushroom-picking, fishing 3km, sea or lake watersports 3km, golf course 25km

PRICE STRUCTURE

3 Bedrooms
La Tour: shower room with wc, double bed: FF300

Coquelicot: shower room with wc, twin beds: FF380

Madras: bathroom with wc, twin beds. FF380

Extra Bed: FF100
Reduction: 4 nights

Capacity: 6 people

——At Cherbourg, take the D901 towards Barfleur. 1km after Tocqueville, turn right on to the D10 and follow the signs. From Quettehou, take the first on the left and follow the signs. From Barfleur, take the D25 and the second on the right and follow the signs.

Olésia DERIEUX

'Manoir du Roueur'

Fauville

50480 STE-MÈRE-EGLISE

Tel: (0) 2 33 41 30 99

manoir-du-roueur @wanadoo.fr www.storm-loader.com/ manoir-roueur/roueurfr.html

Château

35 km - S E - CHERBOURG
Ste-Mère-Eglise: hosts can collect from station, railway station: 10km airport: 40km

PRICE STRUCTURE

5 Bedrooms

ground floor: television, shower room with wc, double bed, twin beds: FF230 (2 people) FF320 (4 people)

first floor: television, shower room with wc, double bed, twin beds: FF230 (2 people) FF320 (4 people)

television, shower room with wc, double bed, single bed: FF230 (2 people) FF270 (3 people)

(2 rooms) shower room with wc, double bed: FF230

Extra Bed: FF50

Capacity: 13 people

50.24 CHERBOURG

Olésia, who has just come back from the Ukraine to live in her beautifully restored manor house again, will give you a really warm welcome. Your accommodation is in the 16th-century outbuildings. After dinner, she will be happy to show you videos on Normandy and the D-Day landings. This village was at the heart of the landings, and the bell tower has become very famous. On sale: Farmhouse cider.

PROPERTY

off-street parking, garden, dinner available, babies welcome, free cot, wheelchair access, hiking, cycling, fishing 4km, bird-watching 7km, golf course 9km, sea or lake watersports 10km

Adequate English spoken

——At Cherbourg, N13 towards Caen. From the centre of Ste-Mère-Eglise head towards Carentan following the signs, for 1.5km.

Laurence LE COUTOUR

'Le Valciot'

14 Chemin des Costils

50340 SIOUVILLE-HAGUE

Tel: (0) 2 33 52 93 15

Château

25 km - S W - CHERBOURG
Siouville-Hague:
ferry port: 25km
airport: 40km
car essential

50.32 CHERBOURG

This young couple welcome you to their family manor house, only 300m from the sea. Climb the impressive staircase to reach your well-equipped room, with a view over the sea and garden. There is a ferry to the Channel Islands 2 km away. Excellent value for money.

PROPERTY

off-street parking, garden, hosts have pets, dinner available, babies welcome, free cot, hiking, cycling, fishing, sea or lake watersports, interesting flora 15km, gliding 15km, golf course 22km

Basic English spoken

——From Cherbourg take the D904 as far as Les Pieux, and then the D23 towards Siouville. In this village, facing the cemetery, turn left and then turn right at the 'Stop' sign. Then take the first on the right. The house is 500m further on, on the right.

PRICE STRUCTURE

**1 Bedroom and
3 Apartments**

Tourelle: bathroom with wc, double bed: FF260

Bureau: kitchen, bathroom with wc, double bed: FF300

Les Meurtrières: kitchen, shower room with wc, double bed, single bed: FF260 (2 people)
FF290 (3 people)

La Mansarde: lounge, kitchen, bathroom with wc, double bed: FF300

Extra Bed:50FF

Reduction: 01/09–20/12 & 05/01–30/06
and 4 nights

Capacity: 9 people

Pat & Tony BROOKER

'Le Perchoir'

Ste-Croix

50630 TEURTHEVILLE-
BOCAGE

Tel: (0) 2 33 54 67 57/
06 03 10 93 23

Fax: (0) 2 33 54 67 57

brookerpat@wanadoo.fr

Private Home

18 km - S E -
CHERBOURG
Teurtheville-Bocage:
ferry port: 18km
airport: 12km

PRICE STRUCTURE

3 Bedrooms
first room: double bed,
2 single beds:
FF300 (2 people)
FF500 (4 people)

second room: double bed,
single bed:
FF300 (2 people)
FF400 (3 people)

third room: double bed:
FF300

Capacity: 9 people

50.34 CHERBOURG

Only 30 mins. from Cherbourg, Le Perchoir is the ideal place for an overnight stop. Your hosts are English, and their house, in the heart of the country, is full of owls – stone owls, wooden owls and even some real ones in the barn. Children will love playing with the chickens and goats. There is wonderful seafood to be enjoyed only 5 mins. away. On sale: Eggs.

PROPERTY

private parking, garden, tv lounge, hosts have pets, pets not accepted, telephone, dinner available, babies welcome, free cot, non-smoking, 1 shared shower room with wc, hiking, fishing 6km, sea or lake watersports 7km, riversports 10km, cycling 12km, golf course 18km

Fluent English spoken

———From Cherbourg, D911 towards St-Pierre-Eglise. At Hamel, right on to the D24 to Le Theil for 5km. Turn left on to the D56 towards Quéthou for 7km. Follow signs to 'Le Perchoir' for 2.5km. (From Valognes, take the D902 towards Quethou for 10km. Left on to the D119 towards Teurtheville.)

Regula & Denis COEPEL

'Château des Poteries'

50310 FRESVILLE

Tel: (0) 2 33 95 02 03

Fax: (0) 2 33 95 02 03

Regula.Coepel
@wanadoo.fr

Private Home

30 km - S E - CHERBOURG
Fresville:
railway station: 12km
airport: 30km
car essential

50.38 CHERBOURG

This 19th-century château has magnificent grounds, which you should not miss visiting, with little bridges and a large pond beside the ancient moat. It is situated in the National Park des Marais du Cotentin et du Bessin, just 8km from the sea and 5km from St-Mère-Eglise. Golf and riding can be arranged locally. Fleur de Soleil member.

PRICE STRUCTURE

2 Bedrooms
Bleue: shower room with wc, twin beds: FF280

Rose: shower room with wc, twin beds, single bed:
FF280 (2 people)
FF310 (3 people)

Capacity: 5 people

PROPERTY

✹ ✹ ✹

private parking, garden, pets not accepted, hiking, cycling, bird-watching 8km, sea or lake watersports 8km, golf course 10km, fishing 10km

English spoken

——On the N13 Caen-Cherbourg road, turn off at Fresville. Turn right at the church, and after 800m turn left, and continue for 200m.

Odile & Didier VIEJO

'Manoir de Bunehou'

50340 ST-GERMAIN-LE-
GAILLARD

Tel: 02 33 93 54 48

didier.viejo@wanadoo.fr

Château

25 km - S W -
CHERBOURG
St-Germain-le-
Gaillard:
ferry port: 25km
airport: 25km
car essential

PRICE STRUCTURE

1 Apartment
wheelchair access,
television, telephone,
kitchen, shower room with
wc, double bed: FF310

Extra Bed: FF70

Capacity: 2 people

50.41 CHERBOURG

The location on its own is worth 3 'suns'! Situated in the countryside but close to the coast, several buildings dating from the 14th and 17th centuries make up this manor, surrounded by a magical garden where each plant is listed and labelled. The apartment integrates beautifully with the style of the place. Odile goes out of her way to make your stay as pleasant as possible. The boats leave for excursions to Jersey and Guernsey only 10km away.

PROPERTY

off-street parking, extensive grounds, pets not accepted,
kitchen, babies welcome, free cot, non-smoking, wheelchair
access, hiking, cycling 5km, sea or lake watersports 5km,
gliding 16km, interesting flora 20km

Basic English spoken

——From Cherbourg take the D924 towards Le Carteret. 1km
after Les Pieux, turn left on to the D131 for St-Germain.
Continue towards Le Vrétôt as far as the manor, which is on
the left.

Hélène POSLOUX

'La Moinerie de Haut'

Les Hauts Champs

50200 NICORPS

Tel: (0) 2 33 45 30 56

Fax: (0) 2 33 07 60 21

Residence of
Outstanding Character

4 km - S -
COUTANCES
Nicorps: hosts can
collect from station,
railway station: 5km
airport: 80km
car essential

50.21 COUTANCES

Hélène is sweet and pleasant. She bakes delicious croissants
and muffins, and her husband takes part in gymkhanas. The
farmhouse has been restored with excellent taste. Make sure
you can handle the rather steep staircase and if you can, stay
several days to really get the most out of this lovely place.

PROPERTY

off-street parking, garden, tv lounge, hosts have pets, dinner
available, babies welcome, free cot, riding, hiking, cycling,
hunting, mushroom-picking, riversports 6km, golf course
10km, fishing 10km, sea or lake watersports 10km,
gliding 10km

Adequate English spoken

——At Coutances, follow signs to Villedieu-les-Poëles (D7) for
2km. Then turn left on to the D27 towards Nicorps. Continue
for 2km as far as the signpost 'Les Hauts Champs'.

PRICE STRUCTURE

**3 Bedrooms and
1 Apartment**

Franck: along corridor
shower room with wc, twin
beds: FF200

Nicolas: shower room with
wc, double bed: FF200

Attic – Frédérique: twin
beds, single bed (child-size):
FF150 (2 people)
FF180 (3 people)

Apartment: 2 nights
minimum stay, lounge,
kitchen, shower room with
wc, double bed: FF250

Extra Bed: FF50

Reduction: 1/11–1/03 and
2 nights

Capacity: 9 people

Jacqueline MICONNET

'Le Clos Serena'

Les Landes

50320 ST-LÉGER

Tel: 02 33 90 63 46

Fax: (0) 2 33 90 63 46

Residence of
Outstanding Character

12 km - S E -
GRANVILLE
St-Léger:
airport: 100km

50.31 GRANVILLE

This is an old house near the 12th-century Lucerne Abbey. It is in a very peaceful location, where you can go walking in the forest or by the sea. One room has been adapted for disabled people. On sale: Cider, Calvados.

PRICE STRUCTURE
3 Bedrooms and 2 Suites

Marie-Louise: bathroom with wc, double bed, single bed: FF220 (2 people) FF280 (3 people)
Gaelian: wheelchair access, kitchen, shower room with wc, double bed, single bed: FF220 (2 people) FF280 (3 people)
Tiphaine: bathroom with wc, double bed, single bed: FF220 (2 people) FF280 (3 people)
Annaik: shower room with wc, double bed + en-suite room Claude: double bed, single bed: FF220 (2 people) FF500 (5 people)
Maxime: bathroom with wc, double bed, single bed + en-suite room Nathan: 2 double beds: FF220 (2 people) FF620 (7 people)

Extra Bed:60FF
Capacity: 21 people

PROPERTY

off-street parking, garden, tv lounge, hosts have pets, telephone, kitchen, babies welcome, free cot, wheelchair access, fishing 1km, mushroom-picking 1km, hiking 2km, golf course 10km, sea or lake watersports 10km

Fluent English spoken

——From Granville, take the D973 towards Avranches. After 4km, turn left on to the D309 and follow the signs for the 'Abbaye de la Lucerne'. 'Clos Serena' is 900m from the abbey.

Madeleine
STRACQUADANIO

'Le Vieux Presbystère'

35610 VIEUX-VIEL

Tel: (0) 2 99 48 65 29

Fax: (0) 2 99 48 65 29

Residence of
Outstanding Character

13 km - S - MONT-
ST-MICHEL
Vieux-Viel: hosts can
collect from station,
railway station: 20km
airport: 50km
car essential

35.06 MONT-ST-MICHEL

In the heart of the Bay of Mont-St-Michel, Jean and Madeleine will welcome you with charm and kindness to their 17th-century presbytery, with its beautiful interior furnished with antiques. It is well worth the detour, not least for the wonderful cooking (their 'canard en cocotte' is a master-piece). On sale: Wine.

PROPERTY

private parking, garden, tv lounge, hosts have pets, pets not accepted, dinner available, packed lunch, babies welcome, free cot, closed: 15/01–30/01, mushroom-picking 4km, hiking 5km, cycling 5km, golf course 15km, sea or lake watersports 30km

Basic English spoken

——In Pontorson, take the N176 towards Dol-de-Bretagne, then turn left on to the D219 towards Sougéal where you turn right towards Vieux-Viel. The house is by the church.

PRICE STRUCTURE

5 Bedrooms

ground floor – Les Nones: shower room with wc, washbasin, 2 double beds: FF250 (2 people) FF420 (4 people)

Baldaquin-Les Papes: shower room with wc, washbasin, double bed, single bed: FF260 (2 people) FF390 (3 people)

Right wing – Le Moine: shower room with wc, washbasin, double bed: FF250

Les Curés: bathroom with wc along corridor, double bed + room ess Vicaires: bathroom with wc along corridor, 2 single beds: FF250 (2 people) FF380 (4 people)

Extra Bed: FF70

Capacity: 14 people

M. F. BARRÈRE & Alain
SCHROTTER

'Château de La Ballue'

35560 BAZOUGES-LA-
PÉROUSE

Tel: (0) 2 99 97 47 86

Fax: (0) 2 99 97 47 70

Château

20 km - S - MONT-
ST-MICHEL
Bazouges-la-Pérouse:
hosts can collect
from station,
railway station: 12km
airport: 30km

35.25 MONT-ST-MICHEL

From the windows, you will admire the beautiful gardens 'à la française'. The large bedrooms are spacious and very comfortable. Your hosts will let you try some very refined 17th-century dishes and, in the summer, famous artists exhibit their work here. On sale: Books, modern art.

PRICE STRUCTURE

4 Bedrooms and 1 Suite

Victor Hugo: shower room with wc, double bed, 2 single beds: FF850

Diane: bathroom with wc, double bed, single bed: FF750

Perse: bathroom with wc, twin beds, single bed: FF750 (2 people) FF950 (3 people)

France: lounge, bathroom with wc, double bed, 2 single beds + en-suite room twin beds: FF950 (2 people) FF1300 (6 people)

Florence: bathroom with wc, double bed, 2 single beds: FF850

Extra Bed: FF200

Capacity: 20 people

PROPERTY

private parking, extensive grounds, tv lounge, hosts have pets, pets not accepted, babies welcome, free cot, 2 nights minimum stay, closed: 01/01–31/01, hiking, cycling, hunting, mushroom-picking, interesting flora 15km, golf course 18km, fishing 20km, sea or lake watersports 20km, bird-watching 25km

English spoken

——From Mont-St-Michel, take the N175 towards Rennes and, at Antrain, follow the signs to the château (Monument Historique).

Régis de ROQUEFEUIL

'Château de Bouceel'

50240 VERGONCEY

Tel: 02 33 48 34 61

Fax: (0) 2 33 48 16 26

chateaudebouceel
@wanadoo.fr

www.chateaudebouceel.
com

Château

14 km - S E - MONT-
ST-MICHEL
Vergoncey:
railway station: 38km
airport: 60km
car essential

50.39 MONT-ST-MICHEL

This very comfortable château, which is a listed historic monument, has been in the same family since 1763. It is 16km from Mont-St-Michel. You will feel its history as you climb the grand staircase under the watchful eye of the ancestors of the Count and Countess, who maintain the family tradition of hospitality. Be sure to stroll in the romantic, English-style grounds, with their lake, island, chapel and ancient trees, one of which was donated by George Washington.

PROPERTY

✳ ✳ ✳ ✳

private parking, extensive grounds, tv lounge, hosts have pets, babies welcome, free cot, hiking, fishing, cycling 15km, sea or lake watersports 30km, golf course 38km

Fluent English spoken

From Pontorson, take the N175 towards Avranches for 500m. Turn right on to the D30 towards La-Croix-Avranchin for 10km. Turn left on to the D363 to Vergoncey.

PRICE STRUCTURE

2 Bedrooms and 2 Suites

Oncle François – Baldaquin & BA-ME: shower room with wc, bathroom, (queen size) double bed: FF800

Nelly: shower room with wc, twin beds + en-suite room single bed:
FF750 (2 people)
FF850 (3 people)

Le Petit Salon: shower room with wc, bathroom, double bed + en-suite room single bed: FF900 (2 people)
FF900 (3 people)

Extra Bed: FF100

Capacity: 10 people

Danielle VOISIN TCHEN

'Les Vieilles Digues'

Route du Mont-St-Michel

50170 BEAUVOIR

Tel: 02 33 58 55 30-06 13
74 11 73

Private Home

4 km - S - MONT-ST-MICHEL
Beauvoir:
railway station: 5km
airport: 45km
car essential

PRICE STRUCTURE

6 Bedrooms
(4 rooms) wheelchair access, shower room with wc, double bed: FF325

shower room with wc along corridor, double bed, single bed: FF325 (2 people) FF425 (3 people)

Vue sur le Mont: shower room with wc along corridor, double bed, single bed: FF325 (2 people) FF425 (3 people)

Extra Bed: FF100
Reduction: 1/11–1/04 and groups

Capacity: 14 people

50.40 MONT-ST-MICHEL

Danielle and Kim are a Franco-Vietnamese couple, who are completely tri-lingual. They have combined their skills and cultures to great effect, to restore this large family home and give a warm welcome. The décor is elegant, the garden well-tended and there is a bar in the guests' lounge. The Coasnon river is a stone's throw from the house and there is a lovely walk along its banks for 3km as far as Mont-St-Michel.

PROPERTY

private parking, garden, tv lounge, pets not accepted, wheelchair access, hiking, cycling, fishing, bird-watching, mushroom-picking 15km, interesting flora 25km, riversports 25km, golf course 30km

Fluent English spoken

——From Pontarson, take the D976 towards Mont-St-Michel. It is the first house on the right as you leave Beauvoir. The house is set back from the main road.

50.42 MONT-ST-MICHEL

This majestic, impressive house is on a farm behind fields of carrots and potatoes. It has an uninterrupted view of the Mont-St-Michel from the garden, which is separated from the road by a thick hedge. Here, everything runs professionally and is well-organised. On sale: Cider, Pommeau, Calvados.

PROPERTY

off-street parking, garden, lounge, hosts have pets, wheelchair access, closed: 15/11–8/02, hiking, fishing, hunting, bird-watching, cycling 5km

PRICE STRUCTURE

5 Bedrooms and 1 Apartment

first room: wheelchair access, television, shower room with wc, double bed: FF290

second room: television, shower room with wc, 2 double beds, single bed: FF290 (2 people) FF545 (5 people)

third room: television, shower room with wc, double bed: FF290

fourth room: wheelchair access, television, shower room with wc, double bed, single bed: FF290 (2 people) FF375 (3 people)

fifth room: wheelchair access, television, shower room with wc, double bed, 2 single beds: FF290 (2 people) FF460 (4 people)

Apartment: wheelchair access, television, kitchen, shower room with wc, double bed, single bed: FF325 (2 people) FF410 (3 people)

Reduction: 9/02–1/05

Capacity: 19 people

Claudine BRAULT

'La Jacotière'

Ardevon

50170 PONTORSON

Tel: 02 33 60 22 94

Fax: (0) 2 33 60 20 48

lajocotière@wanadoo.fr

Working Farm

2 km - S - MONT-ST-MICHEL
Ardevon:
——When you are on the D976 Pontorson to Mont-St-Michel road, 7km from Pontorson turn right on to the D275. Continue for 300m and the farm is on the left.

Michel & Marie-Thérèse
GUESDON

'Au Jardin Fleuri'

Route de Servon -
2, La Mottaiserie

50220 CEAUX

Tel: (0) 2 33 70 97 29

Fax: (0) 2 33 70 97 29

aujardin@club-internet.fr

Private Home

10 km - E - MONT-
ST-MICHEL
Ceaux:
railway station: 10km
airport: 65km
car essential

MONT-ST-MICHEL (Avranches)

PRICE STRUCTURE

5 Bedrooms
first floor-first room & third
room & second floor-fifth
room: shower room with wc,
double bed: FF210

first floor-second room:
bathroom with wc, double
bed: FF210

second floor-fourth room:
television, shower room
with wc, double bed: FF210

Extra Bed:30FF

Capacity: 10 people

50.06 MONT-ST-MICHEL

**The charm of your hostess will make you want to spend
several nights here, in her stone-built house. Not far from
Mont-St-Michel and Avranches, the surroundings are relaxing
with a beautiful view. There is a restaurant 100m away.**

PROPERTY

off-street parking, garden, tv lounge, hosts have pets, hiking,
cycling, mushroom-picking, sea or lake watersports, fishing
3km, bird-watching 5km

Adequate English spoken

——Leaving Mont-St-Michel, turn left on to the D275 towards
Courtils then Ceaux. Opposite the 'Hotel du Petit Quinquin',
go in the direction of Servon for 50m. First entrance on the
right.

François & Catherine
TIFFAINE

'la Gautrais'

50240 ST-JAMES

Tel: (0) 2 33 48 31 86

Fax: (0) 2 33 48 58 17

Working Farm

20 km - S E - MONT-
ST-MICHEL
St-James:
airport: 60km
car essential

50.07 MONT-ST-MICHEL

This old house has been beautifully restored, with old beams and an open fireplace in the living room. Furnished with antiques, one of the bedrooms has a balcony. The terrace overlooks a large garden and the green valley beyond. Cycles may be hired.

PROPERTY ✳✳✳

private parking, garden, tv lounge, hosts have pets, pets not accepted, dinner available, kitchen, babies welcome, free cot, riding, hiking, cycling, fishing, sea or lake watersports 10km

Adequate English spoken

——On the A84, Exit 32, St-James. Follow signs to the supermarket 'SuperU' (on the D12) then, after 900m, you will see the sign 'Ferme la Gautrais'.

PRICE STRUCTURE

4 Bedrooms

Bleue: shower room with wc, bathroom, double bed, single bed:
FF200 (2 people)
FF270 (3 people)

Verte: shower room with wc, bathroom, double bed:
FF230

Balcon: bridal room, shower room with wc, bathroom, 2 double beds:
FF230 (2 people)
FF300 (4 people)

Frisette: kitchen, shower room with wc, bathroom, double bed, single bed:
FF230 (2 people)
FF300 (3 people)

Extra Bed: FF50

Reduction: 3 nights

Capacity: 12 people

Marie-Pierre
LEMOULAND

'La Ferme de la Ruette'

50220 DUCEY

Tel: (0) 2 33 70 95 90

Fax: (0) 2 33 70 95 90

Working Farm

8 km - E - MONT-ST-MICHEL
Bas Courtils:
airport: 70km
car essential

PRICE STRUCTURE

5 Bedrooms
first floor: (2 rooms)
shower, washbasin, double
bed: FF190

second floor – Mansardées :
(1 room) along corridor
bathroom, washbasin,
double bed: FF190

second floor – Mansardées:
(2 rooms) shower,
washbasin, 2 double beds:
FF190 (2 people)
FF260 (4 people)

Extra Bed: FF60

Capacity: 14 people

50.11 MONT-ST-MICHEL

We love Marie-Pierre, who is a kind, strong character. Hers is a classic Normandy stone farmhouse on a working farm specialising in rearing sheep on the salt marshes – well worth seeing. This place is deal for families on a budget. The family are members of a cycling club. On sale: Cider.

PROPERTY

off-street parking, garden, tv lounge, pets not accepted, kitchen, 2 wc, closed: 25/10-02/11, cycling, sea or lake watersports 1km

Basic English spoken

——Leaving Mont-St-Michel, turn left on to the D275 towards Courtils. In Bas-Courtils, take the D288 towards Roche-Torin for 200m. The farm is on the right.

Isabelle & Christian
FARDIN

'Ferme du Grand Rouet'

Le Grand Rouet

50220 JUILLEY

Tel: (0) 2 33 60 65 25

Fax: (0) 2 33 60 02 70

c.fardin@wanadoo.fr

Working Farm

15 km - S E - MONT-ST-MICHEL
Juilley:
railway station: 15km
airport: 70km
car essential

50.37 MONT-ST-MICHEL

This 150-year-old stone farmhouse is only 18km from Mont-St-Michel and is situated in the total quiet of the Normandy countryside. It has a delightful garden, with ducks and a pond. Apart from the dairy production, Christian and Isabelle raise horses. This is a great place in which to relax. For dinner, try the 'ferme auberge', only 3km away.

PROPERTY

off-street parking, extensive grounds, tv lounge, pets not accepted, kitchen, hiking, cycling, fishing, sea or lake watersports 32km

Basic English spoken

——From Mont-St-Michel, take the N175 towards Avranches (A84, Exit 33 to Ducey). Then head towards St-James, via the N998. Pass Juilley without going into the village and, after 1km, turn left on to the D566, signposted to 'La Ferme du Grand Rouet'.

PRICE STRUCTURE

4 Bedrooms
first room: shower room with wc along corridor, double bed: FF240

second room: shower room with wc, double bed: FF240

third room: shower room with wc, double bed, single bed: FF240 (2 people) FF290 (3 people)

fourth room: shower room with wc, double bed, 2 single beds: FF240 (2 people) FF340 (4 people)

Extra Bed: FF60
Capacity: 11 people

Hervé & Annick
LAGADEC

'Manoir de la Porte'

50870 STE-PIENCE

Tel: (0) 2 33 68 13 61

Fax: (0) 2 33 68 29 54

Château

NORMANDIE

10 km - S W -
VILLEDIEU-LES-
POELES
Ste-Pience:
railway station: 10km
airport: 90km
car essential

VILLEDIEU-LES-POELES

PRICE STRUCTURE

50.12 VILLEDIEU-LES-POELES

2 Bedrooms
(2 rooms) lounge,
bathroom with wc, double
bed, single bed:
FF280 (2 people)
FF370 (3 people)

This house was originally an old priory, dating from the
15th century. It is situated in a pleasant spot with beautiful
grounds and a lake. The whole family is charming. Barbecue
available in summer.

PROPERTY

Extra Bed: FF90

Capacity: 4 people

off-street parking, extensive grounds, tv lounge, pets not
accepted, dinner available, non-smoking, 2 wc, hiking, cycling,
mushroom-picking, fishing 10km, interesting flora 10km,
riversports 10km, golf course 20km, sea or lake watersports
20km

Fluent English spoken

———At Villedieu-les-Poëles, take the N175 towards Avranches.
At the crossroads 'Le Parc', turn right towards Ste-Pience and
follow the signs.

Daniel & Maryclaude DUCHEMIN

'Le Cottage de la Voisinière'

La Voisinière
50410 PERCY

Tel: (0) 2 33 61 18 47/
06 85 81 81 75
Fax: (0) 2 33 61 43 47

cottage.voisinière
@wanadoo.fr
http://perso.wanadoo.fr
/cottagedelavoisinière/

Private Home

10 km - N -
VILLEDIEU-LES-POELES
Percy:
car essential

50.23 VILLEDIEU-LES-POELES

Stop at Mary-Claude's and admire her extraordinary English garden. She has a passion for flower-arranging, as well as her ornamental pond and water lilies. For the children there are sheep and a temperamental donkey. Delicious and unusual home-made jams. Very close to Hambie Abbey. On sale: Honey, Calvados.

PROPERTY

off-street parking, garden, hosts have pets, kitchen, fishing 1km, hiking 5km, interesting flora 8km, golf course 30km, sea or lake watersports 30km, riversports 30km

Basic English spoken

——A84:Exit 38. At Villedieu-les-Poëles, go towards Percy. At Percy, turn left on to the D98 towards Sourdeval, and continue for 1.5km.

PRICE STRUCTURE

5 Bedrooms

first floor – Lavande: shower room with wc, double bed, single bed (child-size):
FF240 (2 people)
FF330 (3 people)

first floor – Fuschia: shower room with wc, twin beds:
FF240

Outbuildings:
ground floor – Magnolia & first floor – Camélia: shower room with wc, double bed:
FF240

first floor – Cyclamen: shower room with wc, double bed: FF270

Extra Bed: FF70
Capacity: 11 people

Nathalie DE DROUAS

'Les Boulais'

50800 ST-MARTIN-LE-
BOUILLANT

Tel: (0) 2 33 60 32 20

Fax: (0) 2 33 60 45 20

Château

12 km - S -
VILLEDIEU-LES-
POELES
St-Martin-le-
Bouillant: hosts can
collect from station,
railway station: 13km
airport: 110km
car essential

PRICE STRUCTURE

3 Bedrooms
Carnière: bathroom with
wc, double bed: FF430

Chant d'oiseau: bathroom
with wc, double bed: FF350

Bain de Mer: shower room
with wc, single bed:
FF250 (1 person)

Extra Bed: FF100

Capacity: 5 people

50.30 VILLEDIEU-LES-POELES

The rooms of this château are in surprising, unusual, bright colours. It is surrounded by spacious grounds on a hill, near to the beaches. Your hostess is lively and has two labrador dogs. Outside the main season, the château is used as a language school.

\PROPERTY

off-street parking, extensive grounds, lounge, hosts have pets, dinner available, packed lunch, babies welcome, free cot, closed: 23/12–2/01, hiking, fishing, hunting, mushroom-picking, interesting flora 20km, bird-watching 20km, cycling 25km, golf course 25km, sea or lake watersports 25km

Fluent English spoken

——From Villedieu take the N175 then the D924 towards Viré. Then take the D999 towards Brécey. After Chérencé-le-Héron follow signs to St-Martin-le-Bouillant. When you reach this village continue as far as the saw mill (Scierie Norgeot). Then turn right towards Loges-sur-Brécey. After 10m, before the Mairie (Town Hall) and the church, take the drive up to the château which is on the left.

Ginette & Claude
PELLETIER

'Le Fay'

72600 VILLAINES-LA-
CARELLE

Tel: 02 43 97 73 40

Private Home

18 km - S E -
ALENCON
Villaines-la-Carelle:
hosts can collect
from station,
railway station: 25km
airport: 15km
car essential

72.28 ALENCON

Why not take a comfortable and relaxing break chez Ginette and Claude, who are retired farmers? There is a wonderful view over the vast landscape and the Forêt de Perceigne from the magnificent bay windows of their dining room. The blue bedroom is particularly suitable for couples with a small baby.

PROPERTY

off-street parking, garden, tv lounge, hosts have pets, pets not accepted, dinner available, packed lunch, kitchen, babies welcome, free cot, non-smoking, hiking, fishing, mushroom-picking, cycling 6km, sea or lake watersports 6km, golf course 20km

——From Alençon, take the D311 towards Mamers for 18km and then turn left towards Villaines-la-Carelle. In the village, go towards St-Longis for 2km then turn left to Le Fay.

PRICE STRUCTURE

3 Bedrooms
Bleue: television, shower room with wc, double bed: FF280

Verte: television, shower, wc, double bed: FF280

Brique: television, shower room with wc, twin beds, single bed:
FF300 (2 people)
FF380 (3 people)

Extra Bed: FF80
Reduction: 4 nights

Capacity: 7 people

Joseph Le MOTHEUX
du PLESSIS

'La Miotière'

61400 LE-PIN-LA-
GARENNE

Tel: (0) 2 33 83 84 01

Working Farm

10 km - S -
MORTAGNE-AU-
PERCHE
Le-Pin-la-Garenne:
railway station: 30km
airport: 130km
car essential

PRICE STRUCTURE

3 Suites

Maison 1: lounge, shower
room with wc, double bed +
en-suite room 2 single beds
+ en-suite room single bed:
FF400 (2 people)
FF650 (5 people)

Maison 2 : lounge, kitchen,
bathroom with wc, double
bed + en-suite room twin
beds: FF400 (2 people)
FF650 (4 people)

Maison 3: lounge, kitchen,
bathroom with wc, double
bed + en-suite room single
bed: FF400 (2 people)
FF600 (3 people)

Extra Bed: FF80

Reduction: groups
and children

Capacity: 12 people

61.03 MORTAGNE-AU-PERCHE

**Madame du Plessis is charming. You will stay in a little house
on this working farm. It has a lot of class and has been
furnished with great taste and character. In September, there
is a programme of cultural events. A region with beautiful
forests. Fleur de Soleil member.**

PROPERTY

off-street parking, extensive grounds, lounge, hosts have pets,
pets not accepted, dinner available, babies welcome, free cot,
wheelchair access, hiking, mushroom-picking, golf course
10km

Basic English spoken

——In Mortagne, take the D938 towards Le-Pin-la-Garenne. In
the village, turn right on to the D256 towards St-Jouin-de-
Blavou for about 1km. First lane on the left.

ALDEBERT Sophie &
ASSOULY Olivier

'La Champinière'

61190 BUBERTRÉ

Tel: (0) 2 33 83 34 77

Fax: (0) 2 33 83 34 77

Residence of
Outstanding Character

10 km - N -
MORTAGNE-AU-
PERCHE
Bubertré: hosts can
collect from station,
railway station: 18km
airport: 130km
car essential

61.08 MORTAGNE-AU-PERCHE

Sophie and Olivier have just taken over this beautiful house in the Perche National Park. It is on the edge of the forest, and near to the Perche-Canada museum and the château of the Comtesse de Ségur. On sale: Regional produce.

PROPERTY

off-street parking, garden, tv lounge, hosts have pets, pets not accepted, dinner available, packed lunch, babies welcome, free cot, wheelchair access, hiking, cycling, interesting flora, mushroom-picking, fishing 4km, sea or lake watersports 4km, hunting 5km, gliding 12km, golf course 15km

Adequate English spoken

——From Mortagne turn right on to the N12 towards Paris as far as the exit to Tourouvre. Then take the D32 towards Moulins de la Marche and Bubertré. Follow the signs to 'chambre d'hôtes'.

PRICE STRUCTURE

4 Bedrooms
Soléiado: shower room with wc, double bed: FF290

Mistral: shower room with wc, double bed, 2 single beds: FF290 (2 people) FF490 (4 people)

Capéo: shower room with wc, twin beds: FF290

Ventoux: bathroom with wc along corridor, double bed: FF290

Extra Bed: FF100
Capacity: 10 people

Madeleine FAUQUET

169, rue du Colombier -
D108

76730 AUPPEGARD

Tel: (0) 2 35 85 20 43 06
68 44 43 75

Fax: (0) 2 35 85 20 43

Private Home

12 km - S - DIEPPE
Auppegard:
car essential

PRICE STRUCTURE

1 Bedroom
lounge, shower room with
wc, 2 double beds, single
bed (child-size), cot:
FF240 (2 people)
FF470 (5 people)

Extra Bed: FF70

Capacity: 5 people

76.01 DIEPPE

If you are looking for a typical little timbered Normandy cottage, not far from Dieppe, just for you, then this is the address. Breakfast is served in the rustic dining room – a wonderful experience.

PROPERTY

private parking, garden, lounge, hosts have pets, pets not accepted, dinner available, sea or lake watersports 10km

Adequate English spoken

——At Dieppe, take the N27 towards Rouen for 12km. Turn right on to the D108 towards Auppegard and continue for 2km. The house is on the right.

Catherine DEMARQUET

'Manoir de Beaumont'

Beaumont

76260 EU

Tel: (0) 2 35 50 91 91/
06 83 44 08 44

Fax: (0) 2 35 50 19 45

Château

30 km - N E -
DIEPPE
Eu: hosts can collect
from station,
railway station: 3km
airport: 100km
car essential

76.17 DIEPPE

This is a former hunting lodge, beautifully restored and in a quiet location. Catherine gives a very special welcome in this really authentic setting, and is a mine of information to help you plan your visits. One of our most inviting stops.

PROPERTY

off-street parking, garden, lounge, hosts have pets, pets not accepted, babies welcome, free cot, hiking, cycling, interesting flora, mushroom-picking, bird-watching, fishing 2km, sea or lake watersports 2km, riversports 3km, golf course 30km

Fluent English spoken

——From Dieppe, take the D925 towards Le Tréport/Eu. As you leave Eu, before you reach the D49 towards Ponts and Marais, take the Beaumont road on the right and follow the signs 'chambres d'hôtes' for 2 km.

PRICE STRUCTURE

2 Bedrooms and 1 Suite

Louis XVI: lounge, shower room with wc, double bed, 3 single beds: FF290 (2 people) FF490 (5 people)

Pitou: kitchen, shower room with wc, double bed + en-suite room twin beds, single bed: FF290 (2 people) FF490 (5 people)

Entente Cordiale: shower room with wc, double bed: FF290

Extra Bed: FF70

Reduction: 15/11–15/12 & 08/01–30/01

Capacity: 11 people

Jean-Michel & Maryse
PERROY

'Domaine de
Champdieu'

Les Hameaux

76590 GONNEVILLE-
SUR-SCIE

Tel: 02 35 34 38 46-06 89
09 13 19

Fax: (0) 2 35 34 38 46

Château

20 km - S - DIEPPE
Goneville:
railway station: 6 km
airport: 40 km
car essential

PRICE STRUCTURE

4 Bedrooms

Pivoine: wheelchair access,
bathroom with wc, single
bed: FF615 (1 person)

Rose Trémière: shower
room with wc, twin beds,
single bed: FF600 (2
people) FF735 (3 people)

Jonquille: shower room with
wc, twin beds: FF600

Chèvrefeuille: shower room
with wc, double bed, single
bed: FF600 (2 people)
FF735 (3 people)

Reduction: 3 nights and
groups
Capacity: 9 people

76.21 DIEPPE

This is a typical Normandy timbered house, dating from the
17th century, with a warm and refined interior. Be sure to
wander through the 4 ha of grounds, reputed for their
topiary, or enjoy the swimming pool. Even more important,
be sure not to miss dinner.

PROPERTY

off-street parking, extensive grounds, tv lounge, hosts have
pets, telephone, dinner available, swimming pool, hiking,
cycling, interesting flora, golf course 15km, sea or lake
watersports 15km

Fluent English spoken

——From Dieppe, heading towards Rouen on the A151, Exit
Biville-la-Baignarde. Then turn right towards Baoqueville, then
Gonneville-sur-Scie.

Alain & Claudine RAS

'Ferme des Quatre Brouettes'

76280 TURRETOT

Tel: (0) 2 35 20 23 73

Fax: (0) 2 35 20 23 73

Working Farm

10 km - S - ETRETAT
Turretot: hosts can collect from station, railway station: 7km airport: 15km

76.06 ETRETAT

You will be charmed by Claudine's warm welcome, and this traditional Normandy house and flower garden. It is 10km from Etretat, 2km from the main Le Havre–Fécamp road, and 7km from the equestrian centre. You will love the fireside dinners. On sale: Farm produce.

PROPERTY

Private parking, garden, tv lounge, hosts have pets, dinner available, packed lunch, kitchen, babies welcome, free cot, hiking, cycling, sea or lake watersports 7km, golf course 10km

——In Etretat, take the D940 towards Le Havre. Turn left on to the D32 towards Gonneville-la-Mallet. Cross the village and take the D125 towards Turretot. Cross two junctions, the farm is on this road, 1km on the left, towards Hermeville.

PRICE STRUCTURE

4 Bedrooms and 1 Apartment
Coquelicot: lounge, kitchen, shower room with wc, double bed: FF250

Pervenche: kitchen, shower room with wc, double bed: FF220

Camélia: kitchen, shower room with wc, double bed, single bed: FF280

Myosotis: shower room with wc, double bed, single bed: FF220 (2 people) FF280 (3 people)

Rose: along corridor shower room with wc, double bed, single bed: FF200 (2 people) FF260 (3 people)

Extra Bed: FF60

Reduction: 3 nights

Capacity: 13 people

Brigitte & Serge
QUEVILLY

'Le Manoir'

5, place des Anciens
Elèves - Route d'Etretat

76280 CRIQUETOT-
L'ESNEVAL

Tel: 02 35 29 31 90

Fax: (0) 2 35 29 31 90

Château

8 km - S E -
ETRETAT
Criquetot-l'Esneval:
hosts can collect
from station,
railway station: 15km
airport: 12km

PRICE STRUCTURE

5 Bedrooms
first floor – first room:
lshower room with wc,
bathroom, double bed,
single bed: FF350 (2
people) FF400 (3 people)

first floor – Bleue: shower
room with wc, double bed,
single bed: FF350 (2
people) FF400 (3 people)

first floor – Mme Maugean:
shower room with wc,
bathroom, double bed:
FF350

second floor – Vitrée & du
Fond: shower room with wc,
double bed, single bed:
FF300 (2 people)
FF350 (3 people)

Extra Bed: FF60

Capacity: 14 people

76.24 ETRETAT

Brigitte and Serge, a couple of retired farmers, have left the Normandy countryside to settle down in the manor house of their dreams, 8km from the famous cliffs of Etretat. This is a charming little town, full of flowers. The surrounding meadows have that idyllic, pastoral look, with flocks of sheep grazing under the trees. Brigitte will offer you a glass of cider and you will probably leave with a whole bottle, another souvenir of 'la douce France'. There is a see-saw for the children and Calvados for the grown-ups!

PROPERTY

private parking, extensive grounds, tv lounge, pets not accepted, dinner available, hiking, cycling, mushroom-picking 2km, fishing 3km, golf course 8km, sea or lake watersports 8km *Basic English spoken*

——From Etretat, take the D39 towards Criquetot-l'Esneval. The manor house is on the square, leading to the church.

Marie-Cécile LAMBERT

'La Ferme de Vivier'

88, route de Duclair

76150 ST-JEAN-DU-CARDONNAY

Tel: (0) 2 35 33 80 42

Working Farm

7 km - N W - ROUEN
St-Jean-du-Cardonnay:
railway station: 6km
airport: 15km
car essential

76.07 ROUEN

A 17th-century timbered Norman farmhouse in the heart of the country, with a duck pond. You could visit the abbeys in the region but you are more likely to decide to stay and be enthralled by the warm smile and welcome of Marie-Cécile. On sale: Cider, home-made jam.

PROPERTY

off-street parking, garden, lounge, telephone, kitchen, non-smoking, wheelchair access, riversports 4km, golf course 15km, sea or lake watersports 45km

Basic English spoken

——At Rouen, take the A15 towards Dieppe/Le Havre for 3km. Take the 2nd exit to St-Jean-du-Cardonnay. On the 2nd roundabout take the D43 towards Duclair. Continue for 2km, the house is on the right.

PRICE STRUCTURE

5 Bedrooms

Rose: television, shower room with wc, double bed: FF230

Bleue: television, shower room with wc, twin beds: FF230

Iris: television, shower room with wc, double bed, single bed: FF230 (2 people) FF340 (3 people)

Palmiers: television, shower room with wc, double bed, 2 single beds: FF230 (2 people) FF450 (4 people)

Rhododendron: television, shower room with wc, washbasin, double bed: FF230

Extra Bed: FF45/110

Reduction: children

Capacity: 13 people

Annie & Roger
AUDIBERT

Cidex 21
76690 FRICHEMESNIL

Tel: (0) 2 35 33 59 13

Residence of
Outstanding Character

25 km - N - ROUEN
Frichemesnil:
railway station: 3km
airport: 40km
car essential
——From Rouen, take
the A28 towards
Abbeville. Take Exit 11
and N29 towards Totes.
After 6km, left on to the
D151 towards Bosc-le-
Hard, then Frichmesnil.
The cottage is the third
house after the church.

76.16 ROUEN

This is an authentic, 350-year-old Normandy half-timbered cottage, in a landscaped garden. The little village has a listed church, and from here you can travel the roads of Haute-Normandie. On sale: Farm produce.

PROPERTY

private parking, garden, tv lounge, pets not accepted, dinner available, babies welcome, free cot, 1 shared bathroom with wc, hiking, cycling 3km, interesting flora 3km, golf course 8km, sea or lake watersports 30km

Adequate English spoken

PRICE STRUCTURE
3 Bedrooms
first room: bathroom with wc, double bed, twin beds: FF250 (2 people) FF460 (4 people)

second room: double bed + room double bed: FF250 (2 people) FF500 (4 people)

Extra Bed: FF100; Reduction: 3 nights; Capacity: 4 people

Joël & Maryna
AUBERVILLE

'Les Vernelles'
Le Bout de Bas
76890 VARNEVILLE-
BRETTEVILLE

Tel: 02 35 34 08 04

Private Home

25 km - N - ROUEN
Varneville:
railway station: 7km
airport: 40km
——From Rouen, A151
as far as Tôtes. Exit
Tôtes-Centre and right
on to D25 for 250m.
D101 on the right for
2km as far as the hamlet
of Le-Bout-du-Bas. 'Les
Vernelles' is on the right
as you leave the hamlet.

76.19 ROUEN

Your accommodation will be in a real timbered cottage with a thatched roof, not far from Joël and Maryna's house. Their landscaped garden is a joy to behold. There are flowers everywhere and a small lake, an ideal appetizer for the 20 other botanical gardens which can be visited in this area. Your hearty breakfast will be served in the cottage.

PROPERTY

off-street parking, garden, tv lounge, hosts have pets, pets not accepted, babies welcome, free cot, cycling, interesting flora 3km, riversports 7km, golf course 20km, sea or lake watersports 25km

Adequate English spoken

PRICE STRUCTURE
1 Bedroom
double bed, single bed: FF280 (2 people) FF400 (3 people)

Extra Bed: FF120

Capacity: 3 people

76.20 ROUEN

You are only 15 mins. drive from the centre of Rouen, yet this modern house, on a landscaped development, is so quiet. It is also very close to the superb regional forest. Marie-Hélène, who is retired, will put you at ease and be delighted to tell you about the famous Route des Abbayes. Be sure not to miss visiting the streets of timbered houses in Rouen.

PROPERTY

off-street parking, garden, tv lounge, pets not accepted, babies welcome, free cot, hiking, golf course 5km, sea or lake watersports 60km

Basic English spoken

PRICE STRUCTURE

1 Bedroom
shower room with wc, double bed: FF230

Capacity: 2 people

Marie-Hélène DE BEAU-REPAIRE

Les Longs Vallons   40, rue des Cormorans

76960 NOTRE DAME DE BONDEVILLE

Tel: 02 35 74 94 37

Private Home

10 km - N - ROUEN
Notre-Dame-de-Bondeville:
railway station: 7km
airport: 12km
——From Rouen, N15 towards Dieppe. At Maromme, right towards Mont-St-Aignan, then Les Longs Vallons. Third road on the right to Residence St–Gervais.

Jérôme LANQUEST

'Le Brécy'

72, route du Brécy

76840 ST-MARTIN-DE-
BOSCHERVILLE

Tel: 02 35 32 69 92

Fax: (0) 2 35 32 00 30

Residence of
Outstanding Character

10 km - N W -
ROUEN
St-Martin-de-
Boscherville:
railway station: 10km
airport: 20km
car essential

NORMANDIE

ROUEN

PRICE STRUCTURE

1 Bedroom

lounge, telephone, kitchen,
shower room with wc, twin
beds: FF350

Extra Bed: FF100

Capacity: 2 people

76.22 ROUEN

This place is only 10 mins. from Rouen, and next to the abbey. It has the atmosphere of the old family homes of yesteryear, when large families spent the summer together in the garden, by the River Seine or in the forest. The 17th-century dining room is furnished with antiques. Be sure to take the advice of your hostess, who is a guide at the abbey and can also advise you on things like the Route des Abbayes, dovecotes, gastronomy and the Impressionist painters who loved this region.

PROPERTY

private parking, extensive grounds, lounge, hosts have pets, pets not accepted, telephone, kitchen, babies welcome, free cot, wheelchair access, hiking, interesting flora 1km, mushroom-picking 1km, golf course 10km, sea or lake water-sports 10km, riversports 10km *English spoken*

——Head for the north-west side of Rouen (on the A15, A150 or A151), and take the D982 towards Duclair. At St-Martin, take the D67 towards St-Pierre. After the place de l'Abbaye, the route du Brécy is the second on the right.

Michèle DESREZ

'Manoir de Captot'

Route de Sahurs

76380 CANTELEU

Tel: 02 35 36 00 04

Fax: (0) 2 35 36 00 04

Château

7 km - W - ROUEN
Canteleu: hosts can
collect from station,
railway station: 5km
airport: 10km
car essential

76.23 ROUEN

Just a few minutes from the historic centre of Rouen, you will be surprised by the charm and comfort of this 18th-century manor house at the edge of the forest. Stroll in the extensive grounds, full of ancient beech trees, and listen for the call of the deer in the autumn. Michèle guarantees a warm welcome and will serve her delicious home-made jam with breakfast, taken in a beautiful and enormous dining room worthy of nobility. Of course, be sure not to miss Monet's garden at Giverny and the famous Route des Abbayes.

PROPERTY

off-street parking, extensive grounds, tv lounge, hosts have pets, babies welcome, free cot, hiking, golf course 5km

Basic English spoken

——Head for the north-west side of Rouen (on the A15, A150 or A151), and take the D982 towards Duclair. At Canteleu, take the D351 towards Sahurs. The manor house is by the first sharp bend.

PRICE STRUCTURE

2 Bedrooms
Toile de Jouy: bathroom with wc, double bed: FF400

bathroom with wc, double bed: FF350

extra room: 2 single beds: FF200

Extra Bed: FF100

Capacity: 6 people

ENGLISH CHANNEL

Dieppe

Cherbourg

Le Havre

76

ROUEN

Le Havre

CAEN

Lisieux

St. Lô

*Jersey
(to UK)*

50

14

**NORMANDIE
page 328**

27

Evreux

Vire

Argentan

Dreux

Lannion

St. Malo

Avranches

61

28

Guingamp

Dinan

Fougères

Alençon

Chartr

St. Brieuc

**BRETAGNE
page 158**

RENNES

53

72

Châteaudun

Pontivy

35

Laval
page 397

Le Mans
pages 398-402

Vendôme

41

56

Châteaubriant

Vannes

Redon

**PAYS DE
LA LOIRE**

44

Angers
pages 390-393

Tours

**CENT
page**

Lorient

St. Nazaire

49

Saumur
pages 394-396

37

NANTES
pages 387-389

Cholet

Châtellerault

Châte

85

La Roche

Fontenay-le-Comte
pages 403-405

79

POITIERS

les Sables-d'Olonne

Niort

86

*ATLANTIC
OCEAN*

La Rochelle

87

Rochefort

**POITOU
CHARENTES
page 404**

LI

Saintes

16

Royan

Cognac

17

Angoulême

**LIMOUSIN
page 107**

PAYS-DE-LA-LOIRE

384

Antonio FALANGA

'Château de St-Thomas'

44360 ST-ETIENNE-DE-MONTLUC

Tel: (0) 2 40 85 90 60

Fax: (0) 2 40 86 97 62

Château

25 km - N W - NANTES
St-Etienne-de-Montluc:
airport: 20km
car essential

44.05 NANTES

A peaceful 19th-century château surrounded by woods, with a lake. You will be captivated by the charms of this young Italian host and his French wife. There are stables and archery in the grounds. An ideal place for playing golf and discovering the marshlands.

PROPERTY

✸ ✸ ✸ ✸

private parking, extensive grounds, tv lounge, hosts have pets, pets not accepted, dinner available, babies welcome, free cot, riding, hiking, cycling, fishing, golf course 8km, bird-watching 30km

At Nantes, take the N165 towards Vannes and leave it at St-Etienne-de-Montluc. In the village, after the large town hall square (Mairie), take the 2nd road on the left.

PRICE STRUCTURE

5 Bedrooms
Saumon: television, bathroom with wc, double bed: FF700

Verte: bathroom with wc, twin beds: FF700

Bleue: bathroom with wc, double bed: FF700

Rouge & Romantique: bathroom with wc, double bed: FF650

Extra Bed: FF100
Reduction: 01/10–31/05

Capacity: 10 people

Marcel & Yvonne
PINEAU

'La Mercerais'

44130 BLAIN

Tel: (0) 2 40 79 04 30

Private Home

30 km - N - NANTES
Blain:
airport: 35km
car essential

PRICE STRUCTURE

3 Bedrooms
Rose: shower room with wc,
2 double beds, single bed:
FF265 (2 people)
FF460 (5 people)

Bleue: shower room with
wc, double bed, single bed:
FF265 (2 people)
FF330 (3 people)

Bas: double bed: FF265

Extra Bed: FF15/65
Capacity: 10 people

44.08 NANTES

From the welcoming apéritif on arrival, Marcel and Yvonne will receive you like friends of the family and give you tips on the attractions of their region. The house has a beautiful flower garden and is near the forest of Gâvre and La Baule.

PROPERTY

private parking, extensive grounds, lounge, pets not accepted, non-smoking, 1 shared bathroom, wc, cycling, fishing 1km, bird-watching 25km, sea or lake watersports 30km

——At Nantes, take the N137 towards Rennes for 22km. Turn left on to the D164 towards Blain/Redon. At Blain, turn right on to the N171 towards Nozay. After 3km at the cross, turn right and right again.

Annick & Didier
CALONNE

'Château Plessis Brézot'

Le Plessis Brézot

44690 MONNIERES

Tel: 02 40 54 63 24

Fax: (0) 2 40 54 66 07

a.calonne@online.fr
www.chateauplessisbre-
zot.com

Château

22 km - S E -
NANTES
Monnières:
railway station: 3km
airport: 20km
car essential

44.17 NANTES

This beautiful 17th-century residence, in the heart of the Nantais area, has been wonderfully restored by Annick and Didier. It is quiet and peaceful, and the panelling, furniture and impressive entrance door are very attractive. The inside is even more beautiful than the outside. They will let you taste their own wines, Muscadet and Gros-Plant, and show you around the cellars. Wonderful moments, to which can be added walks in the scented gardens or just lazing by the pool.

PROPERTY ✹ ✹ ✹ ✹

private parking, extensive grounds, lounge, hosts have pets, babies welcome, free cot, wheelchair access, swimming pool, hiking, cycling, fishing, vineyard, golf course 15km

Fluent English spoken

——At Nantes, take the N249 towards Cholet, then the N149 towards Clisson. In Monnières, turn right and then take the D76 towards Gorges and follow the signs.

PRICE STRUCTURE

5 Bedrooms
(1 room) wheelchair access, shower room with wc, double bed: FF470

(2 rooms) wheelchair access, shower room with wc, bathroom, washbasin, double bed: FF470

(2 double or twin rooms) wheelchair access, shower room with wc, bathroom, washbasin, twin beds: FF670

Extra Bed: FF100

Capacity: 10 people

Peter & Susan-Ann
SCARBORO

'La Chaufournaie'

49500 CHAZE-SUR-
ARGOS

Tel: (0) 2 41 61 49 05

Fax: (0) 2 41 61 49 05

Residence of
Outstanding Character

35 km - N W -
ANGERS
Chazé-sur-Argos:
railway station: 35km
airport: 100km
car essential

PRICE STRUCTURE

5 Bedrooms

Mme de Fontenay & Miss
France: shower room with
wc, double bed: FF270

Miss Guadeloupe & Miss
Orléanais: shower room
with wc, twin beds: FF270

Miss Paris: shower room
with wc, double bed, single
bed: FF270 (2 people)
FF350 (3 people)

Extra Bed: FF80

Capacity: 11 people

49.04 ANGERS

Susan and Peter, a friendly English couple, have painstakingly restored this 1850's farmhouse, situated in 18 ha of grounds. It is 15km from a racecourse and in a region that counts no less than 8 golf courses. In each room there are tea- and coffee-making facilities. There is a full-size snooker table in the lounge, and Russian billiards.

PROPERTY

off-street parking, extensive grounds, tv lounge, hosts have pets, pets not accepted, telephone, dinner available, hiking 3km, fishing 3km, mushroom-picking 12km, cycling 15km, riversports 20km, golf course 25km, bird-watching 30km, sea or lake watersports 30km

Fluent English spoken

——At Angers, take the N162 towards Laval. At Le Lion d'Angers, turn left on to the D770 towards Candé. The house is on this road, 3km after Vern-d'Anjou.

François de VALBRAY

'Château des Briottières'

49330 CHAMPIGNÉ

Tel: (0) 2 41 42 00 02

Fax: (0) 2 41 42 01 55

briottieres@wanadoo.fr

www.briottieres.com

Château

25 km - N - ANGERS
Champigné:
railway station: 25km
airport: 110km
car essential

49.12 ANGERS

Totally authentic. Not a 'château-hotel' but a real château whose floors creak and which has been lived in by the same family for six generations. The grounds are magnificent with a lake, swans and charming little nooks. Real class, relaxation, luxury – sheer pleasure. On sale: Anjou wine, honey.

PROPERTY

private parking, extensive grounds, tv lounge, pets not accepted, telephone, dinner available, packed lunch, swimming pool, riding, hiking, cycling, fishing, vineyard, golf course 3km, riversports 7km, hunting 60km

English spoken

——From the A11, Exit 11 (Durtal). Head towards Châteauneuf-sur-Sarthe and Champigné, where you follow the signs. (From Angers, take the N162 towards Laval. Turn right on to the D768 towards Champigné.)

PRICE STRUCTURE

15 Bedrooms and 3 Suites and 2 Apartments

Château-Rose: bridal room, television, telephone, bathroom with wc, shower, double bed: FF2,620
Château-Etang: telephone, bathroom with wc, shower, twin beds: FF1,730
Château-Petite Rose: telephone, bathroom with wc, shower, double bed: FF1,330
Amis: telephone, bathroom with wc, shower, double bed: FF1,030
Fruitier-Cottage: telephone, bathroom with wc, shower, double bed: FF1,030
Fruitier-Cottage 2 : telephone, bathroom with wc, shower, twin beds, single bed: FF1600 (3 people)
Extra Bed: 2,10FF
Reduction: groups
Capacity: 13 people

389

Marie-Claire & Bernard
BOMPAS

'Domaine les Etangs de
Bois Robert'

Route de Candé

49370 BECON-LES-
GRANITS

Tel: (0) 2 41 77 09 89
Fax: (0) 2 41 77 31 00

Residence of
Outstanding Character

20 km - W -ANGERS
Bécon-les-Granits:
hosts can collect
from station, railway
station: 20km
airport: 28km
car essential

PRICE STRUCTURE

1 Suite
Martin Pêcheur: bathroom
with wc, double bed: FF350
(2 people)
FF630 (4 people)

+ en-suite room La Tour:
lounge, shower room with
wc, twin beds (FF450)

Extra Bed: FF90

Capacity: 4 people

49.24 ANGERS

This pleasant property is on the châteaux route, situated in
the middle of a 6 ha estate, with several lakes. Breakfast is
served in a bright room overlooking the countryside, or in
the garden beside the lake, the home of Napoléon the black
swan and his family.

PROPERTY

private parking, extensive grounds, tv lounge, hosts have pets,
dinner available, cycling, fishing, hiking 1km, golf course
20km, bird-watching 20km, sea or lake watersports 20km,
hunting 25km

Fluent English spoken

——From the A11, Exit 18. Then take the D963 towards
Châteaubriant, as far as Bécon-les-Granits. The property is on
the right, as you leave the village.

Florence & Richard SENCE

'Le Frêne'

22, rue St-Sauveur

49520 CHATELAIS

Tel: 02 41 61 16 45

Fax: (0) 2 41 61 16 45

Residence of Outstanding Character

45 km - N W - ANGERS
Chatelais:
railway station: 45km
car essential

49.25 ANGERS

This is a really tempting stop between Brittany and the châteaux of the Loire Valley, in an old village that has grown up on a Merovingian archaeological site. This beautiful bourgeois house is enhanced by many superb water colours, painted by Florence, who also gives lessons. There is a courtyard, a garden with yew trees and a delightful view over the countryside. Richard loves reading, and also plays the bagpipes, which will liven up your evenings. Here you just soak up the atmosphere of 'la vieille France', and the relaxed way of life typical of this region. On sale: Watercolours.

PROPERTY

off-street parking, garden, lounge, hosts have pets, dinner available, packed lunch, babies welcome, free cot, hiking, cycling, fishing, riversports *Fluent English spoken*

——At Angers, D129 towards Lion d'Anger, D863 for Segré. D923 towards Château-Gonthier for 3km, left on to the D863 to Craon. At l'Hôtellerie de Flée, D180 on the left as far as the centre of Chatelais, first street on the left in the village.

PRICE STRUCTURE

3 Bedrooms and 1 Suite
Bleue: shower room with wc, double bed: FF300

Rouge: shower room with wc, twin beds: FF300

Papillons: bathroom with wc, twin beds. FF300

Suite Familiale: lounge, shower room with wc, twin beds + en-suite room twin beds: FF250 (2 people) FF400 (4 people)

Extra Bed: FF70

Capacity: 10 people

Jean-Pierre GAZEAU

'Le Moulin de Couché-La Ponote'

49260 LE-PUY-NOTRE-DAME

Tel: (0) 2 41 38 87 11

Fax: (0) 2 41 38 86 99

Residence of Outstanding Character

20 km - S W - SAUMUR
Le-Puy-Notre-Dame:
railway station: 20km
airport: 140km
car essential

PRICE STRUCTURE

7 Bedrooms and 2 Suites
Coquelicot & Géranium: television, shower room with wc, double bed: FF350
Lilas & Pensée: lounge, television, shower, wc, double bed: FF320
Primevère: double bed + en-suite room: television, shower room with wc, double bed: FF560 (4 people)
Cyclamen: television, shower room with wc, double bed + en-suite room double bed: FF560 (4 people)
Violette: television, shower room with wc, double bed: FF350
Hortensia: television, bathroom, wc, double bed: FF350
Bleuet: lounge, television, shower room with wc, 2 double beds: FF560 (4 people)
Capacity: 24 people

49.08 SAUMUR

Impossible to describe until you have experienced it. The wonderful, friendly atmosphere at this 15th-century watermill, in the heart of the Saumur wine country, has convinced us that you must stop here! Jean-Pierre can advise you on the best wine-cellars in the area. The restaurant is in the restored barn; the bedrooms are in the old mill house.

PROPERTY

private parking, extensive grounds, tv lounge, hosts have pets, telephone, dinner available, packed lunch, closed: 15/10–01/04, hiking, cycling, vineyard, riversports 7km, sea or lake watersports 20km

Fluent English spoken

——At Saumur, take the N147 towards Loudun-Poitiers. At the 2nd roundabout at Montreuil-Bellay, take the D938 towards Thouars for 4km. Turn right on to the D158 towards Passais-Sanziers. The 'Moulin' is on the left, after the bridge on the river (signposted).

Michel & Françoise
TOUTAIN

'Le Prieuré de
Vendanger'

D62 - Vendanger

49150 LE GUEDENIAU

Tel: (0) 2 41 67 82 37/
06 16 66 17 23
Fax: (0) 2 41 67 82 43

info@vendanger.fr
www.vendanger.fr

Residence of
Outstanding Character

30 km - N -SAUMUR
Vendanger: hosts
can collect from
railway station: 40km
airport: 30km
car essential

49.13 SAUMUR

This 15th-century priory, converted into a 'gentilhommière' in the 19th century, has been restored by your hosts to its original Baroque décor. The 5 ha of grounds are surrounded by woods and there is also a lake where fishing is permitted. Billiards, golf lessons, hunting, themed holidays, candlelit dinners, a piano, a large open-air swimming pool – brilliant! On sale: Coffee, home-made jam. sculptures.

PROPERTY

off-street parking, extensive grounds, tv lounge, hosts have pets, pets not accepted, telephone, dinner available, packed lunch, babies welcome, free cot, swimming pool, hiking, cycling, fishing, hunting, mushroom-picking, golf course 12km

Adequate English spoken

——On the A85 Saumur to Tours, Exit Longué. Take the D948 towards Baugé and, 3km after Jumelles, take the D62 towards Mouliherne.

PRICE STRUCTURE

4 Bedrooms and 1 Suite

Chantepleure: bathroom with wc, double bed, single bed + en-suite room twin beds: FF395 (2 people) FF565 (5 people)

Cannelle: bathroom with wc, double bed, single bed: FF375 (2 people) FF460 (3 people)

Jabloir: bathroom with wc, double bed: FF375

Cascaret: bathroom with wc, double bed: FF375

Clairette: bathroom with wc, 2 single beds: FF375

Extra Bed: FF85

Reduction: 1/01–1/06 & 1/10–31/12 and 3 nights and children

Capacity: 14 people

Carmen & Hervé TATÉ

'La Closerie'

Le Bourg

49160 ST-PHILBERT-DU-PEUPLE

Tel: 02 41 52 62 69

Private Home

PAYS-DE-LA-LOIRE

SAUMUR

15 km - N -SAUMUR
St-Philbert-du-Peuple:
railway station: 18km
airport: 150km
car essential

PRICE STRUCTURE

**2 Bedrooms and
1 Apartment**

first room: shower room
with wc, double bed: FF250

second room: shower room
with wc, double bed, single
bed: FF220 (2 people)
FF280 (3 people)

floor: lounge, television,
kitchen, shower room with
wc, bathroom with wc, twin
beds + room double bed:
FF300 (2 people)
FF550 (4 people)

Reduction: 3 nights

Capacity: 9 people

49.17 SAUMUR

'La Closerie' is, in fact, and old farm dating from the 15th and 17th centuries. There is a family atmosphere in this quiet and relaxing location. The garden is a cool oasis, much appreciated after visits to châteaux and vineyards. Carmen is an English teacher, and her husband a retired restaurateur, so be sure to try his tempting dishes, accompanied by a good vin de Loire.

PROPERTY

off-street parking, garden, hosts have pets, dinner available, hiking, cycling, hunting, mushroom-picking, golf course 15km, riversports 18km, gliding 18km, sea or lake watersports 25km

Fluent English spoken

——A85 Saumur–Tours, Exit Longué and go towards St-Philbert-du-Peuple. The house is in the centre of the village (signposted).

François-Charles &
Annick WILLIOT

'Château du Bas du Gast'

6, rue de la Halle aux
Toiles

53000 LAVAL

Tel: (0) 2 43 49 22 79

Fax: (0) 2 43 56 44 71

Château

LAVAL:
hosts can collect
from station,
railway station: 1km
airport: 65km

53.01 LAVAL

A quiet, historic house, right in the centre of the town. The spacious bedrooms have a lot of class. Your hosts have conserved the ancient box trees that date from the 18th century. You will enjoy meeting these hosts, who speak perfect English.

PRICE STRUCTURE

3 Bedrooms and 1 Suite
Napoléon: bathroom with wc, shower, double bed, single bed: FF750 (2 people) FF1050 (3 people)

Jaune: bathroom with wc, double bed: FF650

Jouy: bathroom with wc, twin beds: FF700

Bleue: bathroom with wc, double bed + en-suite room
Verte: shower room with wc, twin beds: FF750 (2 people) FF1350 (4 people)

Extra Bed: FF200/300
Capacity: 11 people

PROPERTY

private parking, extensive grounds, lounge, hosts have pets, closed: 1/12–31/01, cycling, golf course 4km

Fluent English spoken

——In the centre of Laval, Follow signs to the 'Salle Polyvalente' or the 'Bibliothèque Municipale'. Le Bas du Gast is close by.

Michèle & Michel
LETANNEUX

'La Chataigneraie'

72500 DISSAY-SOUS-
COURCILLON

Tel: (0) 2 43 79 45 30

Residence of
Outstanding Character

40 km - S E -
LE MANS
Dissay-sous-
Courcillon:
railway station: 5km
car essential

PRICE STRUCTURE

1 Bedroom and 1 Suite

Suite: bathroom with wc,
double bed + en-suite room
single bed:
FF260 (2 people)
FF460 (3 people)

2 single beds: FF240

Capacity: 5 people

72.14 LE MANS

**Michèle and Michel will enjoy welcoming you to this very
restful and verdant part of the country. The wooded grounds
and the view of the Middle Ages château are very pleasant.
You are in the valley of the Loir, 35km from the châteaux of
La Loire. On sale: Jam.**

PROPERTY

extensive grounds, hosts have pets, dinner available, 1 shared
bathroom, wc, tennis court, closed: 30/10–15/04, hiking,
fishing, hunting, bird-watching, mushroom-picking 5km, sea
or lake watersports 6km, riversports 6km, golf course 15km

——At Le Mans take the N138 towards Tours for 45km. At
Dissay follow the signs on the left for 1km.

Eliane & Jean-Louis
BRAZILIER

'Les 14 Boisselées'

Route de Château du
Loir

72800 LE LUDE

Tel: (0) 2 43 94 90 65

Private Home

30 km - S -
LE MANS
Le Lude:
railway station: 10km
airport: 30km
car essential

72.17 LE MANS

Eliane and Jean-Louis are teachers and adore conversation.
There is a family atmosphere here and you will certainly feel
at home. Their cooking is refined and of a high quality.
There are many trails for hikers and mountain-bikers in the
Vallée du Loir, and the Château de Lude should not be
missed.

PROPERTY

private parking, extensive grounds, lounge, pets not accepted,
dinner available, babies welcome, free cot, non-smoking,
hiking, fishing, mushroom-picking, cycling 2km, golf course
40km

Adequate English spoken

PRICE STRUCTURE

2 Bedrooms
ground floor: shower room
with wc along corridor,
double bed: FF250

floor: bathroom with wc
along corridor, double bed:
FF250

Extra Bed: FF80

Capacity: 4 people

——From Le Mans go to La Flèche via the A11 or the N23
towards Angers. Then take the D306 towards Le Lude and the
D305 towards Château-du-Loir for 2km.

Laura ESQUIVEL

'Manoir du Riablay'

Rue St Jean

72500 CHATEAU-DU-LOIR

Tel: (0) 2 43 44 20 20/
06 80 36 95 11

Fax: (0) 2 43 44 20 20

riablay@wanadoo.fr
http://perso.wanadoo.fr
/riablay/

Château

35 km - S E -
LE MANS
Chateau du Loir:
railway station: 2km
airport: 40km

PRICE STRUCTURE

8 Bedrooms
Améthyste & Ambre &
Emeraude & Malachite:
bathroom with wc,
washbasin, double bed:
FF430

Manoir: Saphir & Rubis:
lounge, bathroom with wc,
double bed: FF590

Opale & Turquoise:
bathroom with wc, double
bed: FF430

Extra Bed: FF120/150
Reduction: 2 nights and
groups

Capacity: 16 people

72.18 LE MANS

This listed Renaissance manor house is haunted by the ghosts of Ronsard and Henri IV. The bedrooms are the ultimate in luxury and period style. The cave villages and the châteaux of the Loir valley are well worth a visit. Excellent value for the standards offered.

PROPERTY

off-street parking, extensive grounds, hosts have pets, pets not accepted, dinner available, wheelchair access, swimming pool, tennis court, hiking, cycling, fishing 3km, hunting 5km, sea or lake watersports 10km, mushroom-picking 15km, golf course 18km

——At Le Mans take the N138 towards Tours. There is a sign to the manor on the right of the town hall (Mairie). At the end of the rue St-Jean, level with the square François Verrier, turn left into the road leading to the rue Verte.

Michel SOUFFRONT

'Château de Chanteloup'

72460 SILLE-LE-PHILIPPE

Tel: (0) 2 43 27 51 07/ 06 11 93 21 89

Fax: (0) 2 43 89 05 05

chanteloup.souffront @wanadoo.fr

Château

18 km - N E - LE MANS
Sillé-le-Philippe:
railway station: 20km
car essential

PAYS-DE-LA-LOIRE

LE MANS

72.26 LE MANS

This family château is only a few minutes from Le Mans, in the magnificent setting of grounds with a lake, and provides five bedrooms with the highest standards of comfort in the converted outbuilding. There are hostesses to welcome you to this wonderful place, with its pleasant swimming pool, games room, tennis court and, in high season, restaurant.

PROPERTY ✳ ✳ ✳

off-street parking, extensive grounds, tv lounge, pets not accepted, telephone, dinner available, swimming pool, tennis court, closed: 30/09–01/05, hiking, cycling, fishing, golf course 10km

Fluent English spoken

——From Le Mans, take the D301 towards Bonnétable. The château is on the right, before Chanteloup.

PRICE STRUCTURE

5 Bedrooms
kitchen, shower room with wc, double bed, single bed:
FF400 (2 people)
FF450 (3 people)

(2 rooms) shower room with wc, twin beds: FF350

shower room with wc, twin beds: FF300

lounge, shower room with wc, double bed, 2 single beds: FF450 (2 people)
FF550 (4 people)

Reduction: 2 nights

Capacity: 13 people

Michel & Nelly JUZEAU

'Le Pré du Doué'

4 rue de Trange

72700 PRUILLE-LE-CHETIF

Tel: 02 43 47 16 41

MICHEL.JUZEAU
@wanadoo.fr

Private Home

11 km - W -
LE MANS
Pruillé-le-Chétif:
railway station: 8 km
airport: 150 km
car essential

PAYS-DE-LA-LOIRE

LE MANS

PRICE STRUCTURE

2 Bedrooms and 1 Apartment

Jaune & Rustique: double bed: FF260

Apartment: lounge, television, shower room with wc, double bed: FF350

Capacity: 6 people

72.27 LE MANS

This place is only a few minutes away from the Le Mans 24-hour motor-racing circuit and the picturesque old town of Le Mans. Nelly and Michel's house is modern and cosy, and its large conservatory leads into their pleasant, wooded and undulating grounds with a small lake.

PROPERTY

private parking, extensive grounds, tv lounge, hosts have pets, pets not accepted, non-smoking, hiking, cycling, fishing, interesting flora, mushroom-picking, golf course 12km

Adequate English spoken

——From Le Mans, take the N157 towards Laval for 1km. Turn left on to the D246 towards Rouillon and Pruillé-le-Chétif. Le Pré du Doué is in the village on the route de Trangé. (From the autoroute, Exit Le Mans-Ouest and head towards Laval on the N157.)

Michèle BONNISSEAU

9, impasse de la Fosse

85420 BOUILLE-COURDAULT

Tel: (0) 2 51 52 42 17

Private Home

10 km - S E - FONTENAY-LE-COMTE
Bouillé-Courdault: railway station: 17km
car essential

85.11 FONTENAY-LE-COMTE

Michèle has cleverly combined the typical characteristics of this region in the dining room, with modern, functional bedrooms. The Japanese-style bedroom is very unusual and attractive. This is a comfortable place to stop, and excellent value for money.

PROPERTY

✵ ✵ ✵

off-street parking, garden, lounge, pets not accepted, kitchen, closed: 15/09–1/06, hiking, cycling, fishing, interesting flora 6km, riversports 10km, sea or lake watersports 50km

Fluent English spoken

PRICE STRUCTURE

2 Bedrooms

Chambre 1: bathroom with wc, washbasin, double bed: FF220

Japon: bridal room, shower, wc, washbasin, double bed: FF250

Extra Bed: FF80

Reduction: 2 nights

Capacity: 4 people

——Between Niort and Fontenay-le-Comte (on the N148 or from the A83, Exit Oulmes). Head towards Courdault. In the village, take the road towards the harbour. Then take the cul-de-sac which leads off this road on the right.

Monique FAVRE

'La Pérotine'

23, rue Jean Moulin

85770 LE-POIRE-SUR-
VELLUIRE

Tel: (0) 2 51 52 35 00

Private Home

9 km - S W -
FONTENAY-LE-
COMTE
Le-Poiré-sur-Velluire:
railway station: 25km
airport: 35km
car essential

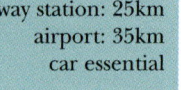

PRICE STRUCTURE

5 Bedrooms

Lavande: lounge, bathroom
with wc, 2 double beds:
FF370 (2 people)
FF740 (4 people)

Rose & Lilas & Muguet &
Pensée: double bed: FF370

Extra Bed: FF100

Capacity: 12 people

85.12 FONTENAY-LE-COMTE

**Monique's house is warm and friendly, and tastefully
decorated. She welcomes you to this house, typical of La
Vendée, in the heart of the Marais Poitevin. They have their
own fishing rights, or will take you on a boat trip through the
Venise Verte, or guide you on rambles in the nearby wildlife
reserve. On sale: Honey, antiques.**

PROPERTY

off-street parking, garden, tv lounge, pets not accepted, babies
welcome, free cot, 2 shared shower rooms with wc, hiking,
cycling, cycling, fishing, interesting flora, mushroom-picking,
gliding 15km, sea or lake watersports 30km, golf course 35km

Basic English spoken

——From the A83 or from Fontenay-le-Comte, head towards
La Rochelle on the D938. After 7km, turn right towards
Velluire and La-Poiré-sur-Velluire. The house is in the centre
of this village.

Mick-Allan LAGAUDE

'La Closeraie'

21 rue de la Paix

85450 CHAMPAGNE-LES-MARAIS

Tel: (0) 2 51 56 54 54
Fax: (0) 2 51 56 55 65

info@closeraie.com

Residence of
Outstanding Character

38 km - W -
FONTENAY-LE-COMTE
Champagne les
Marais: hosts can
collect from station,
railway station: 8km
airport: 26km
car essential

85.15 FONTENAY-LE-COMTE

Your hosts will provide an excellent welcome, in the heart of the fantastic Marais Poitevin and the Baie de l'Aiguillon, famous for its wildlife, flora and fishing. The bedrooms, dating from the 18th century, are furnished with antiques and overlook an internal garden leading to a private swimming pool. Out of season, dinner must be booked in advance. Bicycles for hire. On sale: Local produce.

PROPERTY

private parking, garden, tv lounge, hosts have pets, dinner available, packed lunch, kitchen, babies welcome, free cot, wheelchair access, swimming pool, hiking, cycling, fishing, hunting, interesting flora, golf course 4km, gliding 8km, sea or lake watersports 18km, golf course 26km

Fluent English spoken

——A83, Exit 7, N137 towards La Rochelle. At Moreille, right on to the D10A towards Puyravault for 5km. D25 on the right, for 3km to Champagne-les-Marais. La Closeraie is on this road, in the village after the place de la Mairie, at No.21.

PRICE STRUCTURE

3 Bedrooms and 1 Suite

Richelieu: shower room with wc, twin beds, single bed: FF360 (2 people) FF360 (3 people)

Soleil Bleu: shower room with wc, twin beds: FF320

Océan: shower room with wc, double bed: FF320

shower room with wc, twin beds: FF320

Talmond: shower room with wc, 3 single beds: FF320 (2 people) FF380 (3 people)

Extra Bed: FF60

Reduction: 16/09–14/06 and 3 nights and groups

Capacity: 12 people

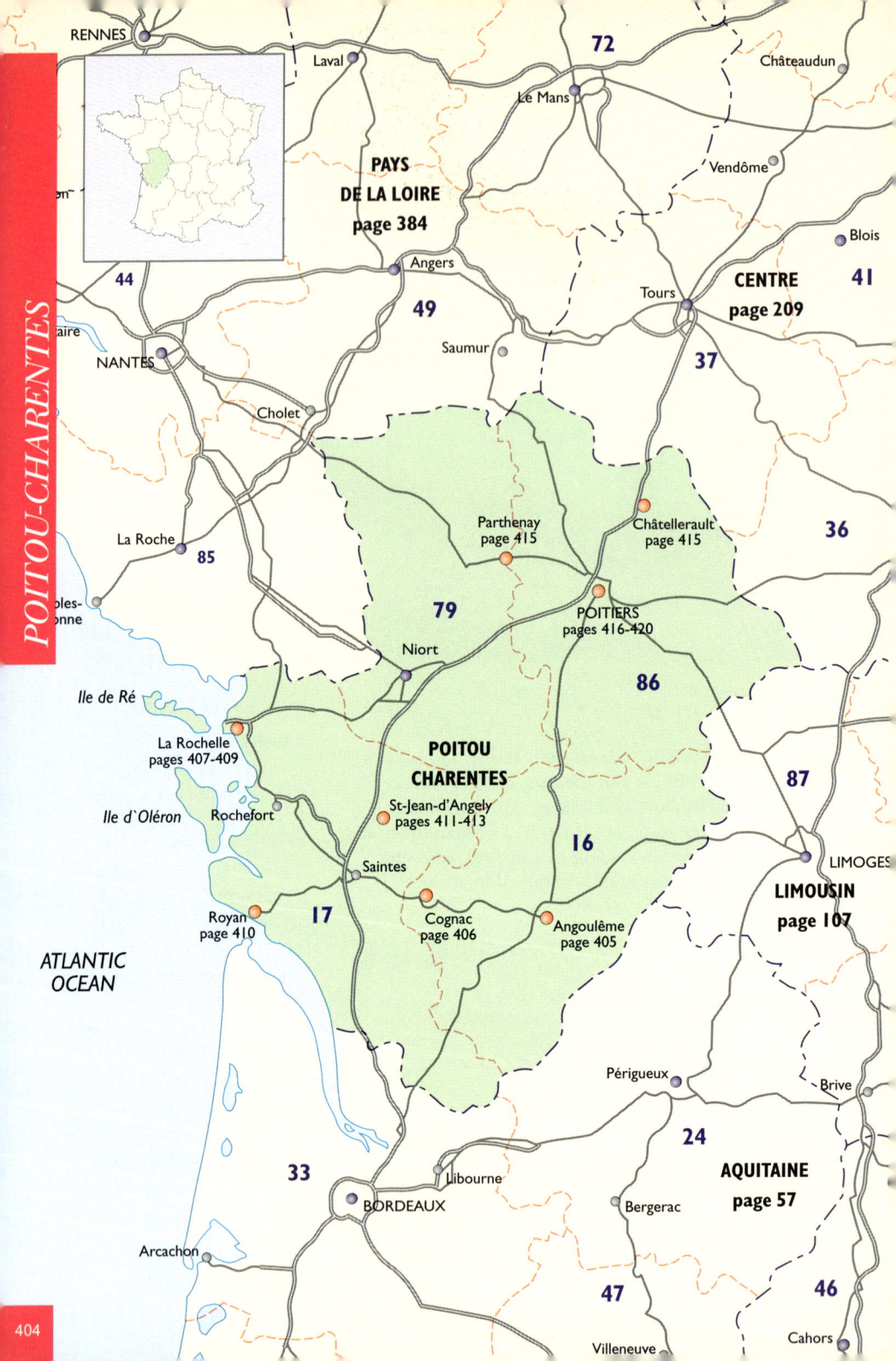

RENNES

72

Laval

Le Mans

Châteaudun

PAYS
DE LA LOIRE
page 384

Vendôme

Blois

44

Angers

Tours

CENTRE
page 209

41

49

Saumur

37

NANTES

Cholet

36

La Roche

85

Parthenay
page 415

Châtellerault
page 415

79

POITIERS
pages 416-420

Niort

86

Ile de Ré

La Rochelle
pages 407-409

POITOU
CHARENTES

87

Ile d'Oléron

Rochefort

St-Jean-d'Angely
pages 411-413

LIMOGES

Saintes

16

LIMOUSIN
page 107

ATLANTIC
OCEAN

Royan
page 410

17

Cognac
page 406

Angoulême
page 405

Périgueux

Brive

24

33

Libourne

AQUITAINE
page 57

BORDEAUX

Bergerac

Arcachon

47

46

Villeneuve

Cahors

Jenny & Derek
FORDHAM

'Les Tilleuls'

Chez Quillet

16290 MOULIDARS

Tel: (0) 5 45 21 59 00

info@les-tilleuls.fr

Residence of
Outstanding Character

20 km - W -
ANGOULEME
Moulidars:
railway station: 16km
airport: 100km
car essential

16.10 ANGOULEME

François Mitterand was born near here, and Jenny and Derek, a young English couple, give you a warm welcome to their authentic old Cognac farmhouse. Beautiful bedrooms with modern bathrooms and great evenings round the dinner table. You will have some good times at 'Les Tilleuls'. On sale: Jam.

PROPERTY

off-street parking, extensive grounds, tv lounge, hosts have pets, pets not accepted, dinner available, hiking, cycling, fishing 3km, riversports 3km, golf course 16km

——From Angoulême, take the N141 towards Cognac for 16km. Then turn left on to the D63 towards Moulidares. 'Les Tilleuls' is 2km further on, on the right.

PRICE STRUCTURE

4 Bedrooms
first room: shower room
with wc, double bed: FF320

second room: shower room
with wc, double bed, single
bed: FF320 (2 people)
FF420 (3 people)

third room: shower room
with wc, double bed, single
bed: FF320 (2 people)
FF420 (3 people)

fourth room: lounge,
shower room with wc,
double bed: FF380

Extra Bed: FF100
Reduction: 7 nights
Capacity: 10 people

Nicolle & Philippe
GIRARD

17, rue Samson

17520 JARNAC-
CHAMPAGNE

Tel: (0) 5 46 49 50 69

Fax: (0) 5 46 49 50 69

Private Home

15 km - S -
COGNAC
Jarnac-Champagne:
railway station: 15km
airport: 120km
car essential

POITOU-CHARENTES

COGNAC

PRICE STRUCTURE

1 Bedroom

television, shower room
with wc, 2 single beds:
FF200

Extra Bed: FF50
Reduction: 4 nights

Capacity: 2 people

17.20 COGNAC

Nicole and Philippe are retired vine-growers and will tell you everything you ever wanted to know about Cognac. Whether you go tasting at the distillery or visit the numerous Roman churches in the area, you are sure to sleep well in the large bedroom. After a wonderful night's sleep, enjoy the delicious 'galette charentaise' for breakfast.

PROPERTY

off-street parking, extensive grounds, lounge, hosts have pets, pets not accepted, babies welcome, free cot, closed: 01/10–31/03, hiking, cycling 15km, golf course 15km

Basic English spoken

——From Cognac, take the D732 as far as Pons. Then turn left on to the D700 towards Archiac. At the second crossroads, take the turn to Jarnac-Champagne and pass the cemetery and the 'Océane' grain silo. Then turn right into an avenue of sycamores, which leads to the house.

Arlette LAFUSTE

'Beaupréau'

48, av Louise Pichon - Rompsay

17180 PERIGNY

Tel: (0) 5 46 27 02 65

Fax: (0) 5 46 27 02 65

Residence of Outstanding Character

2 km - E - LA ROCHELLE
Rompsay: hosts can collect from station, railway station: 2km
airport: 5km

17.13 LA ROCHELLE

This is a family home surrounded by 1 ha of attractive grounds. It is only a few minutes from the beautiful town of La Rochelle, where you should not miss the 'Francofolies' and other festivals in the summer.

PROPERTY

off-street parking, extensive grounds, tv lounge, hosts have pets, telephone, kitchen, babies welcome, free cot, wheelchair access, 2 nights minimum stay (1/07–31/08), hiking, cycling, sea or lake watersports 2km, golf course 3km

PRICE STRUCTURE

3 Bedrooms

Verte & Rouge: bathroom with wc, double bed, single bed: FF290 (2 people) FF375 (3 people)

Bleue: shower room with wc along corridor, 2 single beds: FF270

Extra Bed: FF65

Reduction: 1/10–1/05 and 4 nights

Capacity: 8 people

——At La Rochelle station go towards Niort (Avenue Foch) then take the first road on the right (rue de Périgny) and follow the canal for 2km. The house is on the left.

Françoise SENAN

'Le Chalet du Treuil'

53/55, rue de la Fée au Bois

17450 FOURAS

Tel: (0) 5 46 84 28 80

Fax: (0) 5 46 84 28 80

Private Home

27 km - S - LA ROCHELLE
Fouras: hosts can collect from station, railway station: 20km airport: 20km

PRICE STRUCTURE

6 Bedrooms

Boyard & Ré: television, shower room with wc, washbasin, double bed: FF350

Aix & Loti: television, shower, washbasin, double bed: FF300

Passerose: shower, washbasin, twin beds: FF310

Oléron: shower, washbasin, double bed, 2 single beds (children size): FF300 (2 people) FF480 (4 people)

Extra Bed: FF100

Reduction: 01/09–30/06 and 4 nights

Capacity: 14 people

17.16 LA ROCHELLE

Opposite Fort Boyard of TV fame, le Chalet is situated in the heart of the town, 300m from the beaches, in a leafy location. With its bird reserves and oyster farms, Fouras is a lively resort. Françoise, president of the local radio station, knows her region very well. On sale: Seafood, wine, cheese.

PROPERTY

private parking, garden, hosts have pets, telephone, 2 wc, hiking, cycling, fishing, interesting flora, mushroom-picking, sea or lake watersports, golf course 6km

Fluent English spoken

——From La Rochelle, take the N137 and head towards Fouras. On entering the town, take the Ile d'Aix and La Fumée exit off the 1st roundabout. At the 2nd roundabout, take the 'Le Châlet du Treuil and Le Cimetière' exit. Go straight on for 400m. Nos.53–55.

Nicole & Raphaël PUNTI

'L' Avocette'

23, rue des Groies

17230 CHARRON

Tel: (0) 5 46 01 69 44

Residence of
Outstanding Character

15 km - N -
LA ROCHELLE
Charron: hosts can
collect from station,
railway station: 17km
airport: 15km
car essential

17.19 LA ROCHELLE

This old fisherman's longhouse, 15 mins. from La Rochelle, is full of interest: the brightly decorated bedrooms, the beautiful dining room, the swimming pool... and, of course, a really wonderful welcome from Nicole and Raphaël. Allow time for them to arrange one of their interesting excursions to the Baie de l'Aiguillon on a fishing boat, where you can try mussels on board. Fantastic.

PROPERTY

private parking, garden, tv lounge, hosts have pets, pets not accepted, non-smoking, swimming pool, closed: 01/11–15/11, interesting flora, hiking 2km, fishing 2km, golf course 5km, cycling 10km, bird-watching 10km, riversports 10km, sea or lake watersports 15km *Basic English spoken*

——From La Rochelle, take the D105 for 16km as far as Charron. Then turn right after the church, left after the school and left again after the post office. (From the A83, Exit 7, then the N137 towards La Rochelle. At Marans, take the D105 on the right towards Charron.)

PRICE STRUCTURE

**4 Bedrooms and
1 Apartment**
Ocre & Lavande: shower room with wc, double bed: FF295

Bleu & Jaune: shower room with wc, twin beds: FF295

Studio: kitchen, shower room with wc, double bed, twin beds: FF350 (2 people) FF450 (4 people)

Extra Bed: FF60

Reduction: 7 nights and groups

Capacity: 12 people

Bruno HARMAND

'Maison des Bucheries'

17120 MEURSAC

Tel: (0) 5 46 91 69 68

Fax: (0) 5 46 91 69 68

lesbucheries@minitel.net

Residence of
Outstanding Character

20 km - E - ROYAN
Meursac: hosts can
collect from station,
railway station: 15km
car essential

PRICE STRUCTURE

2 Bedrooms and 1 Suite

Bonheur: shower room with
wc, twin beds, single bed:
FF250 (2 people)
FF320 (3 people)

Paul: shower room with wc,
double bed:
FF250 (2 people)
FF450 (2 people)
& Virginie: 2 single beds:
FF250

Bergère: shower room with
wc, double bed: FF260

Extra Bed: FF70
Reduction: children

Capacity: 9 people

17.18 ROYAN

Bruno sees himself as a 'gentleman peasant'! He welcomes you to his typical Charente house. The bedrooms, which overlook vineyards, are cosy and welcoming and decorated with good taste. Fleur de Soleil member. On sale: Cognac, crafts.

PROPERTY

private parking, extensive grounds, lounge, hosts have pets, pets not accepted, dinner available, babies welcome, free cot, wc, 5 years old minimum age, closed: 1/01–31/01, hiking, cycling, vineyard, fishing 1km, mushroom-picking 3km, bird-watching 5km, interesting flora 10km, sea or lake watersports 12km, golf course 20km

Basic English spoken

——At Royan take the N50 towards Saintes. After Saujon, take the D136 on the right,towards Meursac. There is a sign to 'chambre d'hôtes' on the right before Meursac. (If coming from Saintes, go to Pisany, then to Meursac and at Meursac head towards Saujon on the D136.)

Jack & Margaret
HOWARTH

'Rochebeaucourt'

6, Rue Rose

17400 ST-JEAN-
D'ANGELY

Tel: (0) 5 46 32 03 00

Fax: (0) 5 46 32 03 00

Residence of
Outstanding Character

ST-JEAN-D'ANGELY
St-Jean-d'Angély:
railway station: 1km
airport: 60km

17.05 ST-JEAN-D'ANGELY

Although in the centre of the town, the home of this English couple is a haven of peace – totally quiet with a private interior courtyard. In the garden there are yew trees at least 250 years old. Easy to find, yet only 10 minutes from the autoroute A10. Excellent restaurants within a leisurely stroll.

PROPERTY

private parking, garden, pets not accepted, babies welcome, free cot, non-smoking, closed: 01/11–31/03, fishing 2km, sea or lake watersports 2km, riversports 2km, golf course 20km, bird watching 50km

Fluent English spoken

PRICE STRUCTURE

2 Suites

Bordeaux: bathroom with wc, double bed: FF480

+ Cherry: double bed: FF480

Pine: bathroom with wc, double bed: FF480

+ Twin: twin beds: FF480

Extra Bed: FF100

Reduction: 01/04–31/05 and 3 nights

Capacity: 8 people

——Exit 34 from the A10. Follow signs to Cognac/Saintes for 3km. At the second traffic lights (intersection with the N150), turn right towards the Centre-Ville. Continue for 200m to la rue Rose.

John & Jenny ELMES

'Le Moulin de la Quine'

17350 ST-SAVINIEN

Tel: (0) 5 46 90 19 31

Fax: (0) 5 46 90 28 37

elmes@club-internet.fr

Residence of
Outstanding Character

15 km - S W - ST-JEAN-D'ANGELY
St-Savinien:
hosts can collect
from station,
railway station: 3km
airport: 50km
car essential

PRICE STRUCTURE

1 Bedroom

Parc: shower, bathroom,
double bed, single bed:
FF280 (2 people)
FF330 (3 people)

Extra Bed: FF50
Reduction: 2 nights

Capacity: 3 people

17.06 ST-JEAN-D'ANGELY

Jenny and John, a friendly English couple, have created a really cosy atmosphere here. The bedroom leads on to an attractive and beautifully landscaped garden. You feel as if you are in the depths of the countryside, but can also smell the salt in the air from the ocean.

PROPERTY

off-street parking, extensive grounds, tv lounge, hosts have pets, pets not accepted, dinner available, non-smoking, wheelchair access, hiking, cycling, fishing 3km, golf course 25km, sea or lake watersports 35km

Fluent English spoken

——Take Exit N34 from the A10. Head towards St-Jean-d'Angély, and then turn right on to the D18 as far as St-Savinien. At the traffic lights, turn right and then, under the railway bridge, left on to the D124 towards Bords. At Pontreau, there is a track on the left (by the derelict barn on the corner).

Béatrice & Hubert
PELLETIER

'Domaine de
Fontsauzine'

17430 GENOUILLE

Tel: 05 46 27 27 52

Fax: (0) 5 46 27 31 99

info@fontsauzine.com
www.fontsauzine.com

Residence of
Outstanding Character

22 km - N W - ST-
JEAN-D'ANGELY
Génouillé: hosts can
collect from station,
railway station: 12km
airport: 40km
car essential

17.22 ST-JEAN-D'ANGELY

This beautiful old house was formerly a Charentaise farmhouse, and Béatrice and Hubert give you a very professional welcome to this quiet spot. Located 30 mins. from La Rochelle, in an idyllic country setting with a lake. Here they combine contemporary style with high standards of comfort, without detracting from the character of the house.

PROPERTY

✸ ✸ ✸ ✸

off-street parking, extensive grounds, lounge, hosts have pets, telephone, dinner available, kitchen, babies welcome, free cot, swimming pool, tennis court, hiking, cycling, fishing, bird-watching 25km, sea or lake watersports 25km, golf course 30km

Basic English spoken

——From the A10, Exit 34 St-Jean-d'Angely. Head towards Tonnay-Boutonne for 11km. Then take the D114 on the right towards Surgères. Go through St-Crépin and, 500m after the water tower, it is on the right at the end of a wide avenue.

PRICE STRUCTURE

3 Bedrooms and 2 Apartments

Pavillon Etang: television, telephone, kitchen, shower room with wc along corridor, bathroom with wc along corridor, 2 double beds, twin beds: FF600 (2 people) FF1500 (6 people) Maison du Parc: television, telephone, kitchen, shower room with wc along corridor, bathroom with wc along corridor, 2 double beds, single bed: FF600 (2 people) FF1400 (5 people) Tropiques: lounge, television, telephone, kitchen, shower room with wc, double bed: FF910 Lagon & Corail: lounge, television, telephone, shower room with wc, double bed: FF470 Extra Bed: FF160 Reduction: 1/10–31/03 Capacity: 17 people

Laurence SARAZIN

'Château de Tréguel'

Route de Nantes

86190 CHALANDRAY

Tel: (0) 5 49 60 18 95

Fax: (0) 5 49 60 18 95

Château

20 km - E -
PARTHENAY
Chalandray:
hosts can collect
from station,
railway station: 30km
airport: 40km

PRICE STRUCTURE

4 Bedrooms and 2 Suites
Suite Comtesse & Suite
Honneur: television,
bathroom with wc, double
bed + en-suite room double
bed: FF400 (2 people)
FF600 (4 people)

Comte & Pavillon:
television, bathroom with
wc, double bed: FF280

Jumelles 1 & 2: television,
bathroom with wc, double
bed: FF300

Extra Bed: FF100
Reduction: 3 nights
Capacity: 14 people

86.02 PARTHENAY

This 19th-century château in the heart of Poitou, is in 25 acres of grounds, surrounded by venerable trees. A warm and lively atmosphere reigns. You may start by planning just an overnight stop, but you will not resist the temptation to stay longer in order to visit the Haut-Poitou wine cellars.

PROPERTY

off-street parking, extensive grounds, tv lounge, hosts have pets, dinner available, non-smoking, 2 nights minimum stay (15/11–15/03), hiking, cycling, fishing, mushroom-picking, bird-watching, sea or lake watersports 4km, golf course 15km

Adequate English spoken

——At Parthenay, take the N149 towards Poitiers. 500m before Chalandray, turn right into the lane. Continue for 300m. (Or, Exit Poitiers from the A10, and go on to the N149 towards Parthenay/Nantes.)

Germaine & Jacques BRETON

'La Doiterie'

86220 DANGE-ST-ROMAIN

Tel: (0) 5 49 86 43 77/ 06 81 96 22 32

Fax: (0) 5 49 19 17 71

Residence of Outstanding Character

20 km - N - CHATELLERAULT
Dangé-St-Romain: hosts can collect from station, railway station: 20km airport: 50km car essential

86.23 CHATELLERAULT

This impressive house, quietly situated on a former vineyard, is mid-way between Tours and Poitiers, the capitals of Touraine and Poitou respectively. Germaine and Jacques have travelled widely and are really into the history of the Acadiens, whose story is told in a small museum nearby. There is a beautiful view over the countryside from the terrace, where you will take breakfast.

PROPERTY ✹ ✹ ✹

off-street parking, extensive grounds, tv lounge, hosts have pets, dinner available, packed lunch, closed: 1/11–15/04, hiking, fishing 4km, golf course 25km, sea or lake watersports 25km, riversports 25km

Basic English spoken

PRICE STRUCTURE

2 Bedrooms
Corail: shower, wc, twin beds: FF240

Michel: shower, wc, double bed: FF240

Reduction: 3 nights

Capacity: 4 people

——From Châtellerault, take the N10 towards Tours. When you reach the village, head towards Vellèches (D1 and then the D22) for 3km. 'La Doiterie' is signposted on your right.

Denyse FOUCAULT

10 rue du Gué Rochelin

86190 VOUILLE

Tel: (0) 5 49 54 10 29

Fax: (0) 5 49 54 10 29

Residence of
Outstanding Character

18 km - N W -
POITIERS
Vouillé:
airport: 15km
car essential

PRICE STRUCTURE

1 Bedroom and 2 Suites
Marie Antoinette: shower
room with wc, double bed:
FF360

+ Petit Prince: shower room
with wc, bathroom, twin
beds: FF300

Garden houses:
1 – Le Petit Mazet: kitchen,
shower room with wc,
double bed: FF280

2 – Le Grand Mazet:
kitchen, shower room with
wc, double bed + en-suite
room double bed: FF300 (2
people) FF480 (4 people)

Extra Bed: FF80/120
Reduction: 2 nights
Capacity: 10 people

86.10 POITIERS (FUTUROSCOPE)

Madame Foucault is a charming lady. She has just finished reorganising this new home close to Futuroscope, in order to make her guests more comfortable. She loves medieval cookery and plants and their uses. Be sure to visits the beautiful forest of Vouillé 5km away. Fleur de Soleil member.

PROPERTY

off-street parking, garden, tv lounge, hosts have pets,
non-smoking, swimming pool, closed: 15/11–15/04, riding,
hiking, cycling, fishing, mushroom-picking, sea or lake
watersports 8km, golf course 30km

——In Poitiers, take the N149 towards Parthenay as far as
Vouillé. The house is close to the town.

Alain & Claude GAIL

'Château de Masseuil'

86190 QUINÇAY

Tel: (0) 5 49 60 42 15

Fax: (0) 5 49 60 70 15

Château

10 km - W -
POITIERS
Quinçay: hosts can
collect from station,
railway station: 12km
airport: 10km
car essential

86.15 POITIERS (FUTUROSCOPE)

Alain and Claude will receive you in their magnificent 15th-century château. Their kindness and warmth will ensure that you have an unforgettable stay with this family.

PROPERTY

private parking, extensive grounds, tv lounge, hosts have pets, kitchen, non-smoking, 2 wc, hiking, cycling, fishing, riversports, mushroom-picking 4km, sea or lake watersports 6km, golf course 15km

English spoken

——On the A10 exit Poitiers-Nord. Follow signs to Nantes for 12km. At the bottom of the small descent before Vouillé, turn left. Masseuil is 1.5km further on.

PRICE STRUCTURE

2 Bedrooms and 1 Suite
Empire: lounge, television, kitchen, shower, double bed: FF400

+ Louis XV: shower, double bed: FF400

+ Enfants: lounge, television, kitchen, 2 single beds (child-size): FF200

Louis XVI: shower, twin beds: FF400

Reduction: 3 nights

Capacity: 9 people

Georges REBILLARD

'Château de la
Guillonnière'

86410 DIENNÉ

Tel: (0) 5 49 42 05 46

Fax: (0) 5 49 42 48 34

chateaudelaguillon-
niere@wanadoo.fr

Château

15 km - S E -
POITIERS
Dienné:
railway station: 15km
airport: 20km
car essential

PRICE STRUCTURE

4 Bedrooms and 1 Suite

Napoléon III & George
Sand: bathroom with wc,
double bed: FF600

Les Bucoliques: shower
room with wc, double bed:
FF500

Les Moutons: bathroom
with wc, 3 single beds:
FF600 (2 people)
FF650 (3 people)

Diane de Poitiers: bathroom
with wc, double bed +
en-suite room single bed:
FF800 (2 people)
FF850 (3 people)

Reduction: 3 nights

Capacity: 12 people

86.16 POITIERS (FUTUROSCOPE)

There is a refined and friendly welcome in this superb château. Just as George Sand did, you will appreciate its peaceful atmosphere. The comfortable bedrooms and the extensive grounds are beautiful. Only 20 mins. from Futuroscope. Many magnificent Roman abbeys are nearby.

PROPERTY

off-street parking, extensive grounds, tv lounge, hosts have pets, pets not accepted, telephone, hiking, hunting, interesting flora, mushroom-picking, bird-watching, golf course 10km, fishing 10km, sea or lake watersports 15km

Fluent English spoken

——At Poitiers, take the N147 towards Limoges. At Fleuri, turn right on to the D2 towards Gençay. The château is between Fleuré and Vernon.

Annick & Jean-Noël CURNIS

'Manoir de Beaumont'

12 rue des Portes Rouges

86490 BEAUMONT

Tel: (0) 5 49 85 05 29

Fax: (0) 5 49 85 05 29

jncurnis@aol.com
http://members.aol.com
/jncurnis/index.html

Château

15 km - N E -
POITIERS
Beaumont:
railway station: 15km
airport: 15km
car essential

86.20 POITIERS (FUTUROSCOPE)

You will be charmed by this 15th-century hunting lodge on the Poitou wine trail (Henry IV had an affair with his cousin here!). It has now been totally refurbished, and Jean-Noël is adept at combining traditional features with modern comfort, a demonstration of all that is best in the area. You will be torn between the châteaux or Futuroscope. Fleur de Soleil member.

PROPERTY

✳ ✳ ✳

private parking, extensive grounds, tv lounge, hosts have pets, pets not accepted, telephone, babies welcome, free cot, mushroom-picking, vineyard, hiking 5km, cycling 5km, golf course 5km, fishing 5km, bird-watching 5km, sea or lake watersports 5km, interesting flora 8km

A10 (between Poitiers and Châtellerault) Exit 27. Head towards Poitiers on the N10 for 5km. In the place called 'La Tricherie', D82 towards Beaumont. In the town centre, D82 in the direction of Marigny-Brizay (you are in the rue des Portes Rouges) for 300m. The manor is No.12.

PRICE STRUCTURE

3 Bedrooms and 1 Suite
1900 & Régence : shower room with wc, double bed: FF370

Suite Familiale Directoire: bathroom with wc, shower, double bed + en-suite room 3 single beds:
FF460 (2 people)
FF800 (5 people)

Louis XVI: shower room with wc, double bed (queen size): FF400

Reduction: 3 nights

Capacity: 11 people

Monique & Michel
TABAU

'Château de la Touche'

86800 SAVIGNY-
L'EVESCAULT

Tel: (0) 5 49 01 10 38

Fax: (0) 5 49 56 47 82

Château

15 km - E -
POITIERS
Savigny -l'Evescault:
hosts can collect
from station,
railway station: 15km
airport: 20km
car essential

PRICE STRUCTURE

3 Bedrooms
India: bathroom with wc,
twin beds: FF520

Aurore: bathroom with wc,
double bed: FF520

Algarve: bridal room,
bathroom with wc, shower,
double bed: FF720

Extra Bed: FF90

Reduction: 4 nights

Capacity: 6 people

86.21 POITIERS (FUTUROSCOPE)

Your hosts are from the Midi and have brought warmth and sunshine into this large château. Spacious rooms, especially 'l'Algarve' which is endowed with a harpsichord and a large modern bathroom. M Tabau is the president of a regional cultural association. Fleur de Soleil member. On sale: Jams.

PROPERTY

private parking, extensive grounds, tv lounge, hosts have pets, telephone, dinner available, babies welcome, free cot, hiking, fishing 1km, golf course 5km

Fluent English spoken

——From Poitiers, head in the direction of Limoges on the N147 (Exit 29 from the A10, then towards Limoges). After 5km, Savigny l'Evescault is on the left. In the village, follow the signs for 'Château de la Touche.'

SWITZERLAND

Bourg

01

74

Annecy

Chamonix

Aix-les-Bains

Albertville

Chambéry

73

Vienne

St.-Etienne

St. Jean

38   Grenoble

RHÔNE-ALPES
page 499

Briançon
page 427

ITALY

07   Valence

05

Gap
pages 428-429

Privas

26

Aspres-sur-Buesch
page 402

Barcelonnette
page 422

Valréas
page 498

Sisteron
page 425

04

Bollène
pages 491-494

Digne

06

GUEDOC-
SSILON
ge 260

84   Carpentras
pages 495-496

30

Avignon
pages 485-490

Cavaillon
page 497

Apt
page 484

Moustiers-
Ste-Marie
page 481

Menton
page 441

MONACO

Baux-de-Provence
pages 456-463

Manosque
pages 423-424

PROVENCE-ALPES-
CÔTE D'AZUR

Grasse

Nice
pages 442-446

13   Salon-de-Provence
pages 467-470

Draguignan
pages 476-477

Cannes
pages 430-440

Arles
page 455

Aix-en-Provence
pages 447-454

83

St Raphaël
pages 482-483

MARSEILLE
pages 465-466

Brignoles
pages 474-475

Cassis
page 464   Bandol
pages 471-473

Hyères
pages 478-480

Toulon

MEDITERRANEAN SEA

Olivier TOUSSAINT &
Philippe BALOURDET

'Gîte de la Fourandève'

La Chanenche Haute

04340 MEOLANS-REVEL

Tel: 04 92 81 97 94

Fax: (0) 4 92 81 97 94

info@fourandeve.com
www.fourandeve.com

Private Home

15 km - W -
BARCELONNETTE
Méolans-Revel:
railway station: 70km
car essential

PRICE STRUCTURE

8 Bedrooms
bathroom with wc along
corridor, double bed, single
bed: FF260 (2 people)
FF330 (3 people)

shower room with wc,
double bed, single bed:
FF260 (2 people)
FF330 (3 people)

(2 rooms) shower room
with wc, double bed: FF260

bathroom with wc, 2 single
beds: FF260

shower room with wc along
corridor, 4 single beds:
FF400 (4 people)

shower room with wc, twin
beds: FF260 (2 people)
FF400 (4 people)

bathroom with wc, twin
beds, 3 single beds:
FF450 (5 people)

Capacity: 25 people

04.11 BARCELONNETTE

Olivier and Philippe have chosen a wonderful place to settle down, have now fulfilled their lifetime dream, and offer an excellent Alpine welcome to their guests. Situated beside a spring that pours from the rocks at 1,300m altitude, here you will find the sun and invigorating air of the les Alpes-de-Haute-Provence. Rub your eyes in amazement, but you are not dreaming – this place really is so beautiful.

PROPERTY

off-street parking, extensive grounds, tv lounge, hosts have pets, pets not accepted, telephone, dinner available, packed lunch, babies welcome, free cot, wheelchair access, hiking, hunting, mushroom-picking, fishing 2km, riversports 2km, sea or lake watersports 8km, cycling 10km, gliding 10km, winter sports 16km

Adequate English spoken

——At Gap, take the D900b towards the Lac de Serre Ponçon and Barcelonette for 56km. At Méolans-Revel, turn left on to a small road as far as La Fourandève.

Michèle & Bernard
SANTI

'Le Moulin du Carlet'

Route de Forcalquier

04300 NIOZELLES

Tel: (0) 4 92 75 28 94

Fax: (0) 4 92 75 28 94

Private Home

20 km - N -
MANOSQUE
Niozelles:
railway station: 6km
airport: 100km
car essential

04.07 MANOSQUE

You will find Bernard and Michelle between Le Lubéron and La Montagne de Lure. Their 18th-century watermill is straight out of a tourist brochure, with a small river, view over the lavender fields and many pleasant walks. You will not be disappointed. There are also many arts and crafts workshops around here.

PROPERTY

off-street parking, garden, pets not accepted, babies welcome, free cot, non-smoking, swimming pool, cycling, fishing, bird-watching 7km, hiking 10km, interesting flora 10km, sea or lake watersports 15km, gliding 15km, golf course 25km, mushroom-picking 25km

PRICE STRUCTURE

2 Bedrooms

Lys Orangé: shower room with wc, double bed: FF300

Agapanthe: bathroom with wc, double bed: FF330

Capacity: 4 people

——On the A7, Exit Avignon-Sud, head for Apt/Sisteron. On the A51, Exit La Brillane, head towards Forcalquier. Niozelles is on the N100, between La Brillane and Forcalquier. The mill is 800m from the village, and 4 km from Forcalquier.

Mme CHAMANT

'Campagne Saint Lazare'

04300 FORCALQUIER

Tel: (0) 4 92 75 48 76

Fax: (0) 4 92 75 49 07

stlazare@karatel.fr

Private Home

23 km - N - MANOSQUE
Forcalquier:
railway station: -
car essential

PRICE STRUCTURE

3 Bedrooms
(2 Double or Twin room rooms) bathroom with wc, double bed: FF500

shower room with wc, double bed, single bed: FF500 (2 people) FF750 (3 people)

Capacity: 5 people

04.10 MANOSQUE

Come and discover this region, described by the author Jean Giono, in this typical Provençal farmhouse. Dating from the 17th century, the farm is located in a haven of greenery, bordered by two rivers into which a spring flows. Forcalquier is nearby, with its bustling Provençal street market, as well as the observatory at St-Michel, and the towns of Contadour and Ganagobie. Fleur de Soleil member.

PROPERTY

Private parking, garden, lounge, cycling, fishing, hunting

——From Forcalquier, take the D16, the old route du Dauphin. St-Lazare is 800m further on, on the right (signposted).

Mike, Patricia FRANTZ &
Claude PASQUINI

'Vitaverde'

Le Claus

04230 CRUIS

Tel: (0) 4 92 77 00 89

Fax: (0) 4 92 77 02 33

vitaverde@aol.com

Private Home

20 km - S -
SISTERON
Cruis: hosts can
collect from station,
railway station: 22km
airport: 110km
car essential

04.05 SISTERON

Here in the Alpes-de-Haute-Provence you will find Patricia, Mike and Claude in their 17th-century mas in peaceful surroundings. They are young and friendly, into Green Tourism, and will soon teach you to love this magnificent area. On sale: Organic fruit and vegetables.

PROPERTY

private parking, extensive grounds, lounge, hosts have pets, telephone, dinner available, packed lunch, babies welcome, free cot, non-smoking, riding, hiking, cycling, interesting flora, mushroom-picking, winter sports 20km, gliding 20km, golf course 40km, riversports 75km

Fluent English spoken

PRICE STRUCTURE

2 Bedrooms

Iris: shower room with wc, double bed: FF310

Coquelicot: kitchen, shower room with wc, double bed: FF355

Extra Bed: FF80

Reduction: 08/11–03/04 and 3 nights and groups and children

Capacity: 4 people

——From the A51, take the Exit for Peyruis. Go on to the D951 towards St-Etienne-les-Orgues and Cruis.

Rose-France & René
LEAUTIER

'La Source'

05140 ST-PIERRE-
D'ARGENÇON

Tel: 04 92 58 67 81

Fax: (0) 4 92 58 62 11

Private Home

7km - W - ASPRES-
SUR-BUESCH
St-Pierre-
d'Argençon:
railway station: 7km
airport: 130km

PRICE STRUCTURE

5 Bedrooms
(2 rooms) shower room
with wc, double bed: FF212

shower room with wc,
double bed, 2 single beds:
FF212 (2 people)
FF294 (4 people)

Sous Pente – first room:
washbasin, double bed,
single bed: FF182 (2
people) FF223 (3 people)

Sous Pente – second room:
washbasin, double bed:
FF182

Extra Bed: FF40

Capacity: 13 people

05.04 ASPRES-SUR-BUESCH

This restored old farmhouse is near to a bubbling mineral
water spring, in the shadow of the mountain ridge known as
'serre'. They come from all over Europe to enjoy gliding and
hang-gliding, and some even parascend into the grounds! It is
here that the Alps merge in to Le Midi, and the weather and
the vegetation reflect this. Rose-France will be delighted to
advise on the variety of sports available, such as hiking,
climbing and sailing, or just discovering the local heritage.

PROPERTY

off-street parking, extensive grounds, kitchen, wheelchair
access, 1 shared shower room with wc, closed: 1/10–30/04,
hiking, fishing, hunting, mushroom-picking, gliding, cycling
12km, riversports 25km

——From Gap, take the D994 as far as Aspres-sur-Buesch. At
Aspres, take the D993 for 7km for St-Pierre-d'Argençon, and
the house is on the right after St-Pierre.

Jacqueline LABORIE

'Longue Haleine'

Puy-St-André village

05100 BRIANÇON

Tel: (0) 4 92 21 30 22/
06 84 04 11 72

Fax: (0) 4 92 21 30 22

sudalp@club-internet.fr

Private Home

4 km - S W -
BRIANÇON
Puy-St-André:
railway station: 4km
car essential

05.03 BRIANCON

A friendly couple, in this little village which overlooks Briançon. The house is quietly situated with a magnificent, uninterrupted view. The ski resort claims the record for the most hours of sunshine in France! As for the walks – brilliant. Because of this, it easily deserves 3 'suns'.

PROPERTY

garden, pets not accepted, telephone, non-smoking, closed: 05/01–02/02 & 01/04-31/05 & 09/09–10 /12, hiking, cycling, fishing 4km, sea or lake watersports 4km, riversports 4km, interesting flora 10km, gliding 40km

——As you enter Briançon on the road towards Gap, at the traffic lights take the D35 towards Puy-St-André. As you enter the village it is the third house on the left, down a slope.

PRICE STRUCTURE

1 Bedroom and 1 Suite and 1 Apartment

Jaune: shower room with wc along corridor, washbasin, double bed: FF370

Rose: shower room with wc along corridor, washbasin, twin beds + en-suite room B2. washbasin, 2 single beds: FF370 (2 people) FF620 (4 people)

Apartment: kitchen, bathroom with wc, double bed (queen size), single bed: FF400 (2 people) FF560 (3 people)

Extra Bed: FF100
Reduction: 2 nights
Capacity: 9 people

Donald & Agnès CLARK

'La Combe Fleurie'

Route de Chaillol

05500 ST-BONNET-EN-
CHAMPSAUR

Tel: (0) 4 92 50 53 97/
06 70 21 40 66

Fax: (0) 4 92 50 18 28

l.CLARCK@online.fr

Private Home

15 km - N - GAP
St-Bonnet: hosts can
collect from station,
bus station: 1km
airport: 90km

PRICE STRUCTURE

6 Bedrooms

Mazurka: shower room with
wc, double bed: FF260

Bourrée & Badoise &
Troïka: shower room with
wc, double bed, single bed:
FF260 (2 people)
FF325 (3 people)

Ronde: bathroom with wc,
double bed, single bed:
FF260 (2 people)
FF325 (3 people)

Rigodon: shower room with
wc, double bed, 3 single
beds: FF260 (2 people)
FF400 (5 people)

Extra Bed: FF50
Reduction: groups and
children
Capacity: 19 people

05.02 GAP

This place is on the Grenoble–Gap road, but forget about
your car. Here, you are at the gateway to the Parc National
des Ecrins, where you can walk, ski, breathe the fresh air and
recharge your batteries. Tourism operates here all the year
round, with ski resorts, wonderful countryside, mountains
and many outdoor activities and sports. Wander through the
tempting markets, full of local produce, and ideal for
unusual souvenirs.

PROPERTY

off-street parking, garden, tv lounge, telephone, dinner
available, packed lunch, babies welcome, free cot, hiking,
cycling, fishing, riversports, winter sports

Fluent English spoken

——In Gap, take the N85 towards Grenoble. Turn right to
St-Bonnet. The house is just after the village.

Régine & Alphonse
HAMELIJNCK

Dessous le Serre

05130 SIGOYER

Tel: (0) 4 92 57 93 95/
06 16 89 85 89

QUALITEXT
@wanadoo.fr

Private Home

20 km - S - GAP
Sigoyer: hosts can
collect from station,
railway station: 20km
airport: 180km

05.05 GAP

Régine is German and Alphonse Dutch, and you will love
their home. There is a feeling of space and fresh air in this
large, modern chalet with split level rooms, bay windows and
the lounge designed around the large fireplace. From the
terrace there is a panoramic view over the valley of la
Durance and the Parc National des Ecrins, a paradise for
hikers. The nearby aerodrome specialises in all types of flying
activities, very much en-vogue in this area. Life is good here.

PROPERTY

off-street parking, garden, tv lounge, hosts have pets, dinner
available, hiking, cycling 10km, fishing 10km, hunting 10km,
interesting flora 20km, golf course 30km, lake watersports
30km, riversports 30km, winter sports 30km, gliding 30km

Fluent English spoken

——From Gap, take the N85 (Route Napoléon) as far
as the Tallard
aerodrome. Then take the D219 on the right towards Sigoyer.
The house is on the right, on a bend, 1.5km before Sigoyer.

PRICE STRUCTURE

2 Bedrooms

first room: television, shower room with wc, twin beds,
cot: FF250

second room: shower, wc,
double bed, cot: FF250

Capacity: 4 people

Ariane CHARLIER

623, chemin Argelas

06250 MOUGINS

Tel: (0) 4 93 46 55 84/
06 10 28 79 03

Private Home

4 km - N - CANNES
Mougins: hosts can
collect from station,
railway station: 6km
airport: 20km
car essential

PRICE STRUCTURE

2 Bedrooms
first room: television,
kitchen, shower room with
wc, double bed, cot: FF350

second room: shower room
with wc, double bed, cot:
FF350

Reduction: 01/09–30/05
and 2 nights

Capacity: 4 people

06.05 CANNES

A Provençal house in verdant surroundings only 10 mins. from Cannes. Very quiet, with a large garden on the edge of the forest. Spacious, pleasant rooms, ideal for long stays.

PROPERTY

private parking, garden, tv lounge, packed lunch, babies welcome, free cot, non-smoking, swimming pool, 2 nights minimum stay, hiking, interesting flora, mushroom-picking, golf course 2km, fishing 8km, sea or lake watersports 8km, riversports 13km, gliding 50km

Basic English spoken

——On the A8, Exit 42 Cannes/Mougins. Go down towards Cannes. At the 3rd set of traffic lights, there is a car park on the left with a phone box. Phone your hosts who will come and collect you.

Patrick GUEGUEN

'Marina Cottage'

Villa N°28 - 246 bd des Ecureuils

06210 MANDELIEU

Tel: (0) 4 93 93 59 70/ 06 11 10 96 31

Fax: (0) 4 93 49 90 12

Private Home

2 km - W - CANNES
Mandelieu: hosts can collect from station,
railway station: 5km
airport: 40km

06.08 CANNES

This American-style house on a river is part of a residence run for your comfort and safety. You reach the sea via the marina, and they also organise tennis and diving... and there is a swimming pool.

PROPERTY

private parking, garden, tv lounge, hosts have pets, dinner available, swimming pool, tennis court, hiking, cycling, golf course, fishing, sea or lake watersports, interesting flora 5km, hunting 10km, mushroom-picking 10km, gliding 30km, winter sports 50km

Fluent English spoken

PRICE STRUCTURE

2 Bedrooms

first room: television, telephone, shower room with wc, bathroom, twin beds: FF300

second room: shower room with wc, bathroom, double bed: FF300

Capacity: 4 people

——On the A8 take Exit 40 to Mandelieu-La Napoule. Turn right and right again towards 'Location Orion' in the avenue de la Siagne.

Catherine KING

'La Rivolte'

Chemin des Lierres

06130 GRASSE

Tel: (0) 4 93 36 81 58

Fax: (0) 4 93 36 87 29

larivolte@aol.com
www.larivolte.com

Residence of
Outstanding Character

17 km - N - CANNES
Grasse: hosts can
collect from station,
railway station: 17km
airport: 35km

PRICE STRUCTURE

8 Bedrooms
Jasmin: bathroom with wc,
double bed: FF750
Rose: shower room with wc,
double bed: FF600
Mimosa & Violette:
bathroom with wc, twin
beds: FF500
Lavande:shower room with
wc along corridor , twin
beds: FF400
Lilas: 4 single beds (child-
size): FF250 (2 people)
FF450 (4 people)
Camélia: bathroom with wc,
double bed: FF500
Annexe les Herbes: shower
room with wc, double bed:
FF500

Extra Bed: FF100
Reduction: 1/10–1/05
and 5 nights
Capacity: 18 people

06.09 CANNES

This large 1830s' building is in extensive terraced grounds in perfume country. All bedrooms have a magnificent view over the valley. Everything is geared to keeping the typical style of a traditional, large Provençal family home. They run courses on various themes.

PROPERTY

off-street parking, extensive grounds, tv lounge, pets not accepted, telephone, kitchen, babies welcome, free cot, 1 shared shower room, swimming pool, hiking 3km, cycling 3km, golf course 5km, hunting 10km, mushroom-picking 10km, fishing 15km, sea or lake watersports 16km, riversports 20km, gliding 30km, interesting flora 35km

Fluent English spoken

——Go to Grasse on the N85. At the bus station, go towards Nice via 'Au Thiers'. There, after 300m, take the first left and then immediately right. Then continue 150m to the entrance gate and continue up the hill.

Stella ERBIBO CHAUVET

'Stella's'

5, av Paul Arène

06600 ANTIBES

Tel: (0) 4 93 34 12 14/ 06 03 16 34 54

Private Home

10 km - E - CANNES
Antibes:
railway station: 1km
airport: 17km

06.11 CANNES

When you enter this former laundry, now transformed into a large house, you will find a charming interior garden, peace and quiet and spacious rooms with high ceilings. Stella has created a wonderful, traditional Provençal atmosphere in her home, finished in authentic lime-wash and ochre. On sale: Home-made marmalade.

PROPERTY

garden, lounge, pets not accepted, non-smoking, 12 years old minimum age, 2 nights minimum stay, fishing, sea or lake watersports, cycling 1km, golf course 10km, interesting flora 15km, winter sports 80km

Adequate English spoken

PRICE STRUCTURE

1 Bedroom
shower room with wc, twin beds: FF400

Extra Bed: FF90

Reduction: 1/11–01/03

Capacity: 2 people

——In Antibes, head for the port. After the roundabout continue along avenue de Verdun and it is the second on the right.

Janine & Gérard RONCÉ

'Mas du Murier'

1407, route de Grasse

06220 VALLAURIS-
GOLFE-JUAN

Tel: (0) 4 93 64 52 32/
06 09 57 42 80

Fax: (0) 4 93 64 23 77

Residence of
Outstanding Character

5 km - E - CANNES
Vallauris: hosts can
collect from station,
railway station: 3km
airport: 25km
car essential

PRICE STRUCTURE

2 Bedrooms

first room: lounge,
television, telephone,
bathroom with wc, twin
beds: FF420

second room: lounge,
television, telephone,
bathroom with wc, double
bed, single bed:
FF450 (2 people)
FF550 (3 people)

Extra Bed: FF100

Reduction: 15/10–31/03
and 4 nights

Capacity: 5 people

06.12 CANNES

A superb house in the forest. Your hosts are absolutely charming. The grounds are very well looked after and the interior decor is a great success. This is a little paradise only 4km from the sea.

PROPERTY

private parking, extensive grounds, tv lounge, hosts have pets, telephone, babies welcome, free cot, wheelchair access, swimming pool, 2 nights minimum stay, hiking, cycling, mushroom-picking, fishing 3km, sea or lake watersports 4km, golf course 5km, interesting flora 30km, riversports 30km

Basic English spoken

——In Cannes take the N7 towards Golfe-Juan, then Vallauris. At Vallauris take the road for Grasse.

Laurence GARY

2, rue des Belges

06400 CANNES

Tel: (0) 4 93 38 11 67/
06 82 40 80 32

Apartment

CANNES:
railway station: 1km
airport: 35km

06.13 CANNES

Magic! Right in the heart of Cannes, a few minutes from the Palais des Festivals; two of the bedrooms have a sea view. Take your breakfast on the patio, with its wonderful view over the rooftops of Cannes. A charming apartment, well-soundproofed.

PROPERTY

tv lounge, hosts have pets, sea or lake watersports, golf course 4km

Fluent English spoken

——Head for the centre of Cannes. It is the street which is at right-angles to the Palais des Festivals, between 'La Croisette' and the rue d'Antibes.

PRICE STRUCTURE

3 Bedrooms
Verte: television, shower room with wc along corridor, double bed, single bed: FF380 (2 people) FF510 (3 people)

Saumon: television, shower room with wc along corridor, twin beds, single bed: FF430 (2 people) FF570 (3 people)

Bleue: television, shower room with wc, double bed (queen size): FF430

Extra Bed: FF150
Reduction: 4 nights
Capacity: 8 people

Christiane & Alain
RINGENBACH

'Le Cheneau'

205, Route d'Antibes -
D103

06560 VALBONNE

Tel: (0) 4 93 12 13 94/
06 68 15 82 64
Fax: (0) 4 93 12 91 85

ringbach
@club-internet.fr

Private Home

10 km - N - CANNES
Valbonne:
railway station: 10km
airport: 16km
car essential

PRICE STRUCTURE

3 Bedrooms

Noisette: shower room with
wc, bathroom, twin beds:
FF430

Azur & Violine: shower
room with wc, bathroom,
double bed: FF350

Extra Bed: FF120

Capacity: 6 people

06.14 CANNES

This large house is situated in a beautiful village in the countryside, with easy access. There are lovely bedrooms and pleasant bathrooms with an additional separate entrance to the property. Everything is clean and tidy. You can do as much or as little as you like, with various sporting activities close by. Fleur de Soleil member.

PROPERTY

private parking, extensive grounds, lounge, pets not accepted, telephone, babies welcome, free cot, non-smoking, hiking, golf course, interesting flora, cycling 5km, mushroom-picking 10km, sea or lake watersports 12km, fishing 20km, riversports 20km, gliding 40km, winter sports 60km

Adequate English spoken

——Take the Exit for Antibes on the A8 towards Antibes/ Grasse/Mougins then Sophia-Antipolis. At the Bouillides cross-roads head towards Valbonne (D103) for 3km. 100m after the restaurant called 'Le Bois Doré' and just before the bus stop, go up a small lane. It is the last house at the top, on the left.

Eve & Henri DARAN

'L'Eglantier'

14, rue Campestra

06400 CANNES

Tel: (0) 4 93 68 22 43

Fax: (0) 4 93 38 28 53

Residence of
Outstanding Character

CANNES:
railway station: -
airport: 35km

06.17 CANNES

Your hostess loves meeting people, and will give you a warm welcome to her beautiful, spacious Midi-style house, which dates from 1920. You have everything you need, the place is spotless and decorated with excellent taste. Enormous breakfasts are served all morning in the large dining room You are 10 mins. walk from La Croisette.

PROPERTY

off-street parking, garden, tv lounge, hosts have pets, telephone, non-smoking, wc, sea or lake watersports, golf course 3km

Adequate English spoken

——In the centre of Cannes, take the boulevard Carnot and then the rue R. Viglieno on the right. Go right to the end which leads into the rue Campestra.

PRICE STRUCTURE

4 Bedrooms
Blanche: bathroom with wc, twin beds: FF620

Terrasse – Verte: bathroom with wc, double bed (queen size): FF620

Rez de Jardin – Bleue: bathroom with wc, twin beds: FF620

Rez de Jardin – Rouge: bathroom, twin beds: FF480

Extra Bed: FF140

Capacity: 8 people

Josette & Philippe
BERNARD

'Le Mas des Arts'

219, av de Peygros

06530 PEYMEINADE

Tel: (0) 4 93 09 95 19

Fax: (0) 4 93 09 95 19

Private Home

20 km - N W -
CANNES
Peymeinade:
railway station: 20km
airport: 40km
car essential

PRICE STRUCTURE

06.21 CANNES

1 Bedroom and 1 Suite
shower room with wc,
double bed: FF370

Suite: bathroom with wc,
double bed + en-suite room
twin beds: FF390 (2 people)
FF690 (4 people)

Reduction: 15/09–15/03

Capacity: 6 people

Philippe and Josette, a painter, will give you a warm welcome to their Provençal house, with a wonderful swimming pool and a panoramic view over the hills. Everything is neat and tidy, and the breakfast generous. Josette's charm, the kindness of their daughter and Philippe's warmth easily earn them 3 'suns'.

PROPERTY

private parking, extensive grounds, tv lounge, pets not accepted, wheelchair access, swimming pool, fishing 10km, hunting 10km, mushroom-picking 10km, sea or lake water-sports 10km, golf course 12km, gliding 15km, winter sports 50km

Adequate English spoken

——Go to Grasse on the N85 and take the D2562 towards Draguignan. Go through Peymeinade and, 1km after the village as you reach Jaïsous, follow the signs 'Rivierazur' on your left for 2km.

Christine CAMIA

'Villa Lou Mazet'

7, chemin du Parc Saramartel

06160 CAP D'ANTIBES

Tel: (0) 4 93 61 38 84

Fax: (0) 4 93 61 38 84

lou.mazet@wanadoo.fr

Private Home

10 km - E - CANNES
Juan-les-Pins:
railway station: 2km
airport: 15km

06.22 CANNES

Well-equipped and clean studio-apartment with a kitchenette, separate from the house. An ideal place to spend a few days, as it is only a few minutes from the old town of Antibes. Near the centre of Juan-les-Pins and the beach. Relax and enjoy the garden.

PROPERTY

off-street parking, garden, tv lounge, hosts have pets, babies welcome, free cot, 3 nights minimum stay, closed: 01/11–31/03, riding, cycling 1km, sea or lake watersports 1km, golf course 10km, interesting flora 15km, winter sports 80km

PRICE STRUCTURE

1 Bedroom

television, kitchen, bathroom with wc, twin beds: FF350

Extra Bed: FF100

Capacity: 2 people

——A8, Exit Antibes. From the town centre, go towards Juan-les-Pins/Cap d'Antibes. Take the boulevard du Cap, then right into the chemin du Crouton. Take the first turning on the left (chemin du Parc Saramartel).

Bernadette RAMBAUD

'Le Bellagio'

105, bd Wilson

06160 JUAN-LES-PINS

Tel: -06 60 44 27 47

Private Home

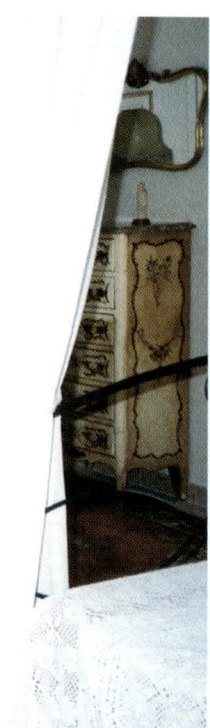

10 km - E - CANNES
Juan-les-Pins:
hosts can collect
from station,
railway station: 1km
airport: 25km

PRICE STRUCTURE

**4 Bedrooms and
2 Apartments**

(2 rooms) Baldaquins:
television, telephone,
bathroom with wc, double
bed: FF500

Baldaquin 3: television,
telephone, shower room
with wc, double bed: FF450

Baldaquin 4: television,
telephone, bathroom,
double bed: FF450

(2 studio rooms) television,
telephone, kitchen, shower
room with wc, double bed:
FF400

Extra Bed: FF100
Reduction: 15/10–15/04

Capacity: 12 people

06.26 CANNES

**Bernadette knows a thing or two about hospitality. She has
given up her 3-star hotel in the north of France and is now
ready to receive guests in the house that she has just
completely renovated. The rooms are spacious and this is an
ideal spot: a villa in Juan-les-Pins near to the beach!**

PROPERTY

private parking, garden, tv lounge, telephone, wheelchair
access, 2 years old minimum age, fishing, sea or lake
watersports, hiking 2km, interesting flora 2km, golf course
10km, riversports 10km, gliding 30km, winter sports 60km,
vineyard 60km

Adequate English spoken

——From the A8, Exit Antibes, head towards Juan-les-Pins and
follow the main boulevard (boulevard Wilson). The villa is on
the left, at the end of the boulevard.

Paul GAZZANO

151, route de Castellar

06500 MENTON

Tel: (0) 4 93 57 39 73

Residence of
Outstanding Character

MENTON
Menton: hosts can
collect from station,
railway station: 2km
airport: 30km

06.02 MENTON

**A south-facing villa in the hills above Menton. This is the
Côte d'Azur as you have always dreamed of it. Paul is Italian
and his wife English and their home exudes warmth and
kindness. Madame is a wonderful cook. Monaco is 9km away.**

PROPERTY

hosts have pets, babies welcome, free cot, swimming pool,
hiking, cycling, sea or lake watersports

Fluent English spoken

PRICE STRUCTURE

4 Bedrooms

(4 rooms) bathroom with
wc, double bed: FF320

Capacity: 8 people

——In Menton, follow the signs to 'Hôtel de Ville'. Pass in
front of l'Hotel de Ville and the fire station then take the road
to Castellar (be careful to take the road called 'route de
Castellar' and NOT the road to the 'Ciappes de Castellar').

Béatrice RONIN PILLET

'Le Clos de St Paul'

71, chemin de la Rouguière

06480 LA-COLLE-SUR-LOUP

Tel: (0) 4 93 32 56 81

Fax: (0) 4 93 32 56 81

leclossaintpaul.hotmail.com

Private Home

17 km - W - NICE
La-Colle-sur-Loup:
railway station: 4km
airport: 10km
car essential

PRICE STRUCTURE

3 Bedrooms
Les Olives: bathroom with wc, twin beds, single bed:
FF360 (2 people)
FF400 (3 people)

Les Blés & Les Pivoines: shower room with wc, double bed:
FF320 (2 people)
FF360 (2 people)

Extra Bed: FF60

Capacity: 7 people

06.10 NICE

This Provençale house is 2km from St-Paul-de-Vence. You will find Béatrice quite charming, and the delightful rooms are tastefully furnished. There is also a 'bar corner' and picnics are available. Good value at this excellent location.

PROPERTY

garden, lounge, hosts have pets, pets not accepted, swimming pool, hiking 3km, fishing 12km, sea or lake watersports 12km, golf course 15km, interesting flora 15km, bird-watching 30km, winter sports 45km, gliding 45km, riversports 60km

——In Nice, go towards Cannes. At Cagnes-sur-Mer, right towards St-Paul-de-Vence. At La-Colle-sur-Loup, pass the church and the roundabout. At the traffic lights, go towards La Rouguière, continue straight on. The house is on the right in the second valley, after the hamlet of old houses.

Pia MALET KANITZ

'Villa Panerâ'

8, av Panera

06100 NICE

Tel: (0) 4 92 09 93 20

Fax: (0) 4 92 09 93 20

Private Home

NICE
Nice: hosts can collect from station, railway station: 5km airport: 10km car essential

06.15 NICE

This small house is set high up in a peaceful location in Nice at the foot of Mont Chauve. Needless to say, there are many wonderful walks close by. The small rooms are elegantly decorated with old furniture. Pia, an artist, provides a warm welcome to her lovely home.

PRICE STRUCTURE

1 Suite
kitchen, shower room with wc, double bed + en-suite room single bed:
FF400 (2 people)
FF600 (3 people)

Extra Bed: FF100
Reduction: 3 nights

Capacity: 3 people

PROPERTY

off-street parking, garden, lounge, hosts have pets, telephone, 2 years old minimum age, 2 nights minimum stay, hiking 1km, cycling 2km, sea or lake watersports 2km, riversports 2km, fishing 5km, mushroom-picking 5km, hunting 15km, golf course 20km, interesting flora 20km

Adequate English spoken

——On the A8 towards Gênes (Genoa) take Exit 54 Nice-Nord. Follow signs towards Gairaut, taking the Aspremont/Le Vens road. After 800m turn left on to the N75 and it is the second house on the right.

Michelle & Guy BENOIT

'L'Olivier Peintre'

136, rue Saint-Claude

06640 ST-JEANNET

Tel: (0) 4 93 24 78 91/
76 30

Fax: (0) 4 93 24 78 77

Private Home

20 km - N W - NICE
St-Jeannet:
railway station: 30km
airport: 20km
car essential

PRICE STRUCTURE

5 Bedrooms
first room: lounge,
television, telephone,
shower room with wc, dou-
ble bed (super king size):
FF600

second room: television,
bathroom with wc, double
bed (king size): FF450

first floor – Apartment: double bed (king size): FF350
(2 people) FF500 (2 peo-
ple)
+ (2 rooms) double bed
(king size): FF350

Capacity: 10 people

06.18 NICE

This house, in the old village of St-Jeannet, has a pleasant garden and a swimming pool. Add to this a wonderful view and peace and quiet. The inside has great charm, and the decor in Room 1 is particularly attractive and the price well justified. Your hostess is very charming, and will be delighted to talk about art, in which she is an expert. It is possible to rent the whole floor as an apartment.

PROPERTY

off-street parking, garden, tv lounge, hosts have pets, pets not accepted, telephone, dinner available, kitchen, babies welcome, free cot, 1 shared shower room with wc, swimming pool, mushroom-picking 5km, golf course 20km, sea or lake watersports 20km, interesting flora 50km, winter sports 80km

Fluent English spoken

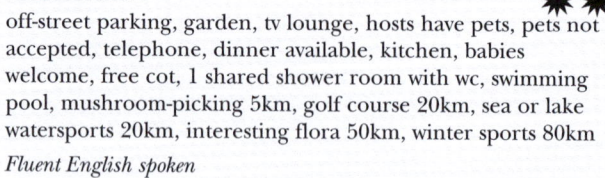

——On the A8 towards Nice, Exit St-Laurent-du-Var. Head towards La Gaude/St-Jeannet (D18) as far as St-Jeannet. In the village, take the main street, then continue to la place Ste-Barbe and go up the rue St-Claude as far as No. 136.

Monique & Pierre ALLIEZ

89 bd Louis Roux

06700 ST-LAURENT-DU-VAR

Tel: 04 93 31 74 35

Fax: (0) 4 93 31 74 35

alliez@club-internet.fr

Private Home

5 km - W - NICE
St-Laurent-du-Var:
railway station: 6km
airport: 2km
car essential

06.23 NICE

This Provençal villa is in a quiet location, at the centre of St-Laurent, 10 mins. from the centre of Nice and 5 mins. from the airport and beaches. There are supermarkets, a yacht harbour and restaurants nearby. This is the ideal base from which to visit the Côte d'Azur, St-Tropez, Menton, Monaco, Nice, Antibes, Cannes, the Esterel, Fréjus and the hinterland, including St-Paul-de-Vence. Windsurfing available. A warm welcome awaits, plus many tips on what to see. Fleur de Soleil member.

PRICE STRUCTURE

1 Suite
shower room with wc,
bathroom, double bed +
en-suite room 2 single beds:
FF380 (2 people)
FF580 (4 people)

Extra Bed: FF100

Reduction: 3 nights

Capacity: 4 people

PROPERTY

private parking, garden, pets not accepted, non-smoking,
closed: 22/1203/01, fishing, sea or lake watersports

——From Nice, on the A8, Exit 49 St-Laurent-du-Var. Follow
the River Var and, at the third roundabout, follow 'Centre-
Ville/Toutes Directions' and at the traffic lights turn right.
The house is No.89, immediately on the left, after the Post
Office.

Marlène DUNESME

'Domaine de Vallestreche'

486, chemin du Tacon

06610 LA GAUDE

Tel: (0) 4 92 11 01 25

Fax: (0) 4 92 11 01 25

dunesme@infonie.fr

Private Home

15 km - W - NICE
La Gaude: hosts can collect from station, railway station: 15km airport: 10km car essential

PRICE STRUCTURE

2 Bedrooms
(2 rooms) shower room with wc, double bed: FF350

Extra Bed: FF100

Capacity: 5 people

06.27 NICE

Charming rooms in this outstanding property, which is more like a habitable sculpture with a view over the sea, Cap d'Antibes, St-Paul-de-Vence, St-Jeannet and the surrounding mountains (Les Trois Baous). It is set in 3 ha of oak and olive woods, where wild thyme grows. Fleur de soleil member.

PROPERTY

private parking, extensive grounds, non-smoking, hiking, fishing 10km, sea or lake watersports 10km, golf course 15km

——From the A8, Exit 49 St-Laurent-du-Var, signposted to Centre-Ville La Gaude, St-Jeannet. At the IBM building, take the middle road at the intersection, which is rue des Serens. At the end, turn left in to rue Berenguier and, after 200m, turn right at the red sign DFCI, in to the chemin du Tacon. It is the last house on the right.

Laurence & René KOLL-WELTER CALMES

'Le Maisnil'

Les Faïsses du Cros

13510 EGUILLES

Tel: 04 42 92 64 37

Fax: (0) 4 42 92 38 52

Private Home

8 km - N W - AIX-EN-PROVENCE
Eguilles:
railway station: 8km
airport: 20 km
car essential

13.30 AIX-EN-PROVENCE

'Le Maisnil' is a superb house in the village of Eguilles, 8km west of Aix-en-Provence. It is built, on terraces, from local stone, and its quiet and sunny location also includes a beautiful view down over the valley, thick with vines. You are only 1 hour from Marseille, Arles, Avignon, the Luberon, Ste-Victoire, Cassis and the beaches. Fleur de Soleil member.

PRICE STRUCTURE

3 Bedrooms
first room: shower room
with wc, double bed: FF450

(2 rooms) bathroom with
wc, double bed: FF450

Extra Bed: FF100

Capacity: 6 people

PROPERTY

private parking, garden, lounge, babies welcome, free cot, swimming pool,

——At Aix, take the D10 towards Berre for 6km. Turn right towards Eguilles. At the roundabout, continue straight on (chemin de la Croix). Then take the street on the left and it is the third house on the left.

Pascale SOLARI

400, chemin St-Simon

13540 PUYRICARD

Tel: (0) 4 42 92 08 92

Fax: (0) 4 42 92 06 85

Private Home

10 km - N - AIX-EN-
PROVENCE
Puyricard:
railway station: 10km
airport: 30km
car essential

AIX-EN-PROVENCE

PRICE STRUCTURE

2 Bedrooms

ground floor – Abricot:
television, bathroom, double bed: FF240

first floor –
Bleue: television, shower
room with wc, washbasin,
twin beds, cot: FF260

Extra Bed: FF50

Capacity: 4 people

13.05 AIX-EN-PROVENCE

**Pascale loves meeting people. Her house is in the country
surrounded by woods and close to Aix. This is the heart of
Provence, cool pine forests and the beautiful town of Aix,
famous for its International Music and Dance Festivals.**

PROPERTY

off-street parking, extensive grounds, tv lounge, hosts have
pets, babies welcome, free cot, wc, swimming pool, hiking,
interesting flora, cycling 10km, golf course 15km, sea or lake
watersports 40km

Basic English spoken

——At Aix on the A8, head for Sisteron and join the D14
towards Puyricard. Continue on D14 towards Puy-Ste-
Réparade. 1.8km after the 'Village du Soleil', turn right into
the chemin St-Simon, then the house is on the right.

Elyane & Joseph
LEONARDI

'Chicalon'

2715, chemin de la
Guiramande

13090 Aix-en-Provence

Tel: (0) 4 42 58 06 54/
06 21 09 20 17

Fax: (0) 4 42 58 06 54

Private Home

AIX-EN-PROVENCE
hosts can collect
from station, railway
station: 5km
airport: 20km
car essential

13.18 AIX-EN-PROVENCE

Only ten minutes from Aix-en-Provence, Elyane and Joseph's villa, nestling between the hills, offers a really warm welcome. If you enjoy food, they will be delighted to serve you their delicious regional and Italian dishes. There is a 'Grande Randonnée' route nearby.

PROPERTY

off-street parking, extensive grounds, hosts have pets, dinner available, packed lunch, babies welcome, free cot, swimming pool, hiking, cycling, hunting, interesting flora 5km, golf course 7km, fishing 20km, sea or lake watersports 20km

Fluent English spoken

PRICE STRUCTURE

1 Apartment
Studio Tara: lounge, television, kitchen, shower room with wc, washbasin, twin beds, single bed:
FF300 (2 people)
FF350 (3 people)

Reduction: 01/09- 31/05 and 3 nights and children

Capacity: 3 people

——At Aix-en-Provence, take the Pont-de-l'Arc Exit, then follow signs to Creps and then continue along the chemin de la Guiramande, as far as number 2715. The house is straight on, at the end of this lane.

Monique & Henri
MORAND

'La Lustière'

442 Petit Chemin d'Aix

13320 BOUC-BEL-AIR

Tel: (0) 4 42 22 10 07

Fax: (0) 4 42 94 13 42

Private Home

7 km - S - AIX-EN-
PROVENCE
Bouc-Bel-Air:
railway station: 7km
airport: 15km
car essential

PRICE STRUCTURE

3 Bedrooms and 1 Suite
Marie-Claude: shower room
with wc, bathroom, twin
beds: FF350

Marie-Caroline & Victoria:
shower room with wc,
double bed: FF350

Pauline: bathroom with wc,
double bed + en-suite room
double bed:
FF350 (2 people)
FF600 (4 people)

Capacity: 10 people

13.37 AIX-EN-PROVENCE

A huge bastide in the style of Aix, dating from the 19th-century, with its painted ceiling, period décor and Provençal furniture. In the old chapel, there is always a crib surrounded by 'santons'. Situated amongst 25 ha of crops and pine trees. Fleur de Soleil member.

PROPERTY

Private parking, garden, swimming pool

——As you are leaving Luynes, on the N8 Marseille–Aix road, take the turning to Gardanne at the roundabout. After 600m, take the D59b on the right, towards Bouc-Bel-Air. After 1,200m, turn left at the white sign 'La Lustière', No.442.

Danielle & Yves
DORBAIS

'Les Roches Rouges'

Chemin de Cassade

13122 VENTABREN

Tel: (0) 4 42 28 94 40

Fax: (0) 4 42 28 94 40

dorbais@caramail.com

Private Home

10 km - W - AIX-EN-PROVENCE
Ventabren:
airport: 15km
car essential

13.40 AIX-EN-PROVENCE

This house is large and modern and situated near the hillside village of Ventabren, typical of Pagnol and Provence. The countryside here is well protected, and there is a magnificent, panoramic view of the valley. Total peace. Large swimming pool. Less than 1 hour from Marseille, Cassis, Avignon, Arles, the Camargue and the Luberon. Fleur de Soleil member.

PROPERTY

private parking, garden, pets not accepted, swimming pool, hiking, cycling, fishing, mushroom-picking, vineyard, golf course 7km, sea or lake watersports 35km, riversports 50km

PRICE STRUCTURE

1 Suite
shower room with wc, double bed + en-suite room bathroom, twin beds: FF450 (2 people)
FF750 (4 people)

Extra Bed: FF100

Capacity: 4 people

——Head for Aix-Ouest-Direct. Then Berre on the D10. After 10.7km, turn left then after 1.4km turn right. Your hosts will be happy to fax a map to you on request.

Joëlle & Paul DI ROSA

'La Bastide'

45, route de Sisteron

13100 Aix-en-Provence

Tel: (0) 4 42 21 56 19

Fax: (0) 4 42 21 56 19

Private Home

AIX-EN-PROVENCE
railway station: -
airport: 20km
car essential

PRICE STRUCTURE

2 Bedrooms

Double or Twin room – 1:
bathroom with wc, double
bed: FF350

Double or Twin room – 2:
bathroom with wc, double
bed: FF400

Capacity: 4 people

13.41 AIX-EN-PROVENCE

This 18th-century bastide has lots of charm, an attractive wooded garden, and is near the town centre. After 20 years travelling the world, Joëlle has decided to settle down in this house, typical of Aix, and her mission is to show Aix and Provence to her guests. Your hosts speak Chinese, Malay and Malgache, should this be of any help! Fleur de Soleil member.

PROPERTY

private parking, garden, closed: 20/12–1/04, hiking, cycling, fishing, mushroom-picking, vineyard, golf course 7km, sea or lake watersports 35km, riversports 50km

——In the centre of Aix, at place Bellegarde, take the 'Route des Alpes' towards Venelles and Sisteron. At the traffic lights, turn right and continue for 20 m and you will see the Résidence des Pinchinats, on the left.

Sarah & Paul
LE MARCHANT

720 chemin de Rapine

13090 Aix-en-Provence

Tel: (0) 4 42 20 44 92

paul.lemarchant
@infonie.fr

Private Home

AIX-EN-PROVENCE
railway station: 3km
airport: 25km
car essential

13.44 AIX-EN-PROVENCE

This is a charming modern house, high up overlooking Aix-en-Provence, surrounded by trees and flowers and absolutely quiet. The festivals at Aix, Avignon and La Roque d'Anthéron should not be missed. Sarah and Paul will be delighted to advise you on all there is to see and do in Provence. Fleur de Soleil member.

PROPERTY ✳ ✳ ✳

private parking, garden, hiking, cycling, fishing, mushroom-picking, vineyard, golf course 7km, sea or lake watersports 35km, riversports 50km

PRICE STRUCTURE

1 Bedroom
Mezzanine: lounge, shower room with wc, double bed: FF350

Extra Bed: FF50

Capacity: 2 people

As you leave Aix on the N7, towards Avignon, turn left just after the hotel 'Le Mas d'Entremont' in to the chemin de Rapine. After 1.2km, you will see a green gate on the left (No.720).

Martine & Joël
BARATHON

'La Villa des Cordeliers'

240, chemin du Faveloun
- Célony

13090 AIX-EN-
PROVENCE

Tel: 06 62 62 64 41

Fax: (0) 4 42 92 23 72

j.barathon@wanadoo.fr

Private Home

4 km - N W - AIX-
EN-PROVENCE
Célony:
railway station: 6km
airport: 30km
car essential

PRICE STRUCTURE

1 Bedroom and 1 Suite
Suite Cézanne: lounge,
television, bathroom with
wc, shower, double bed +
en-suite room twin beds:
FF820 (2 people)
FF980 (4 people)

Mirabeau: lounge,
television, bathroom with
wc, twin beds:
FF540

Reduction: 1/10–31/05
and 10 nights

Capacity: 6 people

13.49 AIX-EN-PROVENCE

Chez Martine and Joël, you really do get the best of Aix-en-Provence. This modern Provençal villa, surrounded by pines and orchards, is in the country yet only a few minutes from the town centre. Each bedroom has its own individual terrace. Aix is a lively town, with thousands of fountains, and is the heart of Provence, close to the Luberon, the Camargue, Avignon and the sea. Writers and poets love this place.

PROPERTY

off-street parking, garden, tv lounge, hosts have pets, packed lunch, babies welcome, free cot, swimming pool, closed: 1/11–1/04, hiking, cycling, mushroom-picking, vineyard, golf course 10km, sea or lake watersports 35km, riversports 50km
Fluent English spoken

——Leave Aix on the N7 towards Avignon. At the traffic lights, after the sign 'Célony', turn right towards 'Le Country Club', and then left 'Lou Camin di Faveloun', which has a sign 'interdit sauf aux riverains'. Continue for 240m.

Roger & Simone
MERLIN

'Le Mas des Colverts'

Route d'Arles

13460 LES-STES-
MARIES-DE-LA MER

Tel: (0) 4 90 97 83 73

Fax: (0) 4 90 97 74 28

Residence of
Outstanding Character

35 km - S W - ARLES
Les-Stes-Maries-de-la-
Mer:
railway station: 35km
airport: 30km

13.02 ARLES

The Provençal mas is situated at the end of a peninsula surrounded by lakes. Your hosts will introduce you to the heart of the Camargue, one of the favourite spots for migrant birds and pink flamingos. The view is unique.

PROPERTY

off-street parking, garden, lounge, packed lunch, babies welcome, free cot, 7 nights minimum stay: (01/07–31/08), hiking, fishing, bird-watching, sea or lake watersports

Fluent English spoken

PRICE STRUCTURE

3 Apartments
(2 studio rooms) kitchen, shower room with wc, double bed, single bed:
FF290 (2 people)
FF325 (3 people)

Flamants: lounge, television, kitchen, shower room with wc, double bed, 2 single beds: FF500 (2 people)
FF550 (4 people)

Reduction: 31/08–30/06 and 7 nights

Capacity: 10 people

——In Arles, take the D570 towards Stes-Maries-de-la-Mer. As you enter Stes-Maries, after the Hôtel Boumian, turn left on to the bridge, before the entrance to the Auberge Cavalière.

Anne-Marie BOUCHEZ

'Mas de la Muette'

Chemin du Mas d'Astre

13520 MAUSSANE-LES-ALPILLES

Tel: (0) 4 90 54 36 46/
06 83 33 68 88

Fax: (0) 4 90 54 36 46

Private Home

3 km - S - BAUX-DE-PROVENCE
Maussane-les-Alpilles:
railway station: 15km
airport: 30km
car essential

BAUX-DE-PROVENCE

PRICE STRUCTURE

2 Bedrooms

first room: shower room
with wc, double bed: FF320

second room: shower room
with wc along corridor, twin
beds: FF300

Extra Bed: FF85
Reduction: 1/1031/03

Capacity: 4 people

13.13 BAUX-DE-PROVENCE

Anne-Marie's country house is at the foot of Les Alpilles, 8km from St-Rémy-de-Provence and its famous Provençal market. There is also Alphonse Daudet's Moulin (at Fontvieille) and les Baux-de-Provence to visit.

PROPERTY

private parking, garden, hosts have pets, hiking 1km, cycling 1km, golf course 1km, fishing 3km, interesting flora 3km, mushroom-picking 3km, gliding 8km, riversports 15km, bird-watching 20km, sea or lake watersports 50km

Fluent English spoken

——At Arles head in the direction of les Baux-de-Provence and follow the D17 as far as Maussane. Cross Maussane and then take the D27 on the right towards St-Martin-de-Crau. At the bull-ring (avenue Frédéric Mistral) turn right and then keep left.

Yvon LUTZ

'Le Mas du Petit Puits'

Chemin Mario Prassinos

13810 EYGALIERES

Tel: (0) 4 90 95 91 18

Fax: (0) 4 90 90 64 43

Residence of
Outstanding Character

15 km - E - BAUX-
DE-PROVENCE
Eygalières:
railway station: 15km
airport: 20km
car essential

13.22 BAUX-DE-PROVENCE

This beautiful mas, furnished in 17th- and 18th-century-style, is only a short distance from Eygalières, a well-known and charming Provençal village. From the swimming pool, there is an uninterrupted view of Les Alpilles. The meals consist of traditional Mediterranean and Provençal dishes. You are 15 mins. from Les Baux-de-Provence. On sale: Wine, olive oil.

PROPERTY

private parking, garden, tv lounge, hosts have pets, telephone, dinner available, packed lunch, babies welcome, free cot, swimming pool, cycling, interesting flora, bird-watching, hiking 1km, fishing 5km, hunting 5km, mushroom-picking 5km, golf course 10km, sea or lake watersports 40km

Adequate English spoken

——From the A7, take the Cavaillon Exit. Head towards St-Rémy-de-Provence. After 12km, turn left towards Eygalières. Go as far as the church and then head towards 'Mas de la Brune' for 300m and turn left. After 100m turn left again.

PRICE STRUCTURE

4 Bedrooms and 2 Suites

No.2: television, bathroom with wc, twin beds: FF530

No.3: television, bathroom with wc, double bed: FF590

No.4: shower room with wc along corridor, double bed: FF430

No.5: television, bathroom with wc, double bed: FF630

Extra Bed: FF100

Reduction: 16/09–15/06

Capacity: 12 people

Solange & Alexandre
RANELLI

'Mas de Beaupré'

24+787 route de St-Rémy

13103 ST-ETIENNE-DU-
GRES

Tel: (0) 4 90 49 02 18/
06 21 30 10 02
Fax: (0) 4 90 49 02 18
mas-de-beaupre
@wanadoo.fr

Private Home

15 km - N W - BAUX-
DE-PROVENCE
St-Etienne-du-Grès:
hosts can collect
from station, railway
station: 8km
airport: 20km
car essential

PRICE STRUCTURE

3 Bedrooms
first room: telephone,
bathroom with wc, twin
beds: FF600

second room: telephone,
bathroom with wc, twin
beds + room Enfants:
telephone, double bed:
FF600

Extra Bed: FF100

Capacity: 6 people

13.23 BAUX-DE-PROVENCE

At the Mas de Beaupré, a warm and genuine welcome awaits
you. Breakfast is served in the dining area of the kitchen –
top quality and very interesting, along with a short verse from
your hosts each morning to get your day off to a good start!
Be sure to take your hosts' advice for your visits and, if you
enjoy walking in Les Alpilles, you can set off directly from the
house. The bedrooms are set back from the road.

PROPERTY

private parking, extensive grounds, tv lounge, pets not
accepted, telephone, packed lunch, babies welcome, free cot,
non-smoking, swimming pool, hiking, cycling, interesting flora
1km, mushroom-picking 1km, vineyard 2km, golf course 5km,
bird-watching 5km, gliding 5km, riversports 20km, sea or lake
watersports 30km *Fluent English spoken*

——Go to St–Remy and take the D99 towards
Tarascon/Nîmes. (From the A7, Exit Cavaillon, then the D99
towards Nîmes.) The house is on the left, 500m before St-
Etienne-du-Grés (there is a sign: '24+787').

Jacqueline ROUX

'Le Mas de L'Esparou'

Route de St-Rémy

13520 LES BAUX-DE-PROVENCE

Tel: (0) 4 90 54 41 32

Fax: (0) 4 90 54 41 32

Private Home

BAUX-DE-PROVENCE hosts can collect from station, railway station: 15km airport: 80km car essential

13.34 BAUX-DE-PROVENCE

You will get a warm welcome from Jacqueline in her quietly-located house, surrounded by pines. There is a fabulous view of the Château des Baux-de-Provence, which is illuminated at night. If you are interested in art, Jacqueline's husband will be delighted to introduce you to watercolours.

PROPERTY

off-street parking, extensive grounds, 1 shared shower room with wc, swimming pool, hiking, cycling, mushroom-picking 1km, golf course 2km, bird-watching 4km, fishing 8km, interesting flora 8km, sea or lake watersports 40km

——Take the D5 from St-Remy with les Baux on your right. Continue for 800m towards Maussane. The house is on the left, after the restaurant 'Le Fabian des Baux'. If you are coming from Maussane, take the D5 towards St-Rémy and, 300m after the aqueduct, take the lane on the right.

PRICE STRUCTURE

3 Bedrooms and 1 Suite

Lavande: bathroom with wc, double bed: FF380

Epi: bathroom with wc, double bed, twin beds: FF380 (2 people) FF580 (4 people)

Olivade: bathroom with wc, double bed, twin beds: FF380 (2 people) FF580 (4 people)

Suite: double bed: FF380

double bed, single bed: FF380 (2 people) FF480 (3 people)

Extra Bed: FF100
Reduction: 1/11–1/03

Capacity: 15 people

Nadine GAUJARD

'Mas dou Calan'

Vallon de la Verdière

13210 ST-REMY-DE-PROVENCE

Tel: (0) 4 90 92 24 18

Fax: (0) 4 90 92 24 18

Private Home

9 km - N - BAUX-DE-PROVENCE
St-Rémy-de-Provence:
railway station: 20km
airport: 80km
car essential

PRICE STRUCTURE

13.39 BAUX-DE-PROVENCE

2 Bedrooms
shower room with wc,
bathroom, double bed:
FF500

lounge, shower room with
wc, double bed: FF500

Extra Bed: FF100

Capacity: 4 people

This single storey mas is located 1.5km from the centre of St-Rémy. Here, you are in the heart of Provence, dominated by Les Alpilles, in a beautiful, quiet setting amongst the pines and the vines. There is a wonderful view and a delightful swimming pool. Tennis, riding and golf are on your doorstep and there are wonderful walks. The sea, if you like wind-surfing, is only 45 mins. away. Fleur de Soleil member.

PROPERTY

private parking, garden, non-smoking, swimming pool, hiking, cycling, fishing, gliding 7km, golf course 8km, interesting flora 30km, bird-watching 45km, sea or lake watersports 45km

——From Les Baux, take the D5 for St-Rémy and Avignon. (From the A7, Exit Cavaillon, and then the D99 towards Nîmes.) 1.5km from St-Rémy, take the route de la Combette, then the chemin Cadenière and Servières.

Nicole POULENARD

'Le Mas des Fleurs'

Quartier Chalamon

13210 ST-REMY-DE-PROVENCE

Tel: (0) 4 90 92 61 86

Fax: (0) 4 90 92 61 86

Private Home

9 km - N - BAUX-DE-PROVENCE
St-Rémy-de-Provence:
railway station: 20km
car essential

13.43 BAUX-DE-PROVENCE

This mas is 1.5km from the village of St-Rémy, and is the place to sample 'la douceur de vivre en Provence'. Relax and enjoy the Alpilles region to the full. Les Baux-de-Provence is only 8km away and Avignon, Arles, the Camargue and the Luberon arc less than an hour's drive. There is a private swimming pool and golf, tennis, cycling and riding nearby. Fleur de Soleil member.

PROPERTY

Private parking, garden, swimming pool

PRICE STRUCTURE

3 Bedrooms
(2 Double or Twin room rooms) shower room with wc, double bed: FF400

Double or Twin room: bathroom with wc, double bed: FF400

Reduction: 2 nights

Capacity: 6 people

——From Les Baux, take the D5 towards St-Rémy and Avignon. (From the A7, Exit Cavaillon and D99 towards Nîmes). Your hosts will send you a map.

Annick RICCI

'Le Mazet des Alpilles'

Route de Brunelly

13520 LE PARADOU

Tel: 04 90 54 45 89/
06 12 14 93 06

Fax: (0) 4 90 54 44 66

www.alpilles.com

Private Home

5 km - S - BAUX-DE-
PROVENCE
Le Paradou:
railway station: 12km
airport: 60km

PRICE STRUCTURE

3 Bedrooms

first room: bathroom with
wc, double bed: FF300

second room: bathroom
with wc, twin beds: FF340

third room: bathroom with
wc, double bed: FF340

Extra Bed: FF100

Capacity: 6 people

13.47 BAUX-DE-PROVENCE

**Annick is an artist, mad about painting, who will welcome you
warmly to her Provençal house. She will be delighted to
advise you on visiting Les Alpilles. There is a delightful
garden, full of flowers and shade, plus air conditioning and a
fridge in the rooms – the little extras that make all the
difference in the summer.**

PROPERTY

private parking, garden, hosts have pets, packed lunch, babies
welcome, free cot, hiking, golf course 4km, vineyard 4km,
cycling 8km, gliding 12km, bird-watching 50km, sea or lake
watersports 50km

Adequate English spoken

——From Les Baux-de-Provence, go to Maussane, and then
take the D17 towards Arles as far as Le Paradou. There, when
facing the bar Le Paradou, turn left in to the route de Belle
Croix, and continue straight along this road, as far as the
roadside cross. Le Mazet is on the left.

Joëlle PHILIPPE

'Mas Monblan'

D27 - La Grande Terre de la Pompe

13520 MAUSSANE-LES-ALPILLES

Tel: (0) 4 90 54 47 43
06 80 41 59 39

Fax: (0) 4 90 54 47 43

Private Home

3 km - S - BAUX-DE-PROVENCE
Maussane-les-Alpilles: hosts can collect from station, railway station: 25km airport: 80km car essential

13.48 BAUX-DE-PROVENCE

Chez Joëlle, you will understand the meaning of the joy of staying in Provence. Your wonderful, welcoming hosts will throw open their spacious, tastefully decorated mas to you, as well as the grounds of 1 ha. Take their advice on excursions into Les Alpilles, and you will find that this is the ideal spot to spend a long holiday.

PROPERTY

off-street parking, extensive grounds, tv lounge, dinner available, non-smoking, swimming pool, hiking, cycling, golf course 5km, vineyard 5km, gliding 8km, riversports 15km, interesting flora 50km, bird-watching 50km, sea or lake watersports 50km *Fluent English spoken*

——From Les Baux-de-Provence go through Maussane, and then turn right on to the D27, and continue towards St-Martin-de-Crau for 3km. On the left, you will see a little stone tower with the sign on it, so turn here and the mas is 150m further on.

PRICE STRUCTURE

3 Bedrooms and 1 Apartment

first room: television, bathroom with wc, double bed (queen size): FF600

second room: television, bathroom with wc, shower, wc, double bed: FF600

third room: television, bathroom with wc, shower, wc, twin beds: FF500

Apartment: shower room with wc, double bed, 2 single beds: FF1000

Extra Bed: FF100

Capacity: 10 people

Maud & Gabriel
APICELLA

'La Bastidaine'

6bis, Av des Albizzi

13260 CASSIS

Tel: (0) 4 42 98 83 09/
06 13 48 45 02

Fax: (0) 4 42 98 83 09

bastiden @club-
internet.fr

Private Home

CASSIS
hosts can collect
from station,
railway station: 1km
airport: 40km
car essential

PRICE STRUCTURE

4 Bedrooms
first room: shower room
with wc, double bed, twin
beds: FF450 (2 people)
FF620 (4 people)

second & third rooms:
shower room with wc,
washbasin, double bed:
FF400

fourth room: shower room
with wc, washbasin, double
bed: FF450

Extra Bed: FF100
Reduction: 15/11–15/03

Capacity: 10 people

13.24 CASSIS

This old vine-grower's bastide is spacious, and the beige-rose colour of the walls sets the tone of a place where you will feel at home. It is easy to find, yet quietly situated amongst the pines. Be sure to visit the famous Calanques de Cassis, where there is also a top sub-aqua centre. Fleur de Soleil member. On sale: Home-made jam.

PROPERTY

private parking, garden, hosts have pets, dinner available, non-smoking, hiking, cycling, sea or lake watersports, vineyard, fishing 1km, golf course 15km

Adequate English spoken

——From the A50, Exit Carnoux. High up above the town, at the traffic lights, head towards the station and Roquefort-la-Bedoule. Turn left at the 1st crossroads. When you are in the avenue des Abizzi, it is 300m further on, on the right.

Martine & Jean-Yves DUSSART

198, avenue de la Panouse

13009 MARSEILLE

Tel: 04 91 41 01 74

Fax: (0) 4 91 41 01 74

Château

MARSEILLE:
railway station: 1km
airport: 30km
car essential

13.29 MARSEILLE

The Château de la Panouse, which overlooks the city of Marseille, is a haven of tranquility between the sea and the mountains. Built in the 19th century by a Marseille ship owner, the property covers over 14,000m2 and is a good starting point for hiking trips into the Massif des Calanques. Fleur de Soleil member.

PROPERTY

✳ ✳ ✳

private parking, extensive grounds, lounge, dinner available, swimming pool, hiking, sea or lake watersports

PRICE STRUCTURE

2 Bedrooms

first room: bathroom with wc, double bed: FF320

second room: bathroom with wc, double bed: FF370

Extra Bed: FF100

Capacity: 4 people

——South-east of Marseille. Map on request.

Tyna & Jacky LEVRAULT-CONTRUCCI

'Villa Souleïado'

2 impasse des Amandeirets

13220 CHATEAUNEUF-LES-MARTIGUES

Tel: (0) 4 42 76 17 17
Fax: (0) 4 42 76 17 17

tynalev@aol.com

Private Home

20 km - N W - MARSEILLE
Chateauneuf-les-Martigues:
railway station: 20km
airport: 10km
car essential

MARSEILLE

PRICE STRUCTURE

2 Bedrooms

Tournesol: shower room with wc, bathroom, twin beds: FF320 (2 people)

Vanille: shower room with wc, bathroom, double bed: FF400

Extra Bed: FF120

Capacity: 4 people

13.45 MARSEILLE

This villa is set amongst relaxing pines, near the Parc des Amandeirets, where the 'cigales' (crickets) sing from June onwards. Only 5 mins. from the beaches and the famous 'calanques', and 35km from Aix-en-Provence and Arles. The Camargue is one hour away, as are Les Alpilles and Cassis. However, you may prefer to stay on the terrace, where breakfast is served beside the swimming pool, with its pool house and barbecue. Fleur de Soleil member.

PROPERTY

Private parking, garden, dinner available, swimming pool, tennis court

——From Marseille on the A55, Exit Gignac-la-Nerthe. (From Arles and Martigues on the A55, Exit Carry-le-Rouet, signposted to Marignane.) Then signs to Châteauneuf and, as you reach the village name sign, turn left before the park. Your host will send you a map on request.

Mireille & Robert
JAUFFRET

55, rue de la Liberté

13980 ALLEINS

Tel: (0) 4 90 59 36 87

Fax: (0) 4 90 57 39 13

Private Home

20 km - N - SALON-
DE-PROVENCE
Alleins:
railway station: 14km
airport: 30km
car essential

13.19 SALON-DE-PROVENCE

If you stay with Mireille and Robert at the heart of this quiet little village, between the Alpilles and the Lubéron, you will benefit from their expert advice on excursions and your choice of which festival to book. In their cute little house you may be lucky to have breakfast served on the terrace (home-made patisseries and jam). You are near to Aix-en-Provence, Avignon and Arles. Fleur de Soleil member.

PROPERTY

private parking, lounge, pets not accepted, babies welcome, free cot, cycling, golf course 2km, hiking 5km

PRICE STRUCTURE

1 Suite
lounge, shower room with wc, twin beds: FF280

Chambre simple: single bed: FF240 (1 person)

Extra Bed: FF100

Capacity: 3 people

——From the A7, Exit 26 Sénas and then take the N7 towards Aix-en-Provence. Turn right towards Alleins. In the village, park on the place de la Mairie and walk down the impasse Lavoisier on the left of the tower.

Diane de LALENE &
Serge DUPONT-VALIN

'La Magnanerie'

Montée de la Glacière

13450 GRANS

Tel: (0) 4 90 55 98 96

Fax: (0) 4 90 55 98 96

sdv@terres-et-lettres.com
www.terres-et-lettres.com

Residence of
Outstanding Character

PROVENCE-ALPES-COTE D'AZUR

5 km - S W - SALON-
DE-PROVENCE
Grans: hosts can
collect from station,
railway station: 7km
airport: 25km
car essential

SALON-DE-PROVENCE

PRICE STRUCTURE

3 Bedrooms
Manon+mezzanine:
television, bathroom, twin
beds: FF500

Aïda+mezzanine: television,
shower, twin beds: FF500

Juliette – balcon: kitchen,
along corridor shower room
with wc, double bed: FF400

Extra Bed: FF100

Capacity: 6 people

13.36 SALON-DE-PROVENCE

The magnanerie is an old silk farm whose golden stones, so typical of the region, are covered in creeper. Its high walls hide a secret garden and a welcoming pool, where jasmine and honeysuckle scent the evening air. Dreams hang on the walls of the chambres d'hôtes – art is present everywhere in light touches. The Camargue, Alpilles and Luberon are very near. Fleur de Soleil member.

PROPERTY

private parking, garden, tv lounge, hosts have pets, pets not accepted, telephone, babies welcome, free cot, wc, swimming pool, fishing, vineyard, hiking 1km, cycling 1km, golf course 7km, sea or lake watersports 10km, gliding 10km, interesting flora 30km, bird-watching 30km

Adequate English spoken

——A7, then the A54 towards Arles. Exit 14 Salon-Ouest/Grans. Your host will send you a map on request.

Monique & Richard BRAUGE

'Le CASTELAS'

Vallon des Eoures

13121 AURONS

Tel: (0) 4 90 55 60 12

Fax: (0) 4 90 55 60 12

lecastelas@aol.com
www.lecastelas.com

Private Home

7 km - N E - SALON-DE-PROVENCE
Aurons:
railway station: 40km
airport: 25km
car essential

13.38 SALON-DE-PROVENCE

The village of Aurons is quite outstanding, and has clung like a spiral staircase around this medieval hill for 11 centuries. This beautiful house, full of character, with its terraced walled garden, blends into the hillside covered in pines, oaks, thyme and rosemary. This is the Provence of Marcel Pagnol, with Les Alpilles, the Camargue and the Luberon on your doorstep. Richard is an antique dealer. Fleur de Soleil member.

PROPERTY

private parking, garden, pets not accepted, non-smoking, golf course 10km

PRICE STRUCTURE

3 Bedrooms

Carthame: bathroom with wc, twin beds: FF380

Lindigotier: bathroom with wc, double bed. FF380

Garance: lounge, bathroom with wc, double bed, single bed: FF420 (2 people) FF520 (3 people)

Extra Bed: FF100

Capacity: 7 people

——A7, Exit Salon. Take the D572 towards Pellissane and then the D68 to Aurons.

Martine ROUX

'Le Mistouflon'

Chemin des Bastides

13116 VERNEGUES

Tel: (0) 4 90 57 38 36

Fax: (0) 4 90 57 37 54

Private Home

9 km - N - SALON-
DE-PROVENCE
Vénergues:
railway station: 9km
airport: 35km
car essential

PRICE STRUCTURE

1 Suite

bathroom with wc, double
bed: FF450 (2 people)
FF700 (2 people)

+ Double or Twin room:
bathroom with wc, double
bed: FF450

Extra Bed: FF150

Capacity: 4 people

13.42 SALON-DE-PROVENCE

Martine welcomes you warmly to her large Provençal bastide, quietly situated amongst the pines, between Avignon and Aix. Vernègues is a town full of craftsmen. You are 4km from the Pont-Royal golf course, and Salon is the town of Nostradamus. Fleur de soleil Member.

PROPERTY

private parking, garden, swimming pool, golf course 4km

——On the N7 at Cazan, head towards Vernègues, and then turn left once, and right and right again. If coming via Salon, follow signs to Centre-Ville, and then to Abbaye de Sainte-Croix (brown signs).

Belle Viste

650, chemin de Maran

83330 LE BEAUSSET

Tel: (0) 4 94 98 62 11

Fax: (0) 4 94 98 62 11

Residence of
Outstanding Character

7 km - N E -
BANDOL
Le Beausset:
hosts can collect
from station,
railway station: 7km
airport: 40km
car essential

83.21 BANDOL

You will be overwhelmed by the taste and originality of this place, with its large swimming pool and magnificent views. Each bedroom opens on to the terrace. The sea, Châteauvallon and Le Castellet are just a few places well-worth a visit.

PROPERTY

private parking, garden, hosts have pets, pets not accepted, telephone, swimming pool, hiking 1km, cycling 1km, golf course 6km, fishing 7km, sea or lake watersports 7km

PRICE STRUCTURE

2 Bedrooms and 1 Suite
first room: shower room
with wc, double bed: FF350

second room: shower room
with wc, twin beds: FF350

Suite: shower room with wc,
double bed + en-suite room
2 single beds (child-size):
FF350 (2 people)
FF600 (4 people)

Extra Bed: FF100

Capacity: 8 people

——On the A50 Marseille–Toulon, Exit 11 for Le Castellet. Follow signs for Le Beausset and take the N8 towards Toulon. At the 2nd roundabout turn right and it is the road after the Shell petrol station.

Patricia BREBION

'Lou Bastidoun'
390, chemin du
Canadeau -
Hameau de la Migoua

83330 LE BEAUSSET

Tel: (0) 4 94 90 26 12-06
09 18 06 48
Fax: (0) 4 94 98 71 54

bastidoun@aol.com
members.aol.com
/bastidoun

Residence of
Outstanding Character

13 km - N E -
BANDOL
Le Beausset:
railway station: 13km
airport: 40km
car essential

PRICE STRUCTURE

2 Bedrooms

Marine: television, shower
room with wc, washbasin,
double bed, single bed:
FF420 (2 people)
FF520 (3 people)

Anglaise: television, shower
room with wc, washbasin,
double bed: FF420

Extra Bed: FF100
Reduction: 3 nights

Capacity: 5 people

83.25 BANDOL

This bastide is out in the wilds, on a hill. Ideal if you are looking for a quiet place with character. The bedrooms are brand new, very well decorated and have a separate entrance. Make use of the swimming pool and enjoy the warm welcome of your hostess. Bandol is a charming little seaside resort and its vineyards produce wine of the highest quality.

PROPERTY

off-street parking, extensive grounds, tv lounge, hosts have pets, babies welcome, free cot, non-smoking, swimming pool, vineyard, cycling 4km, hiking 5km, gliding 7km, golf course 10km, fishing 10km

Basic English spoken

———On the A50, Exit La Cadière, Le Castellet. Head towards Le Beausset. At the first roundabout, turn right towards Beausset Vieux/Le Rouve. 3km further on, in the hamlet of La Migoua, take the chemin du Canadeau on the right.

Magali de ROBIEN

'Villa Chabada'

Chemin Le Vallat - Fabrégas

83500 LA SEYNE-SUR-MER

Tel: 04 94 06 45 56

Fax: (0) 4 94 06 45 56

Private Home

13 km - S E - BANDOL
Fabrégas:
railway station: 8km
airport: 40km
car essential

83.37 BANDOL

Magali will welcome you with a smile to her quiet, spacious studio bungalow, with a cool, shaded terrace. You are only 10 mins. from the autoroute and 200m from the sandy beach. Magali loves to receive guests, and it shows. The area is not built up, as the villas are surrounded by trees and the shore-linc is protected. Whether you choose the coastal path or walks into the Provençal hinterland, you will return enthused by the villages made famous by Pagnol and the wild, yet green, countryside. This is Le Midi as you always imagined it – simple, natural, welcoming, with its climate gentle at any time of the year.

PROPERTY

garden, hosts have pets, packed lunch, kitchen, babies welcome, free cot, wheelchair access, hiking, fishing, mushroom-picking, sea or lake watersports, vineyard 10km, golf course 15km, interesting flora 20km *Fluent English spoken*

——A50 Marseille–Toulon, Exit Six Fours. Map on request.

PRICE STRUCTURE

1 Apartment
Suite Chabada – Double or twin room: wheelchair access, lounge, kitchen, bathroom with wc along corridor. FF350

Extra Bed: FF100

Reduction: 15/09–1/06 and children

Capacity: 2 people

Pierre ROGER
& Jean RIEDINGER

'Chez Pierre'

9, rue Montenard

83890 BESSE-SUR-
ISSOLE

Tel: (0) 4 94 69 79 84/
06 62 66 46 54

Private Home

15 km - S E -
BRIGNOLES
Besse-sur-Issole:
railway station: 35km
airport: 35km
car essential
——On the A8, Exit
Brignoles. Take the M7
towards Le Luc. After 13
km turn right to Besse-
sur-Issole. When in the
village, go as far as the
fountain and the statue,
and then take Rue
Montenard.

83.26 BRIGNOLES

Pierre has decorated this house, on three floors, with great taste and charm. Everything is designed for your well-being. The atmosphere is friendly, yet the location is quiet, in the heart of this 17th-century listed village. The ideal spot from which to explore Provence and enjoy its festivals.

PROPERTY

private parking, garden, tv lounge, hosts have pets, pets not accepted, telephone, 12 years old minimum age, closed: 01/10–31/03, hiking, fishing, sea or lake watersports, mushroom-picking 1km, hunting 2km, golf course 15km

Adequate English spoken

PRICE STRUCTURE
2 Bedrooms

Jaune: shower room with wc, double bed: FF350

Fleurs: bathroom with wc, twin beds: FF350

Extra Bed: FF100

Reduction: 01/04–31/05 & 15/09–31/10 and 2 nights

Capacity: 4 people

PROVENCE-ALPES-COTE D'AZUR

Anne
DEREGNAUCOURT

Le Clavet

83670 FOX-AMPHOUX

Tel: (0) 4 94 80 70 88

Fax: (0) 4 94 80 70 88

Private Home

30 km - N -
BRIGNOLES
Fox-Amphoux:
railway station: 45km
airport: 80km
car essential

BRIGNOLES

83.34 BRIGNOLES

Anne's hobby is repairing old lace, at which she is an expert. From her restored old farmhouse, there is superb view over the countryside, and peace and quiet is guaranteed. You are one hour's drive from the coast and Aix-en-Provence, and 30 mins. from Les Gorges du Verdon. All types of sports and activities are available nearby. Fleur de Soleil member.

PROPERTY

Private parking, garden, pets not accepted, dinner available, swimming pool, hiking, cycling, hunting, interesting flora, mushroom-picking, bird-watching, riversports

PRICE STRUCTURE

2 Bedrooms

shower room with wc, double bed: FF300

shower room with wc, twin beds: FF300

Extra Bed: FF50

Capacity: 4 people

——A8, Exit St-Maximin or Brignoles and head towards Barjols, Tavernes and Fox-Amphoux. Your hosts will supply a map on request.

Michael & Laurence
ALTMAN

'Mas de l'Hermitage'

St-Pons

83830 FIGANIERES

Tel: (0) 4 94 67 94 94/
06 86 56 63 29

Fax: (0) 4 94 67 83 88

Private Home

10 km - N -
DRAGUIGNAN
Figanières: hosts can
collect from station,
railway station: 20km
airport: 95km
car essential

PRICE STRUCTURE
3 Bedrooms and
4 Apartments

Menthe: lounge, kitchen,
bathroom with wc, twin
beds: FF400
Olive: kitchen, shower room
with wc, double bed: FF400
Bergamote: lounge, kitchen,
shower room with wc, twin
beds, 2 single beds (child-
size): FF350 (2 people)
FF550 (4 people)
Thym: lounge, bathroom
with wc, double bed: FF400
Anis : lounge, shower room
with wc, twin beds: FF350
Safran: lounge, kitchen,
shower room with wc, twin
beds: FF400
Santoline: lounge, kitchen,
shower room with wc, twin
beds: FF400
Extra Bed: FF130; Reduction:
01/10–01/04 and 7 nights;
Capacity: 16 people

83.23 DRAGUIGNAN

Take in the lovely open views, with park, woods and play-area
for children, as you enjoy breakfast on the terrace. Laurence
and Michael made the right decision in leaving Britain, and
have created the ideal environment in which to relax, with
Laurence attending to all the little extras that will make your
stay so memorable. Fleur de Soleil member.

PROPERTY

off-street parking, extensive grounds, hosts have pets, pets not
accepted, telephone, dinner available, kitchen, babies
welcome, free cot, wheelchair access, swimming pool, hiking,
cycling, hunting, interesting flora, mushroom-picking, bird-
watching, golf course 12km, sea or lake watersports 28km,
gliding 30km, riversports 38km *Fluent English spoken*

——On the A8 Exit 36 Le Muy, and head towards Draguignan.
At the 2nd roundabout take the D54 towards Figanières for
17km. Carry straight on at the junction with the road to
Fayence, and the house is 150m on the left (sign).

Catherine JOBERT
& Antoine DEBRAY

'Bastide des Moures'

lieu dit les Moures

83340 LE THORONET

Tel: (0) 4 94 60 13 36

Fax: (0) 4 94 60 13 36

catherine.jobert
@libertysurf.fr
www.bastide-des-
moures.com

Private Home

25 km - S W -
DRAGUIGNAN
Le Thoronet:
railway station: 20km
car essential

83.33 DRAGUIGNAN

This 19th-century property is built on a protected site, with 14 ha of grounds,. Some trees over 300 years old. This is the gateway to Provence and you are 5 mins. from the Cistercian abbey of Le Thoronet and 30km from the sea. There are three large bedrooms, decorated in warm Italian colours, a billiard room, a large swimming pool and a sauna. Your hosts cooking is typically Provençal. Fleur de Soleil member.

PROPERTY

private parking, garden, pets not accepted, dinner available, swimming pool, hiking, cycling, golf course, hunting, interesting flora, mushroom-picking, riversports, sea or lake watersports 30km

——From the A8, Exit Le Luc and go to Le Thoronet. Then turn right on to the D84 towards Vidauban for 4.7km, and then turn right at the sign 'Les Moures'. The house is 800m along an unmade road.

PRICE STRUCTURE

3 Bedrooms
Oasis: shower room with wc, bathroom, double bed: FF600

Arlequin: shower room with wc, double bed: FF600

Lavandin: bathroom with wc, double bed: FF600

Extra Bed: FF100

Capacity: 6 people

Pierre & Jacqueline
BRUNET

'Li Rouvre'

Chemin de Beauvallon
Haut

83400 HYERES-LES-
PALMIERS

Tel: 04 94 35 43 44

Fax: (0) 4 94 35 43 44

Private Home

HYERES:
railway station: 18km
airport: 6km

PRICE STRUCTURE

2 Bedrooms
Rez jardin: lounge, shower
room with wc, double bed,
2 single beds:
FF350 (2 people)
FF550 (4 people)

Rez piscine: bathroom with
wc, double bed: FF250

Extra Bed: FF50

Capacity: 6 people

83.11 HYERES

Hyères is well-known as being a favourite spot for retired people. Pierre is no exception – a retired engineer who loves bridge and DIY. The house is set high above the town and offers a splendid view of Toulon and Mont Faron.

PROPERTY

private parking, garden, tv lounge, hosts have pets, pets not accepted, dinner available, kitchen, swimming pool, sea or lake watersports

——In Toulon, take the A57 towards Hyères/Nice then the A570 towards Hyères. At the roundabout where the railway station is indicated on the right, take the opposite direction, on the left towards the North. You are advised to phone for complete directions.

PROVENCE-ALPES-COTE D'AZUR

Amélie & Robert
DIDIER

21, chemin des
Marguerites - La Fossette

83980 LE LAVANDOU

Tel: 04 94 71 07 82

Fax: (0) 4 94 71 07 82

Private Home

20 km - E - HYERES
Le Lavandou:
railway station: 40km
airport: 20km
car essential

83.29 HYERES

This villa, in a quiet, wooded garden, has a wonderful view over the sea and Les Isles du Levant–Port-Cros. You are 3km from the town centre and 400m from a sandy beach, where sea fishing, sailing and diving can be enjoyed. Aix-en-Provence, Cannes, St-Tropez, typical Provençal villages and the Gorges du Verdon are nearby. From Le Lavandou, take a boat to Les Iles Porquerolles and Port-Cros. Fleur du Soleil Member.

PROPERTY

private parking, garden, pets not accepted, fishing, sea or lake watersports

PRICE STRUCTURE

1 Suite
bathroom with wc, double
bed + en-suite room twin
beds: FF400 (2 people)
FF650 (4 people)

Capacity: 4 people

——When you are near, ring your hosts and they will come and collect you from the Tourist Office.

Elizabeth & Jean-Pierre
FARAUDO

'Villa Mogador sur le Cap
Nègre'

64-65, Corniche des
Agaves

83980 CAVALIERE-
LE LAVANDOU

Tel: (0) 4 94 05 78 54

Private Home

20 km - E - HYERES
Cavalière:
railway station: 40km
airport: 20km
car essential

PRICE STRUCTURE

4 Bedrooms

(2 rooms) bathroom with
wc, shower, double bed:
FF800

bathroom with wc, shower,
double bed: FF500

bathroom with wc, shower,
double bed: FF700

Extra Bed: FF100

Capacity: 8 people

83.35 HYERES

**The bedrooms here are top quality, equipped to luxury
standards. It is 25km from St-Tropez, calmly situated in a
private residence with 8,500m2 of Mediterranean gardens.
There is an outstanding view of the sea and Les Iles d'Or.
Sandy beaches are only 3 mins. away. Fleur de Soleil member.**

PROPERTY

off-street parking, garden, swimming pool, sea or lake watersports

——At Cavalière, in the commune of Le Lavandou. Contact
your hosts for directions or a map.

83.18 MOUSTIERS-STE-MARIE

A quiet, authentic village very close to the lake of Ste-Croix and the amazing Gorges du Verdon. Admire the view over the lake from the pool or the terraces. Your hosts run a restaurant in the village. On sale: Truffles, honey, home-made orange wine and jam.

PROPERTY

private parking, garden, tv lounge, hosts have pets, dinner available, packed lunch, wheelchair access, swimming pool, closed: 15/11–1/04, hiking, cycling, hunting, fishing 4km, mushroom-picking 4km, sea or lake watersports 4km, riversports 4km *Basic English spoken*

PRICE STRUCTURE
6 Bedrooms

(4 rooms) television, shower room with wc, double bed: FF275

(2 rooms) television, shower room with wc, double bed, single bed: FF350 (2 people) FF425 (3 people)

Extra Bed: FF50

Reduction: 1/10–30/03 and groups and children

Capacity: 14 people

Jean-Pierre BAGARRE

'Le Bosquet'

Quartier le Bosquet

83630 AIGUINES

Tel: (0) 4 94 70 21 02/ 06 81 34 39 92
Fax: (0) 4 94 70 22 09

Private Home

10 km - S - MOUSTIERS-STE-MARIE
Aiguines:
airport: 100km
car essential
——At Moustiers, take the D952 towards Castellanne. Turn right on to the D957 towards Aups and then left onto the D19 towards Aiguines.

Jennifer PRESTON

Les Bas Baudissets

83440 ST-PAUL-EN-
FORET

Tel: (0) 4 94 76 37 58

Fax: (0) 4 94 76 32 82

20 km - N - ST-RAPHAEL
St-Paul-en-Forêt:
railway station: 20km
airport: 70km
car essential
——On the A8 exit Les
Adrets. Take the D37 to
join up with the D562
(Grasse–Draguignan).
Turn left towards
Draguignan. At the 'Lou
Pascouren' auberge on
the D4, turn left towards
Fréjus. In St-Paul, stay on
this road and phone so
that your host can come
and fetch you.

83.20 ST-RAPHAEL

This charming English lady knows so well how to give her guests a great welcome. She has discovered a wonderful place in Provence that is the envy of all those who wish they had found it first. This magnificent village is full of character. You will feel at home here...

PROPERTY

off-street parking, garden, tv lounge, hosts have pets, pets not accepted, dinner available, swimming pool, 6 years old minimum age, 2 nights minimum stay, closed: 31/10–31/03, hiking, cycling, interesting flora 3km, fishing 4km, mushroom-picking 5km, gliding 5km, sea or lake watersports 15km, golf course 20km

Fluent English spoken

PRICE STRUCTURE
2 Bedrooms

first room: television, bathroom with wc, twin beds: FF500

second room: single bed: FF200 (1 person)

Extra Bed: FF100

Reduction: 01/04–30/06 & 01/09–31/10

Capacity: 3 people

Yvette & Guy PONS

947, bd des Nymphes

83380 LES ISSAMBRES

Tel: (0) 4 94 94 60 70

Fax: (0) 4 94 94 60 70

g-y.pons@lycosmail.com

Private Home

15 km - S W -
ST-RAPHAEL
Les Issambres:
railway station: 15km
airport: 75km

83.36 ST-RAPHAEL

This welcoming house is at Les Issambres, with a view over the Golfe de St-Tropez. The bedrooms are very comfortable, each with their own individual character. There is a garden with a swimming pool, and the breakfast, which includes home-made jam, is served on the large terrace. Fishing, tennis, sailing, skiing, hiking, visits to vineyards and the local Provençal markets can all be arranged. In the season, there are numerous arts festivals in this area.

PROPERTY

private parking, garden, pets not accepted, non-smoking, swimming pool, closed: 1/09–1/06, hiking, fishing, sea or lake watersports, vineyard, golf course 28km

——Situated between St-Maxime and St-Aygulf. When you reach San-Peire-les-Issambres, pass the 'Casino' supermarket, then take the 4th on the left. Follow signs to 'Agence de Neuville', and the villa is opposite the agency.

PRICE STRUCTURE

2 Bedrooms
Maison Indépendante:
shower room with wc,
double bed: FF400

Double or Twin room:
shower room with wc, twin
beds: FF400

Capacity: 4 people

Manuelle & Frédéric
MIOT

'Le Moulin de Mauragne'

Route de Marseille

84400 APT

Tel: 04 90 74 31 37

Fax: (0) 4 90 74 30 14

info@moulin-de-mauragne.com
www.moulin-de-mauragne

Residence of
Outstanding Character

APT
car essential

PRICE STRUCTURE

4 Bedrooms

Tabac: bathroom with wc,
double bed (king size):
FF800

Rouge: bathroom with wc,
double bed (king size):
FF850

Bleue: bathroom with wc,
double bed (queen size):
FF700

Verte: bathroom with wc,
double bed (queen size):
FF650

Capacity: 8 people

84.53 APT

What a relaxing spot! Le Moulin de Mauragne was built in the 10th century, at the water's edge in 9 ha of grounds. There is so much to visit in the Luberon, a paradise for hikers. Do not miss the Provençal markets and the pottery workshops... your car boot will never be large enough! Apt is the capital of glacé fruit.

PROPERTY

off-street parking, extensive grounds, lounge, telephone, babies welcome, free cot, swimming pool, closed: 1/11–15/03, hiking, cycling, mushroom-picking, vineyard, golf course 20km, riversports 30km

Fluent English spoken

——At the Apt tourist office, take the D943 towards Lourmarin. At the roundabout, continue towards Lourmarin for 800m. Then take the road on the left and continue for a further 800m.

Marie VIELLEUX

'Mas de Bassette'

Les Sabliers

13570 BARBENTANE

Tel: (0) 4 90 95 63 85

Fax: (0) 4 90 95 63 85

Private Home

10 km - AVIGNON
Barbentane:
railway station: 10km
airport: 10km
car essential

13.46 AVIGNON

Marie used to be one of our hosts at St-Etienne-du-Grès, but she has now moved to this 17th-century Provençal mas, near to Avignon, quietly situated on the edge of a pine forest. She has not lost her taste for running a B&B, and still looks after her guests just as well. She loves theatre, literature, les Arts Plastiques and is a marvellous source of information on everything to see and do in this interesting region. An excellent address.

PRICE STRUCTURE

2 Bedrooms
(2 rooms) bathroom with
wc, twin beds: FF600

Reduction: 1/11–1/04

Capacity: 4 people

PROPERTY

private parking, extensive grounds, tv lounge, hosts have pets, pets not accepted, babies welcome, free cot, swimming pool, tennis court, hiking, cycling, fishing, hunting, interesting flora, mushroom-picking, golf course 2km, gliding 8km, vineyard 15km, bird-watching 20km *Adequate English spoken*

——At Avignon, take the N570 towards Arles. Before Rognonas, take the D35 on the right towards Barbentane. If coming from the A7, Exit Avignon-Sud, then the N7 towards Marseille, and then right on to the D28 towards Châteaurenard, Rognonas and Barbentane.

André & Annie MALEK

'Le Rocher Pointu'

30390 ARAMON

Tel: (0) 4 66 57 41 87

Fax: (0) 4 66 57 01 77

amk@imaginet.fr

www.imaginet.fr/~amk

Private Home

12 km - S W -
AVIGNON
Aramon: hosts can
collect from station,
railway station: 12km
airport: 12km
car essential

PRICE STRUCTURE

**4 Bedrooms and
2 Apartments**

Noix de Coco: shower room
with wc, double bed: FF400

Bleue: shower room with
wc, twin beds: FF400

Clair de Lune: shower room
with wc, double bed, single
bed: FF460 (2 people)
FF560 (3 people)

Ecurie: bathroom with wc,
double bed: FF460

Studio 1: kitchen, shower
room with wc, double bed:
FF590

Studio 2: kitchen, shower
room with wc, twin beds:
FF590

Capacity: 13 people

30.11 AVIGNON

A Provençal mas in green countryside, surrounded by 7 ha of
'garrigue'. Both the bedrooms and the public rooms are
warm and comfortable. Substantial breakfasts served on the
terrace. Guests are welcome to use the swimming pool and
barbecue.

PROPERTY

off-street parking, extensive grounds, tv lounge, hosts have
pets, pets not accepted, telephone, kitchen, babies welcome,
free cot, swimming pool, closed: 1/11–28/02, hiking, fishing
3km, sea or lake watersports 15km, riversports 15km

Adequate English spoken

——In Avignon, take the 'Pont de l'Europe' towards Nîmes.
Just after the bridge, take the D2 along the Rhône towards
Aramon. Before the next bridge, turn right on to the D126
towards the N100, and continue for 2.3km. Then turn left.

Caroline & Vincent
SOULAT CORNILLE

'Les Vertes Rives'

Chemin des Magues

84470 CHATEAUNEUF-
DE-GADAGNE

Tel: (0) 4 90 22 37 10
Fax: (0) 4 90 22 03 31

www.pageszoom.tm.fr

Working Farm

10 km - E -
AVIGNON
Chateauneuf-de-
Gadagne: hosts can
collect from station,
railway station: 15km
airport: 7km

84.03 AVIGNON

We fell in love with Caroline, whose welcome proves how warm the people of the Midi can be. You will be surrounded by ponies, sheep and angora goats. 10 mins. from Avignon. On sale: Honey, eggs, poultry, jam.

PROPERTY

off-street parking, extensive grounds, lounge, hosts have pets, telephone, dinner available, hiking, cycling, golf course 5km, fishing 10km, riversports 15km, mushroom-picking 20km, interesting flora 25km, winter sports 35km

Fluent English spoken

PRICE STRUCTURE

4 Bedrooms and 1 Suite

Colline & Coté Jardin & Village: television, shower room with wc, twin beds: FF285

Ventoux: television, shower room with wc, 4 single beds: FF285 (2 people)
FF480 (4 people)

Suite Lubéron: television, shower room with wc, double bed, 2 single beds: FF285 (2 people)
FF480 (4 people)

Capacity: 16 people

——At Avignon, take the N100 towards Morières, Isle-sur-Sorgue and Apt. At Châteauneuf-de-Gadagne, turn right on to the D6 towards Caumont for 300m. Turn left and continue for 800m. The property is on the right.

Robert & Elisabeth
NEGREL

'La Pastorale'

Route de Fontaine-de-
Vaucluse

84800 LAGNES

Tel: (0) 4 90 20 25 18
Fax: (0) 4 90 20 21 86

Residence of
Outstanding Character

25 km - E - AVIGNON
Lagnes:
railway station: 25km
airport: 15km
car essential
——From the A7, take
exit Avignon-Sud. Go
towards Apt. At Petit
Palais, go towards
Fontaine-de-Vaucluse.
The house is on the D24,
on the short stretch
between the N100 and
the D99. ('La Pastorale'
sign and antique shop).

84.05 AVIGNON

You will be in heaven, sitting in the shade of a 300-year-old plane tree in this green and tranquil haven. An ideal base and an excellent area for antiques. L'Isle-sur-Sorgue, Fontaine-de-Vaucluse and Gordes are only 5 mins. away. On sale: Antiques.

PROPERTY

private parking, extensive grounds, lounge, hosts have pets, kitchen, hiking, cycling, interesting flora 1km, golf course 5km, gliding 20km

Fluent English spoken

PRICE STRUCTURE

4 Bedrooms

Bleue: shower room with wc, twin beds, single bed: FF350 (2 people) FF430 (3 people)

Rose: bathroom with wc, twin beds: FF350

Verte: shower room with wc, double bed, 3 single beds: F350 (2 people) FF590 (5 people)

Brique: bathroom with wc, twin beds, 2 single beds: FF350 (2 people) FF510 (4 people)

Extra Bed: FF80

Capacity: 14 people

Etienne JAMET

'Ferme Jamet'

Chemin de Rhodes -
Ile de la Barthelasse

84000 AVIGNON

Tel: (0) 4 90 86 88 35 06
61 10 88 35
Fax: (0) 4 90 86 17 72

www.avignon-et-
provence.com/ferme-
jamet/

Residence of
Outstanding Character

AVIGNON
Ile de la Barthelasse:
railway station: 6km
airport: 10km

84.31 AVIGNON

An old mas, surrounded by plane trees, on an isle in the middle of the Rhône. This is how you expect Provence to be. Avignon is not to be missed: sightseeing, culture, history, architecture.... Plan on staying several days here.

PROPERTY

off-street parking, extensive grounds, tv lounge, hosts have pets, pets not accepted, telephone, swimming pool, tennis court, 2 nights minimum stay (1/07–31/08), closed: 1/11–1/04, cycling, fishing 2km, sea or lake watersports 2km, golf course 15km, riversports 30km

Fluent English spoken

——From the A7, exit Avignon-Nord. Follow Avignon-Centre and the banks of the Rhône. Take the 1st bridge (Daladier) towards Villeneuve-lez-Avignon. From the bridge, turn right towards La Barthelasse. Follow the signs to Ferme Jamet.

PRICE STRUCTURE

**5 Bedrooms and
6 Apartments**
Matisse: telephone, bathroom with wc, 2 single beds: FF790, Marquet: telephone, bathroom with wc, twin beds: FF690; Dufy: telephone, shower room with wc, double bed: FF690; Derain: telephone, shower room with wc, double bed: FF590; Cézanne: telephone, kitchen, bathroom with wc, double bed, single bed: FF900 (3 people); Manguin & Renoir & Monet: telephone, kitchen, shower room with wc, double bed: FF850; Gauguin: lounge, telephone, kitchen, bathroom with wc, double bed, single bed: FF990 (2 people) FF1150 (3 people)

Extra Bed:150FF
Reduction: 1/10–30/06
Capacity: 27 people

Fabienne & Hervé ALBA

'Le Grand Jas'

Rue du Bariot

84800 LAGNES

Tel: (0) 4 90 20 25 12/
06 81 23 23 65

Fax: (0) 4 90 20 29 17

grandjas84@aol.com

Residence of
Outstanding Character

25 km - E -
AVIGNON
Lagnes:
railway station: 30km
airport: 15km
car essential

PRICE STRUCTURE

4 Bedrooms

Syrah: shower room with wc,
twin beds, single bed: FF420
(2 people)
FF500 (3 people)

Picholine & l'Ocrette:
shower room with wc,
double bed: FF420

Pastillère: shower room with
wc, double bed, single bed:
FF420 (2 people)
FF500 (3 people)

Extra Bed: FF80

Reduction: 16/09–31/05

Capacity: 10 people

84.42 AVIGNON

Fabienne and Hervé live in a mas full of character, very well placed at the foot of the Monts de Vaucluse. Many walking and hiking routes start from here, so it is a good way to get to know this magnificent area. Fleur de Soleil member.

PROPERTY

private parking, garden, tv lounge, hosts have pets, pets not accepted, babies welcome, free cot, non-smoking, swimming pool, hiking, cycling, interesting flora 1km, golf course 5km, sea or lake watersports 5km, fishing 6km, gliding 20km

Fluent English spoken

——From Avignon, take the N100 towards Apt. At l'Isle-sur-Sorgue, continue on the N100 and then turn left on to the D99 as far as Lagnes. Go up into the village, and it is the last house on the left just as you are leaving the village.

Ludovic & Eliane
CORNILLON

'Domaine St Luc'

26790 LA-BAUME-DE-
TRANSIT

Tel: (0) 4 75 98 11 51

Fax: (0) 4 75 98 19 22

Working Farm

14 km - N E -
BOLLENE
La-Baume-de-
Transit:
railway station: 25km
airport: 150km
car essential

26.27 BOLLENE

We got on really well with Ludovic and Eliane, in the heart of Provence. Their welcome to their 18th-century mas, which has been restored with great taste by Ludovic, could not be warmer. Apart from his passion for wine, he will also introduce you to truffles, which Eliane will let you sample as part of her top-quality cooking using fresh regional produce. Be sure not to miss visiting Grignan, reputedly haunted by Madame de Sévigné. On sale: Their own wine.

PROPERTY

off-street parking, garden, tv lounge, hosts have pets, dinner available, swimming pool, vineyard, hiking 1km, fishing 1km, mushroom-picking 1km, golf course 10km

Adequate English spoken

——From the A7 Exit Bollène. Then take the D994 as far as Suze-la-Rousse and left towards St-Paul-Trois-Châteaux. The grounds are on the left on the D117 after 5.5km.

PRICE STRUCTURE

6 Bedrooms
(3 rooms) bathroom with wc, double bed: FF400

(1 room) bathroom with wc, twin beds: FF400

(1 room) bathroom with wc, double bed, single bed:
FF400 (2 people)
FF480 (3 people)

sixth room: bridal room, bathroom with wc, double bed (queen size): FF600

Reduction: groups

Capacity: 13 people

Pierre-Jean & Suzanne
CHAMBON

'Le Mas Chamfrass'

Chemin de Carsan -
Quartier Vallien

30130 ST-ALEXANDRE

Tel: (0) 4 66 39 39 07

Fax: (0) 4 66 39 39 07

Private Home

15 km - S W -
BOLLENE
St-Alexandre:
hosts can collect
from station,
railway station: 35km

BOLLENE

PRICE STRUCTURE

2 Bedrooms

television, shower room
with wc, double bed: FF350

television, bathroom with
wc, double bed: FF350

Extra Bed: FF120
Reduction: 01/10–31/05

Capacity: 4 people

30.12 BOLLENE

A friendly couple in this Provençal mas, surrounded by pine trees. Nudism is allowed, but only around the swimming pool. You must then get dressed to visit les Gorges de l'Ardèche, the Pont du Gard and Vaison-la-Romaine! There are also local festivals.

PROPERTY

Private parking, extensive grounds, hosts have pets, pets not accepted, dinner available, babies welcome, free cot, swimming pool, hiking, cycling, fishing, mushroom-picking, riversports 10km

Adequate English spoken

——From the Exit Bollène on the A7, take the D994 towards Pont-St-Esprit. Take the N86 towards Bagnols-sur-Cèze. Turn right towards Carsan/St-Alexandre and follow the signs.

Bernard PELLOUX

'Mas Canet'

Chemin de Gavanon

30130 ST-PAULET-DE-CAISSON

Tel: (0) 4 66 39 25 96

Fax: (0) 4 66 39 25 96

Residence of
Outstanding Character

15 km - W -
BOLLENE
St-Paulet-de-Caisson:
railway station: 50km
airport: 70km
car essential

30.18 BOLLENE

An old silkworm farm, renovated with great character. Here you can relax or take a dip in the pool. Visit Pont-St-Esprit and explore the Forêt de Valbonne. If you like canoeing, you will know that the Gorges de l'Ardèche are fantastic.

PROPERTY

off-street parking, extensive grounds, lounge, hosts have pets, swimming pool, hiking, cycling, interesting flora, mushroom-picking, fishing 9km, riversports 9km, golf course 40km

Basic English spoken

PRICE STRUCTURE

6 Bedrooms
(3 rooms) shower room with wc, double bed: FF326

(3 rooms) bathroom with wc, double bed: FF326

Extra Bed: FF75
Reduction: 30/09–01/05

Capacity: 12 people

——From the A7, take the Exit for Bollène. Head for Pont-St-Esprit, then D23 in the direction of La Chartreuse de Valbonne for 7km.

Pierre & Monique
CARDINAEL

'Mas Zazézou'

Quartier Malatras

84840 LAMOTTE-DU-
RHONE

Tel: (0) 4 90 40 45 16/
06 85 34 26 20
Fax: (0) 4 90 40 45 16

Private Home

5 km - S W -
BOLLENE
Lamotte-du-Rhône:
hosts can collect
from station,
railway station: 5km
airport: 60km

PRICE STRUCTURE

3 Bedrooms
Sud & Pilote & Océane:
shower room with wc,
double bed: FF300

Extra Bed: FF100

Capacity: 6 people

84.33 BOLLENE

Monique is from Brussels. Her isolated country house is shaded by a 200-year-old weeping willow. The spacious dining room is furnished with good taste. You will enjoy barbecues beside the swimming pool, or try your hand at painting or pottery.

PROPERTY

off-street parking, garden, tv lounge, hosts have pets, dinner available, swimming pool, fishing, cycling 3km, hiking 10km, riversports 15km, golf course 25km

Fluent English spoken

——From the A7, take the Bollène Exit. Then take the D994 towards Pont-St-Esprit. After Lamotte-du-Rhône, at the last roundabout, turn right and follow the signs.

84.08 CARPENTRAS

A wonderful location in the middle of the vines and the Dentelles de Montmirail. Typically Provençal. A warm welcome awaits you here. Your hosts love poetry, literature and painting.

PROPERTY

off-street parking, extensive grounds, tv lounge, pets not accepted, dinner available, babies welcome, free cot, non-smoking, 3 nights minimum stay, vineyard

Adequate English spoken

PRICE STRUCTURE

4 Bedrooms

Oliviers: shower room with wc, twin beds: FF350

Lavandes & Vignes: shower room with wc, twin beds: FF380

Amandiers: shower room with wc, double bed: FF300

Extra Bed: FF50

Capacity: 8 people

Claude & Simone WEIS

'Le Mas de Silvadour'

Les Estaillades

84330 LE BARROUX

Tel: (0) 4 90 65 04 73
Fax: (0) 4 90 65 03 32

Residence of
Outstanding Character

10 km - N E - CARPENTRAS
Carpentras: hosts can collect from station, railway station: 35km airport: 45km
——At Carpentras, take the D938 towards Le Barroux, Malaucène. At Le Barroux, go towards La Suzette. From the sign 'Suzette', continue on the road for 1.5km. Turn right on to the unmade road for 600m and follow the sign to 'Le Mas de Silvadour'.

Marianne MYIN

'Siloé'

Le Canadel

84570 MORMOIRON

Tel: (0) 4 90 61 87 67

Fax: (0) 4 90 61 87 55

Private Home

11 km - E -
CARPENTRAS
Mormoiron:
railway station: 30km
airport: 30km
car essential

PRICE STRUCTURE

3 Bedrooms
(2 rooms) shower room
with wc, double bed: FF330

third room: shower room
with wc, twin beds, single
bed: FF360 (2 people)
FF430 (3 people)

Reduction: 1/09–30/06

Capacity: 7 people

84.47 CARPENTRAS

If you choose Marianne and Jacques' place, you will get a warm welcome, peace and quiet, wonderful countryside and a view over Mont Ventoux, as well as use of the swimming pool. A great place to unwind and recharge your batteries. They organise weekly 'Conversation Française' packages, which include excursions throughout Provence. An excellent way to improve your French and to get to know this area.

PROPERTY

off-street parking, extensive grounds, tv lounge, hosts have pets, pets not accepted, telephone, dinner available, packed lunch, babies welcome, free cot, wheelchair access, swimming pool, closed: 15/12–15/01, hiking, cycling, fishing, hunting, mushroom-picking, interesting flora 15km, bird-watching 15km,riversports 20km *Adequate English spoken*

——At Carpentras, take the D942 towards Mormoiron and Sault. When you reach Mormoiron, continue towards Sault for 300m. Turn right at the sign 'Domaine des Anges' and go towards Le Canadel for 2km. At fire hydrant 21, there is a sign to 'Siloé' on the right.

Didier ANDREIS

'Les Peirelles'

84560 MÉNERBES

Tel: 04 90 72 23 42

Fax: (0) 4 90 72 23 56

les-peirelles
@worldonline.fr

Private Home

15 km - E -
CAVAILLON
Ménerbes:
railway station: 30km
airport: 30km

84.54 CAVAILLON

This place is in a quiet location amongst the pines and cedars, with only the song of the 'cigales' (crickets) to disturb you as you doze beside the pool. Ménerbes is a sought after village in the heart of the Luberon. There is so much to do: Provençal markets, pottery workshops, hiking, museums and so many other charming villages, not forgetting the 'Fête de la Lavande' (lavender festival).

PROPERTY

off-street parking, extensive grounds, pets not accepted, telephone, packed lunch, kitchen, babies welcome, free cot, swimming pool, hiking, interesting flora, mushroom-picking, cycling 2km, vineyard 2km, golf course 10km, riversports 10km

——At Cavaillon, take the D2 towards Coustellet for 7km. Then turn right on to the D3 for Ménerbes. The house is 2km from the village.

PRICE STRUCTURE

5 Bedrooms

Cerises & Lavande: television, shower room with wc, twin beds: FF430

Fleurs: television, shower room with wc, double bed: FF430

Tournesols: television, bathroom with wc, double bed, twin beds: FF (2 people) FF630 (4 people)

Oliviers: television, bathroom with wc, twin beds: FF630 (4 people)

Extra Bed: FF100

Capacity: 14 people

Manuel LEPEZ

'L'Ivernenco'

Route de Colonzelle - Bellevue

84600 GRILLON

Tel: 04 90 35 63 47/ 06 13 21 80 51

Fax: (0) 4 90 35 63 47

ivernenco@wanadoo.fr

Private Home

5 km - W - VALREAS
Grillon: hosts can collect from station, railway station: 20km airport: 120km car essential

PRICE STRUCTURE

3 Bedrooms and 1 Suite

Suite Lilas: shower room with wc, double bed: FF350

+ Tournesol: 2 single beds: FF350

Lavande: shower room with wc, bathroom, double bed: FF380

Olivier: shower room with wc, double bed: FF400

Chambrette enfants: 2 single beds: FF150

Extra Bed: FF80

Reduction: 15/09–15/03 and 3 nights

Capacity: 10 people

84.51 VALREAS

Deep in truffle country, amongst vineyards and lavender, Manuel welcomes you to his restored old silk factory, surrounded by extensive grounds. The bedrooms are spacious and very relaxing. You may be tempted to spend the day dozing in the sun, but there is too much to be seen in the neighbourhood, such as Madame de Sévigné's château at Grignan, famous for its literature. Manuel also has a one-hole golf course on the premises. The location earns this place three 'suns'.

PROPERTY

private parking, extensive grounds, hosts have pets, telephone, dinner available, babies welcome, free cot, wc, hiking, cycling, fishing 2km, riversports 35km, golf course 40km

Fluent English spoken

——From the A7, Exit Montélimar-Sud, and head towards Valréas, Nyons. The house is 4km after Grignan.

89

70 Vesoul Belfort L
90

21 DIJON BESANÇON 25
page 49

Beaune Dole FRANCHE-COMTE

Autun Pontarlier SWITZERLAN

Chalon-sur-Saône 71 39 Lons

BOURGOGNE page 122

Moulins Macon

03 69 Bourg page 500

Vichy Villefranche-sur-Saône page 519 01 Annecy pages 522-523 74 Cluses page 527

Thiers Roanne page 514 LYON pages 517-518 Aix-les-Bains Chamonix pages 524-526

CLERMONT-FERRAND 42 Vienne Albertville

63 St-Etienne pages 515-516 RHÔNE-ALPES Chambery page 521 73

AUVERGNE page 107 Annonay page 501 38 St. Jean

43 Tain-l'Hermitage page 508 Grenoble pages 511-513

le Puy Valence pages 509-510 Romans-sur-Isère pages 502-507 Briançon

07 Privas 05

48 Aubenas page 520 26 Gap

Mende

Millau 84 Digne 04 06

Alès Carpentras

30 Avignon PROVENCE-ALPES-CÔTE D'AZUR page 421 MONAC

LANGUEDOC-ROUSSILLON page 260 Nimes 13 Grasse Nice

Béziers Arles Draguignan 83

34 MONTPELLIER Aix-en-Provence

MARSEILLE

Toulon

MEDITERRANEAN SEA

RHÔNE-ALPES

ITALY

Nicole LOZANO

Les Chatonnières

01370 ST-ETIENNE-
DU-BOIS

Tel: 04 71 30 53 20

Private Home

11 km - N E -
BOURG-EN-BRESSE
St-Etienne-du-Bois:
railway station: 8 km
car essential

PRICE STRUCTURE

2 Bedrooms

la Bourguignonne &
La Catalane: double bed:
FF250

Capacity: 4 people

01.07 BOURG-EN-BRESSE

Make sure you arrive early at Nicole and Etienne's place, as they will welcome you warmly and ensure that you enjoy their magnificent garden. It is full of flowers from May through to September and has won several prizes. You will take your meals on the terrace and the bedrooms share one superb, spacious bathroom. They really do deserve three 'suns', in spite of there only being one bathroom.

PROPERTY

off-street parking, extensive grounds, tv lounge, pets not accepted, dinner available, babies welcome, free cot, non-smoking, 1 shared bathroom with wc, hiking, mushroom-picking, golf course 9km

——From Bourg-en-Bresse head towards Strasbourg/Lons-le-Saunier. After the Cafétéria Casino continue for 7km towards Lons-le-Saunier.

Danièle & Jacques
LABERE

'Auberge du Château de
Bobigneux'

Bobigneux

42220 ST-SAUVEUR-
EN-RUE

Tel: (0) 4 77 39 24 33

Fax: (0) 4 77 39 25 74

Château

20 km - W -
ANNONAY
St-Sauveur-en-Rue:
railway station: 26km
airport: 80km
car essential

42.12 ANNONAY

An auberge in the 'Parc du Pilat', kingdom of forests, green
pastures and open spaces. The château dates from the 16th
century. Jacques spends a lot of the time in the kitchen and
he will probably tell you about Greenland where he lived for
20 years. On sale: Cheese and charcuterie.

PROPERTY

off-street parking, extensive grounds, tv lounge, hosts have
pets, telephone, dinner available, packed lunch, babies
welcome, free cot, wheelchair access, closed: 01/01–28/02,
hiking, cycling, fishing, hunting, interesting flora, mushroom-
picking, winter sports 10km, golf course 15km, riversports
30km

Basic English spoken

——At Annonay, take the N82 towards Bourg-Argental. The
auberge is on the D503 between Bourg-Argental and St-
Sauveur.

PRICE STRUCTURE

6 Bedrooms

first room: shower room
with wc, washbasin, double
bed, single bed: FF260 (2
people) FF310 (3 people)

second room: shower room
with wc, washbasin, twin
beds: FF260

(2 rooms) shower room
with wc, washbasin, double
bed: FF260

fifth room: shower room
with wc, washbasin, 2
double beds: FF260 (2
people) FF335 (4 people)

sixth room: lounge, shower
room with wc, washbasin,
double bed: FF260

Capacity: 15 people

Jacques & Renée
CRAMMER

'L'Eygalière'

Quartier Coussaud

26300 ALIXAN

Tel: (0) 4 75 47 11 13

Fax: (0) 4 75 47 13 35

jcrammer@easynet.fr

Private Home

8 km - S - ROMANS-
SUR-ISERE
Alixan: hosts can
collect from station,
railway station: 12km
airport: 8km
car essential

PRICE STRUCTURE

3 Bedrooms

first room: bathroom with
wc, double bed (king size):
FF350

second room: shower room
with wc, double bed: FF350

third room: shower room
with wc, double bed (queen
size): FF350

Extra Bed: FF100
Reduction: children

Capacity: 6 people

26.22 ROMANS-SUR-ISERE

You could stay here for a day, a week or a year without getting bored. The warmest of welcomes, wonderful furnishings, a magnificent flower garden, superb swimming pool, a trout stream... and the most charming of hosts. Fleur de Soleil member.

PROPERTY

private parking, garden, tv lounge, hosts have pets, babies welcome, free cot, swimming pool, closed: 4/11–01/03, cycling, fishing, golf course 4km, gliding 8km, hiking 12km, mushroom-picking 12km

Fluent English spoken

——From the A49 Valence–Grenoble, take Exit 6 and then follow the D538 towards Crest. At Alixan, turn left on to the D101 towards Besayes. 500m from the village, turn left and continue for 100m.

Isabelle MAGNIN

Le Petit Chantuzet -
Quartier les Ariennes

26260 ST-DONAT

Tel: (0) 4 75 45 02 84/
06 87 08 07 13

Fax: (0) 4 75 45 02 84

Residence of
Outstanding Character

15 km - N -
ROMANS-SUR-
ISERE
St-Donat: hosts can
collect from station,
railway station: 15km
airport: 100km
car essential

26.29 ROMANS-SUR-ISERE

A typical Provençal house on top of a hill in peaceful surroundings, amongst the apricot trees. Admire the beautiful view over the Vercors. You can relax in the flower-filled garden, swim in the nearby lake or enjoy the Bach Festival. On sale: Honey, apricots, walnut oil.

PROPERTY

off-street parking, garden, tv lounge, dinner available, babies welcome, free cot, non-smoking, hiking, cycling, mushroom-picking, fishing 2km, sea or lake watersports 2km, golf course 20km, interesting flora 30km, bird-watching 30km, winter sports 50km

Adequate English spoken

PRICE STRUCTURE

2 Bedrooms
Bleue: television, shower room with wc along corridor, double bed: FF250

Rose: shower room with wc, washbasin, double bed, cot: FF250

Extra Bed: FF100
Reduction: 01/11–31/03 and 3 nights and children

Capacity: 4 people

——Take the Tain l'Hermitage Exit from the A7 and then the D67 for Saint-Donat. From there, head in the direction of Châteauneuf-de-Galaure, then at the next roundabout, turn left to the town centre. Take the second left after the cemetery towards 'Les Ariennes'. The house is at the top of the hill.

Jacques & Thérèse
BLANCHY

'Le Rucher de Jabelin'

26100 ROMANS-SUR-
ISERE

Tel: (0) 4 75 02 36 97

Residence of
Outstanding Character

ROMANS-SUR-
ISERE:
railway station: 3km
airport: 90km
car essential

PRICE STRUCTURE

4 Bedrooms
(2 rooms) shower room
with wc, double bed, single
bed: FF320 (2 people)
FF400 (3 people)

(2 rooms) shower room
with wc, double bed: FF260

Extra Bed: FF80
Reduction: 4 nights

Capacity: 10 people

26.30 ROMANS-SUR-ISERE

Close to the capital of the shoe industry and 30km from the Vercors, this couple, who are also beekeepers, will welcome you into the tranquility of their home. You will love their house, both inside and out. The bedrooms are spacious and comfortable with beautiful antique furniture. You will never want to leave. On sale: Honey and other beehive products.

PROPERTY

off-street parking, extensive grounds, tv lounge, hosts have pets, babies welcome, free cot, swimming pool, hiking, cycling, hunting, bird-watching, fishing 2km, mushroom-picking 5km, gliding 5km, sea or lake watersports 14km, golf course 18km, winter sports 50km

Adequate English spoken

——At Romans, head towards the Centre-Hospitalier and take the small road on the left. Follow the signs and the house is 800m further on.

ROMANS-SUR-ISERE

'Le Sert'

26190 ST-JEAN-EN-ROYANS

Tel: (0) 4 75 47 70 53

genevieve.mathon
@wanadoo.fr

Private Home

20 km - E -
ROMANS-SUR-ISERE
St-Jean-en-Royans:
railway station: 20km
airport: 50km
car essential

26.32 ROMANS-SUR-ISERE

Geneviève's house is in Le Vercors, the bastion of the the French Resistance, whose history is immortalised by numerous museums and monuments in this area. It is also wonderful for lovers of dramatic scenery: spectacular caves, impressive gorges, scenic roads and lots of hiking and ski routes in this National Park. The local walnuts, ravioli and goat's cheese are much prized by food-lovers. Whatever you decide to do, you can always come back and rest your legs in the shade in Geneviève's garden.

PROPERTY

private parking, garden, tv lounge, pets not accepted, dinner available, babies welcome, free cot, non-smoking, 1 shared bathroom, 1 shared shower room, wc, hiking, cycling, interesting flora, fishing 1km, mushroom-picking 1km, bird-watching 15km, riversports 15km, gliding 25km, golf course 30km, sea or lake watersports 50km

——A49 Grenoble–Valence, Exit 8 (towards St-Nazaire-en-Royans, then St-Jean-en-Royans), or Exit 9 (towards St-Romans, St-Just-de-Claix then St-Jean-en-Royans).

PRICE STRUCTURE

4 Bedrooms
first room: twin beds: FF250

(2 rooms) double bed,
single bed:
FF220 (2 people)
FF290 (3 people)

fourth room: double bed:
FF220

Reduction: 3 nights

Capacity: 10 people

Anne & Pierre JOSQUIN

'Maison Forte de Clérivaux'

26750 CHATILLON-ST-JEAN

Tel: (0) 4 75 45 32 53

Fax: (0) 4 75 71 45 43

pierre.josquin@kyxar.fr

Private Home

10 km - N E -
ROMANS-SUR-ISERE
Chatillon-St-Jean:
railway station: 20km
airport: 100km
car essential

RHONE-ALPES

ROMANS-SUR-ISERE

PRICE STRUCTURE

4 Bedrooms

Coté Jardin: bathroom with wc, twin beds: FF320

Le Murier: shower room with wc, double bed: FF320

Magnanerie – Double or twin room: bathroom with wc, double bed: FF320

Les Mariés: bathroom with wc, double bed: FF320

Capacity: 8 people

26.36 ROMANS-SUR-ISERE

Clérivaux is typical of the Dauphinois region, with its buildings dating from the 13th to the 19th century, surrounding a fortified house. It has been meticulously restored under the auspices of the Government Historic Monuments Department, using quality materials to provide modern standards of comfort. Set in 10 ha of unspoilt grounds and surrounded by the peace and quiet of the gentle, rolling valleys at the foot of the Alps (Le Vercors). An enchanting and friendly place. Fleur de Soleil member.

PROPERTY

Private parking, extensive grounds, pets not accepted

——At Romans, take the D123 to Chatillon-St-Jean, then continue towards Parnans for 1km. Turn left towards St-Michel. Go through Chatillon, then turn left and it is the second house on the left.

26.37 ROMANS-SUR-ISERE

Should you be travelling on the autoroute through the Rhône valley, when you are near Valence we advise you to make a little detour towards Romans. You are in La Drôme, baked by the sun and full of orchards, typical of Provence. There is also Le Vercors, with its famous valleys and gulleys, ideal for skiing as well as having spectacular hiking routes. As you come in to Romans on the D52, the Abbaye Saint-Antoine is as impressive as Vézelay. Marie-Ange and Frédéric are there to welcome you to their house full of character, just 2 mins. from the old town.

PROPERTY

garden, hosts have pets, telephone, packed lunch, babies welcome, free cot, gliding 4km, cycling 5km, hiking 10km, golf course 15km, lake watersports 15km *Adequate English spoken*

PRICE STRUCTURE

1 Suite

Rouge: bathroom with wc, double bed, single bed (child-size) + en-suite room Lavande: twin beds: FF300 (2 people) FF480 (5 people)

Reduction: 6 nights

Capacity: 5 people

Marie-Ange & Frédéric CAMBEFORT

'Froggy's'

57, Av. Duchesne

26100 ROMANS-SUR-ISERE

Tel: 04 75 02 84 07

Private Home

ROMANS-SUR-ISERE
Romans-sur-Isère:
railway station: 2km
airport: 90km
car essential
——You are advised to phone for directions.

Max & Marie-Thérèse
ANGE

Quartier La Motte -
Chanos Curson

26600 TAIN
L'HERMITAGE

Tel: (0) 4 75 07 31 74
Fax: (0) 4 75 07 31 74

Private Home

5 km - E - TAIN
L'HERMITAGE
Chanos Curson:
airport: 90km
——On the A7, take the
Exit Tain l'Hermitage.
Take the D532 towards
Romans. As you enter
Curson, turn left and
climb up for about 800m
towards 'La Motte'.

26.23 TAIN L'HERMITAGE

A quiet, modern villa with an unobstructed view. Your hosts, a very welcoming couple, offer a small self-contained apartment, which is brand new, with a well equipped kitchen, a lounge, and a garden with barbecue.

PROPERTY

1 shared bathroom with wc, hiking, fishing 6km, golf course 10km, mushroom-picking 10km, sea or lake watersports 13km, winter sports 25km, bird-watching 35km

PRICE STRUCTURE

2 Bedrooms and 1 Apartment

television, kitchen, double bed + en-suite room (2 rooms) double bed: FF250 (2 people) FF500 (4 people)

Capacity: 6 people

Marie-Jeanne
KATCHIKIAN

'La Pineraie'

383, Chemin Bel-Air

26320 ST-MARCEL-LES-
VALENCE

Tel: (0) 4 75 58 72 25

marie.katchikian
@minitel.net

Residence of
Outstanding Character

5 km - N E -
VALENCE
St-Marcel-les-
Valence:
railway station: 7km
airport: 15km
car essential

26.13 VALENCE

Five minutes from the A49 and 10 minutes from the A7, this beautiful house offers you a magnificent view of the Vercors mountains. The breakfasts are served with home-made jam and patisseries. You are on the wine trail. A great place to stay. Fleur de Soleil member.

PROPERTY

private parking, extensive grounds, tv lounge, pets not accepted, babies welcome, free cot, hiking 5km, cycling 5km, fishing 5km, golf course 15km, winter sports 40km

——From the A7, Exit Valence-Nord, and head towards Valence-Centre. Turn left at the fourth set of traffic lights towards Grenoble on the N532. At Saint-Marcel-les-Valence, go to the place de la Mairie and, after the first set of traffic lights, turn left in to the rue de la Mairie and then continue straight on after the 'Stop' sign. Go under the bridge, and continue as far as the bridge with a sign of a coffee-pot on it. The entrance is 30m on the left, after you have made a hairpin turn (do not take the entrance on the right). In all about 400m from the place de la Mairie.

PRICE STRUCTURE

2 Bedrooms
Azur: bathroom with wc, double bed: FF300

Fleurie: shower room with wc, twin beds: FF320

Reduction: 3 nights and children

Capacity: 4 people

Josette DUCOIN

'Place de la Fontaine'

26120
CHATEAUDOUBLE

Tel: (0) 4 75 59 80 26

Fax: (0) 4 75 59 42 86

Private Home

16 km - E -
VALENCE
Chateaudouble:
railway station: 18km
airport: 6km
car essential

PRICE STRUCTURE

2 Bedrooms
first room: shower, double
bed, single bed:
FF240 (2 people)
FF300 (3 people)

second room: shower along
corridor, double bed: FF220

Reduction: 2 nights

Capacity: 5 people

26.28 VALENCE

Stop at Josette's place in this village house and you are on the doorstep of the beautiful Vercors. Josette is retired and loves travel, reading, music and singing. Fleur de Soleil member.

PROPERTY

Private parking, pets not accepted, kitchen, babies welcome, free cot, non-smoking, wc, hiking, cycling, fishing, mushroom-picking, interesting flora 8km, gliding 10km, golf course 20km, hunting 20km, winter sports 20km, riversports 30km

——From the A7 take Exit Valence-Sud in the direction of Grenoble. After 5km turn right on to D68 towards Chabeuil. On entering the town turn left towards Romans and take the D68 again on the right, continuing towards Le Vercors for 5km. Châteaudouble is on the right.

'Vallon Libre'

Les Goirands

38710 ST-SEBASTIEN

Tel: (0) 4 76 34 93 43

Fax: (0) 4 76 34 93 61

Private Home

50 km - S -
GRENOBLE
St-Sébastien:
railway station: 20km
airport: 90km
car essential

38.03 GRENOBLE

You will be enthralled by Marie-France, who is mad about photography and cooking. She has restored this farmhouse and you will enjoy the quiet and the magnificent view over the Vercors. The ecology centre, 'Terre Vivante', is nearby. Try bungee jumping, hiking, riding… as well as bread and pizza from the charcoal oven.

PROPERTY

off-street parking, garden, tv lounge, pets not accepted, dinner available, packed lunch, babies welcome, free cot, non-smoking, 1 shared bathroom, 2 wc, closed: 01/11–31/11, hiking, cycling, mushroom-picking, winter sports 10km, sea or lake watersports 20km

Adequate English spoken

PRICE STRUCTURE

2 Bedrooms
Obiou: washbasin, twin beds: FF240

Châtel: washbasin, double bed: FF220

Extra Bed: FF80
Reduction: 1/09–30/04 and 3 nights

Capacity: 4 people

——At Grenoble, N85 towards Gap. 2km after La Mure, right on to the D526 towards Mens. After the 'Pont de Ponsonnas' (bungee jumping bridge), left on to the D227 towards Cordéac. At St-Sébastien, after the 'Salle des fêtes' & the 'Mairie' (Town Hall), follow the signs for 1km.

Johanna LEGER

'La Chantournelle'

6, chemin des Tilleuls

38700 CORENC

Tel: (0) 4 76 88 06 25/
06 08 02 22 08

Fax: (0) 4 76 88 09 19

Private Home

5 km - N -
GRENOBLE
Corenc:
railway station: 8km
airport: 35km
car essential

PRICE STRUCTURE

6 Bedrooms and
1 Apartment

television, telephone,
shower room with wc,
washbasin, twin beds: FF375

television, telephone,
shower room with wc, twin
beds: FF375

(3 rooms) television,
telephone, bathroom with
wc, twin beds: FF375

television, telephone,
bathroom with wc, double
bed: FF375

Studio: kitchen, shower
room with wc, double bed:
FF375

Capacity: 14 people

38.16 GRENOBLE

Your hosts will welcome you to their family home, built in 1745, which has been completely restored. It is on the edge of La Chartreuse, with a fantastic panoramic view over the Belledonne Plateau and Grenoble. La Chartreuse is a great favourite with hikers and nature-lovers, in the summer or winter.

PROPERTY

off-street parking, garden, tv lounge, pets not accepted, telephone, kitchen, babies welcome, free cot, wheelchair access, hiking, cycling 10km, fishing 10km, hunting 10km, interesting flora 10km, mushroom-picking 10km, winter sports 10km, gliding 10km

Fluent English spoken

——At Grenoble, follow 'les quais', the road that runs along the edge of the mountain, beside the River Isère as far as the road to Le Sappey, Col de Porte, which you will see on the left. At Corenc Village, after the white building, take the first road on the left, and then the first lane on the right.

Marie-Laure
KAEPPELIN

'Les Chamois'

Le Charvet

38250 ST NIZIER-DU-
MOUCHEROTTE

Tel: (0) 4 76 53 42 62
Fax: (0) 4 76 53 42 62

marie-laure.kaeppelin
@wanadoo.fr

Private Home

15 km - W -
GRENOBLE
Saint-Nizier-du-
Moucherotte:
railway station: 20km
airport: 30km
car essential

38.17 GRENOBLE

The Vercors is a delightful region to explore offering many walks, horse riding and paragliding in summer, caves and speleology, and skiing in winter. It is a national historic site of the French Resistance.

PROPERTY

✸ ✸ ✸

private parking, garden, pets not accepted, dinner available, non-smoking, hiking, cycling, interesting flora, mushroom-picking, winter sports

PRICE STRUCTURE

1 Bedroom
Room with Mezzanine:
shower room with wc,
double bed, 2 single beds:
FF320 (2 people)
FF480 (1 people)

Extra Bed: FF80

Capacity: 4 people

——By D106 towards St-Nizier. 2 km before the village, turn right beside the Memorial du Vercors. Go along this lane for 1.8km.

Véronique DESTRE

'L'Echo des Bois'

Place de Verdun

42460 CUINZIER

Tel: 04 77 60 54 09

Fax: (0) 4 77 60 53 92

Private Home

20 km - N E - ROANNE
Cuinzier: hosts can collect from station, railway station: 7km airport: 22km car essential

PRICE STRUCTURE

3 Bedrooms
shower, double bed: FF220

shower room with wc, washbasin, double bed, single bed:
FF220 (2 people)
FF400 (3 people)

shower, washbasin, double bed, single bed, cot:
FF220 (2 people)
FF320 (3 people)

Extra Bed: FF50

Capacity: 10 people

42.14 ROANNE

This old auberge has been completely rebuilt by Véronique and is in the heart of the woods on La Route du Beaujolais. The countryside is really lush and undulating, and Véronique will share with you her passion for this region, its hiking routes and abbeys, which she will explain to you with a friendly smile over a cup of tea (she has a wonderful selection).

PROPERTY

off-street parking, garden, tv lounge, pets not accepted, telephone, babies welcome, free cot, wc, hiking, cycling, mushroom-picking, fishing 10km, sea or lake watersports 15km, vineyard 30km

Basic English spoken

——From Roanne, take the D482 for Pouilly. Then the D487 for Charlieu and the D70 for Cuinzier. The house is in the centre of the village, on a small square next to the hairdressing salon.

Jacotte VERNAY & Elia
CATTEAU

'Chez Jacotte & Elia'

Le Plat

42330 ST-GALMIER

Tel: (0) 4 77 54 08 27/
06 10 19 83 99
Fax: (0) 4 77 54 18 94

jacotte.elia@wanadoo.fr
http://perso.wanadoo
/hebergement.
chambrehote/

Private Home

20 km - N -
ST-ETIENNE
St-Galmier: hosts
can collect from
airport: 12km car
essential

42.05 ST-ETIENNE

Just 10 mins. from the A72, this beautifully restored farm is situated in a quiet area between the Monts de Forez and the Parc du Pilat. A beautiful place with a clear view, where your two hostesses will take care of everything. After a delicious meal, they will advise you on activities and museums in the area. Hard tennis court.

PROPERTY

private parking, garden, tv lounge, hosts have pets, dinner available, kitchen, babies welcome, free cot, tennis court

Fluent English spoken

——At St-Etienne, take the A72 towards Roanne and exit at Andrézieux, Veauche, St-Galmier. Then the D12 towards Chazelles-sur-Lyon. At St-Galmier, follow Chazelles. Opposite 'Citroën', turn right on to the small road signposted 'sous le bois'. Continue for 3.5km. It is the first farmhouse, with sky-blue shutters and a paved courtyard, on the left.

PRICE STRUCTURE

4 Bedrooms

Grande: television, shower room with wc, double bed, twin beds: FF380 (2 people) FF550 (4 people)

Rose: television, shower room with wc, twin beds: FF350

Exotique: television, bathroom with wc along corridor, double bed: FF350

Turquoise: television, shower room with wc, double bed: FF380

Extra Bed: FF100

Reduction: 5 nights

Capacity: 10 people

Roland & Marie-Pierre
VIALLY

'Ferme du Nizon'

Le Nizon

42110 VALEILLE

Tel: (0) 4 77 28 91 50

Working Farm

40 km - N -
ST-ETIENNE
Valeille: hosts can
collect from station,
railway station: 7km
airport: 20km
car essential

PRICE STRUCTURE

2 Bedrooms
(2 rooms) television,
washbasin, double bed,
single bed:
FF200 (2 people)
FF250 (3 people)

Extra Bed: FF50
Reduction: 3 nights

Capacity: 6 people

42.06 ST-ETIENNE

This friendly young couple live on a typical Forez farm. You are at the peaceful heart of this region, full of lakes and thermal springs. The 'Ecopole du Forez' nature reserve is only 10km away. On sale: Garden produce and eggs.

PROPERTY

off-street parking, garden, tv lounge, hosts have pets, telephone, dinner available, kitchen, babies welcome, free cot, 1 shared shower room with wc, swimming pool, hiking, cycling, fishing 3km, bird-watching 10km

Adequate English spoken

——From the A72, Exit Feurs. Then take the N89 towards Feurs and Lyon. Then right on to the D10 towards Valeille, then (before Valeille) right towards Le Nizon.

69.02 LYON

This 18th-century residence is only 40km from Lyon, but beautifully quiet. Vineyards stretch as far as the eye can see from this typical Beaujolais house. Madame Roux welcomes you with charm and kindness to her comfortable home.

PROPERTY

off-street parking, extensive grounds, lounge, hosts have pets, telephone, babies welcome, free cot, closed: 15/12–15/01, hiking, cycling, vineyard, golf course 20km

Fluent English spoken

PRICE STRUCTURE

9 Bedrooms

Patricia & Rose: shower room with wc, double bed: FF710

Valentine & Thibault: bathroom with wc, twin beds: FF710

Bleue & Jaune & Empire: bathroom with wc, double bed: FF710

Gauthier: shower, wc, single bed: FF410 (1 person)

Verte: shower room with wc, twin beds: FF710

Extra Bed: FF210

Capacity: 17 people

Anne ROUX

'Domaine de La Javernière'

La Javernière

69910 VILLIE-MORGON

Tel: (0) 4 74 04 22 71

Fax: (0) 4 74 69 14 44

Château

40 km - N W - LYON
Villié-Morgon:
railway station: 8km
airport: 50km
car essential
——On the A6, take the exit Belleville. In Belleville, take the D37 towards Baujeu. In Cercié, turn right towards Morgon. The property is on the right, between Morgon and Villié-Morgon.

Jeannine EXCOFFIER

'Aux Magnolias'

Le Pavillon de Flore -
9, Cours Albert Thomas

69003 LYON

Tel: (0) 4 72 12 10 14

Fax: (0) 4 72 12 10 14

contact
@lyonmagnoliasbnb.com

www.lyonmagnoliasbnb.
com

Apartment

LYON:
railway station: 1km
airport: 20km

PRICE STRUCTURE

3 Bedrooms
Harmony: television,
bathroom with wc, double
bed: FF315

Laura: television, 2 single
beds: FF295

Flora: television, double
bed: FF295

Extra Bed: FF100
Reduction: 2 nights

Capacity: 6 people

69.07 LYON

**Jeannine used to be an English teacher. Her apartment, with
its private garden full of flowers (what bliss in a city!), is in a
good area, handy for the metro, yet still very quiet. The
welcome is warm and friendly, and you will get on well with
Jeannine, so stay as long as possible.**

PROPERTY

garden, lounge, dinner available, wheelchair access, 1 shared
bathroom with wc

Fluent English spoken

——On the A7 go towards Lyon-Centre, presqu'île. Exit
Bellecour then turn right on to the 'pont de la Guillotière'.
Take the grande rue de la Guillotière then the avenue des
Frères Lumière. At rue des Tuiliers, turn left then left again in
to cours Albert Thomas. Métro: Sans-Souci (Line D).

Alexandra & Olivier
du MESNIL du BUISSON

'Château de Longsard'

4060, route de Longsard

69400 ARNAS-EN-
BEAUJOLAIS

Tel: (0) 4 74 65 55 12

Fax: (0) 4 74 65 03 17

longsard@wanadoo.fr

Château

5 km - N -
VILLEFRANCHE-
SUR-SAONE
Arnas-en-Beaujolais:
railway station: 6km
airport: 30km
car essential

69.08 VILLEFRANCHE-SUR-SAONE

This large 18th-century vine-grower's house, with its superb garden, has views over the idyllic countryside: groves, 100-year-old cedars of Lebanon and an Egyptian obelisk presented in the 19th century by one of Bonaparte's generals. The comfortable interior has been restored in good taste. On sale: Beaujolais, Chardonnay.

PROPERTY

✹ ✹ ✹ ✹

private parking, extensive grounds, tv lounge, hosts have pets, dinner available, babies welcome, free cot, hiking, cycling, fishing 5km, mushroom-picking 8km, riversports 8km, golf course 20km

Fluent English spoken

——At Villefranche-sur-Saône, take the N6 towards Macon. After 6km, turn left towards Arnas. Go through the village, and the château is 1.5km further on, on the right.

PRICE STRUCTURE

5 Bedrooms
Musique & Rose: bathroom with wc, double bed: FF600

Beaujolais Bleu: bathroom with wc, double bed (super king size): FF600

Suite Est: bathroom with wc, double bed: FF750

Suite Ouest: bathroom with wc, double bed: FF750

Extra Bed: FF80

Capacity: 10 people

Véronique CHAYNE

'Domaine le Vernadel'

Le Chadenet

07600 ASPERJOC

Tel: (0) 4 75 94 67 92

Fax: (0) 4 75 94 67 92

Residence of
Outstanding Character

12 km - N -
AUBENAS
Le Chadenet:
hosts can collect
from station,
railway station: 7km
car essential

PRICE STRUCTURE

4 Bedrooms and
1 Apartment
Acacia: kitchen, shower
room with wc, washbasin,
double bed: FF350

Tilleul & Bruyère: shower
room with wc, washbasin,
double bed, single bed:
FF340 (2 people)
FF430 (3 people)

La Castagne & La Merle:
shower room with wc,
washbasin, double bed:
FF340

Extra Bed: FF70
Reduction: 2/10–31/05 and
children
Capacity: 12 people

07.01 AUBENAS

This stone-built house dates from 1652 and is set amidst magnificent scenery dominated by chestnut trees. The Chayne family will be delighted to introduce you to the secrets of their region: the flora and fauna, rock climbing or caving and, at the end of a hard day, their local dishes. On sale: Honey, jam, chestnuts.

PROPERTY

private parking, garden, lounge, hosts have pets, dinner available, packed lunch, babies welcome, free cot, swimming pool, 7 nights minimum stay (15/07–28/08), hiking, mushroom-picking, sea or lake watersports

Adequate English spoken

——In Aubenas, take the N102 towards Vals-les-Bains, then take the D578 towards Antraigues. Turn left on to the D243 then right on to the D543. Go over the bridge, then follow the signs for 3 km (yellow and green signs).

Solange RIVIER

'Le Pigeonnier'

Le Château

73670 ST-PIERRE-
D'ENTREMONT

Tel: (0) 4 79 65 89 74

Fax: (0) 4 79 65 89 74

Private Home

25 km - S -
CHAMBERY
St-Pierre-
d'Entremont:
hosts can collect
from station,
railway station: 25km
airport: 25km
car essential

73.11 CHAMBERY

**Your lively hostess has almost finished the work to her brand
new home. There is a superb view of La Chartreuse and you
are only a few minutes from one of the most beautiful rock
formations. Wonderful walking country and also good for
downhill skiing, as well as gentler slopes for family skiing
holidays. On sale: Honey, jam, paintings, glass.**

PROPERTY

off-street parking, tv lounge, hosts have pets, telephone,
dinner available, packed lunch, kitchen, babies welcome, free
cot, non-smoking, wheelchair access, hiking, interesting flora,
mushroom-picking, winter sports, fishing 2km, cycling 6km,
gliding 12km

PRICE STRUCTURE

4 Bedrooms
(2 rooms) television,
kitchen, shower room with
wc, washbasin, double bed,
2 single beds:
FF290 (2 people)
FF470 (4 people)

(2 rooms) television, shower
room with wc, washbasin,
double bed: FF490

Reduction: groups and
children

Capacity: 16 people

——In Chambery, D912 towards the 'Col du Granier' and 'St-
Pierre'. Follow the sign 'Le Château' at the end of the village.
(From Grenoble, take the D520 in Voreppe.).

Jean-Paul DAVIET

'Auberge de la Ferme de la Caille'

18,Chemin de la Caille

74330 LA-BALME-DE-SILLINGY

Tel: (0) 4 50 68 85 21

Fax: (0) 4 50 68 74 56

Working Farm

12 km - N W - ANNECY
La-Balme-de-Sillingy:
airport: 8km
car essential
——From the A41, exit
Annecy-Sud. N508
towards Bourg-en-Bresse.
At La Balme, D3 towards
Pont de la Caille and
follow the signs.

74.08 ANNECY

This place is organised rather like a family holiday complex. It is modern, the bedrooms are small but pleasant, all in the style of a Savoy mountain chalet, with a large rustic dining room. Les Ponts de la Caille are very impressive and should not be missed.

PROPERTY

off-street parking, garden, hosts have pets, pets not accepted, dinner available, babies welcome, free cot, wheelchair access, tennis court, cycling, fishing, mushroom-picking 1km, hiking 2km, golf course 2km, interesting flora 8km, sea or lake watersports 10km, riversports 20km, gliding 25km, winter sports 30km

PRICE STRUCTURE
7 Bedrooms

first room: television, telephone, bathroom with wc, double bed, 2 single beds: FF535 (4 people)

second room: television, telephone, bathroom with wc, 4 single beds: FF535 (4 people)

Sympa: television, telephone, bathroom with wc, double bed, 3 single beds: FF565 (5 people)

Petites (3 rooms) television, telephone, bathroom with wc, double bed: FF365

television, telephone, bathroom with wc, shower, twin beds: FF305

Capacity: 21 people

Carole
BARRUCAND-FONT

'Les Charretières'

428, route des Mongets

74320 SEVRIER

Tel: (0) 4 50 52 43 30/
06 80 45 90 64

Fax: (0) 4 50 52 43 30

Private Home

5 km - S - ANNECY
Les Mongets:
railway station: 6km
airport: 12km

74.09 ANNECY

Carole now runs her mother Nicole's pleasant, flower-filled house. The bedrooms are small and quiet. Close to Annecy, this place is a good base for visiting this region and for enjoying the lake, which is only 50m away.

PROPERTY

off-street parking, garden, tv lounge, pets not accepted, dinner available, kitchen, babies welcome, free cot, 2 wc, cycling, fishing, sea or lake watersports, hiking 1km, interesting flora 1km, mushroom-picking 1km, golf course 10km, winter sports 10km

PRICE STRUCTURE

6 Bedrooms
(6 rooms) shower, double bed: FF260

Extra Bed: FF30/60
Reduction: 01/09–01/07

Capacity: 12 people

——From the A41, take the Exit Annecy-Sud and then the N508 towards Albertville. At Sevrier, turn left immediately after the 'Bowling'.

Manu & Laurence
LUCOT DOS SANTOS

'Chalet Beauregard' 182,
Montée de la Mollard
74400 CHAMONIX
MONT-BLANC

Tel: (0) 4 50 55 86 30/
06 61 82 11 03
Fax: (0) 4 50 55 86 30

manu-laurence
@chalet-beauregard.com
www.chalet-
beauregard.com

Private Home

CHAMONIX:
railway station: 1km
airport: Genève
80km

PRICE STRUCTURE

5 Bedrooms and 1 Suite

L'Aiguille du Goûter:
television, shower room
with wc, twin beds:
FF405 (2 people)
La Verte & Les Drus: shower
room with wc, double bed:
FF405 (2 people)
L'Aiguille du Midi:
bathroom with wc, double
bed: FF405
Le Mont Blanc: shower
room with wc, double bed,
2 single beds: FF505 (2
people) FF608 (4 people)
Le Paradis: bathroom with
wc along corridor, double
bed, single bed: FF405 (2
people) FF505 (3 people)
+ Le Brévent: 2 single beds:
FF305
Extra Bed: FF100
Reduction: 7 nights
and children
Capacity: 17 people

74.11 CHAMONIX

Chamonix is a really attractive little town, with a worldwide reputation. Mont Blanc, La Mer de Glace and la Vallée Blanche are fairytale names for children, and wonderful places for adults to explore. You are fortunate to stay with Manu and Laurence in their typical mountain chalet, near to the town centre, and a short walk from the cable cars to l'Aiguille du Midi, le Brévent and Flégère. The bedrooms have a balcony and a magnificent view over Mont Blanc and the glacier.

PROPERTY

private parking, garden, tv lounge, pets not accepted, telephone, non-smoking, 2 years old minimum age, 2 nights minimum stay, closed: 20/10–20/12, hiking, cycling, interesting flora, mushroom-picking, riversports, winter sports, golf course 2km *Fluent English spoken*

——At Chamonix-Sud, head towards Téléphérique du Brévent. After two roundabouts and a set of traffic lights, turn left at the third roundabout, and take La Montée de la Mollard. It is the fourth chalet on the right after the Gendarmerie.

Danièle & Marcel
FRASSERAND

'Chalet à l'Orée du Bois'

Fond de Taconaz

74310 LES HOUCHES

Tel: (0) 4 50 54 46 80/
(0) 4 50 55 53 14

Fax: (0) 4 50 54 54 73

chalet@oreedubois.net

www.oreedubois.net

Private Home

9 km - S W -
CHAMONIX
Les Houches:
railway station: 5km
airport: Genève
70km

CHAMONIX

74.16 CHAMONIX

This chalet, typical of the Chamonix Valley, is covered with masses of hanging baskets. There is a wonderful view of Mont Blanc from the balcony. Marcel is a blacksmith who knows this area in depth and Danièle is a wonderful cook, famous for her local dishes. This place is well worth a visit at any time of the year. Half-board available: 238FF (reductions for children) except on New Year's Eve.

PROPERTY

private parking, garden, hosts have pets, pets not accepted, telephone, dinner available, babies welcome, free cot, non-smoking, wheelchair access, hiking, cycling, fishing, hunting, interesting flora, mushroom-picking, riversports, winter sports 2km, golf course 5km, gliding 18km

——From the A40, take the N205 towards Chamonix. Go through Les Houches and, 1km after the petrol station, turn left towards Les Bossons and then left after 400m, under the bridge.

PRICE STRUCTURE

4 Bedrooms and 1 Suite

Amis: television, shower room with wc, bathroom, double bed, 2 single beds: FF472 (4 people)

Alain: television, bathroom with wc, double bed: FF276

Valérie : television, shower room with wc, double bed, single bed + en-suite room France: television, single bed: FF276 (2 people) FF517 (4 people)

Drus: television, shower room with wc, double bed, single bed: FF276 (2 people) FF379 (3 people)

Brevent: television, shower room with wc, double bed: FF256

Extra Bed: FF100
Reduction: children

Capacity: 15 people

Fabienne CHAMOUX

'Chalet Khachöma'

2101, Route de vaudagne

74310 LES HOUCHES

Tel: 04 50 47 22 08/
00 41 79 2050015

Fax: (0) 4 50 47 22 08

Residence of
Outstanding Character

10 km - S W -
CHAMONIX
Les Houches:
railway station: 6 km
airport: 75 km
car essential

PRICE STRUCTURE

2 Bedrooms
shower, wc, double bed
(king size): FF500

Chalet Mazot: shower room
with wc, double bed: FF600

Capacity: 4 people

74.20 CHAMONIX

You will be especially well received in this beautifully and elegantly furnished chalet. Your young hostess is mad about mountaineering, and knows the Himalayas just as well as the Alps. There is also an adorable little chalet (or 'Mazot'), separate from the main house.

PROPERTY

off-street parking, garden, lounge, hosts have pets, pets not accepted, packed lunch, non-smoking, closed: 16/09–31/01 & 30/04–15/06, hiking, winter sports 3km

Fluent English spoken

——From the A40, Exit Les Houches-Centre, Prarion and Bellevue. Opposite the Téléphérique Bellevue, take the street on the right towards Prarion. After the télécabine, continue straight on towards Vaudagne. The road climbs up through the forest and, when it descends, look for 2101, a chalet with large bay windows.

Hélène ESNAULT

'Chalet le Nanty'

600, route du Pontet - la Frasse

74300 ARACHES

Tel: (0) 4 50 90 32 76/ 06 20 79 20 19

Private Home

10 km - E - CLUSES
Araches:
railway station: 10km
airport: Genève 55km
car essential

74.19 CLUSES

Hélène is a wonderful cook, specialising in the cuisine of the Savoy and Lyons regions. She will welcome you warmly to her quiet chalet, from which there is an uninterrupted view over the mountains. You are not far from Chamonix. Although there are only 2 bathrooms for 4 bedrooms, we had to make an exception and give this place 3 'suns', mainly because of Hélène's wonderful welcome and the outstanding location.

PROPERTY

off-street parking, garden, tv lounge, pets not accepted, dinner available, 2 shared shower rooms with wc, 6 years old minimum age, closed: 30/09–15/12 & 15/04–15/06, hiking, mushroom-picking, cycling 4km, hunting 4km, interesting flora 4km, riversports 4km, winter sports 4km, fishing 6km, golf course 10km *Adequate English spoken*

——From the A40, Exit 19 to Cluses-Centre, and then head towards Les Carroz d'Araches/Flaine. In the village of Araches, turn right towards La Frasse/Village de la Frasse. It is the first road on the right, the route de Pontet.

PRICE STRUCTURE

2 Bedrooms and 1 Suite
Haut: Romme: double bed: FF350

Haut: Le Chevran: double bed: FF350

Bas: Le Platé: double bed: FF350

Bas: Le Pré des Saix: double bed: FF300

Reduction: 5 nights

Capacity: 8 people

INDEX

INDEX

Index

Reservation Form (Part 1)

Number of Persons: ....

ADULTS Mr / Mrs / Ms	First Name	Family name

Send this Form
with your payment to :

Bed & Breakfast (France)
94–96 Bell Street
Henley-on-Thames,
OXON RG9 1XS
United Kingdom

Fax:
from Britain: 01491 410806
from outside Britain:
+ 44 1491 410806

CHILDREN Age on Arrival	First Name	Family name

Reservations (bed & breakfast)

Stop No	Date of Arrival	Date of Departure	No of Nights	1st Choice	2nd Choice	Dinner

Normal arrival time is between 5pm and 7pm unless you have made alternative arrangements with your host. Give the Host Numbers of your 1st and 2nd choices. Put a tick in the column 'Dinner' if you would like dinner on your 1st evening (if indicated that dinner is provided). You will pay your host directly for dinner.

Address:
....

....

Town:.................................Post Code: ....Country: ....

Telephone:.............................Fax:.............................E-mail: ....

How are you travelling round France? ....

Reservation Form (Part 2)

Deposit to Pay: £30.00

☐ * The host numbers given are the only ones that are acceptable to me. I understand that if each one of these is not available, the deposit will be refunded. (If you do not tick this box, we shall find you a host as close as possible to your original request.)
* See Conditions of Reservation No. 2b

☐ I am covered by Cancellation Insurance and enclose a copy of my valid policy. It is mandatory that you are covered by Cancellation Insurance and, unless you enclose proof that you have your own valid cover, a small premium will be added to your invoice.

Recommended forms of payment

☐ Sterling cheque on UK bank made payable to 'Bed & Breakfast (France)'
☐ Travellers cheques in sterling signed twice
☐ International Money Order in Sterling
☐ VISA or ☐ MASTERCARD

I authorise Bed & Breakfast (France) to debit £.................. non-refundable deposit
All credit card transactions will be debited by us in £ Sterling (Pounds)

Card Number: ☐☐☐☐ ☐☐☐☐ ☐☐☐☐ ☐☐☐☐

Expiry Date: ☐☐☐☐

Other form of payment: ....
(Please add a £25 supplement for all other forms of payment.)

TOTAL TO PAY NOW: £ ....
I enclose my payment. I have read, understood and accept the Conditions of Reservation of Bed & Breakfast (France) for myself and all the members of my party.

Please sign below.

Date   Signature

Le Feedback

Please tell us what you think of the places at which you stayed, taking account of VALUE FOR MONEY, COMFORT, WELCOME, LOCATION, FOOD and SPECIAL INTERESTS. It is our policy to pass on all guests' comments to our hosts. If you do not wish us to do this, tick the box below.

☐ I do not wish my comments to be passed on to the hosts.

☐ I booked direct   ☐ My reservation number is: ....

Please give the Host Number of each place.

....

....

....

....

....

....

....

....

....

....

....

Name:

....

Address:

....

....

Town:..Post Code: ....Country: ....

Telephone: ....Fax:...................................E-mail: ....

Please return to :
Dept BBF, Thomas Cook Publishing, PO BOX 227, Thorpe Wood,
Peterborough PE3 6PU, U.K.
or email:
bookings@bedbreak.demon.co.uk

BAB FRANCE

BED & BREAKFAST (FRANCE)

BOOK AHEAD, TO BE SURE OF A BED

To book direct with your host :
either telephone or complete this letter and mail or fax it.
Be sure to mention Bed & Breakfast (France)

Date : ....

Madame, Monsieur,

Nous souhaiterions séjourner chez vous. Vous trouverez ci-dessous les informations concernant notre demande de réservation. Voulez-vous nous dire très rapidement si les dates souhaitées vous conviennent et ce que nous devons faire pour confirmer cette réservation. Dans l'attente du plaisir de vous rencontrer, nous vous prions d'agréer, Madame, Monsieur, nos salutations distinguées.

Signature : ....

Number of Adults: ....Number of Children (with Ages):...

Room arrangement:..

Date of Arrival:...Date of departure: ....

Number of nights:...........

Station pickup (with contribution towards car expenses) from:... station requested.

Dinner requested Yes/No: ....

Mr / Mrs / Ms   First Name - Surname

....

Address:

....

....

Town:...Post Code: ....Country: ....

Telephone:...Fax:...

E-mail: ....